DORSET
and the
SECOND LEGION

New Light on a Roman Campaign

Norman H. Field

Foreword
Professor S. S. Frere

DORSET BOOKS

First published in 1992 by Dorset Books

Copyright © 1992 Norman H. Field

ISBN 1 871164-11-7

British Library Cataloguing-in-publication Data
CIP Catalogue Record for this book is available from the British Library

DORSET BOOKS
Official Publisher to Dorset County Council
1 Chinon Court
Lower Moor Way
Tiverton EX26 655
Tel 0884 243242
Fax 0884 243325

Designed for Dorset Books by
Topics Visual Information,
397 Topsham Road,
Exeter, Devon EX2 6HD

Typeset by ICON, Exeter, Devon
Printed and bound in Great Britain by BPCC Wheatons Ltd, Exeter, Devon

Foreword

Roman roads have long been attractive antiquities either for the casual walker or for the serious fieldworker. Many of them survive in lanes or paths and appear on Ordnance Survey maps; but in parts of the country where they have disappeared from the modern landscape, recovery of the ancient course is not easily or quickly achieved: it calls for experience, a skilled eye and the energy to excavate. By good fortune this county has seen a succession of workers with these qualities, of whom Norman Field can be hailed as the latest. In Dorset very few Roman roads are described in the standard work of I. Margary or shown on the Ordnance Survey Map of Roman Britain, and their absence has inevitably coloured our thoughts on the nature of the Roman occupation in these parts. How wrong these earlier conclusions were is now apparent.

The spark which fired off Field's long programme of exploration was the discovery of a large mid-first-century base at Lake Farm, near Wimborne, and the realization that the presence of a Roman legion here must mean that Lake Farm was the hub of Roman regional control in its earliest – military – phase. He gives an account of the original discovery of the Lake Farm site in the early 1960s, where no surface indications of fortification betrayed its presence, and how further work progressively led to the conclusion that this was no normal Roman auxiliary fort, but a fortress of about 40 acres, later reduced in size to just over 30. A fortress of 40 acres is large enough to house a mid-first-century legion, and there can be little doubt that it was for a time the base of Legion II Augusta, and may even have been established by the future emperor Vespasian while he commanded that legion in the years between 43 and 46 or 47.

If roads radiate from Lake Farm, they must be contemporary with the short period of its importance, and they must have been built to communicate with military sites. Wareham is shown to be very probably one of these: but the really interesting discovery is that many of the roads lead to Iron Age hillforts. One of these, Hod Hill, still has its Roman fort in good condition; and now that we know of others elsewhere (Hembury, South Cadbury, Brandon Camp) which were briefly occupied by Roman garrisons, an exciting possibility opens up. We must hope for the return of more liberal times, when large-scale research excavations can again be mounted and this hypothesis tested. If it turns out to be correct, our

1

present picture of the tactics of the Roman advance will have been shown to be very defective.

The book, then, is an account of archaeological fieldwork and observation by a first-rate practitioner; but it is also far more, presenting well-argued conclusions which affect the history of Roman Britain itself. With the book in hand, the active worker may reach his own conclusions about many of the features presented, but the evidence is there on the ground waiting to be observed. The armchair reader, on the other hand, has a great deal of new information to contemplate, his task made easier by the lucid style in which the material is described. There is much food for thought, for the final chapters go deeply into the probable course and timing of the Roman campaign of conquest and into its impact on the native population, bridging the divide between local and general history. This is in the best tradition of local studies.

S. S. Frere

(Professor Sheppard Frere is Emeritus Professor of the Archaeology of the Roman Empire in the University of Oxford.)

Contents

Acknowledgements

Acknowledgement is made to the following for illustrative material:

The British Museum, for Illustration 11.1, reproduced by courtesy of the Trustees.

Royal Commission on Historical Monuments (England) for Illustrations 3.1 and 3.3.

A & C Black, for Illustration 2.11 from Anne Johnson, *Roman Forts* (1983).

Gertrude Aitken and the Dorset County Museum, for Illustrations 1.3 and 6.3.

Priest's House Museum, Wimborne, for Illustrations 1.3 and 4.1.

Ancient Monuments Laboratory for Illustration 4.4.

Mrs F. Radcliffe for Illustration 5E.6.

Keith Jarvis and Poole Museums Service for Illustration 4.4.

List of Illustrations

Figures unless marked as **Plates** (b/w photographs)

IN MEMORIAM

Norman Field 1917-1992

It was with deep sadness that we learnt of the author's death only weeks before the publication of this book. In Norman Field's obituary, carried in the *Independent*, on 8 May this year, Roger Peers wrote:

Archaeology continues to spawn talented amateurs who confound the professionals. One such, Norman Field, ranks among the most distinguished Wessex archaeologists who, over the past 150 years, have done their best to record, and save, some part of the archaeological richness of their region from the apparently inevitable vandalism wrought by economics and development...

His mild manner masked a steely, even stubborn will. He saved numerous crucial sites from destruction, and found others, including an important first-century Roman fort to the west of Wimborne Minster. Here he had to contend with scepticism, even scorn, of professional archaeologists, but was triumphantly justified by subsequent large-scale excavation....

Field knew Dorset. He had an eye for the lie of the land, an instinctive feeling for the likely route of a road, or the position of a settlement. He felt deeply the need to protect the surviving ancient sites by all means possible.

The publication of this work, originally planned for 1991, was disrupted by the impending collapse of a major publishing empire. The author's calm determination to share his life's work with others, his courage in the face of failing health, and his faith in seeing his book through to the final stages, are here worthy of record. It is a tragedy that he was unable, at the last, to share in the pleasure of its publication.

The Publisher
May 1992

Introduction

During the 1960s, a series of relatively minor excavations took place in the river meadows of the Stour valley, at Lake Farm near Wimborne. It emerged that this was the spot where the Romans had set up a major military base in Dorset, soon after their invasion of Britain. By the end of that decade, an area of more than 16 hectares (40 acres) had received recognition and protection as a scheduled ancient monument. In its day the Roman site at Lake Farm must have played as important a role in the conquest as those that underlie Exeter and Lincoln. There could now be little doubt that the course of the well-known Roman road from Hamworthy was originally laid out to serve that military base, whence the route had continued at least as far as Badbury Rings. Equally, the site at Lake must soon have been linked by other roads to outlying garrisons in the countryside, of which the most obvious lay inside the native stronghold at Hod Hill.

I had been associated with the work at Lake from the start, having a particular interest in this problem of the early Roman roads. However, at the time, I was able to carry out only limited survey and excavation to seek evidence for the line of a Roman road from Badbury Rings towards Hod Hill. I also found it possible to take a look at evidence for the road that should have connected the newly identified Roman fort at Waddon Hill with Dorchester, where a military fort would certainly have preceded Roman Durnovaria. In the early 1970s, I organized the cutting of a section across a short, but significant, stretch of early road at Lazerton Farm, close to the foot of Hod Hill. Was there indeed, as already suspected, a direct link from there to Lake Farm and Poole Harbour, via Badbury Rings? Meanwhile further excavation at Lake showed that the Romans had kept a military presence there until after the rebellion of Boudicca (A.D. 60–61), although it by no means followed that the size and purpose of the site had remained the same. On the face of things, a Lake–Badbury–Hod military road (strongly suggested by the work at Lazerton) made no sense whatsoever without the existence of a direct road westwards from Lake towards Dorchester and Exeter that would have avoided a double crossing of the Stour. The well-known Roman road from Badbury to Dorchester simply could not have served the military station at Lake Farm.

9

The breakthrough came from a chance remark by a farmer at Corfe Mullen, who spoke of a parched streak showing in a field during dry weather. From that point, details steadily accumulated by normal means: ground survey, selective excavation, air photographs, tithe maps and so on. One road led to another, in the proper sense, and a surprisingly coherent pattern has emerged of Roman road communications laid out in Dorset after the invasion, Dorset is not a large county, but we can now add 160 kilometres of military road to the 130 or so kilometres already known. Even some of the latter distance can also be ascribed to the army. The core of this book describes and explains that early road network. Traces must still await discovery in the county and, as we shall see, will further throw light on a Roman campaign long steeped in mystery.

Roman roads, whether military or civil in origin, and given normal layout and build, should remain one of the most enduring elements in our archaeological record. After the conquest their vital role in human activity continued and expanded in the later civil life of the Roman province. Every villa worthy of the name had to be connected with a road leading ultimately to the cantonal or provincial capital. Archaeologists have always been understandably reluctant to accept claims for the Roman origin of lengths of ancient road, unless the evidence was buttressed at critical points by further survey and by excavated sections. Yet it is impossible to over-emphasize the confusion that has reigned in this part of the country over the origin and extent of the local Roman road system. Did the Roman army build any of the roads hereabouts? If so, which? Could proof be offered for the date of construction in particular examples? Importantly, where were the roads serving the known early forts in Dorset? These questions had already been answered negatively by some authorities, an attitude which had never seemed satisfactory, given the long-accepted view that road construction was essential to Roman military thinking. Others, by contrast, have taken it for granted without seeking proof that, in this area, the known Roman roads at least were the work of the army. The remarkable details that have emerged in Dorset may still not prove sufficient to convince those confronted by basically new conceptions. Fortunately elements of these roads are there to be looked for on the ground, although increasingly threatened by what is called progress and development.

A short while ago, my conclusions about what happened to certain hillforts after the invasion would have seemed controversial in the extreme, even with the new evidence that they were served by Roman military roads. But recent discoveries outside the county have encouraged fresh thoughts about the early campaigning strategy of the Roman army. A few years ago, in Herefordshire, the foundations of Roman military buildings were identified within the Iron Age hillfort of Brandon. To quote the report on Brandon:

> Discoveries ... in Luxemburg and ... southern Germany among other places, as well as occasional accounts in ancient authors such as Caesar's record of his *hiberna* at Bibracte (B.G.vii, 90), have made us aware that during the years of conquest the Romans sometimes stationed troops in native hillforts; but until recently examples of the practice have been scanty. Hod Hill (Dorset) is the best known site of this type in Britain. There the hillfort was too large for the proposed garrison, which constructed a new fort in one corner.[1]

Professor Frere went on to refer to work at Hembury in Devon and at South Cadbury Castle in Somerset, two other native sites where the Roman military presence has been identified. Since hillforts are the most widespread and massive of all vestiges of the Early Iron Age in southern Britain, the average reader may well wonder why it has taken so long for this connection to be spotted. In general, the likely reason is that hillforts have long been protected by law, so that thorough excavation has had to be justified in terms of research and expense. Not every hillfort will have had a Roman garrison, but without large-scale investigations the vital evidence for a brief Roman sojourn might be missed or misconstrued. If the right questions are not asked, the answers cannot be forthcoming. Certainly, military roads, if they existed (and an over-wintering garrison required one), are difficult to trace and prove. But many hillforts possess so-called 'modern' or 'post-Iron Age' surface features or alterations that have attracted little attention, yet may well have been the work of the Roman army.

A few words on the format of this book will not be out of place. The main archaeological work on the roads and associated earthworks, as detailed in Part II and the Appendices, might have appeared in one or other of the learned journals dealing with such matters. However, I felt that the discoveries were proving too lengthy to be suitable for the normal publication channels. There was also a wider readership beyond, who might like to share the excitement of seeking and finding in the Dorset countryside some lost pages of our early history. The question marks ending the chapter titles 6 to 8 are purely cautionary, acting as an invitation and a challenge to future work with the spade. Part I begins, therefore, with two introductory chapters aimed at those unfamiliar with the Dorset scene in the 40s A.D., when Briton and Roman came face to face. The third chapter, completing Part I, attempts to sum up how our knowledge and understanding of the Roman arrival in the county have developed up to the present. Part III deals with the shadowy score of years of military presence in Dorset, concluding with thoughts on the not insubstantial debt that arguably we now appear to owe to the brief sojourn of the Second Legion.

Acknowledgements are gratefully made to various people and organizations. I owe particular thanks to Professor Frere for looking through the finished text and making helpful suggestions. The basic spadework, cutting section-trenches, owed much to Ian Groves, Len Norris, John Day, Ken Smith and others unnamed; general encouragement came from Laurence Keen (County Archaeological Officer), the Dorset Archaeological Committee, the Wimborne Archaeological Group and the East Dorset Antiquarian Society. Thanks are due to the Society of Antiquaries of London, for a grant at an early stage; Dr Grace Simpson, for reporting on the Wareham samian; A. D. Mills, for comment on the location of a significant place-name; Teresa Hall and Len and Pam Norris, for certain illustrations; John Boyden and Francesca Radcliffe, for help with air views; Tim Toogood and John Alford, for their care with the general maps; Robin Bowers, head of the Dorset College of Agriculture and Horticulture, for vital assistance at Stinsford; and my wife, for walk and talk in out of the way places and the chores of proof-reading.

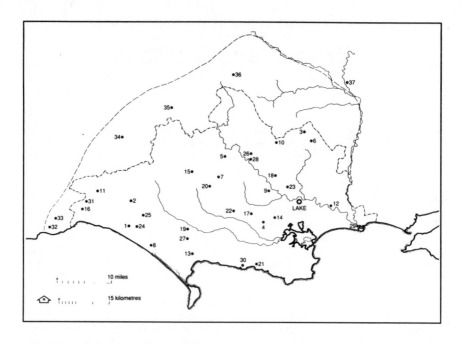

1.1 The tribal area of the Durotriges ('Greater Dorset')

Key to hillforts:

Hillforts of this tribe lying within the modern county of Dorset

1 Shipton Hill	12 Dudsbury	23 Badbury Rings
2 North Poorton	13 Chalbury	24 Chilcombe
3 Mistlebury Wood	14 Bulbury	25 Eggardon
4 Woolsbarrow	15 Dungeon Hill	26 Hambledon Hill
5 Banbury	16 Coney's Castle	27 Maiden Castle
6 Penbury Knoll	17 Woodbury	28 Hod Hill
7 Rawlsbury	18 Buzbury	29 Hengistbury
8 Abbotsbury Castle	19 Poundbury	30 Bindon Hill
9 Spetisbury Rings	20 Nettlecombe Tout	31 Lambert's Castle
10 Bussey Stool Park	21 Flower's Barrow	
11 Pilsdon Pen	22 Weatherby Castle	

Hillforts, probably of this tribe, lying outside the modern county of Dorset and mentioned in the text:

32 Hawkesdown Camp	34 Ham Hill	36 White Sheet Castle
33 Musbury Castle	35 Cadbury Castle	37 Old Sarum

PART I
Britons and Romans

1
Dorset before the Invasion

The Second Legion Augusta, which arrived in Dorset[1] around A.D. 44, shared a single objective with the invading forces elsewhere: to bring the native barbarians within the pale of Roman civilization. By blocking the left flank of the Roman advance, albeit only temporarily, the Dorset tribe came to enter the annals of recorded history, for Caesar's short campaign a century before had not extended so far west. Those Iron Age peoples who opposed Vespasian's disciplined units have long seemed shadowy figures indeed, known mainly as the builders of the massive and mysterious earthworks we call hillforts. However, since Victorian times, there has been a slow, but steady, accumulation of facts about pre-Roman Dorset, thanks, in particular, to the pioneering research of General Pitt-Rivers, followed in the twentieth century by major excavations at three of the tribal strongholds: Maiden Castle, Hod Hill and Hengistbury Head. Even though there remains much that we would like to know, it is now possible to say something positive about the life and work of the people who faced the Romans in the 40s A.D. and severely tested the efficiency of the legion and its auxiliaries.

The inhabitants of Dorset on the eve of the invasion were known as the Durotriges, a name we owe to the Alexandrian geographer Ptolemy, who listed the settlements of Roman Britain in the second century A.D. He gave one of them as a township of that tribe, with its location plainly set in central southern Britain, a signficant detail to which return will be made in a later chapter. There is reason to believe that the Durotrigian people, who would have spoken a Celtic tongue, had been dominant in Dorset for several hundred years. Recently, it has been customary for archaeologists to restrict the tribal name to the material culture that immediately preceded the Roman conquest – that is, perhaps from 100 B.C. to A.D. 43. Yet there is little doubt that the Iron Age farmers of Dorset had been tilling their fields and tending their flocks without disturbance for very much longer. If conservative by habit, they could be energetic on occasion, as the construction of the hillforts suggests, even if we do not know what part was played by forced or voluntary labour. Like other Celtic tribes, the Durotriges probably formed a loosely knit community owing allegiance to local chieftains, who in turn may have served on a tribal council under a traditional overlord. This assumption is based on analogy elsewhere in Britain and Gaul. However,

13

1.2 Jar of native Durotrigian ware from Lake Farm, 1962. Height 24.5 cm (Priest's House Museum, Wimborne)

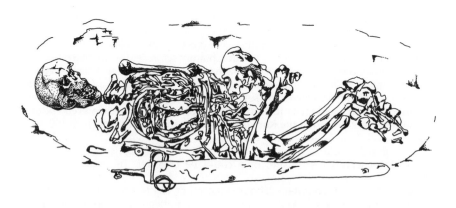

1.3 The Whitcombe warrior in his grave – an artist's impression (Dorset County Museum)

the Durotriges seemed to have lacked a single pre-Roman tribal capital, which has reinforced the notion that the tribe formed a loose federation rather then a monolithic nation.

The majority of the Durotrigian people were peasant-farmers, with a sprinkling of craftsmen, fishermen and traders (who would also have farmed). By contrast, the hillforts remind us that those in control of the centres of power enjoyed the prime place in tribal society. It is instructive to compare the situation across the Channel in Gaul. Caesar describes two privileged classes in that country: first, the 'knights', whom we might call the chieftains, together with their families, retainers and serfs; and second, the Druids, responsible for religious festivals and law-making in a non-literate community.[2] Intriguing clues to such notables have come from excavations in Dorset. At Hod Hill, a round hut with unusual features had been specially picked out for Roman attack. It was thought by the excavator to have belonged to a high-ranking personality within the hillfort, probably its chieftain. Again, inside Maiden Castle, a similar Iron Age hut lay at the head of a cobbled street and appears ultimately to have had a successor in the dwelling of the priest serving the fourth-century Roman temple. It is difficult not to see the original hut as that of a respected tribal elder, whom Caesar would have termed a Druid.

It was only in the 1950s that the territory of the Durotriges could be established with any accuracy, the boundary being based on the distribution of their coins and pottery. As the most westerly of the coin-issuing tribes of southern Britain, the Durotriges lay between the coinless Dumnonii of Devon and Cornwall and the more civilized peoples of the south-east with their close continental contacts. As was customary, the tribal coinage had been copied at long remove from the gold *stater* of Philip II of Macedon. A particular aspect in the local case was the absence of an inscription identifying a ruler by name, a fact that may well support the existence of a tribal federation.

Of more practical importance, given the frequency of broken sherds, is the recognition by form and fabric of typical Durotrigian pottery belonging to the years before the Conquest.[3] This development of ceramic uniformity stems partly from the relative isolation of the Durotriges at that period and partly from the growth of specialist pottery-making, particularly along the southern shore of Poole Harbour. This was an activity later encouraged by the Roman garrison in Dorset. There is a close correlation between the find-spots for both coins and pottery, so that it is possible to trace the bounds of the tribe as a coherent unit holding sway over what we might call Greater Dorset, since it encompassed the fringes of Wiltshire, Somerset and Devon. The archaeological evidence (limited though it may often prove) is that hillforts like Castle Ditches and Winkelbury in Wiltshire, South Cadbury and Ham Hill in Somerset, and Musbury Castle in Devon were culturally all within the ambit of the Dorset tribe. On the pottery evidence it is probable that the Nadder valley and possibly that of the Wylye, too, lay within the limits of the neighbouring Belgic tribe, living to the north, north-east and east of modern Dorset.[4] The recent inclusion of the Bournemouth–Christchurch conurbation inside the county of Dorset has brought the Hengistbury settlement back to its ancient allegiance. Certainly, in tackling the problem of the Roman army face to face with its Durotrigian adversaries, we should be looking at a Dorset extending a little beyond its present boundaries. Fortunately, the post-1972 confines of the county include a vital area involved in the Roman campaign and leading to a coherent story in itself.

What kind of life-style did the Durotrigian people lead on their tribal lands before the coming of the Romans? Hillforts must have played a key role, with over thirty of these impressive structures within the modern county out of the forty-odd they are thought to have controlled. We can hardly exaggerate their importance as social centres, yet it is surprising how many problems remain unsolved. Certain facts have long been commonplace: hillforts are strongly defended enclosures, sited on prominent positions, their construction presumably the work of a sizeable number of tribesfolk. But were they permanently occupied? Did they contain what may be called 'towns' or was there ample space for the grazing or herding of stock? In particular, what was the relationship between neighbouring hillforts belonging to the same tribe and between the individual hillfort and its surrounding farms? Not all these questions would be answered even if the interior of one Dorset hillfort had been fully explored, which is far from being the case. There is more certainty about the dating and function of perimeter defences, since a section cut through such bold features can, with care, tell an intelligible story. Whether its rampart was fronted by a single ditch or multiple ditches, each hillfort challenged direct attack and access was made difficult by the design of the entrance passage of its gateways. The advent of sling warfare has long been held to explain the widening of defence systems during the later Iron Age. It is true that caches of slingstones occur inside hillforts, and Balearic slingers were being employed at that time in Roman auxiliary regiments. However, to judge by other evidence, the ordinary native warrior relied on the simple equipment of spear, sword and shield, with body-protection, if he had any, from no more than a leather jerkin. It is worth quoting here a description of the unusual burial at Whitcombe near Dorchester, now reconstructed in the Dorset County Museum. The remains were those of a young man, who surely enjoyed high rank in the tribe. He was:

> ...unique in the region in being buried with iron weapons as well as ornaments. These had consisted of a sword 2 1/2 ft long, lying by the right side in a bronze-mounted wooden scabbard, probably attached by two rings to a belt or baldric, a spear, perhaps grasped in the right hand, and a hammer-like weapon with chalk pommel on the left. A bronze brooch ... lay above the right shoulder and a bronze ring with stud on the breast probably to fasten clothing or a baldric. This burial must be presumed prior to the Roman conquest.[5]

Dorset hillforts were set among farmland, both arable and pastoral, where the typical homestead lay inside its own ditched and blockaded enclosure of small size. The most intensively farmed parts of Dorset lay on the light, easily tilled higher downlands of the north-east, centre and south. But there had already been some clearance of natural woodland, as at Bulbury, unusually placed on heavier clay soil. The average tribesman-farmer probably lived a more or less self-sufficient existence in respect of basic wants like food, fuel and clothing. The large-scale excavation at Gussage All Saints, however, has added a new possibility. If Gussage is typical, some settlements may have specialized for generations in some technical skill; there, it was metal-working, notably the manufacture of bronze-fittings for chariots.

There are also signs that craftsmen and hawkers were moving around the countryside or turning up at fairs and markets to bring local farmers a wider choice of products. Thus, if one feature of the Iron Age landscape was the hillfort, another must surely have been the schematic arrangement of small so-called 'Celtic' fields characteristic of the farming of that period. Little is left now of what was a common sight when the Romans first ventured forth to reconnoitre, but there are notable survivals, as on Smacam Down, north of Cerne Abbas. Amid such field-patterns, single farmsteads or scattered hamlets continued their way of life little changed through Iron Age times. As Pitt-Rivers showed at Woodcutts and Rotherley, some of these settlements remained on their farm-holding until the close of the Roman period, while others either disappeared or developed into prosperous villas.

If the Durotrigian farmer largely provided for all his own daily needs, what else did he receive by way of trade, traceable on the archaeological record? Certainly, with the passage of time in the Iron Age, it became more and more possible to obtain small objects of some intrinsic value, like brooches and rings, often of bronze. One group of semi-luxuries, which was being produced on the Isle of Purbeck by what we would now call a cottage-industry, must be singled out. Kimmeridge shale was used for bracelets and bangles, as well as other hand-carved objects, which proved to be popular in the tribal area and beyond. It is certain, too, that there was trade in other goods of wood, leather and wool, which have left little mark today.

Pottery was becoming a specialist occupation and by the time of the Conquest much was probably being made in the vicinity of Wareham and Poole Harbour. In that respect at least, the self-sufficiency of the family was giving way to marketing in the tribal unit. By the mid-first century A.D. the southern shore of Poole Harbour was somehow engaged in overseas trade, replacing Hengistbury, which, a little earlier, had taken a major part of this activity.

A striking feature of Durotrigian life in the century before the Conquest has been considered to be its relative isolation, both from its neighbours and from continental influences. It is true that minor changes in fashion emanated from tribes in the south-east of the country; some of whose 'Belgic' pottery forms were imitated by Durotrigian craftsmen. Indeed, the recent view was that from the end of the second century B.C. until the Caesarian campaigns of the 60s, 'south-western Britain shows signs of intensive trade with the Armorican peninsula and beyond. But after Caesar's conquest of Gaul this trade declined, to be replaced by even more intensive contacts between the Roman world and the pro-Roman tribes of eastern Britain.'[6] However, it is now known[7] that sophisticated pottery imports were reaching Ower on Poole Harbour from continental sources before the Roman invasion, while they had dried up at Hengistbury. What was being sent from Dorset to pay for such luxuries is still a mystery, nor is there yet much indication that they reached settlements inland in any quantity. While this discovery shows that continental contacts were not entirely severed, there is still cause for thinking that the Durotriges had a deep traditional resentment of Roman power.

The distribution of coins and pottery within the tribal territory implies that tracks existed of various kinds and in regular use. Certainly, the open downs and heaths must have had a network of such routes going back to remote times. These apart, two major categories possessed clear topographical advantages and, as we shall see, the Roman army profited by some of them to move troops in the initial stages of the campaign, and then upgraded them into military roads.

The first category was the ridgeway, which followed chalk and limestone crests on a reasonably level gradient, so avoiding wooded valley bottoms and steep spurs. One notable example appears to have led across the county since Neolithic times, from the direction of Salisbury Plain in the north-east, through central Dorset and then in a wide sweep around the north of the Marshwood Vale. It was joined west of Dorchester by a second ridgeway which started on the Purbeck Hills near Swanage and then ran parallel to the south coast. The siting of many hillforts supports the belief that these ridgeways were an integral part of the everyday scene when the Romans invaded Dorset.

In the second group of tracks we find routes that skirted the course of a river, usually running close to the top of the valley slope. Thus, beside the Stour, a string of prehistoric finds pinpoints the ways inland leading from Christchurch Harbour and linking hillforts on both banks. There are signs along the Frome, too, that, for long stretches, there were similar tracks on both banks.

If we wish to visualize members of the tribe as individuals, we have no recorded names like Caratacus or Cogidubnus to provide dramatic authenticity. There are only the buried remains of nameless folk, such as were found in the 'war cemetery' at Maiden Castle. From that evidence, it appears that men and women were then markedly shorter than today, males averaging 5 ft 6 in. (1.65 m) and female adults barely 5 ft (1.52 m). Life expectancy seems to have been about forty years, with the oldest perhaps sixty. These figures, always subject to improvements in technical assessment, were normal for English populations until the better diet and medical care of modern times. The crouched posture of those burials is commonly taken to recall the pre-natal position of the deceased on his or her return to Mother Earth. This was an ancient custom among prehistoric peoples and had been the practice in Dorset during the earlier Bronze Age. Was this a sign of the strength of Durotrigian tradition? It is interesting that, while the tribe observed this kind of inhumation, the British tribes in the south-east, probably under continental influences, were cremating their dead. Furthermore, grave-goods in the shape of pottery vessels and joints of meat were increasingly being interred with the burials. Were these old rituals due to a growth in the influence of the Druids? Archaeology is unlikely to give a satisfactory answer to such a question, but the circumstances might underline the aloof independence of the Durotrigian tribe when confronted by the Roman threat.

2

The Roman Army

In Wales and in northern England, the problems of troop movements and garrison strengths during the Roman occupation extend over several hundred years. There are many military sites in the zone south of the Wall, and beyond it, too, to complicate the picture, while, over such an extended period of time, relationships between Roman authority and the various native tribes cannot have remained static for long. By contrast, the association of the Second Legion Augusta with Dorset lasted barely fifteen years, if as long, and was basically concerned with a single sustained campaign in one tribal territory only. These temporal and spatial limitations should greatly help us to understand Roman strategy in Dorset during the actual invasion and Roman policy in the few years of pacification that followed. Two simple factors have held up investigation in the past, again a contrast with Wales and the North: the shortage of identifiable forts and military posts, and the failure to recognize the system of early roads created by the Roman army. Part II will endeavour to remedy some of those deficiencies. In this chapter, something will be said about the Roman imperial forces and how their activities may still be traceable after an interval of nearly two thousand years.

There are excellent accounts of the typical organization of officers and men within a legion[1] and this is not the place to repeat them. Nor will the scanty details of earlier campaigning by the Roman army in the British province be retold here.[2] It will be useful simply to remind ourselves that, whatever details the Roman historian Tacitus may have written about, events in this region have long been lost. In the case of Dorset and the West Country, the information still stored in the ground remains our only source of knowledge. But, to begin with, certain general questions will be asked by the reader. How do we know, for example, which legion was involved in this county? What, in brief, was the likely composition of that body of men and its auxiliaries in the mid-first century A.D. ? Can we visualize the normal camp or fort, used by the invaders to establish their hold on the countryside? What about roads, traditionally the most obvious contribution of a Roman taskforce to the landscape?

There is little difficulty in identifying the Roman legion that operated in Dorset and the West Country. Around A.D. 120, the Roman geographer, Ptolemy of

Alexandria, compiled details for a map of the empire and named a settlement in this part of Britain: *Isca Legio II Augusta*.[3] This is always taken to be a reference to Exeter, although the argument is extended in Chapter 11. However that may be, an even more important clue comes from the Roman historian Suetonius (Chapter 3 below). He refers specifically to the capture of the Isle of Wight by the Second Legion under its commander Vespasian, later to become emperor.

No reminder should be needed that in the ancient world the regimented discipline of the Roman army was the key to its success. In Britain, nothing comparable existed by way of organized soldiery until Cromwell's New Model Army more than 1500 years after. It is true that what had been a citizens' force in Italy was now recruited at the lower levels on a mercenary basis. However, the career prospects of the common soldier were well protected and promotion through the ranks was a normal feature, at any rate as far as the respected rank of centurion. At the time of Claudius, staff officers still came generally from members of the Roman gentry, although it seems likely that half the 'other ranks' were by then of non-Italian origin. *Esprit de corps* was always high, founded on loyalty to the commander and to the emperor, whose person embodied all the Roman virtues.

A legion had come to be composed of 10 cohorts, each of which was made up of 6 centuries. In turn, the century had a nominal roll of 80 fighting men to give the cohort a figure of 480 and the legion as a whole 5280. Additionally, the legion, as a self-contained force, also included craftsmen and specialists, like armourers, clerks, carpenters, hospital staff. Some of these may have doubled as ordinary legionaries, which would affect the total. On campaign, the legion was accompanied by auxiliary troops, possibly equal in numbers and also organized in cohorts. The *auxilia* consisted of either cavalry or infantry or part of each, and, though entirely non-Roman volunteers, their commander was normally a Roman nobleman of standing. Thus the number of fighting men available to the legionary legate amounted to over 10 000, even if some of these could not be counted as combatant.

This reasonable certainty about the normal numerical strength of a legion and its auxiliary forces does not extend to the manner in which the various units were stationed on the ground. The relationship between the identity of garrisons and the size of forts ought to throw light on the dispersal of Roman forces after victory. If we knew the location, dimensions and dating of every fort in a given territory, important conclusions would emerge, though, even then, only after substantial excavations. But some knowledge as a guide is better than none, for gaps can be filled by modest reasoning, a process in which Dorset, as already suggested, offers advantages. So the next step in assessing the Roman military situation must be how to recognize forts of the Claudian period.[4]

The basic distinguishing feature that the Roman fort had developed by the mid-first century A.D. is always taken to be the playing-card shape of the defence-perimeter. This was typically a rectangle with rounded corners and gateway-gaps, which were set midway in the short sides, and, in the long sides, off-centre, but still opposite each other. In early forts, the earthen rampart was bounded by a single external ditch, increased for security, if need be, to two or three. Such a military site may well be betrayed to modern eyes by small finds of pottery, coins or fragments of a soldier's gear, and their importance is discussed below. It is, however, only when the defence system is identified that the presence of a fort can be finally assured. In the mid-first century, when the playing-card outline had not been universally adopted, the less stereotyped shapes of Augustan times seem to have persisted to some extent. In Britain, the forts at Hod Hill (Dorset) and The Lunt (Warwick) possessed curving sides that look old-fashioned for

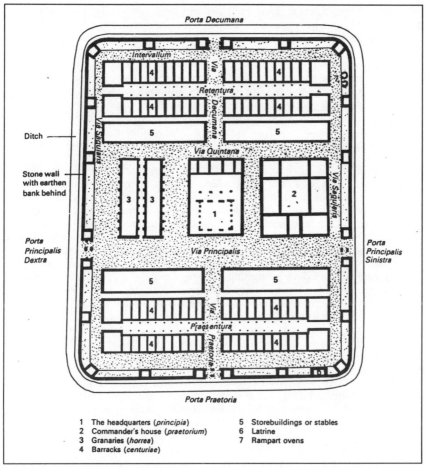

Porta Decumana

Intervallum

Via Decumana

Retentura

Via Quintana

Via Principalis

Praetentura

Porta Praetoria

Ditch

Stone wall
with earthen
bank behind

Porta
Principalis
Dextra

Porta
Principalis
Sinistra

1 The headquarters (*principia*)
2 Commander's house (*praetorium*)
3 Granaries (*horrea*)
4 Barracks (*centuriae*)

5 Storebuildings or stables
6 Latrine
7 Rampart ovens

2.1 Plan of a typical Roman auxiliary fort (Anne Johnson)

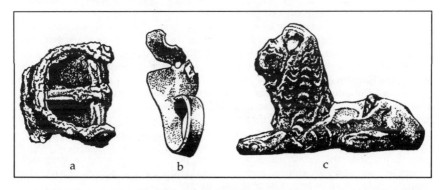

a   b   c

2.2 Military finds of bronze from Lake Farm, near Wimborne – a: strap-end, b: cuirass-hook, c: statuette of lion (*Proceedings* **87** [1965], 101)

21

their date of construction. Hod Hill, perhaps understandably, had only three gateways, one of which was in a corner. At Lake Farm, near Wimborne, the evidence of 1967–70 was for a gate near the south-west corner, which also served to introduce an aqueduct. The Waddon fort was considered by its excavator to be 'abnormally narrow';[5] not surprising, he thought, in a period of 'evolution'. But, in general, what we recognize as the traditional shape came gradually into use, with proportions close to the 3:2 of later years, although the square, or something akin, was still being adopted, as at Longthorpe in Northamptonshire.[6]

How is it possible for a fort to remain so long undetected in a county as well documented as Dorset? Ploughing, over a long period of time, may be one reason; the major base at Lake Farm falls into that category of vanished sites. It was first suspected only when deep trenching brought to light fragments of Roman military gear. Such finds tell us that the Roman army was in the vicinity, but do not establish the size and importance of its quarters. Allowance must also be made for the Roman habit (not always effective) of refilling ditches with the rampart material when a camp was being abandoned. Until recently, on unimproved grazing land, such as moor, heath or the open downs, the outline of a fort might still be discernible to the observer on the ground – better still, if he is airborne. The Roman site on Hod Hill is an example, rare of its type, and the writer makes a case for two others decipherable on Holton Heath (Chapter 8B).

Given intensive modern ploughing, the stage may be reached where only an air photograph under the right conditions can pick up what is visible of the outline at ground level – either as a shadow-mark or a soil-mark. If the topsoil is now very deep, the buried ditches may still refuse to reveal themselves. In that event, they may possibly be noted and plotted by geophysical methods, using sophisticated instruments sensitive to disturbances in local terrestrial magnetism. In the last resort, there is always the time-honoured spade, aided by the judicious employment of a mechanical digger. It may happen that, in a town with a long history, a fort's defences have been blotted out by a series of buildings over the centuries. Notwithstanding, a clue to the old circuit may emerge from a study of the medieval street-pattern, although this is more likely where, in later Roman times, worked stone came to replace earth and timber as the main constituent of the fortificiations. However, on farmland and in a built-up area alike, the discovery of the odd potsherd or coin may well make us suspect an early military presence. Thus, in various parts of Dorchester, telltale small finds have come to light over the years, establishing beyond reasonable doubt that Roman Durnovaria began as a fort. True, precise dating and size have remained a mystery, but a solution is offered in Chapter 6.

There remains one category of find recovered from Dorset soil that should be associated with the Roman army of occupation,[7] in spite of not being specifically military in character. This is the imported pottery from Gaul known as terra sigillata, the orange-red 'samian' ware that was later to be universally traded among the Romano-British civil population. If recognizable fragments of uniform or coins of the emperor Claudius are retrieved from the ground, no difficulty arises in suggesting the near presence of the Roman army. Yet, when a Dorset site has produced samian ware of that period (a rare enough circumstance), first thoughts have not normally linked the find-spot with the invasion forces. Thus the discovery long ago of first-century samian in Wareham could have been a pointer towards the existence of a military post of some kind, a case now reinforced by other evidence, and not weakened by the recent recovery of similarly dated pottery from Ower, not far away.[8]

The most conclusive evidence for a fort may come from the fortunate sighting of a section cut through the Roman defensive perimeter as a result of modern developments. This would be best recognized as a substantial ditch and might well come to light in a contractor's trench. Only then can we be confident that the Roman fort has been retrieved from its historical oblivion. The next stage is for some further cross-sections to establish at least one other side, and so determine its area and hence relative importance in the invaders' scheme of operations. Thus, in the first century, it seems that a headquarters base capacious enough to take a whole legion might cover 16 hectares (40 acres),[9] although such bases were normally larger in the later empire. Units of cohort strength needed camps of only half a dozen acres, and smaller detachments even less.

When we want to obtain details of the structures within, the story may be more difficult. Occasional glimpses of construction-slots or post-settings may seem informative, but in these early forts only large-scale clearance offers a real chance of identifying which building was which. To take a notable Dorset example, there has been some criticism of the selective cross-trenching carried out in the excavations on Hod Hill, although the general results remain unquestioned. Richmond demonstrated that the fort held two *praetoria* or houses for commanding officers: one for the senior legionary centurion and the other for the Roman nobleman in charge of the auxiliary cavalry detachment. This discovery supported the view that the garrison consisted of a mixed force of legionary infantry and cavalry troopers, for in Victorian times ploughing had exposed surface finds of military equipment attributable to both kinds of unit. It may be possible, as claimed at Hod Hill, to distinguish between barrack-blocks used by legionaries and those used by auxiliaries, but more certain seems to be Richmond's identification of a stable for cavalry horses. The practice of stationing in a particular fort a mixed garrison rather than a single type of unit was apparently a policy forced on the Romans in these early years in Britain, and has been noted elsewhere than in Dorset.

Other buildings which excavation may reveal in a larger fort include a hospital, a granary, latrines and workshops. A feature almost certain to have left a well-defined trace is provision for water supply. This could take the shape of a ground aqueduct or a leat entering the fort through a gateway, or of individual wells for the officers' quarters.

Within a fort, one of the basic requirements must have been gravel surfacing for the streets that formed the skeletal plan when the layout took place. Such provision, usually traceable today, would have extended as far as the entrances and then beyond, to the approach roadways.

It has always been taken for granted that road construction in newly conquered territory was an essential task for the victorious Roman soldiery. Yet, in Dorset, military roads in general have been denied existence[10] or else relegated to the status of 'romanized trackways'. The latter term begs the question, since if reconstructed in a Roman manner these would be recognized as 'roads'. The point need not be laboured here, since in Dorset no such example has yet been proposed, let alone proven. Yet it has seemed to this writer that the most urgent of reasons must have compelled the Roman command to link outlying garrisons with their bases as soon as possible. A *recognizable* road was essential in a hostile landscape, as soon as a unit was established for more than a few days. In mist or poor weather, and on moonless nights, an emergency relieving force needed to be certain of its way. Under such conditions, a surfaced road, clearly demarcated, was equally important as a guide to movement and an aid to transport. Collingwood took 'romanized trackways' to be a form of specifically 'Roman road', connecting only minor civil sites, and, he said, difficult to trace. He was adamant about the role of the army: 'There is little doubt that most of the main roads were first made for strategic purposes in the course of the conquest.'[11] It is against the background of these differing views that the evidence of Roman military roads in Dorset will be examined in Part II.

At this point, we might remind ourselves of those characteristics that, without excavation, may suggest the existence of a Roman road, whatever its possible date in the Roman period. Basically, there are three:

> **first**, an association with Roman sites of importance, known or awaiting discovery, since a road must run from A to B;
>
> **second**, a layout in straight stretches, normally related in an intelligible way to the terrain being crossed; and
>
> **third**, a build-up of metalling for the cambered causeway.

There has never been any doubt that the surveyors and engineers of the Roman army created their road communications on these lines and, in Collingwood's opinion, at the earliest opportunity in their campaigning. In the highland zones of the North, such roads and their destinations are often still traceable without great difficulty. The relief on Trajan's Column, half a century after the invasion of Britain, illustrates legionaries at work on roads and bridges. There is no reason to suppose that such activity did not take place in Dorset during the fifteen or twenty years of the military presence. Elsewhere in lowland Britain, the same problem has confronted the excavators of the early Roman base at Longthorpe: 'Certainly the fortress must have been served by roads during its brief occupation of some twenty years, but the absence of clear traces of them suggests that consolidation of the road system took place later.'[12] In this county the failure to recognize the early military roads can be partly explained by the recentness of the discovery that Lake Farm near Wimborne was the first base of the Second Legion in the West Country. Thus there appeared no special reason to look for a road from the well-known fort at Hod Hill that would be running down the Stour valley, even though the new Roman entrance, the Ashfield Gate, pointed in that direction.

Once mapwork and observation in the field have strongly supported the existence of a Roman road, the importance arises of digging cross-sections to confirm its existence and establish its construction. It is curious that insufficient attention seems to have been given to a classic account of road construction by Statius, writing towards the end of the first century A.D. He describes[13] a methodical approach almost certainly military in origin and forming current practice at the time. As we shall see, the Second Legion was building its roads in very much the same fashion. According to Statius, the first task was to dig side-furrows (*sulcos*) to create limits to the road. One of these at least probably ended up as a side-ditch. In the next stage, topsoil and some bedrock were removed over a strip the width of the intended carriageway. Statius then stated that the bed of the depression was to be given a suitable foundation, followed by the actual surfacing. Finally the road-material had to be kept in place by lateral kerbs and by driving in pegs at intervals. In lowland Britain, when suitable stone was lacking, the last detail needed adaptation. A number of the early Dorset roads were provided with a 'kerbing' for the build-up either by the side wall of the original depression or by a border of heavy gravel and flints.

The retrieval of these early Dorset roads from their obscurity is more than an interesting exercise in archaeological investigation. The results will throw new light on what has always appeared to have been a mysterious campaign, the contradictory hallmarks of which were apparently speed of movement by the victors and ferocity of resistance by the vanquished. These two features in association have never provided a satisfactory explanation for what happened, and the reality was somewhat different.

3

The Invasion and After: some earlier views

The Claudian invasion of Britain in A.D. 43 has been discussed in general terms by a number of writers in recent years and only the broad outline will be presented here. Despite the scantiness of historical record, archaeological discoveries have suggested the strategy of the Roman command, namely to control the lowland triangle of the British mainland, defined by the east and south coasts and by the Exeter–Lincoln line (later followed by the Fosse Way). After the three-pronged landings in Kent and Sussex, the battle of the Medway followed, in which Vespasian distinguished himself. The Thames was crossed and a base-camp set up at Colchester, near the apex of the triangle. From there it would appear that the Roman forces lost no time in operating northwards towards the Wash and Lincoln, to form the right wing of the campaign drive, and north-westward to form the central advance. The left wing of the Roman thrust was soon working westwards from the base near Chichester, identified in the 1960s. In this region the story was tersely summarized in the oft-quoted words of Suetonius (already mentioned in Chapter 2), which have always been recognized as the starting-point for understanding the Roman conquest of southern Britain:

> On Claudius' accession Vespasian was indebted to Narcissus for the command of a legion in Germany; and proceeded to Britain, where he fought thirty battles, subjugated two war-like tribes and captured more than twenty towns, besides the entire Isle of Wight. In these campaigns he served at times under Aulus Plautius, and at times directly under Claudius...[1]

All the evidence indicates that, on its transfer from Strasbourg, the Second Legion Augusta, one of the four legions involved in the invasion, was under Vespasian's command. Given his recorded activity on the Medway (and so, presumably, that of his legion), together with the build-up that apparently took place at Fishbourne, Vespasian can hardly have begun military operations in Dorset before 44 or even 45. It was then that a major base was set up at Lake Farm, near Wimborne. The discovery of this important site, and subsequent work connected with it, will be discussed in Part II.

Very little factual detail about the first events in the invasion of Britain has come down to us from Latin sources. Imagination for a long time filled the gap and applied conclusions that were uncritically accepted until the arrival of modern archaeology. Thus, if we start in the eighteenth century with Hutchins's *History of Dorset* (1774), the Dorset hillforts were thought to have been constructed by the Romans and to have held garrisons throughout the several hundred years of occupation. Strangely enough, the latter view can now be seen to hold for some hillforts, but for the invasion period only. Then, during the nineteenth century, odd finds began to be recorded and earthworks were more closely examined. By the time of Warne's *Ancient Dorset* (1872), the Roman camp within Hod Hill was recognized for what it was, even if there was still uncertainty about hillforts. Were these the original strongholds of the native Celts or, in some cases, the work of the Romans? Although admitting he was aware of arguments that lacked material proof, Warne made an elaborate case for a Roman advance westward close to the south coast of Dorset; curiously he did not attempt to fit in the role of Hod Hill. A little later, while General Pitt-Rivers did not add details to the story of the invasion itself, his work established in essence what we know of the life-style of the Dorset tribe, both before and after that event.

Early in the present century, odd finds were hinting at a Roman military presence elsewhere in the county, particularly at Dorchester, though the notion of a Roman fort there did not find general agreement. After the First World War, pottery of Claudian date was recovered at Hamworthy and, while this implied that Poole Harbour had served as an early Roman trading port, there was no thought at the time of a close connection with the actual invasion.

The remarkable excavations at Maiden Castle in the 1930s drew attention to the arrival of the Roman army long ago at the mightiest of the Dorset hillforts. It was obvious from the mutilated skeletons in the native 'war cemetery' that this was one of the twenty 'towns' stormed by Vespasian's Second Legion. So Wheeler felt able to write of 'a main line of the Roman advance through Dorset', now that he had the backing of archaeological evidence. There was a shortage of corroborative detail, even if, we conclude, the overall picture seemed authentic: 'Approaching from the direction of the Ise of Wight, Vespasian's legion may be supposed to have crossed the River Frome at the only easy crossing hereabouts – where Roman and modern Dorchester were to come into being.'[2]

The next major step forward in reconstructing the Roman campaign in Dorset occurred in the 1950s with Ian Richmond's work on Hod Hill. He was able reasonably to demonstrate the size and composition of the garrison within the Roman fort and the approximate length of its occupation. Hod Hill held a mixed force of legionaries and auxiliaries numbering 718 men, an unusual combination suggesting a shortage of manpower for policing purposes. Their stay was confidently given as no more than five to seven years, ending about A.D. 50. In the final report (1969), published after his death, Richmond was certain about the absence of any Roman road connecting with Hod Hill: 'The fort belongs to the initial stage of the Roman conquest, before the engineers had begun to transform the tracks blazed by the advancing armies into a settled road-system conforming to the requirements of engineering rather than those of initial strategy.'[3]

In 1946, the West Dorset volume of the Royal Commission on Historical Monuments had drawn attention to a site on Waddon Hill, near Beaminster. Here, in Victorian days, quarrying had brought to light 'mid-first century material of strongly military character'.[4] Excavations at that spot in 1959, and for several seasons after, were carried out by Graham Webster. Despite the previous disturbance, he established details of a major Roman fort. While the Roman army was at Hod from 44 or so to 50, the occupation of Waddon probably lasted from around 50 until at least the start of the 60s. The Hod fort could be fitted, Webster

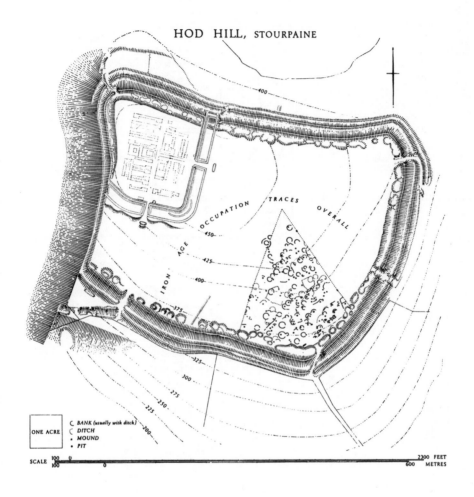

3.1 Hod Hill, plan of the Early Iron Age hillfort and the Roman fort. Prepared by, and published by permission of, the Royal Commission on Historical Monuments (England). (The three entrances on the east side of the hillfort are known, from north to south, as the Steepleton Gate, the Ashfield Gate and the Home Gate.)

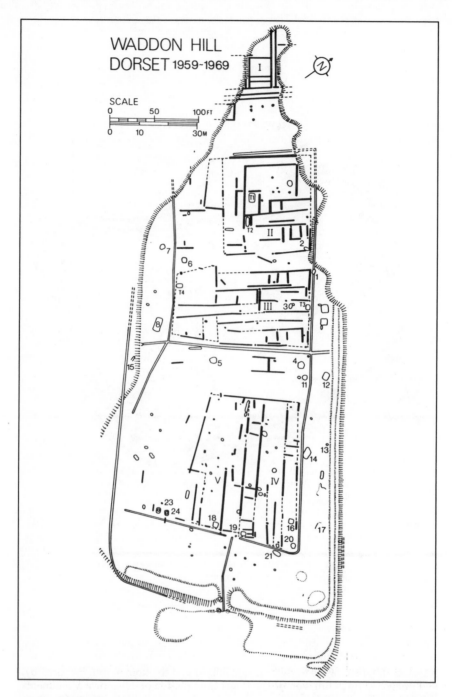

3.2 Waddon Hill, plan of Roman fort; its unusual shape was dictated by the elongated hill-top. (*Proceedings* **101** [1979], 52)

thought, into the rule of the first Roman governor, Aulus Plautius, and possibly for a further year or two, when 'the disposition of units ... was that of an occupying army spread thinly over the newly conquered province with more men on and near the frontier zone to watch the barbarians without who had not yet been conquered nor were under any treaty.'[5] After 48, under the second Roman governor, Ostorius Scapula, faced with the need to confront Caratacus and his followers in Wales, further Roman forces moved into forward positions, so that rearward areas were denuded of troops. It was then that Hod was abandoned and Waddon set up. On roads, Webster expressed a similar view to Richmond's: 'Cleared routes there may have been, but the Roman road in his area is the result of later civil development.'[6]

Before the 1970s, the results from both Hod Hill and Waddon Hill were making it clear that the Roman army must have had a number of other sites in the Dorset tribal area: either larger, in the shape of a supply-base or headquarters; or of like size, to accommodate further garrisons; or, finally, smaller, by way of police-posts and signal-stations. Excavations in various parts of Dorchester, an obvious candidate for a fort, were failing to bring positive structural evidence. However, as we shall see in Chapter 6, certain clues from previous investigations on the County Library site in the town had not been recognized as clues to the fort. South-west of Dorchester, a small earthwork on Blackdown, Winterborne Steepleton, has been claimed as a probable signal-station.[7] Another, inside the hillfort of Abbotsbury Castle, did not yield positive proof of Roman workmanship, when tested by excavation.[8] Aerial photographs taken during the dry summer of 1976 added two probable sites in the Stour valley: a small square enclosure, well ploughed over, on Keynston Down;[9] and a 2.4 hectare (6 acre) fort and annexe near Crab Farm, 1.6 km south-west of Badbury Rings.[10]

Meanwhile, across the river Stour from Badbury, on Lake Farm, near Wimborne, information had slowly accumulated since 1962 for a Roman military establishment of some size, occupied from the mid 40s to the early 60s. It will be interesting at this point to look at views of its importance, as expressed over the last twenty years or so.

The first discoveries at Lake were reported in *The Times* in March 1962, with an emphasis on their military significance. However, it was not until the mid-1960s that it was possible to claim the existence of a large fortress[11] and the site was scheduled as an ancient monument. The information about Lake was too recent for absorption in Webster's survey, *The Conquest of Britain* (1965), but he noted a possible store-base at Hamworthy and the early pottery-kiln at Corfe Mullen. Dorchester retained general preference as the main centre for military operations in this part of Britain and (based on the reading of Ptolemy's *Geography*, discussed in Chapter 10) it was always thought that Exeter would prove the site of a small fort, at least. Frere (1967) added Lake to his list of what he called 'Julio-Claudian' sites in Britain, but he opted for major Roman bases first at Dorchester, then at Exeter. A little later (1974) he included Lake, but not Dorchester, among his 'vexillation-fortresses'. These comprised a series of important military sites, reduced in area from what has been regarded as normal for a full legion at that time. Manning (1976) dealt extensively with the military situation in the West Country around the mid-first century, but thought details from Lake too indeterminate for its importance to be properly judged. In his opinion, a prime factor supporting the existence of a fort at Dorchester was the road-system emanating from the town, in complete contrast to the thoughts of Richmond and Webster on roads, noted above.

A further intriguing pointer linking Dorchester to the Roman army came from the reinterpretation by Bradley (1976) of St. George Gray's work at Maumbury Rings. Long thought to have served as an amphitheatre for the Roman town of Durnovaria, the Neolithic henge monument was apparently converted early in the Roman period into a *ludus* or training-ground for cavalry. But the problem remained: Where precisely was the fort?

The first detailed attempt to examine the military campaign in Dorset and beyond, using the new information about Lake Farm, came from Branigan (1972). He proposed Roman thrusts in three directions from Lake as a base: towards the north-west, up the Stour valley; westward, aiming at the area of Maiden Castle; and northward, along the Avon valley. One point in his argument was that Vespasian reached Exeter and the line of the Fosse Way[12] by A.D. 44, a speed of movement that will be questioned in Chapter 9. Certainly, also in 1972, Eicholz argued contrariwise that Vespasian himself could well have served in Britain until 46 or 47.[13] Notwithstanding, the idea that the Roman forces lost little time in subduing the Dorset tribe continued to receive support, albeit tempered by caution. Manning (1976) was explicit: 'By A.D. 47 the west of England was largely conquered and garrisoned',[14] though the vagueness of that area and the modifying adverb made the statement less useful. His most recent view is different: Vespasian's campaign 'almost certainly' took several seasons and the base at Exeter was set up no earlier than around 55.[15] In 1981 Salway cautiously favoured ' ... the reasonable hypothesis that Vespasian's thrust ... established his wing of the Claudian forces in firm control at least as far west as Exeter before the end of the first governor's tour of duty [i.e. before 47], *even if they had not moved their new fortress there at that point*' (my italics).[16] The uncertainty implied by those words has confronted most Romanists besides Manning. How could rapidity of conquest be reconciled with two signficant factors: the discovery of a major base at Lake Farm and the dating of the major fortress at Exeter?

Yet the notion of a speedy campaign persists and Webster has emphasized (1988) that Vespasian's force 'swept rapidly westwards and took the Britons by surprise'. He also expresses the view that the Lake Farm base was not set up until 48, to replace Fishbourne at the same time as Hod Hill was evacuated.[17] Hod Hill, Richmond told us, probably remained in Roman occupation for some five years or more. There are obvious contradictions in this approach to the problem.

By contrast, the 'three to four years' accorded by Frere (1986) to Vespasian's campaign in the south-west was some acknowledgement of the probable time factor involved. But could the second powerful tribe mentioned by Suetonius have been the Dumnonii, as he proposed? Recent excavation indicates that the involvement of the Roman army in Devon was more complex than has hitherto seemed possible and occurred later (*c.* A.D. 50–60 at Hembury).[18] These circumstances certainly fit the case made by Eicholz on Vespasian's stay in Britain and may point to a period of five to six years overall.

A recent survey of Roman Dorset by Bill Putnam, an archaeologist resident in the county, speaks indeed of 'a bitter war of conquest' lasting 'as long as 15 years' and terminated only by the revolt of Boudicca in 60–61. The arrival at Hamworthy, however, is placed 'late in the year' 43. Putnam estimates that half the legionaries were outposted from Lake Farm, which explains the reduced size of that base.[19] But he did not point out that in the smaller forts (their sites still mainly unknown) legionaries had probably to be quartered with equal numbers of auxiliary troops, as Richmond demonstrated at Hod Hill.

If we are fully to understand the activities of the Second Legion during its stay in Dorset, the case of Exeter and the Fosse Way illustrates the need to look beyond the county boundaries. As already pointed out, the territory of the Durotriges was not limited even to present-day Dorset, marginally enlarged since 1972. Research digs on any scale on hillforts are rare and not lightly undertaken, so it is fortunate that, since the work of Wheeler and Richmond, two have taken place on Durotrigian territory just outside the county. Both have revealed evidence of use by the Roman army. Thus at South Cadbury in Somerset[20] and Hembury in East Devon (above) excavation has brought to light the outlines of Roman buildings of military type, hitherto unsuspected on those sites.

The strategic objective of the Roman command must always have envisaged the eventual control of the entire peninsula in the South-West. In this scheme of things, thanks to the Roman geographer Ptolemy (Chapter 10), Exeter has been considered a possible base for the Second Legion Augusta, despite the possible confusion with Caerleon. Excavations in the city have now revealed that the original Roman settlement was indeed a fortress, with an area of 16.40 hectares (40.45 acres). Furthermore, its initial construction has been placed within the years 55–60 (with the later figure favoured). At North Tawton, 27 km west-north-west, a series of military circuits of various sizes (including a possible vexillation base) has been identified from the air, to add to the earthwork fort already known at that site. Thus, there appears to have been a Roman penetration into central Devon before and after the major base at Exeter was set up. Fragments of this intriguing jigsaw puzzle are beginning to be recognizable, though fitting them together is not straightforward. It is at least recognized that the conquest both of the Durotriges in Greater Dorset and of the Dumnonian tribe in Devon was more drawn out than has often been supposed.[21] By the early 50s, the campaign in Dorset had finally been completed and Exeter was due to replace Lake as the legionary headquarters.

Despite recent advances in knowledge, three aspects of the Roman campaign in Dorset and its environs have remained obscure:

first, what was the role of the base at Lake Farm, recognized now for over twenty years? Did it operate at any time as the legionary headquarters? Is its size determinable at present? Did it undergo more than one phase of construction?

second, what time-scale can we set for the local military operations? If rapidity is no longer the order of the day, can some acceptable precision be established in terms of campaigning seasons?

third, if we are now thinking of years instead of weeks, how were the legion and its auxiliaries disposed through the tribal territory? Where were the outlying forts, whose absence has always posed a problem even before the discovery of the Lake fortress?

PART II

The Roman Fortress at Lake near Wimborne and Subsequent Discoveries

4

The Military Base at Lake Farm

For years, among the many problems concerning the Roman campaign in the West Country there was one in particular that required a solution. Where precisely was the earliest military base? Only when this was located could it be understood how the commander of the Second Augustan Legion set about challenging the hillforts of Dorset and its environs. Such a major site must have existed somewhere in central southern Britain for a short period from the mid 40s A.D. Exeter and Dorchester had been offered as candidates, but growing evidence ruled them out for the Claudian period. The first certainly has been shown to possess a large Roman fortress, but, as noted in Chapter 3, it was occupied only from around 60 onward, possibly as early as 55.[1] The second (of which there is more in Chapter 6) has consistently failed to produce signs of a fortress large enough to have served as a major base. Even Chichester has been brought into the reckoning, but it lay too far east to be of value other than as a supply port. Since the late 1960s there has been acceptance by many that the Roman military site identified at Lake Farm seemed to fit the bill as the missing headquarters of the Second Legion during those crucial early years of the Roman occupation.[2] However, the full report of the most recent excavations from 1972, including those by Graham Webster and Poole Museum, has yet to appear, together with a summary of previous work, while a geophysical survey, carried out by the Ancient Monuments Laboratory with important results, has not yet received the attention it deserves.[3]

This chapter will confine itself, therefore, to three aspects of the Roman military site at Lake Farm:

(a) how the site was discovered and identified (always apparently a matter of interest), with an outline of the first excavations in particular from 1959 to 1971, with which the writer was closely concerned;

(b) a review of the geophysical survey and what it revealed of the size of the base and its subsequent history;

(c) an appraisal of the role of the Lake fortress in the Roman invasion strategy.

4.1 Roman 'honey-jar', Lake, 1962 (Priest's House Museum, Wimborne)

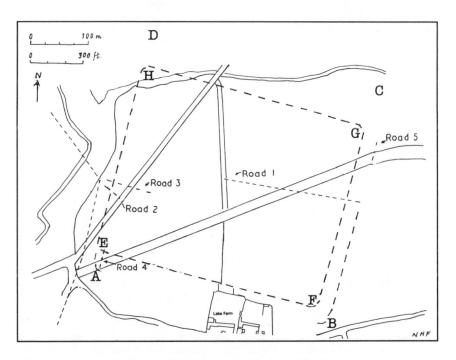

4.2 Roads and other Roman linear features at Lake, 1959–71

33

Discovery

The identification of a Roman military site may be immediate and the labour of confirmation by the spade avoided, if circumstances are in favour. Air photography can provide acceptable proof by revealing the telltale rectilinear shape with rounded corners as a crop- or a soil-mark. Even then, limited excavation is advisable to make certain of its builders and its date. However, as pointed out in Chapter 3, the military presence may remain long unsuspected where the defence-ditches (the best clue to a fort's presence) are deeply buried and when air views prove unhelpful. Scraps of pottery, fragments of military equipment and the odd coin, helpful as they can be, need substantiation. Fortunately, scientific techniques may enable hidden ground disturbances like ditches and pits to be plotted so as to amplify excavated details. This is what has happened at Lake Farm.

The initial work at Lake in 1959–60 investigated a long ridge, tentatively called Road 1, north of the farmhouse. There was no thought at the time that the team of volunteers was digging inside a very extensive Roman site. Before excavation of a cross-section, the ridge looked suspiciously like the causeway of a Roman road, and it is still very visible south of the new Wimborne bypass. Interestingly (and a major reason for testing the feature), this ridge pointed directly at the sharp bend where the Roman road from Poole Harbour turned towards Badbury Rings in the valley meadows of the river Stour. Where sectioned, the ridge was seen to have been laid directly on the old ground level and was a simple construction of soil surfaced with scanty stony metalling. There were flanking side-ditches 12.8 m apart. Though associated with early Roman potsherds, this was too insubstantial to look like a 'normal' Roman road and there was no positive sign of even this build-up when it was dug for in 1965. But the scattered worn potsherds did suggest that, during the first century A.D., there had been activity of some kind in the vicinity on this low valley terrace. In 1962–63, another broad and prominent ridge (Road 2), not aligned with Road 1 and lying on the other side of the modern main road (then the A31), was sectioned in two places, in advance of engineering works. The results were exciting and a number of other trenches were dug to reveal what the writer calls Roads 2 and 3, plus a number of pits and gullies. Finds included a range of pottery both of native and of Roman or romanized wares, coins (mainly Claudian) and fragments of military equipment, including cuirass-buckles and cuirass-hooks. Road 2 bore some resemblance to Road 1 in construction: its causeway was built of soil, but topped by more consolidated gravel, and it also possessed side-ditches 13 m apart. At the eastern end, in 1962, the side-ditch of Road 2 was seen to have disturbed a pit that contained finds belonging to an earlier phase. In 1963, near its western end, Road 2 was associated with pottery scraps occurring not only below the gravel metalling, but also above. Roads 1 and 2 both gave the impression, therefore, that they were later than the first Roman activity in the area. Road 3, however, told a rather different story, being narrower, 4.8 m wide, but laid signficantly on ground cleared of original topsoil, a technique of military type.[4]

Two questions now demanded at least provisional answers: What was the size of this early Roman site and when precisely was it occupied? A report in *The Times* (March 1963) summarized the position: 'Recent finds near Wimborne offer a good chance that further digging will discover a Roman military site connected with Vespasian's campaign in the south-west.' At this stage, the basic requirement was a section dug to reveal a ditch or ditches wide and deep enough to have formed part of the defences of such a site. These ditches could not only confirm the actual location of the military settlement, but also provide a reliable guide to its size and so its relative importance. The work in 1963 did pick up some evidence for a defence-ditch of this kind, but after further work in 1965, to the east of the A31 road again, it was not possible to continue operations on the farmland proper. However, excavations that year showed that Road 3 at any rate, though robbed, could still be traced, together with more pits aligned with it.

It had become clear that the Roman military presence could be detected over an expanse of many acres, north-west and north-east of Lake farmhouse. Pottery and other material were also dug up even further away, a result of modern pipe-laying to the south and test-trenching to the east. Their distance and the lie of the ground precluded these finds from being within or close to a possible defence circuit. The key question still could not be answered: What was the size of this base? It was known that the Roman road from Hamworthy passed very close on the west, and indeed, to judge by its alignment, had been built to serve it. The last stretch of this road down the hill from East End, Corfe Mullen, crossed an abandoned railway track at the point known as Lake Gates[5] in the south-west corner of the extensive area producing the early Roman finds. With excavation on the actual farmland temporarily impossible, the best chance of locating those defence-ditches seemed to lie in digging beside and along the course of the former railway. There was a disadvantage in the shape of the dense scrub (the line had been disused long before the Beeching era). Occasionally, too, pickaxes would be needed to cope with the ballast of the old permanent way. Nevertheless, voluntary workers[6] could take their time – not a bad thing when interpreting difficult ground. The first trench would probably start from the line of that road from Hamworthy, a useful archaeological datum. Traces of a gravelled road with a side-ditch were indeed found, but not fully confirmed in all the later work.

So the years 1966–71 saw trenches up to 80 m long dug from west to east on each side of the old track, while in one place 60 square metres of the old railway-ballast was removed – all this carried out by hand, with no aid from a machine. The results were more interesting than expected. The opportunity is taken here to describe them briefly as they came to be identified, as digging proceeded from west to east. After the edge of the suspected Roman road (much robbed at this point) there came a series of features cut into, or redeposited upon, the valley gravel. First, several ditches and remnants of banks, straight, then curving, were interpreted as the corner of a military circuit (Ditches I, II and III, Banks I and II). Gully I may have acted as a drain between Ditches III and II. Bank II yielded evidence of having had single posts set into it at intervals. Then came a belt of residual re-laid soil and an array of post-holes (interpreted as a rampart). There followed the evidence of a well-constructed aqueduct or water-leat running in from the south and associated with settling tanks (Tanks I and II) aligned parallel with the leat. Next, another metalled road (Causeway = Road 4) was revealed, flanked to its east by a wide depression, probably for drainage (Gully II). A little further a well-shaped flat-bottomed ditch or gully (Gully III) had been cut through a lightly metalled surface, probably an earlier road-surface. This gully ran at right angles to all the previous linear features, as did the next very substantial ditch (Ditch IV), with vestigial remains of a rampart beyond, furthest from the western starting-point.

When the preceding description is related to the plan, it will be seen that the succession of features has been presented in a series of phases, the reasons for which will not be explained here.

It was now possible to estimate the probable maximum size of the Roman base as approaching 16 hectares (40 acres).[7] Further along the old railway track, a trench was cut to locate perimeter features on the eastern side, whose line on the ground could now be estimated with reasonable accuracy. This work revealed a

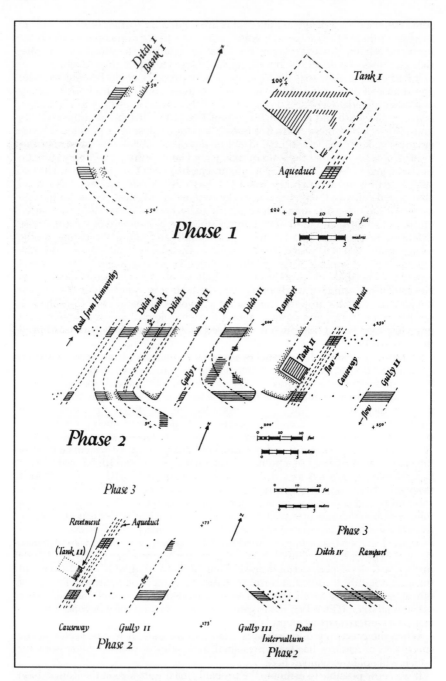

4.4 Discoveries in trenching of 1966–71, Lake Farm. Phases 1 and 2 were then regarded as successive stages of an early defence-circuit (=Lake I?) and Phase 3 to a later reduced circuit (=Lake II ?).

4.5 Military ditch at Lake Farm, with the writer, 1970 – view from north-west (photo: Kevin Allison)

4.6 Water leat, Lake Farm, 1979, view from south-east (Poole Museums)

cross-section of a major linear disturbance that may include remains of a road running north–south (Road 5). Its position and alignment suggest that this might be the internal road within a defence line, the intervallum road or *via sagularis* of one phase of the military site. Subsequent geophysical work tends to support that view.

By 1970, the whole of the ground lying within the probable system of defence had been protected under the Ancient Monuments Acts, at the instigation of the writer, who withdrew from active direction on the site in 1972. For two seasons excavation was directed by Graham Webster, and two large areas were opened up by machinery between the trenches dug in the sixties and by then refilled. This work confirmed some details (Ditch IV in particular, and the existence and alignment of Bank I), but left others uncertain (Webster 1972 and 1973). Thus, as it later happened, the vital point where the water-leat turned into the fortress was not reached and has now been destroyed by the construction of the Wimborne bypass for the A31 trunk road. The new roundabout covers the south-west corner of the military site.

In 1979, before these road improvements, a team led by the late Ian Horsey of Poole Museums examined two swathes of ground, one (Area 1) on the farmland and the other (Area 2) along the line of the old railway, now followed by the bypass. Features picked up included: the water-leat, with the expected change of direction to allow for gravity-flow; the major defence-ditch already located twice previously (recorded as Ditch IV); foundation slots for timber buildings, one of which was possibly a *praetorium* or commander's house; a well, containing much pottery, together with other signs of at least two phases of military activity, one deemed only a 'demolition' phase (Horsey and Jarvis 1979). At the same time, there was little positive trace of the defence system in Poole Museum's Area 1, located in 1966–70 south-west of the causewayed road (Road 4), and the leat alongside. Once again, it was unfortunate that this rescue work did not establish the point at which the water-leat located in 1966–67 had changed direction. That angle should have thrown light on an important gap seen in the perimeter defences of at least one phase.

How did matters stand therefore, in 1980, as a result of previous excavations at Lake Farm? It had certainly been established that the south-west corner of one of the phases of the military site lay in the area affected by the new roundabout for the bypass and just east of that point. But confirmation was still lacking for phasing and size. Roads 3, 4 and 5 could be attributed to the military occupation. Road 1, though probably Roman, was laid after the army had left. Road 2 has always obviously belonged to a later phase, deemed military for several reasons. In 1962, as noted above, its side-ditch cut through the top of a significantly dated pit, probably filled by 55 or so,[8] while in 1963 the road was seen to incorporate, and lie directly on, early Roman material. It was highly unlikely, on general grounds, that this well-built road had been constructed merely for civil purposes to cover only a short distance across the first defence lines identified in the later sixties and described above. The significance of Road 2 is further discussed below.

Fortunately, vital information to confirm the size and phasing of the fortress emerged from the geophysical survey which was carried out by the Ancient Monuments Laboratory between 1976 and 1983.

Geophysical Survey

To appreciate the results of the scientific survey at Lake, one should understand the two basic approaches that are possible. Both methods aim at plotting buried disturbances of various kinds caused by human agency. These include ditches, pits, kilns and even, sometimes, walls and roads. In a resistivity survey, such invisible remains offer differing resistance to a weak electrical current passed between electrodes set at a regular distance apart in the modern ground surface. Previous weather conditions can be important, since dry terrain impedes, and wet soil exaggerates, the passage of the current. In 1970 the Ancient Monuments Laboratory found results at Lake by this method to be inconclusive, owing to what they called a 'lack of discrimination between archaeological and natural variations in soil texture and moisture retentiveness'. In 1976 the laboratory geophysical team started a series of magnetic surveys, which, by comparison, have had marked success. This method depends on the fact that man-made disturbances of subsoil will affect the local terrestrial magnetism and this variation can be recorded continuously along the ground by the requisite instrument, in this case called a fluxgate magnetometer. The surveys continued in 1980, 1982 and 1983 and revealed a 'very complex' situation.

The laboratory's final small-scale plan shows all the major anomalies recorded over the four visits. Isolated blobs which sometimes appear as linear features are interpreted as pits and ovens, while, most importantly, solid lines represent ditches and gullies. What it was hoped would emerge was the 'playing-card' shape that was becoming standard for fort-perimeters in the mid-first century A.D. Such a circuit (EFGH) has been claimed in the final laboratory report, with the east and north sides well defined and the west side suggested by inference from the disappearance of those anomalies indicating minor features within the fort itself. 'All four sides of the rectangle can therefore be positioned with some confidence and a sufficiently large area of the site has now been covered for an overall internal symmetry to be detectable. The fort appears to cover ... 12.8 hectares (31.6 acres) ...' This 1983 report goes on to detail the probable internal sub-divisions, but makes no further reference to the obvious ditch-line BC, explained as a 'boundary' in 1980, when the same term was used to define FG. If it seems surprising that the geophysical team did not suggest ABCD as a second military perimeter, the reason may have been understandable caution on this major site and ignorance of unpublished details from earlier excavations. There is certainly no problem about acceptance of perimeter EFGH as outlined by the laboratory. The magnetic survey has produced a clear visual image and the south side has been sectioned on three different occasions, close to the corner E.

But that is not the end of the story, since there are visibly a number of significant features resulting from the geophysical survey and past excavation that remain unexplained. The writer is convinced that there is a strong case that the outline ABCD represents the perimeter of an earlier and larger fortress. The following reasons can be offered:

1. The ditch-line BC has a straight layout, almost parallel to FG but longer, and can be accorded a military origin. Yet it would not fulfil any specific function in relation to EFGH. It would enclose too narrow a space for what are called 'extra-mural' activities, as it was only 20 m or so wide. The gap, markedly noticeable in the line, would fit a gateway at the other end of Road 3.

2. Of the two north-east and the two south-east corners (G,C and F,B respectively), only the curve of G was unequivocally shown up by the magnetic survey. However, in the south-east sector, the turn of both inner and outer ditches are swamped by what are termed 'industrial' features. These might belong to a period late in the military occupation (a demolition phase, for example) or afterward. Yet the plan does give some indication of linear details proceeding westwards from both F and B and commemorating, it appears, *two* south sides. At the north-east corner assigned to C, we again have definite signs

of magnetic anomalies curving round on the inside of the proposed defence circuit and then continuing vaguely on a westerly course. The military ditch or ditches forming the accepted perimeter EFGH by no means reveal themselves with clarity at every point. This is also the case with ABCD in respect of what was surveyed of its north and south sides, let alone the west side, which in essence appeared to be common to both phases.

(Why do these ditches show up so patchily on the magnetic survey? The laboratory report for 1980 supplies two likely causes: first, the ditches may have been 'infilled after a fairly short time with the relatively non-magnetic material of the banks', which would make the ditches virtually untraceable; second, 'activity on the site might have completed the in-filling of some of the features with more magnetic material to produce more detectable anomalies'; settlement of the soil thrown back into the ditches would occur after some time and provide depressions in which such fresh deposits could accumulate. It is this process possibly that has caused BC to become so obvious to a modern instrument.)

3. Road 5 lay just west to the ditch-line BC and would fit as the *intervallum* road (*via sagularis*) running inside that defence system. It had been cut into by a gully that had silted up with very black occupation soil and it yielded a coin of Claudius. The implication is that intense local activity had continued *after* this road had become disused and that the associated ditch-line BC belongs to the early phase of the military site.

4. The strip separating the two perimeters, the proposed ABCD and the accepted EFGH, can be usefully considered in the light of the existing evidence. The north sides (CD, GH) appear parallel and are separated by some 60 m, although, without opening up the ground, this cannot be checked. On the east the alignments of BC and FG are separated for more than 200 m by a strip with a constant measurement of some 21 m. A third linear feature which is discernible diverging slightly from the northern half of BC should belong to the earlier circuit ABCD and could be the start of a strengthened defence system that would not have been out of place for the vulnerable sides of the first fortress. Along the south, the two lines (EF, AB) have not yet been picked up by excavation. The strip of ground separating them would arguably be parallel again, with a width of around 20 m, a distance noted as separating inner and outer defences during the excavations of 1966–71. What is highly significant, as noted above, is that the water-leat or aqueduct recorded in those years changed direction to take the course seen in 1979 as it crossed through this projected defence-line AB. There was no apparent reason, given the level terrain and the presence of Road 4, why such an angle in the course of the leat should not have occurred at least 20 m further north, if EF were the only defence-line to have existed on this south side.

5. The 1980 laboratory report ended with these words: 'One can only comment on the striking coincidence of the evidence, as it emerges, with Mr Field's hypothesis.' The writer's suggested circuits for a large military site followed by a smaller one were illustrated in that report and approximate closely to the perimeter ABCD. These original findings formed the basis for the area scheduled as an ancient monument, but are now superseded by the plan based on the magnetic survey. However, there were good reasons why these first views were reached (i.e. a large fortress of almost legionary size, followed by a much smaller fort) and why, with the later information, mainly from the magnetic survey, the writer has arrived at his present argument (i.e. a large fortress, followed by a slightly smaller one).

Back in 1968, Road 1 had seemed to suggest the axial line of the military base, the east side of which had conceivably to lie at right angles and also to pass just east of Road 5. The south-west corner having been identified, it was possible to sketch the outline of a fortress of 16 hectares (40 acres) internally. Road 3 and its line had been excavated, but not evaluated, a fact that would have provided a truer alignment for the fortress. The much smaller fort which the writer thought lay inside the south-west angle of the original fortress was supposedly linked by Road 2 to the elbow in the Roman road from Poole Harbour to Badbury Rings. Thus there was evidence for two main phases, as later excavators came to realize. It had always become difficult anyway to reconcile the build and alignment of Road 1 with those of later similar features. After the geophysical survey, it could be seen that linear details of various kinds recorded from 1966 to 1973 closely matched what can now be regarded as the axis of the Roman layout.

What conclusions does the writer offer in the light of the arguments outlined above? It is proposed that excavation over the years and magnetic survey present two main phases in the defence-system at Lake Farm. The first fortress, Lake I (ABCD), enclosed an internal area of 420 m × 400 m (16.8 hectares, 41.5 acres), and was succeeded by Lake II (EFGH) measuring 400 m × 320 m (12.8 hectares, 31.6 acres).

Recognition of the true size of Lake I will no doubt fully emerge only with further trenching to establish its northern defence line. Long before the geophysical results the writer had concluded that the main fortress covered some 16 hectares (40 acres), following field-walking and contour-survey, soil-augering and test-excavation. As will be outlined below, there is a growing presumption from sites elsewhere that this size would be expected for such a legionary campaign base in the mid-first century.

What then of the interior of these phases of the fortress? It hardly needs to be said again that only large-scale excavation can make proper sense of the many internal features revealed by the magnetic survey. Some of the details brought out by that survey almost certainly will be found to betray not only the Roman military occupation, but also much later activities. Notwithstanding, it is possible to comment on certain salient features as clearly belonging to the period under investigation. There is an obvious hint of rectangular arrangements, measuring 80 m by 50 m, which, from comparison with other sites, would fit as legionary barrack-blocks lying in pairs back to back, with room for a third block ranged alongside, and parallel. These zones are outlined in the survey by firm, mainly continuous lines and, in two places, have shown up in limited excavation as gully-ditches, presumably for drainage on terrain that could in winter have proved very wet indeed. Some are likely to belong to Lake II, since traces of timber buildings have been found to pre-date them. The lesson from Longthorpe, a site of similar date and function,[9] is that considerable parts of the earlier layout were probably incorporated in the later, a fact that adds further caution to interpretation at this stage.

The significance of Roads 2 and 3 makes a case in point. The course of Road 3 has been identified on three occasions as noted above and is revealed on the survey by lines of (demolition?) pits, which have also been traced by excavation. There is no doubt that the west gate of at least one phase of the fortress gave access to the Roman road from Hamworthy at the sharp bend leading towards Badbury Rings. While Road 3 would fit as one access for that gate, it is noticeable on the magnetic survey that its projected alignment goes on to bisect those rectangular 'barrack' areas just mentioned and is crossed further east in the interior by a double-ditched feature, almost certainly another road, forming part of the rectangular pattern. Thus, was it the case that Road 3 belonged to Lake I and that the interior of the fortress was re-planned in Lake II? If so, Road 2, certainly later than Road 3, represents the second access to the bend in the Hamworthy road, when the west gate was rebuilt a little further south. It is important that in 1981 a small excavation, the latest work on the site, was undertaken in the mid-eastern area of the fortress (just south of the line of Road 1). It showed, to the satisfaction of the excavators, that the ditch of an internal east-west road had apparently cut through the end of an earlier building. This discovery confirms that extensive changes took place between two main phases.[10]

Thus Road 2 would have linked up with a new street in the re-planned fortress that would have run across at the junction of a central range of rectangular blocks mentioned above. If these two roads are related, as they seem to be, to the internal street-plan of the two main phases of the fortress, can it be that each represents the *via principalis* of one phase? Did the *porta praetoria* lie centrally along the southern perimeter just north-west of the buildings of Lake Farm itself? What of the access (Road 4) near the south-west corner apparently associated with an aqueduct? Is there any confirmation from what is known of Roman military sites at this period? These are questions that will be finally resolved only when further excavation is undertaken. Something may be gleaned, however, at this stage, from a comparison with the conventional internal planning of Roman military sites elsewhere.

A significant statistic inside a Roman fort comes from the ratio of the width of the fore part (between the defence-line of the *porta praetoria* and the *via principalis*) and the width of the central and rear parts (the rest of the fort). Normally the figure varies between 1.7 and 2.1, with some exceptions: the following appear to be the details for the Lake fortress:

LAKE I (if Road 3 is on line of first *via principalis*) = 1 : 1.74
LAKE II (if Road 2 re-aligns along second *via principalis*) = 1 : 2.6

The first of these figures compares satisfactorily with the ratio of 1.71 at Longthorpe I and 1.72 at Neuss, two contemporary fortresses, and fits the case for the defence-line CD. Even more interesting is the ratio from the published plan of the Exeter legionary fortress,[11] which, despite being overall more rectangular than Lake I, has been given the proportion 1 : 1.77. As for Lake II, the ratio seems unacceptably high, but there is strong evidence for the relatively later date of Road 2. We have also the excavated remains of what is thought to be a commander's house, a *praetorium*, which would be suitably sited, if the *via principalis* assigned to Lake II passed just south of it.

There is perhaps nothing to be gained by further discussion at this point. The fortress is there and sometime in the future answers will be forthcoming. Very probably, its planning involved elements that by the time of Claudius were already outmoded.

The Role of the Lake Fortress

It is possible to be more confident about the significance of the Lake base from what we have learned of its defence layout. The areas of Lake I and II can be set against those of comparable Claudio-Neronian military sites in Britain, although none has been totally excavated. The original base at Lincoln covered 16.7 hectares (41.3 acres), short of the 20.25 hectares (50 acres) considered essential for a full legionary garrison. Such reduced headquarters for the Ninth Legion Hispana pointed apparently to a loss of numbers either through outposting to small forts (normally held by auxiliary forces) or through casualties on campaign. However, most interestingly, it is now claimed that the 16.5 hectares (41 acres) at Exeter, the successor to Lake, apparently held enough barrack-blocks for at least a legionary complement to have been able to over-winter within it. By contrast, York, to which the Ninth Legion eventually moved, took in the full 20 hectares. But Lincoln was not occupied until the 60s, so it must be to Longthorpe near

Peterborough that we look for details of the largest military site yet identified on the right flank of the Roman advance into lowland Britain. There, too, as at Lake, two main phases have been established, the larger of 10.9 hectares (27 acres), the smaller and later of 4.4 hectares (11 acres).

The first Longthorpe fortress:

>...belongs to a class of military site virtually unknown until 20 years ago, but of which some 12 examples can now be identified. They vary ... between 20 and 30 acres (8 and 12 hectares) and though only half the size of a normal legionary fortress ... are many times larger than a normal auxiliary fort (3–5 acres). Although some may have served wholly or partly as store-bases, it seems likely that their normal function was a winter-quarters *(hiberna)* for battle groups made up in varying proportions of legionary and auxiliary troops. The term vexillation-fortresses is proposed for them.

In this notable paper, Frere and St Joseph went on to explain the probable reasoning behind the creation of this type of military station. After the immediate conquest 'the reinforcement of scattered auxiliary garrisons and the requirements of strategy could be more efficiently supported by a wider distribution of centres of power than a scheme based on whole legions in single fortresses.' The map of the 'vexillation-fortresses' in southern Britain during the mid-first century shows that in the initial years of the conquest the Roman forces on the right flank had to cover a considerable distance to reach the 'frontier' belt, ostensibly represented by the Fosse Way. On the left flank, however, Lake remained during that time a pivotal centre and its role as a legionary base of less than normal size seems to have been envisaged from the very start of operations. The choice was deliberately made in advance and did not result from mere expediency.

Lake I, Exeter and Lincoln were almost identical in size and, one might also guess, in function. It is apparent that these three military stations form a separate category, each with an area of just over 16 hectares (40 acres), somewhat larger than those listed by Frere and St Joseph, but still somewhat smaller than the 'normal' legionary fortress. There is still a case that legionaries were being outposted to share duties with the auxiliaries at the smaller military sites, including those now known or suspected inside hillforts. A fresh examination of the evidence from far afield, however,[12] suggests that, on first-century sites, it may be more difficult than hitherto thought to distinguish the presence of auxiliary troops from that of legionaries. A legion would then have normally over-wintered in full complement, a view apparently supported by the latest conclusion that the Exeter base held enough barrack-blocks for the whole of the Second Augustan Legion. It follows, on that argument, that Lake I would have served the same end and Hod Hill was a normal outlying auxiliary fort.

On existing evidence, Lake I (figs. 4.3 and 4.4, ABCD), one third larger than Longthorpe I, was replaced, around 55 or a little earlier, by Lake II (EFGH), of equivalent size.[13] It is reliably estimated that Longthorpe I held a maximum of 2800 men of which number from 1440 to 1760, in three cohorts, could have been legionaries, with the remainder as auxiliaries. On the theory of split forces, it would not be unreasonable, therefore, to place six cohorts of the legionary strength of ten in the garrison of Lake I, with four cohorts serving at posts in the countryside. With the establishment of Lake II, the base would be proportionately reduced. Whatever the complement of Lake I, troops could then have been released for active service in Wales or Devon and Cornwall, where they were more urgently needed in the mid-50s. Indeed, the discovery at North Tawton of several phases of a military site, up to the size of Lake II, would suggest the creation of a forward campaigning base. In 60–61, the garrison of

Lake II, at least in part, was still stationed to support outlying units, like Waddon.[14] As discussed below, the Boudiccan rebellion faced the legion with a major problem and only after repressive measures could the movement of the legionary headquarters to Exeter be finally completed.

Despite the general details given so far, some have still thought that 'the site of the original legionary base for the south-west is far from certain.'[15] In the opinion of others, a reduced fortress at Lake Farm may have had a companion at Dorchester, each of these holding half a legion.[16] However, excavation at Dorchester has so far failed to offer proof of a military site of anything like the area of that at Lake Farm. A solution to the main problem at Lake *per se*, encompassing size and sequence, has been outlined in this chapter. The next chapter will reinforce that case by the description of Roman military roads emanating in the first place from Lake Farm.

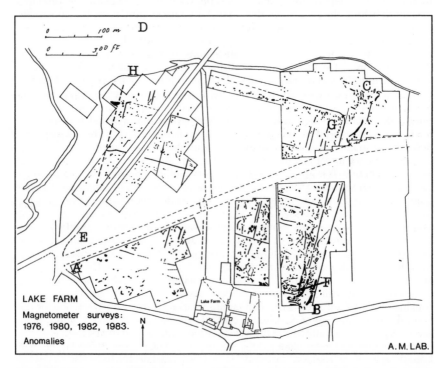

4.7 Lake Farm: geophysical plan showing features plotted by Ancient Monuments Laboratory, 1976–83

5

The Early Military Roads

The roads to be described in this chapter form an impressive monument to the military thinking behind the campaign that the Roman army fought in Dorset during the 40s A.D. There is no problem, indeed, as we shall see, in fitting the roads, as they emerge, into the strategy of the invaders. First things first. The difficulty begins today with the burden of proof that these roads actually existed. Can the network be satisfactorily demonstrated? It has never been an easy task to obtain general agreement even on bridging a gap in an accepted Roman road where most of the track has been for generations. Special conviction may be required, too, in Dorset. Some years back, the county was the subject of the most thorough investigations by staff of the Royal Commission on Historical Monuments (England). Of all the archeological remains, roads would seem to offer the least disturbed evidence of their period, being already at ground level and so often forgotten and buried by later deposits. How, then, to explain why these finds were not made before for their recovery has simply been a question of employing formal and well-recognized methods of field-survey and test excavation?

The overriding reason is the comparative recentness of the discoveries at Lake Farm, near Wimborne, which were not recognized until the late 1960s. The known Roman road from Hamworthy, Poole Harbour, clearly led to that major military site and thereby destroyed the contention of some authorities that the Roman army built no roads as such in Dorset. Given that fact, the least inquiring of Romanists would have suspected the existence of other contemporary lines of communication. Judging by the evidence dug from the ground, there was a military presence at Lake for at least fifteen years. It became more and more obvious that from that site roads must have been laid radiating towards Badbury Rings and Hod Hill, Dorchester and probably Wareham and almost certainly from the direction of Salisbury and Winchester. To establish the roads to Dorchester and Wareham, the writer has, over the last dozen years, carried out a number of investigations in the time-honoured manner, beginning at Corfe Mullen, then extending to other parts of the county. The work has been based on normal observation of surviving surface evidence in the field, reinforced from chance exposures and full length sections cut by machine or dug entirely by

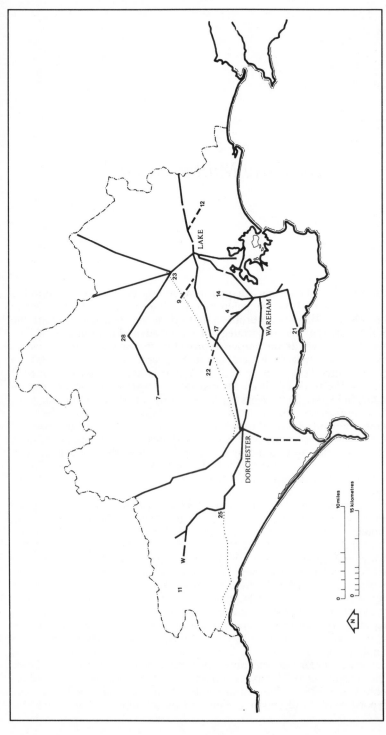

5.1 Roman roads in Dorset, described in Chapter 5. The early military roads shown as heavy lines, the later civil roads as dotted lines. (W=Waddon Hill, 4=Woolsbarrow, 7=Rawlsbury, 9=Spetisbury, 11=Pilsdon, 12=Dudsbury, 14=Bulbury, 22=Weatherby Castle, 23=Badbury Rings, 28=Hod Hill)

hand. Detailed findings from particular points along the roads have been placed in the Appendices. The results form the core of this book. Not only do they add many miles to the hitherto accepted grid of Roman roads in Dorset, they also clarify the progress of an invading force whose movements have long been wrapped in mystery.

Something has been said in Chapter 2 on the traditionally accepted characteristic of Roman roads (of which point-to-point straightness is most typical). To what extent are these features revealed by military roads in Dorset as they will be described? Faced by the need for rapid construction, the army surveyors were much governed by immediate topography and existing native trackways. Long straight lengths, so familiar on the open rolling chalkland of Cranborne Chase, for example, may be replaced by shorter alignments where a ridgeway was being utilized (Dorchester westward) or where woods were being skirted (Lake to Wareham, avoiding Lytchett woods). It is worthwhile recalling what was said many years ago by a great authority on Roman Britain: 'A Roman road does not often run really straight for long together ...when one is walking along the road, it seems straight, even when on a small-scale map it may seem to be almost constantly changing direction...'.[1] On these military roads the camber was gentle; excavation shows that, if we see a high agger today, it could well have been created by successive re-surfacings, often later than Roman times. Thus an early road which found little use after the departure of the army may not long have resisted burial by various agencies, like ploughing or soil-creep, unless an alternative purpose was served, as a local access, for example, or as a boundary of some kind.

Another important detail that distinguishes the early military roads is the manner in which the materials were laid. Later roads, built by civilians, did not necessarily follow the methods adopted by the military. The broad trench in which, we have noted, according to Statius,[2] a road had to be laid, has indeed featured in several cross-sections: Corfe Mullen (Higher Russell's Copse and Cogdean), Stinsford (Butcher's Copse) and probably Stoborough Heath. The method was obligatory on soft, unstable subsoils, but clearance of topsoil may have sufficed on a firmer natural base like chalk, or very stony gravel as at Stourpaine (Lazerton Farm) and Corfe Mullen (Whitehall House).

Some words of explanation are required about the way in which the roads have been depicted. The 'normal' method has been to reproduce strips directly from large-scale Ordnance maps. Here these are replaced by plans specially drawn to avoid extraneous detail. On these, a firm unbroken line signifies that, in the writer's view, the course is reliable and may still be traced positively in one way or another by the observant eye. It will usually have been revealed, for example, by surface traces of an ancient ridge or by other long-accepted indications like parish boundaries or pre-nineteenth-century hedge-lines. In some cases, excavated sections or exposures have been vital. For these stretches of road, the Ordnance Survey might use the term 'certain'. Where the line is shown broken the course on the ground may nevertheless be presumed reasonably certain. Validity here is supported by what can be recognized elsewhere, but the exact positioning may be a few metres either way of what is shown.

The custom has grown up of frequently quoting National Grid References in describing a road. It is felt, however, that these groups of figures interrupt a text otherwise adequately illustrated by maps simplified from Ordnance Survey style six-inch or recent 1:10 000 plans. Such map references have been restricted in general to the Appendices for identifying details of sections and so on.

A final point. During the last ten years major changes have been taking place in some motor-roads indirectly involved in our survey. Each of Wimborne, Bere

47

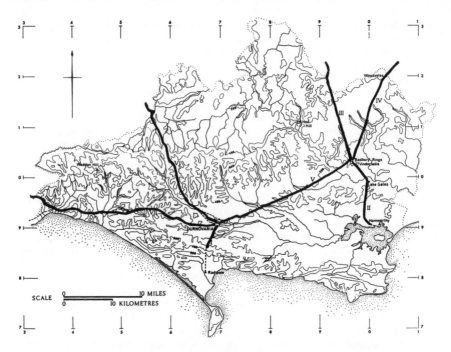

5.2 Roman roads in Dorset, as recognized in 1975 (Royal Commission on Historical Monuments, England)

5A.1 High agger of the Roman road from Hamworthy to Lake Farm, on Barrow Hill, Poole, looking north-east

Regis, Wareham and Dorchester now has its bypass. If almost all the plans have had to be based on older large-scale maps, it is hoped they will prove none the less informative to those in search of knowledge.

(A) **Lake Farm to Poole Harbour**

The course of this road has been for much of its length one of the best recognized in Dorset, because it lay undisturbed across Upton Heath and the high wastes of Corfe Mullen. Its early date of construction has been obvious since the Roman military base was identified at Lake, which was clearly linked to landing facilities set up on the shore at Hamworthy. All the same, precisely where the Romans had their landing-stages for their port and where their road headed inland remain uncertain, despite the unearthing in the 1920s, close to the power-station site, of much first-century pottery. Some of this material had been imported from the Continent and could only have come over with the Roman army, whose nearby presence might have been suspected at the time of its discovery. It is only towards the neck of the Hamworthy peninsula, therefore, that the line of the road can be positively identified[1] at the beginning of the long stretch north-north-east towards the Lake Farm base. The course can still be walked as a bridle-way or a recent modern road, while two lengths of prominent causeway are scheduled as ancient monuments on Corfe Hills and Barrow Hill. For much of the way across the immemorial heathland, so recently developed, the Roman road has served as the parish boundary between Corfe Mullen and Canford, the precise limit being a bank on its western flank. Landscaping by machine not long ago unfortunately buried terracing on a spur midway along where the Roman road descended on heathland to Rushcombe Bottom.

To the north, beyond Higher Merley Lane, having crossed the gravel plateau that separates the harbour waters from the Stour river, the road re-aligns to drop down towards Lake. The exact point where this angle occurs has been lost in old quarry-pits at Cogdean, but the line of this final stretch has been established thanks to excavation and chance exposures (Appendix 15). The sequence of constructional events at various points on this well-used road need not detain us here. We are basically concerned with the road as a link from port to base during the military occupation of Dorset, and there is no question but that the road was the creation of the Roman army. However, it is relevant to note that two early phases have been observed in sections cut through the Roman road in Corfe Mullen, close to the Lake base camp, the first carriageway being only wide enough for one-way traffic. More importantly, at two places on this stretch down to Lake, clues were forthcoming suggesting branch-roads running west and south-west. Obtained under the not ideal conditions that sometimes attend rescue work, the evidence had to await confirmation in various forms from the branch-roads themselves.

The first indication of a possible road-junction occurred in 1977, only 15 m east of the railway bridge (now vanished) at East End and on the north side of the deep cutting (Appendix 15). A double service was performed by the machine-clearance. A precise section chopped through the Roman road from Hamworthy in its several phases, showing it at the same time to be aligned a little more to the east than anticipated. Furthermore, a discovery difficult then to explain was a substantial support of stones, built to take a carpentered post and probably belonging to the second phase of the road. As explained elsewhere, this branch-road, which has proved to be leading to Wareham and Purbeck, forked off at the very spot later destroyed by the railway cutting. It is very probable, therefore, that the stone cairn had been built to hold a sign-post of the 'finger' type, arguably the earliest such traffic indicator yet identified in the British Isles.

Having re-aligned at the top of the descent at East End, the road from Hamworthy ran down towards Lake past the branch to Wareham, which joined it, as noted, east of the former bridge. It then passed under the old cottage that now forms part of the Lamb's Green inn. Another 240 m further downhill, the Roman road was seen and examined in 1981 when Wimborne Road was diverted across it (Appendix 16). The impression here of metalling for a branch-road curving away in a westerly direction could not be followed up at the time, but has since been corroborated at a number of points in lower Corfe Mullen and its ultimate destination shown to be Dorchester. This last stretch of the road from Poole Harbour reached the south-west corner of the military base at Lake under what is now the roundabout forming the start of the Wimborne bypass. From there, the indications are that it ran parallel to and west of the Roman defence-ditches on a very slightly altered alignment, eventually to arrive outside the western gateway of the fortress (Lake I). Thereafter, with a further change of angle, it became the road to Badbury Rings and beyond.

(B) Lake Farm to Badbury Rings and Hod Hill

The Roman road from Lake Farm to the fork north of Badbury Rings has long been authenticated and its course established on the ground, despite its disappearance for much of the stretch towards the hillfort. What was originally regarded without complication simply as the road from Poole Harbour inland took on a different aspect when the sharp bend in the Stour valley was seen to lie at the west gate of a major military site. From that point, the straight alignment towards Badbury can be picked up in the river meadows, and then further on at Abbott Street, as a distinctive low agger. While its initial construction can certainly be ascribed to the engineers of the Second Legion, details along this stretch confirm what excavation has revealed for the southern part from Poole Harbour, namely that the road had several phases of build in the past and what is visible today masks the first military highway. Thus, while in Eye Mead, between the Lake site and the Stour, the road survives with a width of 8 m, a section with another story to tell came to light from a machine-cut trench north of Kingston Lacy House, where the course is buried.[1] A substantial band of pebble metalling sealing medieval pottery, was found to be 6 m wide. Below, the earlier road had two (presumably Roman) phases of gravel-topped chalk make-up, the first of these 3.24 m wide. No signs appeared here of side-ditches at any stage of the road-history. Yet, close to Badbury Rings, where the material for the agger has been completely removed by ploughing on shallow natural soil, buried side-ditches exist, 25.6 m apart. It seems that widely separated side-ditches, particularly those associated with Roman roads running over Dorset downs or heath, belong to a later phase of construction than the military period.

North-west of Kingston Lacy Park, more closely set side-ditches were identified, possibly of later than Roman date, but the plough had removed all trace of the agger from above the chalk.[2] Then, immediately north of Badbury Rings, the road from Lake forked into three in a remarkable manner (1a). It cannot be accidental that the two angles made by the trifurcation are exactly equal, with the implication that the roads from this point towards Hod Hill, Bath and Sarum were all of military origin. A recent excavation in Batts Field,[3] north of that point again, has shown that the side-ditches of the Bath road were laid out to fit in with those of the Dorchester–Badbury–Sarum road, the renowned Ackling Dyke of Cranborne Chase. Since, as already suggested, side-ditches often appear to be of secondary build (and certainly those which lie widely apart), it remains probable that the Roman army created the treble fork and that the road to Dorchester athwart the general line was a later construction.

50

5B.1–5 Roman road from Badbury Rings to Hod Hill

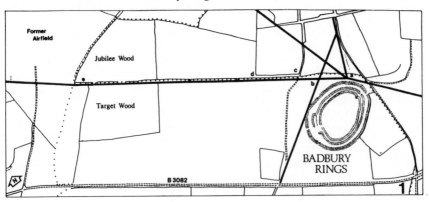

5B.1 Lake Farm to Hod Hill: Badbury Rings

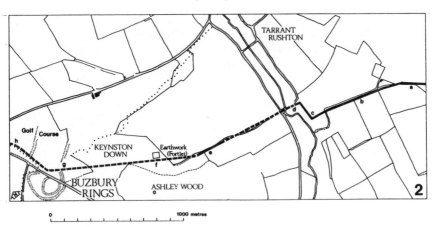

5B.2 Lake Farm to Hod Hill: Buzbury Rings

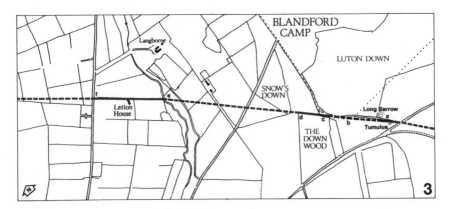

5B.3 Lake Farm to Hod Hill: Snow's Down and Letton

51

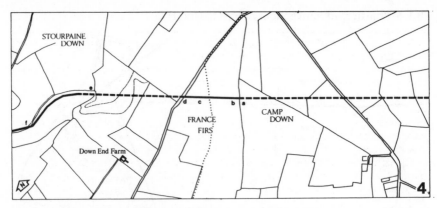

5B.4 Lake Farm to Hod Hill: France Firs

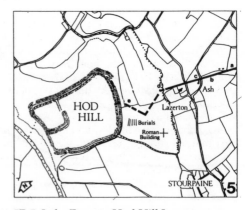

5B.5 Lake Farm to Hod Hill Lazerton

52

After the Badbury junction, which occurs in a small thicket, the road leading towards Hod Hill is soon crossed by the massive agger of Ackling Dyke. On either side of that point, the Hod line has received support from two sources, although nothing now shows on the surface. Firstly, to the east, air photography[4] in the 1920s revealed a late enclosure bank, starting at the outer ditch of the Rings and ending precisely at the expected alignment, which seems to have been flanked by several quarry-ditches. All these features respected the existence of a linear feature, which must have been the Hod road. Secondly, west of the intersection of this road with Ackling Dyke (1b), excavation has revealed a denuded band of flint and chalk material, 4.8 m wide, spread on natural chalk. It lay exactly where anticipated and again is evidence for the lost road (Appendix 24).

The continuation of the Roman line is next suggested by the straight length of parish boundary between Pamphill and Shapwick, to which Codrington drew attention years ago. Recently, three trenches[5] have been cut in the long belt of woodland hiding that parish boundary between Pamphill and Shapwick (1c–1d). In varying degrees of survival, the Roman road has appeared as a band of flint metalling on broken chalk, 3 m wide with a low camber, and 0.25 m thick at maximum. On its north side, it had a side-ditch, probably secondary, which, when filled, had a turf bank built upon it. This became the parish boundary, only to vanish finally under leaf mould. At the end of this stretch of woodland, three parish boundaries are recorded as meeting at the stone inscribed 'Religious Cross'. The stone remains, but there is little to be seen of the boundaries or the road itself (1e). However, the Roman line next goes on to traverse arable, where it could be traced in the 1960s as a dark band with a hard surface which could be picked up by probing. At that time, the Tarrant Rushton airfield was still in operation and, a little further on (1f), a low ridge stood out in the mown grass of the overshoot to the south runway (1f). Approaching Preston Cottages, we find a hedge coming from the south turns to take up the alignment for 200 m before the first marked change of direction (2a) since the junction north of Badbury. So far, the course of 3.2 km has seen a rise and fall of no more than 15 m, and the line moreover (1a–2a), if projected, would lead directly to the ultimate destination at Hod Hill. The re-alignment precisely occurs at the start of the drop to the little river Tarrant, and the low ridge can be traced along the south side of the next hedge. Then, south of the lane, a section-trench in the shallow soil (Appendix 23) revealed slight flint and chalk metalling more than 4 m wide (2b). When the lane swerves away south-westward the Roman line is presumed to have continued, with a minor re-alignment on the steepening slope. There is a complication here in that a white streak seen after ploughing may represent either the old road or the trace of a war-time drain leading down from the former airfield. What is certain is that the final descent to the Tarrant below was effected by a zigzag terraced track (2c), now destroyed and incorporated in an enlarged field. All that is left to remind us of the lost terracing is a modern stile at the lowest point.

The Roman road now goes across the lane to the ford as a stony ridge, which then swings west to form the north hedge-boundary of that lane as a causewayed edge (2d). At the Tarrant, we find signs of two fords: the present one is reached by a slight diversion off the line on the south, but the older ford took the direct route, which the existing footbridge also observes. The causeway can be observed in the triangle of rough ground on the other side of the water, then, beyond the Tarrant valley road, the Roman course is almost coincident for 800 m with Heath Lane. The latter becomes a sunken way and soon wanders a little southward off the Roman line, which has been ploughed out on the north. Then the reverse happens with the agger concealed in the fringe of copse to the south (2e). Near the higher ground a recent diversion of the lane-cum-bridle-path carved a way through the narrow copse and afforded a partial section of the Roman metalling alongside the hollow-way. The gravelled camber was seen to be 5.3 m wide and at least 0.4 m deep in the centre. There was the possibility of a side-ditch to its south.[6]

Even at the time of the first six-inch maps (1886), this area was tree-covered and known as Ashley Wood. The name is preserved by enclosed woodland to the south and by the neighbouring golf-links. Until the arable was extended in the 1970s, it was possible, at the stub-end of the lane, to see where the Roman road re-aligned at the start of a new stretch in the direction of Buzbury Rings. Between that spot and those earthworks, the ancient right of way has been diverted, as noted above, although its recent course was indeed straighter than appears to have been the case when Ashley Wood extended over Keynston Down. Modern farming has smoothed out former boundaries, so that the low squarish shape of the probable Roman fortlet,[7] close to the suggested line of the road is now even more difficult to locate at ground level than a few years ago (2f). Only at the eastern edge of Buzbury does the Roman road betray itself in the shape of a causewayed passage over the outer ditch of the hillfort, allied to a purposeful cutting through the rampart (2g). One fairway of the golf course is set along the wide track of the old road, which has been called a medieval pack-horse route, a view apparently strengthened by the very visible ridging in the turf. We must recognize why the Roman engineers thought it necessary to lay this road through the Rings. As a hillfort, Buzbury is in an inferior category and some relegate it to the status of a mere defended settlement, whatever that may mean. But it was sited on a narrow col between the slope down to the Stour on the south and a pronounced dry valley on the north, and thereby controlled the prehistoric way on that side of the Stour.

Having entered the Rings by means of a causeway and a cutting, the Roman road turns sharply close to the modern Blandford Road to pass from a north-westerly to a north-north-westerly bearing. This re-orientation occurs on the crest of downland that has been subjected to wear and tear over the centuries, as demonstrated by an early air-view in *Wessex from the Air*. That photograph shows a number of old tracks, almost any one of which could qualify as the Roman road on the new alignment. Modern farming and the golf course have somewhat altered the landscape in sixty-odd years, but there is little doubt that for a distance of nearly 1.6 km onward the track of the Roman road is linked directly and indirectly with the behaviour of parish boundaries.

Thus two straight lengths of the boundary between Tarrant Rawston and Langton Long Blandford take the course past the Ashley Wood golf-house and a short way along a lane. This was an important sighting point (3a), for the Roman road was laid out to pass between a round barrow (now in a clump of trees to the south of the lane) and a notable long barrow to the north. The ridge of the old road is still just visible north of the tumulus. Then lane and parish boundary swerve off line on the north-east in a curve, leaving the Roman course to continue, ploughed out, on Little Down (3b), until the next boundary is met by all three linear features. This boundary, coming uphill 'undefined' over Luton Down from the east, separates Tarrant Monkton from Tarrant Rawston. When it meets the Roman line coming across the field, the boundary again combines with it for another tangibly straight length, which offers some particularly important details.

For the first 200 m the straightness of the parish boundary is the only certain evidence. There is no bank, only the stony edge of a copse and ploughed ground. Then, along the north side of The Down Wood estate, a positive agger can be observed, cloaked in trees and brushwood, quite separate from the banked edge to the south. Here, after a small disturbed area at the north-east corner of the estate, the parish boundary appears as a distinct low bank, only 0.15 m high, with the Roman road parallel to the north, 3 m wide and up to 0.2 m high (3c). Since Badbury, this is the first stretch of Roman road to have remained unequivocally recognizable as an abandoned agger, under its thin covering of humus. Over a distance of 50 m, road and boundary thus run together, with the gap between them gradually becoming more pronounced in the shape of a ditch, shallow at first, then deeper (Appendix 34). The bank and ditch forming the parish boundary next turn sharply north-westwards and cut through the agger, which for its part continues for another 150 m as the rest of the well-defined north edge to The Down Wood. Before the agger proceeds to disappear on the long-established arable of Snow's Down, a low bank forming the western limit of The Down Wood runs up to the north-west corner of that enclosure (3d). There it can be seen resting as a later addition on the end of the Roman causeway.

From that point, for 800 m, the plough has been regularly levelling the ground, although a ridge, only just discernible, crosses the field on the right line in the southern part of Snow's Down. The nameless stream flowing south to the Stour is reached after a narrow belt of alluvial meadow, but still nothing shows. Then there immediately comes into view, more particularly on the far bank, evidence for two fords, the northernmost of which is still in farm use. The older one, just to the south, lies most significantly at the end of the projected line (3d–3e) from The Down Wood and can be compared to the older ford noted where this Roman road crossed the Tarrant.

Beyond the stream lies an irregular area of raised ground, marked on early Ordnance Survey maps as a small enclosure. Its north side was then the site of a building apparently erected on the line of the Roman road. This stretch, with a slight change of direction at the stream, can be traced as far as the Salisbury Road, over 400 m up slope, past a new housing development in the grounds of Letton House. A hedge of some age rests upon a distinctively wide, low ridge, varying from 2.5 m to 3 m in breadth and averaging 0.2 m high. It is noteworthy that there is no indication of an accompanying ditch, which would be expected if the feature were a normal field-bank. Indeed the width of the road-ridge is emphasized for some distance by parallel wire-fences along each flank, a procedure observed elsewhere where an extant fragment of road has been adopted as a boundary.

On the other side of the Salisbury Road (the gradient of which has long been eased by a cutting) there is nothing again to substantiate the probable Roman line, which for more than 1.6 km crosses intensively cultivated farmland long known as Camp Down. Visual evidence does not occur until we have entered the mixed woodland, strangely called France Firs. The east margin of this old plantation comprises a solid bank of large flints running athwart the vanished line of the former road. It is not hard to see why traces of the Roman causeway are no longer visible on this approach to France Firs from the south-east. Although a belt of recent woodland borders the lower edge of the bank, there are signs of a sharp negative lynchet, indicative of sustained ploughing in the past before the present trees grew on that side (4a). But west of the bank, a diligent search in the wood will identify the intermittent remains of the road.

The plantation of France Firs is traversed by tracks used by forestry vehicles and the effect of both clearance and occasional traffic of this kind is to throw into relief at points of traverse the hard ridge of the Roman road. Thus the ridge can be seen in the woodland track running just inside the eastern perimeter bank (4b). To the south, that track is also crossed by several parallel furrows that are almost certainly connected with the final use of the Roman road. Since the latter

55

line is now continuing up the slope of a spur inside the Firs, the furrows can be taken to represent secondary routes (packhorse ?) that developed as the original road fell into disrepair – a common phenomenon on such a gradient, where a zig-zag had not been attempted in the first place.

As already noted, the woodland is by no means purely coniferous, and, with the passage of time, there has been a considerable accumulation of humus and decaying hardwood stumps, which does not help the recovery of ground evidence for a low agger. If the Roman line is followed up the slope from the perimeter track (4b), the next clue is given as the higher ground levels out. Here the slight ridge of the road runs through an ancient gap in an unrecorded linear bank of unknown date and length. After passing a mound of recent origin, the Roman road is crossed, some 70 m north-west of the gap, by a new forest track and shows distinctly as a stony band 6 m wide and 0.6 m high. Another 120 m further on, there is again a sighting of the low ridge, where a track of importance from a forest crossroads to the south runs over it (4c). Only 40 m north-east of that spot, in shrubbery west of the track, a fine unrecorded round barrow (diameter 9 m, height 0.6 m) reminds us of what France Firs still conceals. Beyond the intersection at 4c, uprooted stumps belonging to deciduous trees of age and substance lie on the line, which otherwise appears as an occasional stony belt, but finally emerges as a ridge in the western perimeter track beside the present road to Stourpaine (4d).

Across the road, the land continues to rise in the fields east of Down End Farm, but once again regular ploughing has effectively erased surface traces. Some 500 m north-east of Down End, the road must have reached the summit of a col between yet higher ground south-west and north-east. Thereafter the course of the Roman road gently descends as far as the head of the dry valley (4e) that leads to Ash, Lazerton, the Iwerne stream and finally Hod Hill. From that point, a broad terraced way, some 7 m wide, skirts the spur on the south side of the valley, running along the north-facing slope well above the lowest terrain. This terrace runs level for 600 m keeping contour-wise a little higher than the 70 m (200 ft) contour, until the course has curved round the spur and straightened for the last stretch towards Hod Hill. It is then crossed and re-crossed by the tarred road that now leads up this valley from Ash Farm (4f). East of two cottages, the remnant of the old (untarred) lane, now bypassed, begins that last alignment. Then, still terraced, the course passes south of the cottages (5a), where the Roman road coincides with the modern lane (5b). Next the lane shifts a little northward to leave the Roman line running under a well-established hedge with trees. This hedge bounds the higher field to the south, with the farm-lane parallel to the north, and there has been considerable soil accumulation down towards the boundary. If inspection is made from the lower level of the lane the stony metalling of the old road can be discerned beneath the build-up of soil. The Roman alignment continues as the access alongside the farmhouse itself and then passes into the grounds of Lazerton on the west of the Blandford–Shaftesbury road. While slight indications occur in garden-beds and lawns near the house, it is the last 130 m of this alignment towards the Iwerne (4f–5d) that now demand attention.

In the grounds of Lazerton, a series of ponds has been constructed, served by the adjacent water-supply, although they have not functioned for a long time. One of the long, empty depressions lying west-east to the north of the house is flanked along its north side by a prominent earthwork like a high causeway. This feature continued the line we have been following which aims at the Ashfield Gate now near at hand up on Hod Hill. It also formed a manorial boundary, on the face of things older than the pond-system. Excavation in the early 1970s and later (Appendix 25) indicated a probable Roman origin and subsequently most of the earthwork, for a length of about 100 m, was scheduled as an ancient monument. The further work in 1986, close to the stream, on an unscheduled portion, amplified the findings. Of three phases of build, the first was a road about 3 m wide, with a gently cambered surface 0.15 m high, of chalk fragments topped by flints and on a base of larger stones set in the natural chalk. Then metalling was added in the later Roman period and finally, in the eighteenth century, spoil from the adjoining pond was thrown up to widen what was no longer in use as a road. For half a dozen metres towards the Iwerne there has been disturbance from the creation of a conduit for the ponds, so that it is not possible on the east of the stream to establish whether the Roman army made use of a bridge or a ford (5d). Once on the other bank, only a formidable 1:4 climb was needed to take the alignment straight up to the Ashfield Gate. It is strange that over the years the problem of access to and from the Gate and the Roman fort within has not been investigated. There is a strong clue in the terrain at the eastern end of the causeway, well illustrated in the Royal Commission hachured plan of Hod Hill.[8] Movement from that point was guided towards the south-east, for the outer Iron Age ditch has been further refilled to provide access in that direction. Notably, too, a small defensive feature, now seen only as a straight edge, appears to have prevented a direct approach on to the causeway. This outwork could have been a *titulus* like that fronting the *porta praetoria* of the Roman fort itself. One method chosen by Roman engineers for tackling a stiff gradient was a zigzag approach, and on the terrain in question this would have required terracing or shelving the roadway into the slope. By this means a more acceptable incline of 1:8 was possible. With the passage of time, the terraced road, once abandoned, would fill with soil-creep, but should at least remain faintly discernible from the air. Since the site was first photographed for Plate I of *Wessex from the Air*, views of the hillfort taken on various occasions have not seemed helpful. Fortunately, one oblique view with the sun and the field growth in favour is revealing. The upper stretch of such a zigzag or dogleg can be seen as a long, narrow furrow (5e) in the field south-east of the Gate, which appears to be its goal.

Two further details reinforce the case that this was how the road from Lake Farm and Badbury ended. First, the south-east approach offers a slightly easier slope than that to the north-east of the Gate. It would be the logical choice for the Roman engineers. Second, just south of the angle of the zigzag, lies 'Great Bournes', a Romano-British building uncovered in 1860, when a number of burials were also found further up the slope. It would be logical enough for a settlement of some kind to have used the road entry set up by the military into the hillfort and for a small cemetery to have been sited close to that access. Indeed the burial ground might have begun as an army affair, while the permanent enclosure inside the native fortress cannot have failed to attract local farming once the legion had left.

(C) Lake Farm to Dorchester

The road branches off from the Hamworthy–Lake Roman road 150 m south of the south-west corner of the fortress, a fact first suspected in 1980 during rescue work before the construction of the Wimborne bypass. The road from the harbour was sectioned where earth clearance had already exposed its line (Appendix 16) and it was noted that the latest stony metalling was beginning to curve round westwards (1a). Investigation of this apparent junction could not be completed, but the details were sufficient to fix the location for the trench that was cut in 1983 less than 20 m to the west (Appendix 20). At that point the early

5B.6 Roman Road from Badbury to Hod Hill at Buzbury Rings, looking east

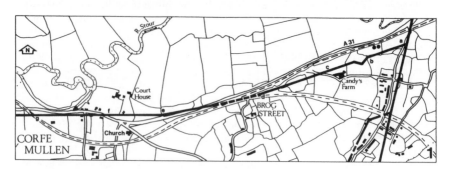

5C.1 Roman road from Lake Farm to Dorchester: Corfe Mullen

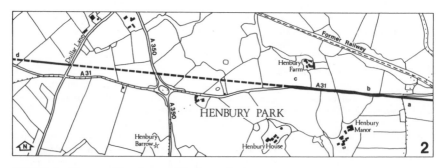

5C.2 Lake Farm to Dorchester: Henbury Park

road proved to be 2.75 m wide, with a *margo* or walk-way joining it on the south. The curving edge of the possible branch-road seen in 1980 tied in with the spread of later metalling at a higher level. Potsherds associated with the low surface were contemporary in date with the military occupation at Lake Farm. Only the slightest of ridges is visible in this field and the line of the road passes under the corner of the site now occupied by a sewage plant. Much defaced by pipe-trenches, the course then emerges in the next field-corner, north of a prominent spur (1b). The earthworks associated with this higher ground are discussed later (Chapter 8A). The evidence, in the writer's view, is that they were intimately connected with the first alignment of the road and with the everyday functioning of the Roman base itself.

At the foot of the spur, the remains of a low bank, possibly the edge of a medieval field, runs parallel with the Roman line for a short distance. Beyond the next north-south hedge (also a boundary of considerable antiquity) the road enters the large field east of Candy's Farmhouse and now makes a sharp zigzag southward following the slope of the plateau gravel. This zigzag, well marked in dry weather, may have been engineered to avoid an obviously wet re-entrant in London Clay, or else it may have some link with the earthworks on the spur. Back on its original alignment, the road shows as 70 m of agger, 4 m wide, which served in the 1960s to take a pipe-trench to the sewage works. North of Candy's Farmhouse, the road is not visible in the disturbed ground of a former orchard, although it was still to be seen in the next field until levelled by ploughing not long ago. It reappears crossing the garden of no. 2, Carter's Cottages, as a short length of well-preserved causeway (1c). The agger continues to show less prominently in the garden of no.1, where a small investigation was possible in 1984 (Appendix 21). The evidence here, and further west, indicates that the *margo* now lay on the north, a change that probably occurred at the earthworks on the spur to the east. Beyond Carter's Cottages, the causeway crosses the entrance to the small caravan park, and the office hut is sited upon it. The course of the road passes transversely to the other side of Candy's Lane and is commemorated by an angle in the opposing hedge. It now runs more or less parallel to Candy's Lane and, for some distance, has been destroyed by quarrying, building and landscaping.

The next indication is a terraced section (1d) coming into view between Brog Street Lane (a significant name ?)[1] and the former railway track (now with a house upon it) from Blandford to Broadstone. After some defacement at the start of the lane, the road-terrace is well preserved on the north-facing slope for some 80 m with a cambered profile 2.4 m wide. Along this stretch, the Roman engineers kept the road level along the side of the hill and above a re-entrant from the Stour valley, through which several streamlets still flow.

The first alignment of 1.1 km ends at about the point where the Brog Street Lane cuts across the terrace and under a disused railway bridge. For the next 400 m, the former railway junction and the present A31 trunk road have removed all traces until the ridge reappears on the lower ground in Lower and Higher Russell's Copse. Here (1e), a perceptible ridge runs for over 100 m, slowly diverting from the modern road and accompanied on the south by a substantial bank. Excavation (Appendix 18) in the Copse has shown that the road was 4.25 m wide with a *margo* on its northern margin and had a long history of local use. Just before emerging from the Copse, in thick brambles, the alignment changes to a more westerly track on the low terrain near the river. In the meadow between the bungalow at Court Farm and the A31, the course of the road has been noticed in dry summers as a straight, brown strip, unrelated to nearby medieval field earthworks. South-east of Whitehall House, little is to be seen, but an excavated section (Appendix 17) showed the early road as having a width of 3.75 m, and falling out of service in early medieval times (1f). A little way onward and the course reaches a brook now bridged by the A31, but in pre-turnpike days the site of a ford. For some 300 m the Roman course runs just south of, and parallel to, the main road, here called Mill Street, until the turnpike-cum-trunk road makes a sharp and dangerous swerve off the alignment at the entrance to the Wessex Water Laboratory. A section-trench (Appendix 19) cut 75 m south-east of the old Bailey Gate level crossing (1g) confirmed the line of the Roman road and showed that it had a revival of use in the early medieval period. In the field west of the old railway track there are slight surface signs of the ridge as the A31 comes back to rejoin the older couse (2a). Surveyed profiles, combined with probing, indicate a width of 4 m here for the buried agger. The behaviour of the parish boundary between Corfe Mullen and Sturminster Marshall is significant, for it makes a sharp angle where it crosses the Roman road to the south of the present thoroughfare. A very small change of alignment occurs in this field, and in this next stretch of 500 m the course of the old road, once past the parish boundary, moves over to the north margin of the A31 (2b–2c) for 1 km. Just west of the entrance to Henbury Farm, the A31 trunk road moves away from the line.[2] From here to the Lion Gate of Charborough Park, across the old medieval fields of Sturminster Marshall, surface evidence is lost. North-west of the Dullar Lane–A31 crossroads, a check on the precise line was obtained from the digging of a Wessex Water pipe-trench, which revealed a buried stony agger 2.5 m wide, with a broad, evenly cut ditch on its north side.[3] It was the slow expansion of that field-system that pushed the old route southward to the present course of the A31.

Just south of the Gate (3a), there was apparently a major re-alignment of the Roman road to a more westerly direction, betrayed inside the Park, as far as the Sturminster–Morden parish boundary, by soil marks on air vertical photographs.[4] The critical point lies on that boundary (3b), since from there westward a first-class stretch of the road has survived at the southern margin of the area reserved for deer-grazing (3b–3c). East of 3b, on air views, a medieval track or road ran north-eastward towards Sturminster village, acting also as the headland for a system of furlong fields and not aligned with the old road in the Deer Park. But from 3a, Lion Lodge, a track points towards 3b, but forks before reaching it. This second track takes the line 3a–b–c–d and is older than the furlong fields. Then, from 3b to 3c, an abandoned cambered road, with ditches 7 m apart, pursues a course for 300 m in downland grass, with a group of beech trees (diameters not less than 1 m) growing athwart it to emphasize long disuse. In Old Nursery, this fine section has been erased by successive tree-plantings, although the road-profile is visible where it is crossed by the tranverse north-south path. From the air,[5] however, the course of the Roman road shows up as a thinned line of trees relatively stunted in growth, a fact not readily noticeable on the ground. A perceptible ridge emerges for some 30 m from Old Nursery on to parkland grass before passing aslant into arable to the north. Slight swelling marks the line until it reaches the top of a prominent knoll in thick vegetation north-east of Peacock Lodge (3d). Here, at a height of 50 m, we reach the end of a long ascent (2 km) from Lion Lodge (height 33 m). This was an obvious point for a re-alignment for there was good sighting along the crest south of the Winterborne stream, as well as back to Badbury Rings and the Stour valley, now being left behind.

In the early eighteenth century the Roman road from 3b to 3d was still being used as a boundary skirting Charborough Park, since Taylor[6] shows the land to the north of 3b–d as 'New Field' (1773–76). We have seen that a road from the direction of Sturminster Marshall joined the Roman line at 3b and the two

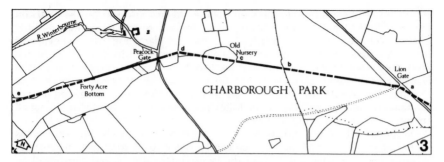

5C.3 Lake Farm to Dorchester: Charborough Park

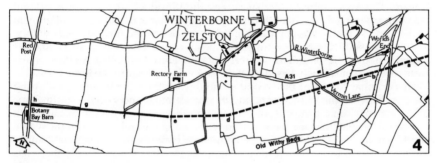

5C.4 Lake Farm to Dorchester: Winterborne Zelston

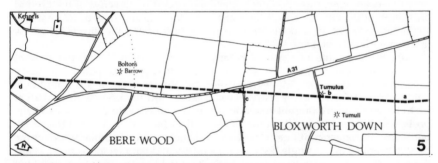

5C.5 Lake Farm to Dorchester: Bere Wood

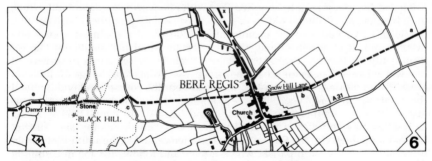

5C.6 Lake Farm to Dorchester: Bere Regis

O Metres   1000

61

continued as one not only to the high point at 3d, but also south-westwards on the new Roman alignment. Starting from 3d, where the new angle is now difficult to trace close to the junction of arable and plantation, the medieval and Roman roads coincide for 260 m in a now overgrown strip of land. They run absolutely straight, and once marked the Park limit on this side. Then, while the Roman course presumably went on in the same line, the later road curves away (3e) and back again before the two part once more. Nothing is to be seen here of the Roman course, now taken to be following a spur-slope (4a) down to a small stream, tributary to the Winterborne.

On the far side of this stream, there are again no signs of the Roman road as such, but in other ways its presence can be detected. A tongue of the former Almer parish projected south from the Winterborne stream and comprised an ancient land-holding of some 10 hectares (25 acres), probably a consolidated virgate. This was centred on what is now the World's End tavern, the present building having only a sixteenth-century origin. What is notable is the alignment of the two old roads crossing this holding, and also of the furlong-fields within. They all lie parallel to the presumptive Roman course (4b), which also coincides with one of the field-boundaries (surviving until erased recently). All these linear features were consciously based on the medieval successor to the Roman road.

This original course of the 'World's End' layout then climbs again, following the crest between the Winterborne and its small tributary now on the south. Signs of the agger become visible again near the north-west end of Vermin Lane (4c). On the east side of the lane there is a stony spread in the arable, and on the west a short 30 m length of causeway appears in grass between hedges in a field-angle. The track of the Roman road disappears over the next 600 m, where there has long been ploughing on light downland soil. After a straight course of 3 km from near Peacock Lodge, this alignment must have ended on the crest of the ground (4d) south of the Old Rectory. Westward from 4d to 4e and then onward after a slight re-alignment, field-boundaries have commemorated the line as far as the junction with Rectory Lane (4f).

From Rectory Lane to north of Botany Bay Barn, some 670 m, the straight section 4e–4h is continued with significant details. Up to the parish boundary separating Zelstone and Anderson (4f–4g), the Roman road, again acting as a field division, survives in the shape of a substantial low bank 5 m wide and 0.6 m high. Its width in its present function has necessitated a double row of fence-posts, which lie on either side of the 2 m wide flat central strip. West of the parish boundary, the agger continues (4g–4h) as a shallow ridge of similar width at the edge of arable, but the single hedge is now off-set and parallel to the north. Thus the ridge evoked a different response in the later field arrangements on each side of the boundary.

Beyond the minor road linking Red Post with Bloxworth, the downland, which once bore traces of several old routes, has been heavily ploughed. Barrows that not long ago could still be prominently made out have almost completely disappeared. It is not surprising that the remainder of the alignment (4g–4h) from south of Rectory Farm has left no certain trace on the surface here of Bloxworth Down. The evidence from further west points to a change of direction about 270 m beyond Botany Bay Barn, which kept the course level and avoided the climb up to Bere Wood. The new alignment (5a–5d) crosses an old lane just south of a prominent, if damaged, round barrow (5b) where two opposing field-gates may be relics of the final use of the old road. Passing over further well-ploughed terrain, the Roman line is commemorated at the south-east corner of Winterborne Kingston parish, where it joins and follows for 150 m a straight section of the parish boundary (5c).

62

Here a bungalow has been built on an unusual triangle of land where the A31 trunk road, of medieval and turnpike ancestry, curves away from the angle formed by that boundary. In the eighteenth century, several tracks from across Bloxworth Down to the east united at this point to form the old way, which then still followed the Roman line. At the angle it was joined from the south by a lane – now vanished – through a gateway traceable today, but long abandoned.

Westward of this straight stretch (5b–c), now marked only by a hedge, the modern road and the parish boundary combine to take a sinuous course, with the Roman line invisible on arable just to the north. The A31 then swerves away towards the south-west, and the parish boundary towards the north, but it is only at the end of this alignment (5d) that the Roman road can be identified again. It makes a surface reappearance on the hillside where there is a major turn of 60 degrees south-westward. The ridge, now conspicuous, begins in the middle of an arable field and runs mid-slope for some 450 m. Today constantly ploughed, it is nevertheless prominent enough from the A31 road below, although its profile is best preserved 8 m wide and 0.4 m high where crossed by another lane close to 5d. This linear feature was completely ignored by the strip cultivation of Bere Regis, recorded in 1776, which it clearly ante-dates. Importantly, too, south-west of the farm-road leading to Muddox Barrow Farm (6a), the 1845 tithe map has a field-boundary marked along the road-line, which can no longer be observed on arable.[7] A little further onward, a vast defile has been carved into the landscape by the Bere Regis bypass. But towards Snow Hill the alignment is betrayed again by a 'grass lane' (surviving from the open-field system), which shows as a slightly sunken track in pasture.

At the right-angle bend (6b) of Snow Hill Lane, a ridge crossing over and running along the south-east side of the lane (where it becomes more obvious) is evidence of the early road. From the bend, the course was re-aligned to keep contourwise at the same height on the slope as the preceding stretch from 5d. Along the lane, the agger, now 5 m wide and up to 0.3 m high, first occupies the verge and then has a hedge-bank upon its crest, with signs of a parallel side-ditch well within the field. At the southern end of this short alignment, a new residential road has cut through a hedge-bank wider (3.5 m) than normal and lying directly on the surface of the old road.

From this corner of the downland plateau, the Roman surveyor could obtain a sighting over the Bere valley towards Black Hill. The minimal change of direction (4 degrees) is today marked by the slant of the property boundaries at the junction of Snow Hill Lane and Day's Lane. At this point the course crossed the line of the earlier military road considered to have run from Woodbury to Weatherby Castle (Chapter 5M). From the top of Day's Lane to the steep northern edge of Black Hill, a distance of 1 km, the Roman course has left no certain surface trace, passing first through the town, then down across the meadows by the Bere stream and finally up the long-cultivated arable of Shitterton. On the north bank of the stream a shrubby ridge may indicate where the road crossed. There are various earthworks just south of the stream, including gravelled ridges which seem to unite at the line of the vanished road.

At the foot of the sharp rise to Black Hill (6c), west of a projecting copse masking an old quarry, traces of a ridge towards the lower field-fence appear to indicate the end of the stretch from Day's Lane. Confirmation comes from among the bracken and undergrowth of the undisturbed 1:6 slope. A terraced track, with a camber still visible in places, 2.5–3 m wide, climbs obliquely up as the first part of a 'dog-leg'. After 50 m, this diversion reaches a boundary bank and a path running contourwise where the gradient is much less. Beyond that point, surface vestiges are lost in ground covered in bracken and thick humus, while gorse takes over at the top, with even a recorded tumulus difficult to locate. However, once the vegetation thins out on the high plateau, an irregular line of birch and fir trees lies close to the course, which was evidently re-aligned slightly at a point north-west of the tumulus. With a ridge beginning to be visible in places, the agger finally becomes apparent on this stretch just east of a crossing made by two heath-tracks, which run north-east to south-west and north-west to south-east respectively. For a further 130 m, the former track accompanies the heather-covered Roman road, distinctly separate on its west side, 3–4 m wide and 0.2 m high, and flanked for some way to the west again by a small ditch and a later bank.

Close to a notable group of tumuli there has been gravel-quarrying in the past, with some interference to the remains of the early road. The latter, it would appear, makes a short dog-leg or zigzag west of the Devil's Stone, a monolith of heathstone, where the previous alignment is resumed. The alteration of line was evidently to lead the road off the plateau through a deep cleft on the southern flank of Black Hill. By terracing this rise on its east it was possible for the road to resume its direction after the Stone on descending to the valley of the Piddle. The terrace is partly masked by gorse, bracken and scree from the slope for some 75 m, but the causeway becomes plainer when it reaches the intermediate shelf of high ground which extends to Damer Hill (6e). The bridle-path, which has been skirting the Roman course, now crosses diagonally over the line and, before Damer Hill, runs for some 90 m on its west as a well-developed hollow-way. Along this stretch, the Roman road is seen as a prominent agger, 4 m wide, flanked on the east by a ditch and the remnants of an old laid hedge.

As on the north side, a zigzag leads off the high heathland and down to the Turners Puddle fields, and the present broad lane effecting this manoeuvre incorporates the original line. At the foot of the gradient (6f), the straight pre-enclosure lane is the successor of the Roman road and its direction exactly resumes that of the two alignments across Black Hill. The old road is to some extent visible under the south-east hedge (7a). East of Turners Puddle Church there appears to be a slight deviation when the course reaches the edge of the river meadows. Where the valley road, with its modern surface, crosses the line, a marked hump probably pinpoints the start of the short stretch now buried in dark reedy soil alongside the Piddle. At the river (7b), there are indications of flint and chalk bridge abutments that preceded the present ford and, significantly, are aligned to serve this invisible stretch over the low ground.[8] In addition, a strong case can be made that this river-crossing gave its name to a local medieval tithing called *Streteford*. Place-names derived from the combination of *street* and *ford* have usually been associated with Roman roads (Appendix 29). Beyond the Piddle, a new alignment takes the course some 3 km over to the Frome valley (7b–8b) with only a minor correction on the intervening crest.

On the first stretch (7b–7f), positive evidence survives at several points:

- at Throop (7c): a short length of ridge behind Piper's Cottage with a small outbuilding on it;
- south-east of Landshare Coppice (7d): 65 m of causeway, 0.4 m high and 4 m wide, in an early nineteenth-century plantation;
- near the eastern edge of a more recent plantation (7e): a footpath shown on early Ordnance Survey maps following the Roman line in disturbed terrain;
- at the summit of the rise (7f), on a virgin corner of Bryantspuddle Heath in an angle between two modern roads: 75 m of causeway forming a continuation in thick gorse of the aforesaid footpath;

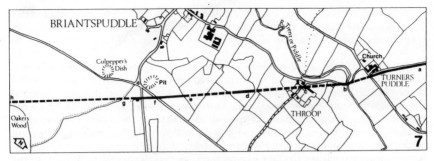

5C.7 Lake Farm to Dorchester: Briantspuddle (Bryantspuddle)

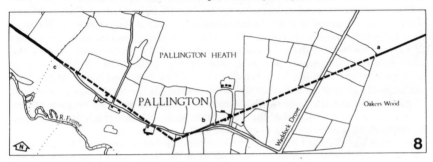

5C.8 Lake Farm to Dorchester: Pallington

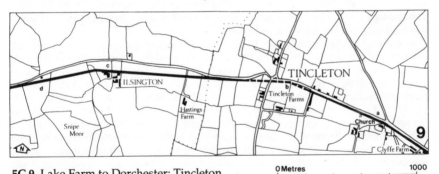

5C.9 Lake Farm to Dorchester: Tincleton

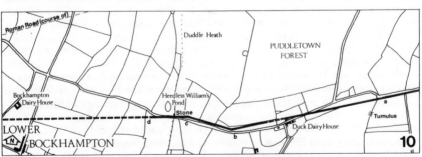

5C.10 Lake Farm to Dorchester: Lower Bockhampton

65

– at the north-east end, 4 m wide and 0.3 m high, but more prominent at the south-west end by development of lateral hollow-ways, so that width and height reach 4.2 m and 0.5 m.

On the other side of the modern road between Bryantspuddle and Bovington stands Heath Cottage, aligned with and sited on the remains of the agger visible in the garden. Since that residence dates only from 1857, it may be concluded that the footpath-cum-Roman road was still distinct enough then to influence building-lines. Some 30 m south-west of the cottage, the agger can again be briefly observed before it vanishes for some 600 m in the intensively furrowed forestry plantations, which were open heathland only a generation or so back. Somewhere near Heath Cottage occurs the slight re-alignment of 3 degrees, the only one between the rivers Piddle and Frome.

The new line is next discernible as the north boundary of Oakers Wood (7h–8a), an enclosure of considerable antiquity, with a place-name earlier than the fourteenth century. This stretch of bank, 300 m long, was built of heath-turves laid on or, for a short distance, beside, the track of the Roman road. Where the line of the latter meets the east end of the bank (7h), its presence is commemorated by an old track parallel to the bank, but soon both coincide and the underlying agger is increasingly obvious towards the west end of the length of bank (8a). Here the road-ridge is 4 m wide, with the bank set on its northern edge, and there is a shallow southern ditch (original side-ditch?) and a deep northern ditch (contemporary with the bank?).

In two places the road-plus-bank crosses two combes, so creating in the distant past dams against surface drainage. Although the dams have now been mainly washed away, boggy ground is still noticeable to the north, the combes being scoured and eroded to the south. This man-made phenomenon of blocked watercourses has been associated with Roman roads elsewhere in southern England as a mark of genuine antiquity.[9]

At the end of this straight length of Oakers Wood boundary (8a), the turf-built bank is replaced by one of different construction, which turns away north-west, leaving a low ridge, 15 m long, continuing as the evidence for the Roman road. This ridge is then interrupted by a north-south sunken way, parallel to the manorial boundary between Affpuddle and Bryantspuddle, which today serves to divide Oakers Wood from the arable fields of Waddock Farm. Trace of the Roman road is now lost for 1.2 km until it can be picked up exactly on line at Pallington (8b). From that point almost to Dorchester, the medieval/modern road from Waddock Cross to Dorchester through Tincleton plays a major part in the story.[10]

East of Pallington that road makes a sharp bend as it negotiates a spur projecting onto the Frome valley bottom. On the north side, within a thicket, some 30 m of old causeway can be identified, 4 m wide and 0.6 m high (8b). It forms the precise end of the alignment from Heath Cottage and Oakers Wood (7g–7h–8a). Today, it merges here with the existing road to Dorchester, which on early maps led at this point from enclosed fields to the west on to Pallington Heath to the east. The banked hedge north of the causeway still curves away as in the eighteenth century. Thus, at the foot of the spur, the long stretch of Roman road from the river at Turners Puddle now makes a major change of direction to follow the Frome valley. The angle of 60 degrees, interestingly enough, is identical to that for the similar important re-alignment north of Bere Regis (5d).

The next alignment that can be positively identified begins 800 m further west, close to the parish boundary between Puddletown and Affpuddle, where a stretch of the present road must, on several counts, be accorded a Roman origin

(8c–9a). Its straightness on *both sides* of the boundary suggests that it is earlier than enclosures. On the Affpuddle side, the Roman line skirts the northern edge, but the Puddletown section lies under the southern edge. Past the front of Clyffe Farm, part of the agger is visible for 30 m where it has survived alongside the modern road. From the farm-buildings to Tincleton Church, some 250 m, a massive hedged bank lies along the south margin, and a recent cut though revealed a base of stony material, probably residual from the earlier road. The end of this alignment occurs north of the church (9a), where, as at Clyffe Farm, the south slope of the causeway can be observed, into which the churchyard wall has been set.

Modern road and Roman both change direction here and adopt the same line for another 800 m (9a–9b). At first, over ground unenclosed until recently, the two courses closely coincide, but, along the middle stretch, a wide southern verge indicates the probable siting of the earlier route. Parallel with the final length of modern/medieval road from the church, there are signs of a slight ridge in the field north-east of Tincleton Farms. Then, 130 m east of Tincleton crossroads, the next re-alignment must be expected (9b).

Watery Lane, which reaches the crossroads from the south, is set in a deep cleft. However, on its west side, an old raised gateway, standing on the vanished line, apparently goes back to earlier days when the direct road would still have been in use. Other similar diversions off the older Roman line can be noted at Ilsington, Duck Dairy and Bockhampton/Stinsford. North-west of Tincleton Farms, the present road rejoins the Roman line, which has not left any trace in the intervening fields. The two then run together for 300 m, before parting again north of Hastings Farm.[11] The Dorchester road (called Ilsington Road on older maps) makes another diversion to the north before rejoining the Roman course 1.2 km further on (beyond 9d). Meanwhile, the latter is either ploughed out or buried in arable east of Ilsington Farm, but re-asserts itself as 140 m of old lane. The alignment here, skirting the farm, is bounded on that side by a long wall and barns set length-wise, which show that not too long ago the route was still a public way. West of the farm complex, the line has been interrupted in the past by watercress beds and then to the west again the Roman road, before being diverted, must have made a change of direction to take it on to the next stretch of 2 km (9c). This would have occurred on well-ploughed terrain behind newly erected barns, but nothing now appears on the surface. However, in the next field onward, south of an old barn in a walled yard, the road-ridge is visible for some 50 m on the new line, 4 m wide and 0.2 m high (9d). Here it is crossed by a public footpath passing north-south over the arable that is typical of this part of the Frome valley. At this point and until it is now rejoined by the Ilsington Road, the Roman course was still shown on the 1840 tithe map as the boundary to several fields, with the diversion clearly marked as the later feature.

So, after almost vanishing for a short distance, the Roman course merges into the wide southern margin of the Ilsington Road for 400 m (10a). North of the tumulus (unusually sited on the broad flat valley bottom of the river Frome) the modern road makes an awkward elbow, leaving the original route to continue straight on as a faint hollow-way, formerly accompanied by a hedge. There are no surface signs for a little distance on established tillage north of Duck Dairy House.

Then, west of the Dairy, the Roman line is betrayed by faint ridging (still visible despite ploughing) and, most significantly, by hachuring marked on earlier large-scale Ordnance Survey maps.[12] This part of the course lay on what was then an undisturbed part of Duddle Heath. It can be compared on those maps to hachures depicting the Roman road from Badbury Rings directly to the north on Puddletown Heath. It appears here that the Ordnance surveyor was noting two parallel hollow-ways, which even by the close of the last century had been destroyed on the arable just to the east, close to Duck Dairy. On alignment, there is little doubt that, in the course of time, these hollow-ways had developed on either side of the agger of the Roman road from Lake Farm. Earthworks of similar type were noted on Affpuddle Heath (7f).

The alignment from west of Ilsington Farm has now risen to the higher ground forming the southern spur of Duddle Heath (10b). Duddle Farm is sited nearer the river, but on a hill forming an outlier to the spur, so that there is a well-defined pass between the two high spots. It was through this natural gap that a new Roman alignment was laid out for some 300 m. The agger is north of and parallel to the modern made-up road, plainly visible for some 80 m, nearly 4 m wide and 0.3 m high on the terraced slope of Duddle Plantation (Appendix 34).

At Headless William's Stone, the final re-alignment takes place for the stretch to Dorchester 3 km away.[13] The first few metres of the Roman line are now under the tarmac of the present thoroughfare, and it is instructive to check how this has happened. Between 10c and 10d the combined modern and Roman roads cross the steep head of the re-entrant valley on the west flank of the Duddle spur. While the north edge of the modern road passes the Stone flush with the ground, on the south there is a sharp built-up drop of around 2 m to the field below. Thus, in the recent past, the carriageway that we now see has been widened by the construction of an embankment, the older road presumably having been terraced into the slope.

As the land starts to rise again westward, a field-boundary, which has now disappeared, once continued the straight Roman line for another 80 m past Bhompston Cottage, which has also disappeared without trace (10d). The medieval/modern road, however, turns north-westward in what is to be a long diversion around Bockhampton, Kingston Maurward and Stinsford. Ahead, the Roman road regained the higher ground by way of a small, but convenient dry-valley, which eased the gradient. This plateau, overlooking the Frome to the south, has been intensively farmed or landscaped since Tudor times, so that not until the proximity of Stinsford Church does further surface evidence for the Roman course become apparent. But it is noteworthy that its expected track passed close to Manor Farm (once the seat of the local squire) and its sixteenth-century successor, Kingston Maurward House. South-east of the church and the Old Vicarage, in Butcher's Close, a field under permanent grass, a prominent ridge has been sectioned (Appendix 28) with important results (11a). This feature proved to have been built up by prolonged ploughing against the Roman road, which continued in service until the creation of Kingston Maurward Park around 1700. The road-line can be traced through the southern part of the vicarage garden as far as Church Lane. Beyond, the early road would have skirted the churchyard, but after that point massive garden-works connected with the construction of Stinsford House in the seventeenth century have lowered the ground level and removed all traces as far as the water-meadows.

The alignment has now reached the site of Grey's Bridge, whence there can be little surprise as to how it continued into Dorchester.[14] Its ultimate destination is the subject of Chapter 6, but the course through the town can now be reliably traced, since the general line has been confirmed at Kingston Maurward. The London Road (until 1989, the A31 trunk road) from the Bridge and High East and West Street were long suspected to have had a Roman origin. In reality, there have been exposures in the eighteenth century, and much more recently, which all line up to indicate an ancient road running parallel, in close association, and finally passing just north of St Peter's Church. In noting the earliest of these

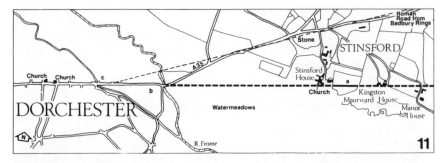

5C.11 Lake Farm to Dorchester: Stinsford

5C.12 Agger at Carter's Cottages, Corfe Mullen, looking south-east. The old resident in the picture remembered when the ridge could be seen in the field beyond.

5C.13 Roman road, Charborough Park, from north-west

5C.14 Roman road, Damer Hill, Turners Puddle, from north-east

5D.1–5 Roman road from Lake Farm to Wareham (and page 72)

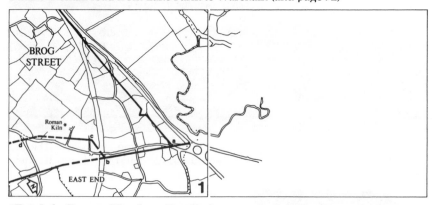

5D.1 Lake Farm to Wareham: East End

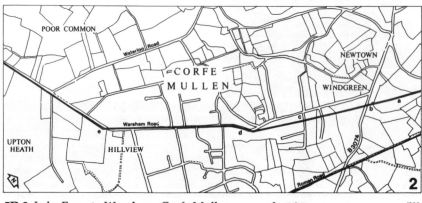

5D.2 Lake Farm to Wareham: Corfe Mullen

exposures (6.1b) Hutchins referred to ' … an old road, almost parallel to the new London Road, paved with flints and stone … near the east end of Dorchester, coming from Stinsford Lane'. He stated with precision that, from Segar's Orchard '… it pointed … to the back of the old jail, the north side of St Peter's and through Trinity Church.'[15] In 1970 a short length of an east–west road was located during rescue excavation at Greening's Court, just north of High East Street, 170 m west of Segar's Orchard (6.1c). Most tellingly, in 1980, 200 m further west again and on the north side of St Peter's Church (6.1d), another fragment of road was identified, apparently on the same alignment.[16]

The course of the road from Lake Farm to Dorchester makes a striking contrast, in more than one respect, to the familiar one running from Badbury Rings to Dorchester. We have been accustomed to looking at maps of Roman Britain where the almost completely straight alignment taken by the Badbury road has been regarded as an essential hallmark of Roman communications in Dorset. Why, then, did the road from Lake behave so differently?

We need first to identify specific features of the Dorchester–Badbury road. It runs almost entirely over chalk downland, and, though crossing several waterways, scarcely deviates for the whole of the 20 Roman miles. There is no reason to think that it was at any point following a pre-existing native track. There is every indication of its having been laid out on open pasture or the marginal arable land of scattered Iron Age farms. An excavated section through a well-preserved part of the road has shown that it had never borne much traffic.

By contrast, the road from Lake appears to have made use of native routes both at the start – along the south bank of the Stour – and at the end – along the north bank of the Frome. The direct line to Dorchester presented obstacles that could best be avoided by following age-old tracks along river-valleys. Thus, on the clayey sands of the London and Reading Beds between Corfe Mullen and Bere Regis, there was dense woodland, later commemorated by names like *Bere* (Anglo-Saxon 'woodland') and *Lytchet* ('grey wood'). Additionally, the direct line would have had to rise to over 76 m – Bere Wood – when a simple deviation (the actual route) took it through a gap – Bere Regis. Incidentally, the argument made elsewhere for an early military road from Woodbury to Weatherby Castle has some interesting implications in respect of Bere. The two roads crossed just north of the spot where, much later, the church came to be built, but the fact would explain a possible early settlement, since both roads remained in local use. Nor was the church at Bere the only one to be sited on the Lake to Dorchester road. It is striking that the churches at Corfe Mullen, Turners Puddle, Stinsford, and three inside Dorchester itself all speak eloquently for the longevity of this road.

(D) Lake Farm to Wareham

This road branched from the early Roman road between Lake and Hamworthy at a point (1b) under 800 m south of the fortress, where the slope up from the valley floor begins to level out on the heathland plateau. In the nineteenth century, the exact site of the junction was destroyed by the deep cutting at East End dug for the Somerset and Dorset Railway. However, in 1977, in order to aid the disposal of spoil from road works nearby, the upper north face of the now disused cutting was widened by machine. It became possible (Appendix 15) not only to establish precisely the line of the known Lake–Hamworthy road, but also to plan certain unusual details whose meaning has emerged only later. The Hamworthy road was found to be passing further east than was previously thought and to have possessed three main phases of construction. The first two were ascribed to the military phase, and associated probably with the second of these roads was an unusual structure in the shape of a substantial stone post-support. Until evidence

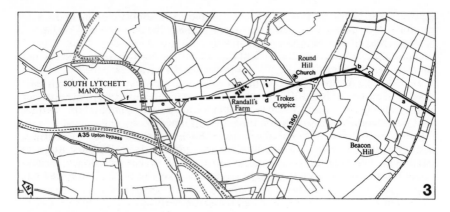

5D.3 Lake Farm to Wareham: Lytchett Minster

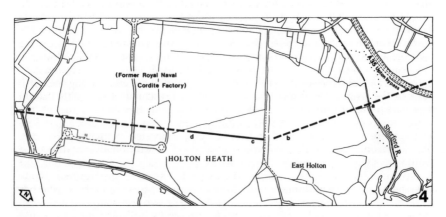

5D.4 Lake Farm to Wareham: Holton Heath

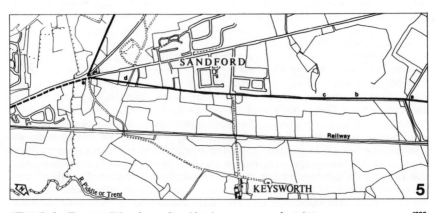

5D.5 Lake Farm to Wareham: Sandford

72

was established for the Roman roads to Wareham, it was uncertain why a post should have stood at this spot in apparent isolation. But the explanation can now be offered that it was a guide-post at an important fork, with arms pointing north to the military base at Lake, south to Hamworthy on Poole Harbour and, finally, south-west towards Wareham, the direction we shall be following.

The first alignment of the road to Wareham can be traced both from the 1840 tithe map and from the ground evidence still visible beyond the cutting, today completely filled back. In the mid-nineteenth century an old lane left the medieval/modern Wimborne road to run south-westwards from the site of the future railway bridge. When this lane reached what is called Wayground Road, it forked, one branch curving north-west, the other being commemorated by a straight field boundary in a south-westerly direction. As far as that fork, the lane extended along the north flank of a short stretch of agger, which can be picked up in the garden of 'Oaklea' as a good camber 3 m wide. There was a sharp re-alignment of 55 degrees (1c) as the road reached the top of the climb from the Stour, and the precise spot lies just south of no. 11 Wayground Road. The north-western boundary of this property coincides with a straight field-edge on the tithe map, while that on the south-east skirts a ridge 5 m wide and is marked by an established laurel hedge. That ridge, though subjected to disturbance over the last century, can still be discerned in gardens west of Wimborne Road, notably nos 83, 85 and 93. In the face of building development close to this line, limited trenching in 1987 and a machine-cut in 1989[1] indicated that the ridge was, in its first phase, some 5 m wide, built on a central *spina* and succeeded by later remetallings on the unexcavated eastern side. After 400 m, this stretch turns southward, just north of the junction of Wimborne Road and Higher Merley Lane, with a change of angle recorded on the tithe map, but since destroyed.

South of the junction, the picturesque late eighteenth-century Appletree Cottage (formerly two dwellings, now one) is set directly on the Roman line (1d). The cambered ridge runs perceptibly along the middle of the garden behind, with the surviving lane parallel to the west.

From this point to the Blandford Road, 500 m southward and uphill, an extensive housing development is changing the landscape, but fortunately not without having provided important confirmation of the track of the early road. After the cottage garden, the line could be traced through a thicket, and then a field, as a swelling ridge. In the middle of a second field, the buried agger was exposed and sectioned (Appendix 22), remarkably well preserved, with side-ditches and a *margo*, precisely where expected (2a). The alignment then ran more or less invisibly alongside a straight length of hedge before interruption by a deep ditch. Suddenly, in the grass of OS parcel 0658, behind no. 66 Blandford Road, the ridge shows up distinctly for 80 m, with a width of 4 m and a maximum height of 0.3 m (Appendix 34). Most interestingly, it changes course half way along, whereas the old field bank, almost parallel to its east, runs straight and true, clearly a construction of medieval date. This slight re-alignment is not unexpected as we have reached the level high ground, but the sight of such a well-defined angle on a Roman road is certainly unusual.

Ground clearance for the new roundabout at Windgreen yielded a little more information on the line of the early road (2b), after which further housing development of various dates has destroyed evidence for some 300 m. It is significant that the stretch of Wareham Road to the west was at some time laid out parallel to the Roman line, which presumably remained visible hereabouts, although not used as a property boundary. Beyond South Road, however, the causeway is well observed (2c) in several of the gardens behind houses fronting on Wareham Road, particularly nos 59, 65 and 71, and in the footpath east of 71.

The average width is 4 m, and in places there is an accompanying ditch on the west. Worthy of notice is the behaviour of the present Wareham Road, presumably a post-medieval construction. From its junction with Blandford Road, it was laid parallel to the Roman road to Wareham, which must still have been a visible feature. It then swings to join the older line, where both negotiate the col between the Waterloo valley to the north and the head of the deep chine known as Rushcombe Bottom to the south. A short strip of the old road has survived here, still covered in gorse (2d). Thence, for 900 m, the modern road and the Roman form one as far as Hill View at the other end of the plateau. Here, an excellent sighting place, there was a marked change of direction from the south-south-west to south-west. The wide cambered ridge is conserved amid gorse and small trees to the south of the existing turn (2e), the present carriageway having been cut through the inside angle of high ground, an improvement certainly earlier than 1840. Alongside the causeway, signs of a hollow-way show that the final abandonment came after a long period of use.

After following the heathland heights from the area of Windgreen, the direction and layout of the road (3a) were still governed by local topographical demands: firstly, to continue skirting the broken terrain and woodland of Lytchett by staying on the level gravel plateau, albeit lower now; and secondly, to avoid the twin obstacles of Round Hill and Beacon Hill, which loomed ahead.

So, from Hill View, the present road again coincides with the Roman for nearly 1.6 km, constituting a straight alignment that descends on to lower ground and then passes from Corfe Mullen into Lytchett Minster. It is a commentary on the antiquity of the road that this part of it is, on the visible evidence, very much older than a normal enclosure road. The land in each parish has long belonged to different estates, and there are no records of a common agreement to set up a straight road across what, until the eighteenth century, would have been open heathland.

Some 500 m south-west of the Holme Bush inn, the modern tarmac of this stretch swings south, just inside the ridged angle of the older road visible in the allotment garden beyond (3b). This major turning-point is precisely at the watershed separating the Stour valley from Poole Harbour, whose waters come into sight if we look along the new alignment passing between the two hilltops. There are few signs of the course immediately beyond the angle, save for extra stoniness in Maylyn Road, long unmade, since housing and gardens lie athwart the line as far as the crossing of Wareham Road with the nineteenth-century Lower Blandford Road from Hamworthy. The former rejoins the Roman line on the other side of the crossroads before the existing carriageway deviates south of Round Hill (3c). The old course continues into the adjacent field and climbs a slight slope by a hollowed cleft, whence it runs onward, betrayed by ridging in grass up to the ground of Troke's Coppice. Here, this stretch of the Roman road has reached a prominent edge looking south and well sited for the next alignment of over 3 km, down slope to Sherford river and then gently up to Holton Heath.

Within the garden of Troke's Coppice, a former tennis court has destroyed some evidence, but fortunately an impressive fragment of agger, 16 m long, remains amid orchard grass (3d). The ridge is 6 m wide, 0.25 m high, with a substantial ditch on the north-west side. It lies at the point where the new alignment starts, clearly aiming at the minor height of East Holton in the distance.

Down from Troke's Coppice, past Randall's Farm, there is little to be seen in the cabbage fields; then the line is taken up by a short entrenched length of Randall's Lane, which sharply deviates left at One Elm Cottage, leaving the

Roman course to run straight on. However, little shows in the arable west of the cottage. The course then crosses the old Poole–Lytchett Matravers turnpike. From this point, almost to the Sherford river, the Roman road once acted as the central route through the oval framework formed by the arable fields of Lytchett Minster village.[2] By the nineteenth century, the function of the old road had disappeared, replaced by lanes around the perimeter of the former enclosed land. Today the chief reminder of the old line is a massive positive lynchet (3e) that runs for some 150 m, south of the turnpike, inside Lytchett Manor park. After the lynchet, there are slight ridges visible on both verges of the approach drive (now occupied by caravans in summer), at a distance of 70 m from the entrance gates. South again, a hedge that grew along the line in 1838 has gone, but there is still a broad ridge discernible in places on this rise (3f), with a stream parallel to the west, flowing from the direction of Randall's Farm. Traces are then lost in shrubbery, and the course then passes under the modern road from Upton to Lytchett Minster, built as recently as 1907.

Beyond the park now, and on long-standing permanent arable, no surface indications remain as far as the Sherford river. A thick alluvial cover has accumulated on either side of the waterway, further camouflaged by reeds on the southern bank. Where the actual crossing took place (whether by ford or bridge) is not now apparent. However, the alignment from Troke's Coppice soon reaches a spur of higher ground on Holton Heath and it is probable that the critical crossing-point (4a) lay some 600 m east of King's Bridge, of late medieval origin, which takes the A351 over the Sherford towards Wareham. Between there and King's Bridge, the tithe map of 1838 marked the site of Holton Bridge, which still appears as a footbridge on large-scale maps. It is not very far west of the likely Roman (and early medieval?) crossing. Logically, the known rise in sea level over the last two millenia could have moved the lowest bridging point upstream for precisely that distance.

The Roman line goes next into a conifer wood at the eastern end of Holton Heath, a feature that seems to have arisen with less disturbance than is common on much forestry land, often deeply furrowed before tree-planting. While this circumstance might seem to have favoured the survival of good ground evidence, it is not surprising that the relatively low agger of an early road like this should have been masked by thick pine-humus or a multitude of tree-stumps. Only towards the end of the alignment from Troke's Coppice does a short length of hollow-way appear in undergrowth, some 120 m north-east of the spot where the Roman road changed direction towards Sandford and Wareham. The angle of this re-alignment (4b) was located close to the eastern perimeter fence of the former Cordite Factory, where the estate road runs to East Holton, 500 m east-south-east. The course of the re-aligned road receives interesting support, however, within the factory grounds, now a nature reserve.

During a period spanning two world wars, the Royal Naval Cordite Factory isolated 1.25 square kilometres of heath from the public and substantially altered the land-surface in the western half of the enclosure.[3] Fortunately, in the eastern interior, little more was done than to set up scattered temporary huts, linked by gravel or cinder tracks through the heather. One of these tracks (4c) re-used the Roman agger, which was oriented conveniently for the dispersal of dump storage. On the 1948 factory plan, the Roman course is shown as a 'cinder roadway', running for more than 300 m past huts nos 13 to 16 from the spot close to the factory fence where the change in alignment probably occurred. The terrain has now gone back entirely to heather, gorse and small trees, with the square platforms of the huts grown over. The camber of the old road has certainly been heightened in places during the recent Admiralty phase, but there is no mistake about what happens after 300 m. Then the modern remetalled road swerves off line to leave the earlier ridge heading straight on westwards for another 200 m. The Roman course is well visible in heather and gorse, and the platforms of huts nos 7 and 12 are the only disturbance to it. Thereafter, in the western part of the former naval establishment, industrial building, both past and present, seems to have respected a belt of trees, which for some distance conceals evidence of the old road.

We pick up the Roman line again where the road from Organford bends sharply (4e/5a) as it heads south to the former Holton Heath railway station, then forming the east boundary to the Keysworth manor. The Roman and medieval road constitutes the northern limit of that estate, clearly denoted by a series of stones along it. West of the car-park at the bend, the Roman road can be discerned after some 200 m into the wood, past the first Keysworth stone, running on the north side of its medieval counterpart. The latter is skirted by turf banks, suggesting that it had acted as a drove road. Then, for another 260 m, the agger is comparatively undisturbed (5b) amid occasional pines and gorse, separate from, but clearly influencing, its later counterpart. Then, beyond a second boundary stone, both courses, Roman and medieval, unite in terrain much broken by former quarrying and continue together as a stream is negotiated (5c). Thus the stretch from East Holton eventually completes nearly 3 km, with only minor adjustments. It ends today about 200 m beyond the drive to Keysworth Farm from the north-west, but field boundaries continue the line. A final slight re-alignment introduces the stretch of 600 m that runs to the stream-crossing responsible for the name Sandford and now bridged for the A351 road. Close to the descent down to the water, the agger shows up in a slight deviation through a small wood (5d). It is flanked today by a disused clay-pit and a restaurant, before emerging from thick undergrowth to join the modern road at the bridge. Here it was joined by the branch to Bulbury (5e).

From Sandford Bridge as far as the North Causeway, the course of the Roman road coincided with that of the old turnpike road, which is shown to be running absolutely straight on tithe maps and Ordnance Survey plans (if we allow for the diversion for the level crossing created in 1840). On the way, there was a further branch running to Woodbury (5G.1p), but all surface details of these junctions have been lost for a variety of reasons. East of the Railway Tavern and west of the new road-bridge, the evidence for more than one pre-railway road running south-west by north-east has recently been observed.[4] In close association were a number of burials, also clearly of early date (5G.1q). It seems that the Roman road underlies the North Causeway into the town only from the new roundabout, where the straight length through the North Gate runs into the town. There have been signs from excavation[5] that, in antiquity, North Street did not bend to the west opposite Dollins Lane, but held its straight alignment southward (5G.1r). The ulitimate goal of this road, as of others running into the Wareham area when they were first constructed, was arguably a Roman military post somewhere in the south-east sector of what was to become the Saxon town.

It is immediately noticeable that this road branched sharply from the Poole Harbour road and then re-aligned to run for some distance not far off to the west. This sharp deviation raises a pertinent question. Why did the Wareham road not fork off either earlier or later so as to avoid what seems to be a short duplication of constructional effort? Several possible answers can be offered. First, the branch starts only a little east of the well-known pottery kiln site discovered in the 1930s. There is little doubt that production of both Romanized and native wares was carried out here soon after the Conquest, and a communication between this spot and the Roman fortress in the valley below would have been an early requirement. The behaviour of the branch-road is strongly suggestive that some such local need was being served, in addition to the link with distant Wareham. But there is a second explanation of why the branch occurred where it did and not a little further south. Just before it descends into the Stour valley, the road from the harbour crosses two deep chines, today known as Rushcombe Bottom and Happy Bottom. The road from the Harbour negotiated these physical obstacles without diverting and certainly one of these was crossed at an angle which lessened the gradient for traffic. Military haste must have been the governing factor here, with the overriding need to lay down the nearest route between fort and port. Later it must have seemed good sense to start the branch-road where these chines could be avoided. A third point is the essentially military advantage that the branch, by occurring where it did, was soon able to skirt the low-lying woodland of the Waterloo valley. In addition, from the high ground, a watchful eye could be kept westward, in the direction of what was still hostile country when the road was buit. A final and possibly not insignificant detail. In Victorian times, quarrying uncovered an early Roman cremation south of the point where the branch road began. Is it possible that thereabouts, alongside the Hamworthy road, lay the military cemetery of the Lake fortress? The information is scanty, but the circumstance would make another reason for siting the fork to Wareham further to the north.

From upper Corfe Mullen to the mouth of the Sherford river, the Wareham road continued to keep closely to the junction of the sandy Bagshot heath and the wooded clayland of the London and Reading Beds. The bends in the route reflect the problems of the terrain. Beyond the Sherford river, the re-alignment at East Holton followed valley gravels without impediment as far as the Sandford stream-crossing.

(E) Wareham to Flower's Barrow and Purbeck

The South Causeway, like its northern counterpart, has long been a feature of the local scene, and the case must be made that it formed a continuation of the early link-road traced from Corfe Mullen to Wareham. The first place-name that can be connected dates only from 1620, but there can hardly be any dispute about the antiquity of the 900 m of straight alignment from the Frome Bridge, through Stoborough, to the junction with Grange Road. Fortunately, from that point southward, evidence is abundant to explain the behaviour of the military road from Wareham, once it had passed through the village of Stoborough. It is curious indeed that the facts have not been appreciated since they appear very suggestive on large-scale maps and find strong support on the ground.

The present main road (A351) from Wareham to Corfe Castle and Swanage is now joined south of Stoborough by the new bypass from the north-west, but before that point it makes its first angle where Grange Road branches off to Creech and East Holme (5G.1y). There are reasons for suspecting that the straight stretches of the A351 across the heath towards Corfe Castle are of Roman civil origin,[1] but the early military road that we are following continues this alignment at the Grange Road junction and then runs for over 1.6 km as far as the tumulus at Hill View. The first 300 m of the course have been lost in what would have been medieval arable, but, behind a modern bungalow on the main road intriguingly named 'Wayzgoose', a short length of ridge can be seen with an old barn almost set upon it (5G.1z). From here, where a lane crosses at right angles, a hedge and wet ditch take us another 300 m on the right line, but with no sign of the old road, which once lay parallel on the west, on what is now arable. However, matters become clear once the housing development at Stoborough Green is reached on the east, which faces heathland on the other side of the

5E2–6, 5E2(A) Roman road from Wareham to Flower's Barrow

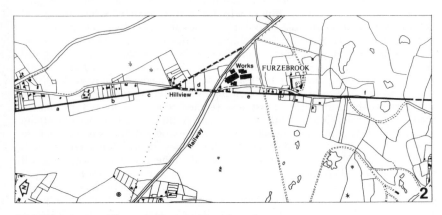

5E.2 Wareham to Flower's Barrow: Furzebrook

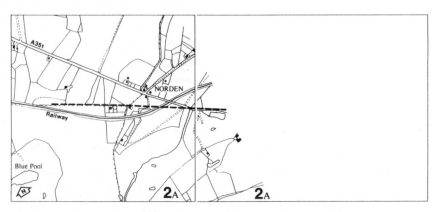

5E.2A Wareham to Flower's Barrow: Branch road towards Corfe Castle

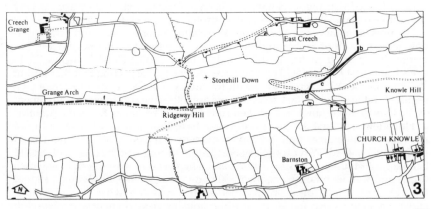

5E.3 Wareham to Flower's Barrow: Ridgeway Hill

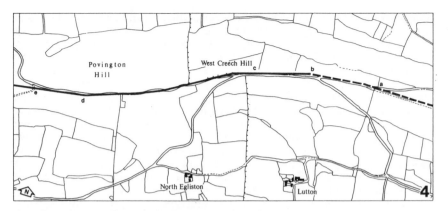

5E.4 Wareham to Flower's Barrow: West Creech

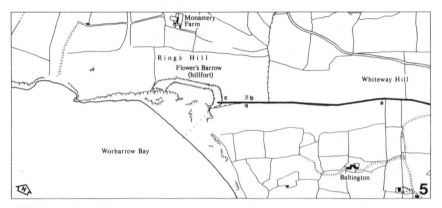

5E.5 Wareham to Flower's Barrow: Flower's Barrow

5E.6 Flower's Barrow, air view of the eastern approach, from the south (Mrs F. Radcliffe)

Roman course. At first disturbed, the agger becomes increasingly visible, 3–4 m wide with a footpath between it and the old property boundary in the shape of a bank and ditch. Gorse occasionally masks the causeway, which nevertheless stands in contrast to the often water-logged heath. West of Hyde Hill, where the Wareham bypass now breaches the line, excavation in advance has established details of the road-build (5E.2a – Appendices 27 and 34). The Roman course soon passes on to a belt of land reclaimed from the heath comparatively recently. Here, as the result of ploughing, the ridge has been lost, but the bank and ditch forming the old property boundary continue, together with the traditional footpath and its right of way (2b). South-west of nos 96 and 98 Furzebrook Road, two nineteenth-century semi-detached cottages, the causeway is again in evidence across open common (2c), around 3 m wide for a distance of 250 m up to the high point at Hill View. There has been some disturbance in places from tracks and ditching, with thick gorse another difficulty. But the route is still assigned a right of way following the agger, while, significantly, property boundaries no longer enter the picture.

As its name suggests, Hill View is a spot of noticeable prominence in the slowly rising terrain between the Frome river and the Purbeck Hills, being situated about half-way in the intervening distance of 5 km. There are indications that the military road from Wareham divided into two at this major sighting point. One branch, its recognition depending largely on the behaviour of a parish boundary, led towards Corfe Castle and the heart of Purbeck; its apparent course is noted at the end of this chapter. The main route, after a slight angular adjustment to the south, coincides with the Furzebrook Road (2d) to beyond the railway bridge. It then goes straight on, while the later road swings east and runs parallel to rejoin the Roman predecessor after 500 m. This straight stretch finds confirmation in further property boundaries, some of which date after the tithe map (1844), where the Roman line shows as an independent feature crossing undeveloped waste. The agger is visible here and there (2e) in a belt of thick gorse until it is rejoined by the medieval/modern road opposite Furzebrook House.

After another 370 m the tarmac road swings away again, this time in a semi-circle to the west. The old alignment continues, marked in undergrowth by a short stretch of ridge and then more definitely on the east of the footpath by a substantial bank and ditch, the latter bearing a laid hedge of some antiquity (2f). By now, scrub on either hand hides abandoned clay-pits of Victorian or later date. The present metalled road returns from its semi-circular diversions only to move away finally on a more westerly track. For its part, the Roman line leaves the clay-pit zone and crosses long-established arable. In the first field, west of the Furzebrook villa, no surface traces are visible. But then the lost course, projected from the Hill View alignment to the north, coincides with a massive lynchet that forms the eastern edge of the next field and of the little triangular copse known as Lillyhays (3a). From the south-east corner of the copse, a hedge (now vanished) pursued the line as far as the incised bed of the stream flowing in the shallow vale from the direction of East Creech. We have now arrived at the last field before the steep scarp of the Purbeck Hills. This was obviously a critical point in the layout of the early road which basically, with only two minor angular changes, had maintained a steady alignment from Wareham. To the south of the stream, a farm track runs over a rise in the ground where the Roman way must have passed. However, it is only much closer to the field bank, at the foot of the wooded hill-slope, that a stony, chalky ridge can be spotted, turning sharply in the arable towards the south-west (3b). It is probably relevant that a right of way cuts through the bank at this place, though the existing footpath is transverse to our route. Following the 30 degree angle of the turn, the track of the lost road is not difficult to follow as a band of stonier material up to 5 m wide on the north side of the bank. Towards the upper, western end of the field, which narrows considerably, the course is revealed by a break in the terrain, now showing slightly away from the field-bank. It seems that this slight edge represents the beginning of a terraced way (3c), which, after being once crossed by a Victorian tramway, climbs the abrupt north face of Knowle Hill. This well-engineered stretch of road, hitherto unrecognized for its date and original purpose, is unusual enough to merit independent comment (Chapter 8D). It is sufficient to say here that the single-track vehicular road, with its purpose-built side-walk, takes us to the high ground and through a cutting (3d), also of military construction.

At the hill-top, known as Bare Cross, the metalled road of today comes up by a separate zigzag and then goes over the crest and down south into the Purbeck country. Eastward, along the crest, one finds no signs whatsoever, in that direction, that the route was ever a made road or even very much used. Westward, up what is interestingly called Ridgeway Hill, the story is different. There are various indications of an original causewayed road following the ridge and eventually arriving at the hillfort of Flower's Barrow, some 2.5 km away. The agger, typically laid out in short straight stretches and varying in width from 3 to 5 m, has been much defaced, worn or replaced by a metalled surface. It is usually accompanied by a turf-and-flint bank, either parallel to, or on the side of, the former road itself.

From Bare Cross, the line of the old road can be picked out in the ascent up Ridgeway Hill with the bank on its south. For some distance, the agger is flanked by later vehicular tracks before the bank twists to run close to the old course again. The agger then appears 4 m wide and 0.3 m high, the present farm-track being of a similar width and now on the north only (3e). Halfway up the east slope of Ridgeway Hill, where the modern track takes a right angle northwards, the boundary bank moves on to the edge of the old causeway. A cart-track (disused, but shown on Ordnance Survey) then skirts the south side, accompanied now by the Church Knowle–Steeple parish boundary, which eventually turns away to the south at a boundary stone. Some 400 m west of the stone, the boundary bank along the ridge, and the perceptible agger on which it rests, enter a belt of undergrowth. Hereabouts, there is a change of alignment in the bank, which is soon seen to be running on the north of a perceptible ditch and a causewayed strip, with the existing track alongside to the south (3f). At the Grange Arch, the bank has been partly removed and the ditch filled, but the profile of the underlying causeway is visible in the turf. Beyond the open space cleared for the Arch, the best of trees and undergrowth gives way to arable, and the existing track swings back on to the line of the original road. Bank and track together follow the Roman line and soon a straight length of some 900 m is reached, which is joined by the motor-road climbing from Creech Grange (4a).

From that point to the top of Whiteway Hill, the Roman line continues in half a dozen alignments averaging 400 m in length. In the first of these stretches, the ridge is faintly visible as the north edge of the modern tarmac road as far as the turning to Steeple (4b). After a slight re-alignment here, opposite the army guard post, the ridge continues on the north edge. Arable soil has here built up so as to mask it, until it emerges most clearly (4c) close to where a spacious parking-area has been created on the site of an old gravel pit. Bramble and gorse now thickly conceal the line until, close to the angle of the Steeple–Tyneham parish boundary, the terrain is given over to a small coppice, long unploughed. The agger briefly appears as a clear and separate low feature, just opposite the next turning to Tyneham. The line is now interrupted by a semi-circular manoeuvring space for army vehicles. It is soon resumed by the parish boundary-bank resting on the old road amid gorse, brambles and small trees. Some 160 m past the Tyneham turning, the boundary-bank with the Roman road beneath re-aligns slightly. The present road cuts through this next stretch of 300 m at what was called Maiden's Grave Gate, where the boundary between Steeple and Tyneham departs northward. The low Roman agger runs on westward to the south, taking the same straight alignment, now with a smaller bank set on it. A little way past the next car-park and viewpoint, beyond the crest of Povington Hill, the modern road gradually diverts downslope on its way to East Lulworth. A metalled predecessor, however, probably medieval, wanders on and off the Roman agger, which otherwise bears a residual bank (4d).

After Lawford Sheard Gate (4c), the Roman road continues up the next rise as a low separate ridge on an unchanged line, now flanked by a well-defined boundary bank on its south, and by a gravelled bridleway on the north. From the top of Whiteway Hill (5a), these three linear features proceed in two alignments to reach the Outwork (5b) east of Flower's Barrow (fig. 5E.6). Thereupon, the low bank, now a parish boundary, diverts from the line and runs off to the south-east corner of the hillfort, close to the eroded cliff and down to the shore. The Roman road, however, still a low, but perceptible ridge, with its accompanying track, a twentieth-century phenomenon, passes straight through the Outwork and then the first defences proper (5c) of the Iron Age stronghold. The causeway and cutting required in each case to negotiate a ditch and a bank or a rampart have never evoked comment, curiously enough. Yet, in terms of effort on this remote and wind-swept height, they must be claimed as examples of Roman military engineering comparable to the terraced way and cutting further east, at Bare Cross, Church Knowle.

What needs to be explained first about this route is its sharply right-angled course to reach the hillfort from Wareham. Why did the Roman engineers not strike directly south-westward across the heathland from the south bank of the Frome? Very likely, the Roman road on its southward line followed for at least part of the way a native track which took this gently rising route towards the Purbeck Hills. It was clearly the shortest distance between the Frome and the ridge, an important military detail since command of that high ground was tied up with the control of Flower's Barrow, so that rapid access was the order of the day. It is understandable that such a native track would have forked to reach the Corfe Castle gap, which must always have been a passage of great local importance in prehistoric times as well as later. The evidence is that the significantly named point at Hill View was also ideally placed for the Roman army to survey a branch to that central gap in the hills. The main Roman road went on, as we have seen, to reach the top of the ridge by the remarkable terraced climb at Bare Cross, whereas the native route would have taken an easier ascent up the dry valley between Stonehill Down and the Purbeck chain proper. The latter track presented no problems to herdsmen or traders passing through friendly territory, but, in respect of terrain and visibility, enjoyed no military advantage whatsoever for a hostile force. Along the Purbeck heights the Roman course is not always easy to discern, but one point is immediately obvious. Eastward from Bare Cross to the Corfe Castle gap there are no clues to suggest any kind of metalled track along the ridge. Westward, however, as far as the hillfort, the course can be traced from existing bridleways, field and parish boundaries, modern roads and, in the most significant sections, frequent sightings of the low camber of an ancient route. The distinctive feature of those

6.5 km is the series of short straight stretches, so characteristic of a Roman military layout on difficult terrain.

The probability of a branch-road from Hill View, noted earlier (5E.2 and 2A) stems from the recognition that early Roman access into the heart of Purbeck must have used part of this original military road to Flower's Barrow. Hill View was an ideal point from which to lay out a sight-line for a road. There is a strong clue in the behaviour of the parish boundary running east-north-east, separating Church Knowle from Holy Trinity, Wareham (now Arne). Unfortunately, that boundary has more than half vanished owing to the construction first of the railway and then, recently, of an oil terminal. It is, however, well documented as three straight lengths for 1.6 km. When the parish boundary turns away at the angle,[2] the alignment coninues, after brief interruption, clearly leading towards the gap at Corfe Castle. Here, for a little distance, a broad pebbly ridge can be traced parallel to, and south of, the southern boundary of Catseye Cottage (a dwelling bearing the date 1710). This short length of old road on reclaimed heathland was probably recorded as the 'Stone Way' (*stanwei*) of a tenth-century charter.[3] The key gap at Corfe Castle was always the target of this military road, and marble quarrying inside Purbeck implies that the Roman command soon established a positive link for that purpose. The Roman route taken beyond the present village of Corfe Castle must remain conjectural and difficult to prove, but the siting of Kingston may not be without significance. The association of the place-name 'Kingston' with Roman roads surviving in Saxon times has long been regarded as a probability and will be noted in Chapter 5K. How early were the alignments represented by East Street and by the obviously old road leading to Kingston, which makes such a determined zigzag across Corfe Common to reach the foot of the limestone plateau?

(F) Wareham to Woodbury

To the casual traveller and to anyone perusing the Ordnance Survey maps alike, this route must always have offered the possibility of being a Roman road, distinguished as it is by straight alignments and a purposive direction. And in the case of the road to Sherford on the east, a number of factors have always argued against this conclusion. There were apparently no other Roman roads serving Wareham and no reason to connect the latter settlement (of doubtful status in Roman times) with the hillfort of Woodbury or with Bere Regis nearby, neither of which had proof of being connected with Wareham at that period of history. The fact that the course to be described had been turnpiked as early as 1765 was a twofold obstacle to recognizing its early origin. On one hand the precise layout of this 9.6 km road in its several stretches was taken to be the work of eighteenth-century surveyors, and, on the other hand, if at any point details could be seen of an old causewayed construction, they presumably did not have to be any earlier than the turnpike era. Yet the case that this road simply supplanted a series of heath tracks 200 years ago is not borne out by ground examination and documentary evidence.

It is only needful at this point to note the curious destination of this supposedly Georgian road, aiming at the main entrance to Woodbury instead of more directly to Bere Regis. The explanation that the turnpike was designed to serve Woodbury Fair as well as the village is implausible. When the turnpike was built the ancient September market was in decline, with the tolls halving between 1730 and 1770. Fortunately, there is evidence enough to demonstrate that the construction simply took the form of improvement to an existing route which had survived until recently on the open unenclosed heath. The original road was laid out in four distinct alignments, basically followed by turnpike and modern carriageway, but with very revealing divergences off line at two places that will be noted: Cold Harbour and Triangle Plantation.

The first stretch therefore branched from the Lake Farm–Wareham Roman road at Northport (fig. 5G. 1), represented by the present Bere Regis road. The course climbs steadily from low ground to gain the Seven Barrows ridge after 1 km. Passing between the barrows (1a), the road re-aligned northward on the second stretch across Northport Heath for a further kilometre. Although at first there are parallel ridges on either side of the modern road the one on the west is flanked by a pronounced ditch on the far side and remains visible until the high point (spot height 34.7m) is reached at the end of the stretch (1b).

This is the beginning of the third part of the Wareham–Woodbury Roman-cum-turnpike road. The well-marked change of angle towards the north (1b) gave a typical sighting for a straight length of more than 4 km. In the descent past 'Forest Lodge', the modern road and turnpike divert very slightly south-westward, cutting most visibly across the line of an excellent ridge, 4 m wide and up to 0.5 m high, with a defined east side-ditch, which now appears on the east. This part of Northport Heath was open ground in living memory and the agger here has fortunately been left undisturbed in the wide belt of forestry fire-break. The Roman line continues as a discontinuous feature marking the east boundary of an old wood and the modern road,[1] as we reach Cold Harbour Heath. The inn that represents the settlement of that name has been renamed in modern times, first the Angel Inn, now the Silent Woman. *Cold Harbour*, reached after 300 m from the angle of re-alignment, was a term often applied in the past to a refuge beside an old highway, particularly, it appears, a Roman road. This is, in the circumstances, an interesting generic place-name, applied, in the present case, to an early land-holding that clearly suggests the pre-existence of this Roman road. Certainly, there is proof here that the straight alignment of our road is independent of, and significantly older than, the days of the turnpike. Hutchins in 1774 recorded 'six small tenements' at Cold Harbour, otherwise 'North Cary', and the field system of this settlement can easily be identified within the bounds of the holding. One of the earliest of these fields encroached on to the straight line of the original road from Wareham. As a result, the carriageway followed by the turnpike and its modern successor has been forced to divert before coming back on its course northwards. For a distance of 150 m, the present road is separated from its predecessor by an old laid hedge and the track of the older road, now on the south-west side, is occupied by a flat belt of ground along the foot of the gentle slope rising to the west. To the north of this diversion, the western hedge bounding the modern road smartly resumes the straight alignment (1c), emphasizing the interruption created by the bulge at Cold Harbour.

This slight hiccup in the straight alignment past Cold Harbour goes far to establish the age of the road as well before the eighteenth century. The evidence from the bounds of the old Cold Harbour land-holding reinforces the case (Appendix 32) and provides a clue to the branch-road that led away to connect with the small hillfort at Woolsbarrow. Further evidence for a pre-medieval origin soon emerges from this long stretch which ends at Sugar Hill, some 3.5 km to the north.

For some distance there is a wide verge on the west of the present road, but that appears to be part of the turnpike improvement, since the line of its Roman predecessor must prove to lie to the east, marked by a substantial hedge-bank. Thus we reach Triangle Plantation on the east (2a), at the point where it will be shown that the Romans formed a branch-road by upgrading a native track leading towards the north (Chapter 5I and Appendix 22). Close to the edge of the Plantation, a prominent ridge of typical profile can be followed through the

5F.1–3 Roman road from Wareham to Woodbury

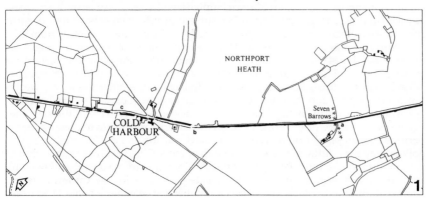

5F.1 Wareham to Woodbury: Cold Harbour

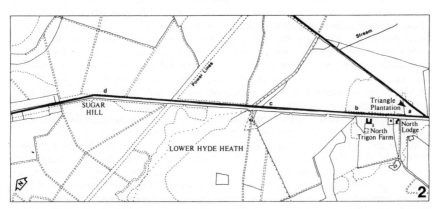

5F.2 Wareham to Woodbury: Hyde Heath

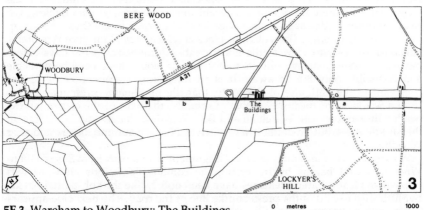

5F.3 Wareham to Woodbury: The Buildings

85

woodland, parallel to, and east of, the modern road. It is 4–5 m wide and up to 0.6 m high and its antiquity is at once emphasized by the number of beech trees of considerable girth growing on it. The surface-profile from west of the modern road to east of this prominent agger underlines its separate identity from the turnpike, and a gap of as much as 10 m develops between the nearer edges of each (Appendix 34). Midway along Triangle Plantation, the ground drops into a shallow dell, which is drained north-eastwards by a small water-course. Hereabouts, the turnpike road was provided with side-ditches and the water flows in zigzag fashion from west to east through a culvert under the tarmac road.

Towards the north of the Plantation this wet-ditch is diverted through the agger. There was sufficient obstacle to progress here for vehicles to have required perhaps a small plank bridge. When it thus diverts, the wet-ditch is replaced by a hollow-way for a little distance opposite the gate to Trigon. Thus, momentarily, we can observe the unusual circumstance of Roman road, medieval hollow-way and turnpike-cum-modern road side by side. At this point the causeway is re-aligned slightly westwards, its centre having been at maximum some 11 m from the edge of the present tarmac. The Roman line passes into dense undergrowth, gradually re-joining the present road (2b) as the vegetation thins 200 m beyond North Trigon Farm which lies on the other side.

This third alignment, continuing towards Sugar Hill, goes straight down to Stroud Bridge (2c). A medieval road certainly passed this way and support for the antiquity of this line comes from several sources. In the first place, the word *stroud* ('marshy ground with brushwood') can be traced back locally to the thirteenth century, and a belt of such peaty terrain drains south-west in this area for several kilometres. Stroud Bridge takes the road across a drier gap in the middle. This bridging point has long been in service, certainly preceded by a ford, for there is a ramp up from the water-course on the north bank, east of the bridge. A second detail is that four parish boundaries join here, so that this spot clearly once had special significance in the open heathland.

There are other particular features to note about this middle part of the Wareham–Woodbury road, that is, the northern stretch of the third alignment from Stroud Bridge to Sugar Hill and the southern stretch of the final alignment after Sugar Hill. 'Improvement' by afforestation with conifers has reached this area of heathland comparatively recently. Twin turf banks, possibly of medieval date, border the road, with a wider verge and hints of a ridge on the east. These details might suggest an old drove or they could belong to the turnpike era. However, their presence is closely associated with the straightness of the alignments and there is nothing comparable on recent open ground flanking the road. From the bridge at 16 m above sea-level, the present road thus takes us up to 36 m on Sugar Hill (2d), an obvious place at which to re-align since Woodbury Hill now comes into view to the north-west. Additionally, in the days before pinewoods, Woolsbarrow with its minor hillfort would have been both visible and accessible only 800 m away. It is an interesting comment, certainly not irrelevant to the antiquity of the route, that the place-name *sugar* may derive from a Saxon word meaning 'robber'. Certainly, this part of the course, on the heath half-way between Wareham and Bere Regis was lonely and hazardous in the Middle Ages, but no doubt it saw much traffic each autumn, before and after Woodbury Fair.

We are now on the fourth and final alignment which runs from Sugar Hill to Woodbury and begins by traversing the conifer plantations on what was Bloxworth Heath. Lateral features have been noted, like the substantial banks, but little else to hint at the pre-turnpike line of the road. The next clue appears 1 km onward from Sugar Hill where the road crosses the parish boundary between Bloxworth and Bere Regis, which arrives from the north in the shape of a double bank with ditches (3a). This positive linear feature then curves away westward beside the turnpike road, leaving the boundary to continue southward, marked 'undefined' on the earliest Ordnance Survey maps. The implication is that here, when the heath was still waste and common, the road itself was adopted as a land-boundary to a holding on the north. A further guide to the use of the road as a medieval drove emerges just to the east, where there is a break in the lateral bank on the north to accommodate a pond, which probably acts as one source for the Sherford stream. We can recognize this for a watering-place for animals on their way to or from the traditional Woodbury Fair.

Between the passage of that parish boundary and Woodbury itself the straight course of the modern road runs between late enclosed fields (2b) and is closely hemmed in by a ditch and hedge on each side as far as the intersection with the A35. Beyond the crossroads, for the last 800 m, a typical profile athwart the existing road furnishes helpful information. If we start well to the south-west, the surface of the field on that side rises over a defined ridge 4 m wide topped by a hedge; then follows a narrow verge and the modern (turnpike) road, also 4 m wide; finally, on the other side, a small verge and ditch, with a hedge set on a bank. The ridge under the first hedge represents the Roman original and its appearance on the south-west ties in with an off-set in the alignment to the south-east of the A35 crossing. The ridge can be traced parallel to the present road almost to a spot opposite the south-west entrance to Woodbury, where an old building, recorded in 1776, now only a barn, stands upon it.

(G) Wareham to Dorchester

Given the argument that an early Roman military site is apparently located in the vicinity of Lady St Mary's cemetery, it is not surprising that this road, on the evidence, should have begun in the area of that church and then run westward to join the line of the present Worgret Road at a significant bend nearly 500 m beyond West Walls. Abbot's Quay originated on the course (1a) and the pattern of the block of buildings based on Holy Trinity Church also appears to conform. Then, in the grounds of Castle Close, the site of Wareham Castle, the recent construction of a tennis court revealed several layers of stony metalling highly characteristic of an old road, terraced into the top of the slope (1b). The disposition of the metalling and its general alignment were precisely on the anticipated course, which is effectively earlier than the West Walls as we now see them (Appendix 26).

It is indeed outside the southern ditch of West Walls that the next indications emerge. Some 50 m from the south end of those western defences (1c) occurs a steepish edge at an angle to the ditch, so that it lies parallel to the projected Roman course, which should be forming the 'shelf' just to the north. The private road leading to 'Frome Harbour' has cut deep through this edge and revealed a stony deposit, looking like disturbed metalling. It is possible to explain this scarp as partly natural, a process begun by the Roman agger and accentuated by soil-creep, on what must have been arable, both before and after the Saxon fortifications were built. This sharp slope, gradually becoming less pronounced, can be traced athwart the line of the brick wall between Westport House, the district council offices, and the house to the south, no. 9 Westport Road. The latter road is narrow, unmade and flat as far as the scarped edge, which here has a more natural appearance. However, a band of heavy flints across the road has been exposed and may represent upper metalling of the Roman course.

The line now runs long-established private gardens and the scarp curves away south-westward, before we reach Encombe Crescent, south of the police station.

5G.1–9 Roman road from Wareham to Dorchester

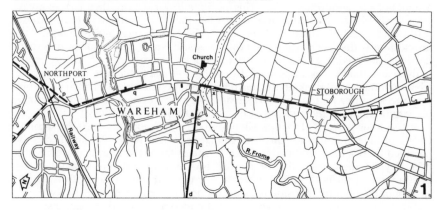

5G.1 Wareham to Dorchester: Wareham

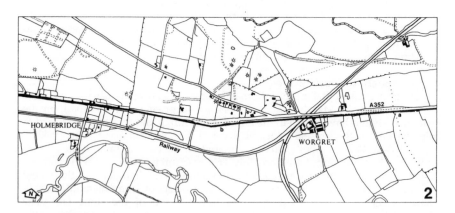

5G.2 Wareham to Dorchester: Worgret

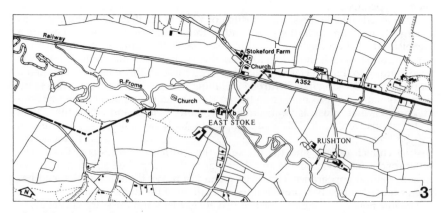

5G.3 Wareham to Dorchester: East Stoke

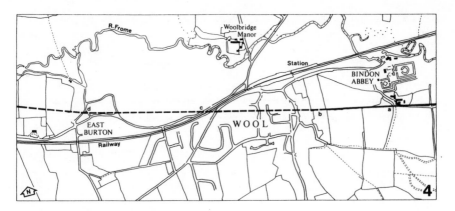

5G.4 Wareham to Dorchester: Wool

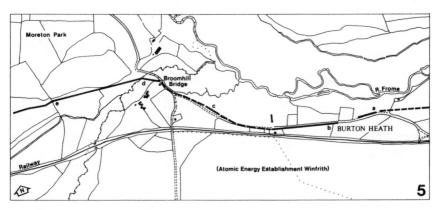

5G.5 Wareham to Dorchester: Broomhill

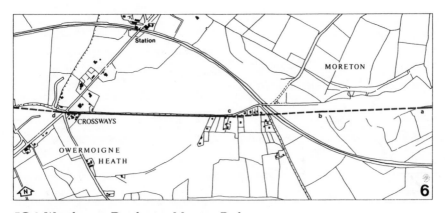

5G.6 Wareham to Dorchester: Moreton Park

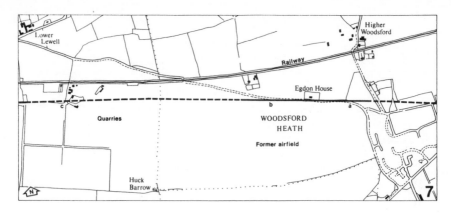

5G.7 Wareham to Dorchester: Woodsford Heath

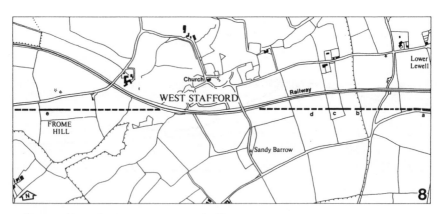

5G.8 Wareham to Dorchester: West Stafford

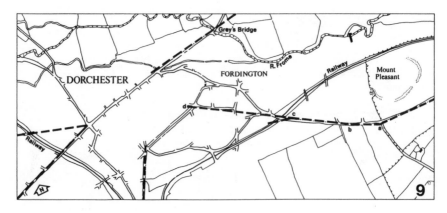

5G.9 Wareham to Dorchester: Fordington

This is an area of extra-mural Wareham developed only recently and, despite the housing, useful evidence still survives on the ground. Through the back gardens on the north side of the Crescent, some 50 m of low ridge can still be followed, visible also on aerial photographs (1d). We can next pick up the alignment just before it merges with the southern fringe of Worgret Road (1e). Two houses (nos 26 and 28) stand high on a wide ridge, while west of no. 28, a short length of agger survives across the access, 0.15 m high and 6 m broad. Its occurrence here is doubly important. First, a hedge-bank rests on the north side of the camber, emphasizing that the latter had an earlier, independent origin. Second, after arriving on a straight alignment, the modern/medieval road is demonstrably bending away towards the Westport gateway, in a manner typical of a diversion.

The Roman alignment next follows the southern edge of Worgret Road (2a) and both run together as far as the hill at Worgret (though now interrupted by the new bypass). *Worgret* is from a Saxon word meaning 'gallows', a grim reminder that this spot was a prominent feature in the landscape. It was at this excellent sighting point on a spur that the first Roman stretch from Wareham ended after 2.5 km and a view could be had forward along the Frome valley. As it re-aligns on the slope round this critical corner, the Roman road takes a terraced course for more than 100 m, mainly hidden in gorse and bracken, the earliest metalling well-covered in humus (2b). On its south there are remains of a later bank, while on its north, between it and the modern/turnpike road, the medieval Wareham–Dorchester highway shows as a deep hollow-way, that finally cuts across the line. The new alignment is soon revealed by a fragment of the embanked road close to East Stoke post office, lowly set beside the old course.

Thus, for another 2.5 km, an almost straight course is followed by the present A352 up to the beginning of the bend at St Mary's Church. This track from Worgret, with two minor adjustments of line, has been attributed to the turnpike engineers, 'a new construction replacing the older way through Rushton'. As it happens, however, a manorial map for East Stoke, dated 1732,[1] shows that this straight length was in existence, with fields abutting it, thirty years before the Wareham Trust started work in 1765. East of the church (a Victorian replacement for the ruined church across the river), older maps show a sharp curve in the hedge-line, at the end of the alignment (3a). It is undoubtedly here that the Roman engineers organized a major re-alignment to cross the Frome.

The course now ran south and gained the other bank east of the bridge at Stoke Mill, where there is an obvious old ford (3b). From there, for a distance of 500 m, a medieval road once led in a straight line west-south-west, passing south of the deserted earthworks of old East Stoke to reach a meander of the Frome. Despite development at the Freshwater Laboratory, the Roman route is defined for most of this stretch by a fine hollow-way (3c–d), which peters out at the bend alongside a short, but prominent, ridge surviving between it and the river.

It is difficult to explain this ridge as other than covering a fragment of the early road. The north flank has been eroded to expose a depth of stone-free soil over a stony layer, hardly the material for a flood-bank. Although this ridge is sited almost on the projected line over the river flats between 'new' St Mary's Church and, as we shall see, Long Coppice just south-west, it is definitely aligned with the hollow-way to the east. There can be little doubt that the river was negotiated by this zigzag rather than by the direct line for which there is no evidence.

Beyond the Frome meander, the Roman road re-aligned after crossing a small stream draining into the main river. Its course can then be traced along the slope running down to the low ground at the edge of or inside Long Coppice (3e): either as a low ridge 3 m wide, set with remnants of an old laid hedge, or, midway along, as a terrace cut into a spur around which the field boundary has

91

been diverted. It is clear that the medieval version of the road kept, on this stretch, to the east of its older counterpart and this juxtaposition is displayed to the south of Long Coppice, where, in the open field, there is a ploughed hollow-way with the earlier spread of stones to its west. Towards the middle of that field the hollow-way peters out (3f) at the end of the long cross-valley sighting from the north bank of the Frome.

The next alignment (3f–5a) will be found to run almost completely straight for nearly 5 km up the valley, parallel to the river. A small stream or wet-ditch provides the first evidence of the changed course by bending sharply as it crosses the road-line, which then shows up clearly west of that point as a typical low ridge. This merges into the north side of the present road that passes Bindon Abbey on its way to Wool. South of the Abbey there is a right-angled bend, but the early road continued in line as a well-recorded hollow-way (4a–4b) amid 'settlement remains, formerly part of Wool village. This road was already blocked by a cottage in 1770'.[2] A high ridge (revealed by contouring on Ordnance Survey maps) runs for more than 200 m along the north side of the hollow-way and, as at Long Coppice, is a firm pointer to the original Roman course.

Within Wool, north–south thoroughfares in the shape of Spring Street and High Street have removed traces of the first road along which the village seems once to have been sited. However, west of High Street, old property boundaries belonging to cottage gardens are broadly based on that alignment and the evidence is strengthened by a hedge-line beginning 130 m west of the former vicarage. This field boundary, some 400 m in length, once formed the north side of a block of medieval strips and, it must be claimed, of the Roman road. Its last 100 m also coincided with the parish boundary between Wool and East Burton, which was significantly indented at this pointed (4c), but does not figure on current maps.[3]

Again, ground evidence has gone, thanks to the railway and recent housing, and beyond the East Burton road there was apparently a minor re-alignment of the Roman course. It then continued over slightly lower terrain, though still above the flood level of the Frome. This area, called 'The Moors', was once intensively strip-cultivated, which might explain the disappearance of the early line. The medieval/modern road takes a sweep, contour-wise, to the south and then regains the probable Roman line for 100 m at Burton Farm. This type of diversion occurs also west of Burton and exemplifies what might happen when an old road was forced to go *round*, instead of *through*, arable land.

In the heart of the village, where a trace of the old road might more easily have survived the ravages of the plough, there is a significant short stretch of agger west of the stream. Here that water-course is deeply incised, some 5 m wide. Of necessity it is negotiated today by a footbridge, which clearly has a long ancestry and lies, moreover, close to the projected line. On the western bank, from the stream to the lane, some 30 m of independent ridge, 3 m wide and 0.25 m high, shows on grass (4d). It is sited transversely to the footpath, its successor, so that erosion has exposed gravel metalling. The continuation of the agger in both directions is blocked by a building of seventeenth-century date or later.

After the stream-crossing, the Roman line, as given by the ridge, has shifted slightly northward to follow level ground over the arable once known as Northbrook. Having moved away again, the medieval/modern road to Broomhill returns to rejoin the older one where another stream emerges from a marshy side-vale and flows into the Frome. Until recently the passage of the stream was effected by a ford and a footbridge. This had survived as a fair-weather route, since there used to be a higher, drier track to Moreton starting at the last bend, but now cut by the railway. At the old ford the stream-bed has been widened and we now find a brick road-bridge, but beyond, despite local changes, the landscape is still recognizably what was called Burton Common or Heath.

In this relatively undisturbed setting, with patches of original gorse, the low ridge of the old road can usually be traced as far as Broomhill on one side or other of the tarmac. If we follow the course in detail, on the short re-alignment up from the ford (5a), the ridge is first hidden on the north side in thick gorse, then appears 3 m wide and some half a dozen metres from the edge of the present road-surface. There is an interruption by a small site working for the Atomic Energy Authority, then the two courses re-align together at the top of the slope (5b).

The old ridge is now on the south flank, barely independent of the modern surface, but revealing its stony metalling in a number of places. From here to Broomhill the route basically involved four alignments along the southern upper edge of the Frome valley. The first extends past the turning to Hyford, with the ridge on the south of the modern road. The second is short and angular, presumably concealed under the present tarmac; and continuing as the third, which runs up and over a sharp spur, where the route has been eased by a small cutting of uncertain date at the highest point. After the spur, the ridge, re-appears (5c), now on the north side, and is very distinct in pasture a little further on, just before the beginning of the fourth stretch. Finally, the latter, on indirect evidence, is in the main followed by the modern road as far as the first of the Broomhill bridges. Before the stream, recent building has removed any indication there might have been for terracing into the slope.

There are three bridges at Broomhill taking the road to Moreton over the several channels of the Maynewater, a small tributary flowing east into the Frome. The southernmost bridge stands at the start of the original crossing, where the existing road and its Roman predecessor reach the present main-stream. An ancient passage, over the low ground beyond, may be still partly in use as an irregular slight hollow-way (5d) now followed by cattle from the farm that have crossed at the ford alongside the first bridge. On the other side of the meadow-flats, it soon becomes clear that the original road hereabouts linked, not with the sinuous one to Moreton, but with an age-old route aiming west towards Dorchester. Where the ground rises from the valley bottom, through a thicket, there is a masking cover of deep black humus. Nevertheless, eventually, a telltale break in the ground merges into a remarkable causewayed lane, with a broad side-ditch on its north flank. It now links with the Moreton road, but it is clearly a much older line skirting Moreton Park on its south.

We are at the start of an unmistakeable alignment that can be traced, with minor adjustments, for more than 10 km, as far as Frome Hill, just short of Dorchester (5d–8e). The first part, fringing the park, has been called 'an attractive old road with some magnificent oak trees'.[4] In a changing world this description fortunately remains basically true, even if it was then applied to a road considered only medieval in origin. Certainly this route must have witnessed long service before travellers from Dorchester and the west tended to be diverted through Moreton on the north. The fine agger and the straightness of alignments simply confirm its real antiquity.

After more than 600 m, the Roman line adjusts slightly at the foot of a considerable spur projecting from the north (5e). Just beyond this point (where a trench was cut for a major water-pipeline in 1989),[5] we can spot for a little distance slight terracing into the slope, which kept the original road on course, north of the present track. The latter swings away and then back to run parallel to the Roman course and on its south, a prominent feature normally well covered in bracken and brambles. Another 130 m further, past the spur, the gravel track moves away following easier level ground. The Roman agger is here exposed, lower and free of later embanking, as it climbs a wooded hill beside old quarries on the northern side. After another slight change of alignment (6a), beyond this hill and as far as the railway, gravel-pits and afforestation have erased traces of the Roman line, except in one spot. Extending south from South Lodge of Moreton Park there is a long-established path which still survives in a narrow strip of undisturbed heathland. It is crossed by the low ridge of the Roman road, showing up as a stony band, some 30 m south of, and parallel to, the gravel-track (6b). Indeed that track merges into the embanked entrance avenue to Moreton Park and the fact that both are equidistant from the Roman line demonstrates that the latter was still a notable local landmark until recent times.

Immediately west of the railway, the parish boundary between Moreton and Owermoigne takes a straight course for nearly 1.6 km to Crossways. For most of the way, the present road from Moreton follows this, as the successor of the recognized medieval road from Broomhill. It appears to be built on an older causeway like that noted south of Moreton Park, aligned along the south side under the parish bank of turf (6c). Beyond Crossways, the parish boundary zigzags across the probable Roman line, no positive trace of which remains in an area of former arable and now of houses and gardens. Less then a kilometre west of Crossways, the meeting place of four present roads, a footpath and a parish boundary bears the interesting name of Dick o' th' Banks. The Roman line passes unseen through to the north of the road junction and across what was part of Woodsford Heath. There was once a gravel pit nearby, followed by an army post, and now the area is arable.

While a slight ridge and a parallel depression have been left here, the old alignment finds striking confirmation when the road from Crossways to West Stafford through Dick o' th' Banks swings back on to the Roman course east of Egdon House. The Roman road is commemorated as a massive linear feature (7a), buried in thick gorse on the north edge of the present road, which here suddenly straightens. At its eastern end this earthwork has been chopped through to reveal a stony base, but westward its line is gradually traversed by the road to West Stafford, a development that took place comparatively recently. Before 1840 the medieval successor to the Roman road went on for 600 m on the south side of the earthwork, which must have been built up as a boundary to substantial proportions. Some 250 m west of Egdon House, after the tarmac road has thus cut through the line towards the level crossing and West Stafford, there was still evidence on the ground for the western end of this substantial earthwork aligned in the direction of Dorchester (7b). It will be useful at this stage to consider this information in relation to the topography of the Roman route from Broomhill.

From that bridging point, the Roman and medieval road followed precisely the crest of plateau gravel separating the Frome valley to the north from the narrower tributary stream of the Maynewater flowing on the south. As the high ground broadened towards Crossways on Moreton Heath, the road was maintained close to the northern edge, taking full advantage of the terrain that extended towards Dorchester. That obvious line between Broomhill and Dorchester may have offered too many gaps to merit proper consideration as the lost road between Wareham and Dorchester, but clues still remain to throw light on the problems. If we then pursue the projection westward of the alignment past Egdon House, we may note that an eighteenth-century road appears to be recorded as coincident for 3.2 km as far as Highgate Lane, which runs north over the ridge from West Knighton to Lewell. Where the modern road was seen to divert towards the level crossing, a fragment of causeway-cum-bank, 5 m wide and 1 m high, subsists in brushwood on the south (7b). This is an area much disturbed in the past by gravel pits and a war-time airfield so that the alignment can be picked up only after another 800 m beyond the gate to English China Clay land (7c). This is obviously the eighteenth-century road, but with an asphalt surface, built on the original line. Some 250 m west, the roadway swerves to the south; between it and the copse to the north a low ridge, 40 m long, proclaims the first straight layout (8a). Oak trees set in a turf bank continue the line a little way, when the made-up road swings south towards West Knighton. A deep re-entrant from the Frome valley to the north must now have created a problem. Did the old road make a zigzag to keep level around what is now arable or did it drop down and rise to the other side of the dip? Certainly in the far hedge there is a notch in the West Stafford–West Knighton parish boundary (8b), associated with a fragment of ridge where the road-alignment was regained.

From this point onward to Frome Hill, the evidence, both visual and documentary, is tenuous, even though the relatively direct course from Broomhill has already been satisfactorily traced for 7 km out of the 10. This major gap was created in the first place by the diversion of local traffic through Lewell and West Stafford in medieval times, leading to fragmentary use or disuse of the original road. A number of public ways were altered or extinguished in West Stafford at the close of the eighteenth century, but it is not easy to be certain of their track from description only.

After the anomaly in the parish boundary noted above, the line crosses four fields in 800 m before reaching the railway. In the second and third of these, a break in the slope accompanied by a broad stony band in the arable is on alignment and should be relevant (8c–d). The presumed course then runs under the railway and through the new housing south of West Stafford village. It has long been lost in the field west of the old rectory, where ridge-and-furrow survives in grass alongside the South Winterborne stream. This is the one area between Broomhill and Frome Hill where the road has had to descend to low terrain, always subject to the later routine ploughing so inimical to residual earthworks. The course, tentative here, then passes back under the railway embankment on to further arable and climbs the eastern slope of the chalk outlier known as Frome Hill.

This high ground possesses a small capping of Bagshot Beds, sands and gravels, traversed by the actual modern/medieval road from West Stafford to Dorchester as well as our Roman line, both of which merge shortly to the west. Some 100 m south of the prominent tumulus on the hill a straight band of local gravel a few metres wide has been seen from the road (8e). Its location identifies it as a stretch of buried causeway revealed by the depth of machine-ploughing.

The final 600 m of the long alignment from Broomhill now coincide broadly with the West Stafford road that joins the A352 from Wareham, south of the Mount Pleasant henge monument and the Conquer Barrow. Major road alterations in this area have destroyed the obvious primacy of that stretch of the minor road (9a). North-westward from the junction (9a, now a roundabout), with a slight change of line north-westward (9b), the first part of this 800 m alignment of the early military road runs as far as the railway bridge. The Roman course has unquestionably been concealed under Alington Avenue, which in turn has suffered bisection by the new bypass.[6] The line is briefly lost until, in Fordington, it reaches the right angle where King's Road joins Icen Way. Despite the modern origin of its name, the latter is a street of considerable antiquity, incorporating a straight length of 200 m that betrays an early predecessor as far as Gallows Hill

(9d). Here, the military road re-aligned for the last time, aiming for the high ground at Top o' Town, in the north-west of Roman and medieval Dorchester.

Is it possible to be confident about the precise course of the Roman road from Wareham as it reaches Dorchester? The case for the stretch from Mount Pleasant as far as the railway bridge has always been regarded as purely 'circumstantial',[7] with the burials strung out close-by forming 'the only tangible evidence'. A cemetery alongside a major road, but outside city walls, was normal practice in Roman times and the discoveries did suggest that the early road probably lay under the present avenue. Recent discoveries at Alington Avenue add to the indirect evidence for the stretch between 9b and 9c, while a well-recorded observation of Victorian days can now be accepted as showing how that final stretch passed onward from Gallows Hill:

1. In excavations by the Trust for Wessex Archaeology,[8] a number of ancient property boundaries and building lines were found to run at right angles or parallel to the avenue on its south side. They were clearly related to a highway precisely ancestral to Alington Avenue (now almost unrecognizable after alterations connected with the bypass). The fragment of milestone, dating to the third century, which was recovered during the work, had probably not wandered far from its original location. Furthermore, a length of early road metalling was seen to emerge from under the avenue at its western end near the railway bridge 9c). It was interpreted, probably correctly, as aiming at the *south* gate of the Roman town. But there is equally no reason why it should not be regarded as *branching* from the original approach road, which would explain its change of alignment at that point. With the development of civil *Durnovaria*, traffic from Wareham entered the town through the south gate.

2. Around 1865,[9] a 'very hard, smooth, cemented roadway, about three yards wide' was traced for 60 m across the garden of Culliford House, running in a west-north-west direction from Gallows Hill. Most importantly, it was seen to be earlier than the remains, since removed, of the Roman civil rampart. Nevertheless, since 'it conforms in no way ... with what is known of the Roman street pattern' the date of this road has been in doubt. However, the case of the Dorchester fort, argued in Chapter 6, reinforces the evidence for this as a military road and as the logical termination of the road from Wareham. Can it be a coincidence that this last stretch was parallel with, but offset by 200 Roman feet from, the alignment of the road that left Dorchester for Ilchester? This is a pointer to both routes having been laid out to serve the identical destination.[10]

(H) Sandford to Bulbury

Most of the course of this road has been readily identifiable from large-scale Ordnance Survey maps and distinguishable as a feature earlier than the modern road which resulted from turnpike improvements. No doubt, as in the case of other roads connecting Wareham with neighbouring hillforts, a Roman attribution will still be difficult to swallow. The facts on the ground must be allowed to speak for themselves.

The place-name *Sandford* (5D.5e) belongs to the spot where the Roman road from Lake to Wareham crossed the small nameless stream running from Northport Heath down to the Piddle and the sea. No fewer than four other alignments of various kinds and various dates converge on Sandford. We shall be following the line of the most westerly, which is first traced (1a) opposite Laurel Cottage and marked on early maps as a boundary swinging round north-north-west. It is still immediately obvious, despite building development, that this line

5H.1–2 Roman road from Sandford to Bulbury

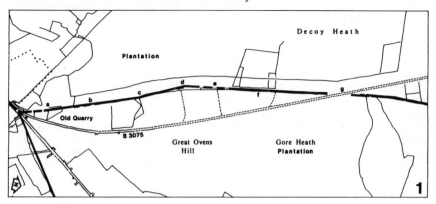

5H.1 Sandford to Bulbury: Gore Heath

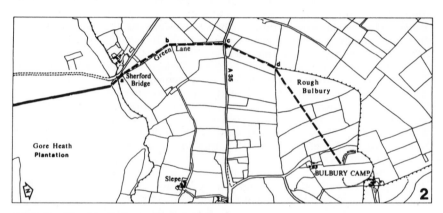

5H.2 Sandford to Bulbury: Rough Bulbury

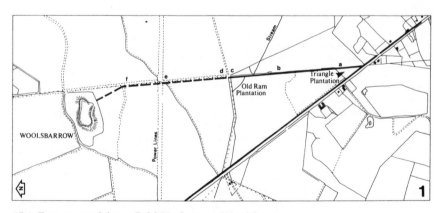

5I.1 Roman road from Cold Harbour to Woolsbarrow

was a pre-turnpike road. We can first pick it up some 220 m north of the cottage and north of a 'ranch house' bungalow called 'Sherwood' which has been built across the old line. The stony edge of the 3–4 m wide low ridge has been exposed by ground-levelling 20 m west of Morden Road, the start of which is now blocked from through traffic.

After shrouding by gorse, the line of the road emerges for 50 m as a wide grassy low agger, with a hollow-way skirting its west side. The course is then cut through by a gully of probable nineteenth-century date and intended to drain the former clay-pits now coming into view on the east (1b). There continues to be a footpath wandering along the course, though it is not marked as a public right of way. The walker now begins to ascend through the cluster pines of twentieth-century planting. In the recent past, quarry-working respected the old track, which for a short distance runs with a scarp to the east (artificial) and a scarp to the west (natural). The narrower original agger, though much chopped about, is still a discernible feature. Half-way up this rising ground, which forms an outlier to Great Ovens Hill, the footpath moves away westward over the road-ridge, while the latter plunges straight onward into thick gorse and brushwood that now bar the way. Somewhere and sometime in the scrub, between that point and the flatter plateau beyond (1c – called on old maps 'Nundico'), the agger has been strongly defined by turf addition so as to stand 0.6 m high with side-ditches, a distinct, but unexplained feature on the Ordnance Survey. It now pursues a prominent gorse-covered course across open heath, fortunately spared from the conifer planting that has taken place a short distance to the west.

The first major change of direction occurs at the top of Great Ovens Hill where there is a fine view northward towards Sherford, now 2.5 km away. An east–west gravel track runs across the line (1d), and then the Roman course separates from the ditched and embanked feature that has commemorated it across Nundico and descends into a dell that marks the west side of the Hill. The intention of the Roman surveyors was to bring the road down from the high ground by a gentler gradient than the single turf-bank that appears on the Ordnance Survey map. There is thick vegetation at this spot, but a cutting was apparently created at the head of the dell, with a subsequent terrace into the slope along the western edge of Great Ovens Hill. A short length of hollow-way here, alongside the fine cambered ridge, points to considerable usage of this route in pre-turnpike days. All the way down for some 250 m, the agger of this old road, 2.5 m wide is undisturbed in heather and bracken. This important unrecorded stretch of old cambered road is completely independent of the turf-bank activity of post-Roman times that forms the alignment 'recognized' by the Ordnance Survey along the upper slope above the dell.

Official mapmakers acknowledged a problem by their use of double lines (= bank and side-ditches) that change to a single line (= turf-bank) on Great Ovens Hill and then back to double lines (= embanked road) on the lower ground to the north. To complicate matters, there are other post-Roman linear features diverting north-east from the turf-bank.

When the dell emerges on to a gentler downhill slope, the Roman agger, slight in relation to the turf features to its east, is crossed by another east–west present-day track (1e) leading from the car-park by the Morden Road. North of this track the Roman course re-unites with the turf-bank after its diversion. Thick gorse makes close observation difficult, but the line of the Roman road, visible as a low ridge, is now enclosed by twin banks 12 m apart (1f). This development is associated for some 300 m with enclosures of possible late medieval date,[1] constructed on the heath alongside the old road and to its west. Opposite the end of the second enclosure, yet another footpath, ungravelled, runs athwart the line from the east. The two parallel banks again become one feature set on the original road, 2.5 m and 0.6 m high with deeply cut side-ditches.

The alignment continues in this fashion until it reaches (1g) the existing Morden Road (B3075), which is the successor of the turnpike of 1765. Where the two courses intersect obliquely, clearance of a broad belt of heathland has removed traces of the older road, particularly on the west. On the eastern side of the Morden Road the alignment is again preserved within twin banks 10–12 m apart in scrub and woodland. In this way it arrives (2a) just south of the Sherford river as a most perceptible feature on the ground and on Ordnance Survey maps, with a slight re-adjustment of line on a high point east of Morden Road. At Sherford a bridleway (now a forest walk) of probable medieval ancestry, which follows the southern river-bank, traverses and obliterates the end of the line. However, on both sides of the water deep clefts mark the site of the old ford a few paces east of the bridge, which was itself first recorded in 1683.

The crossing of the Sherford river is reached from Sandford by the present Morden Road basically in three straight stretches, the turnpike engineering being deceptively like Roman construction. There are indeed signs of an older road alongside in the last section down to the bridge. These might belong to a medieval way, for the date of the bridge and its siting off the line of the ford and the Roman course suggest that the latter was already out of service in the seventeenth century, before the bridge-road was turnpiked.

Beyond the river, on its north bank, the behaviour of the two roads is of particular importance in deciding origins. After a sharp re-alignment, what is of certainly the later road from the bridge takes present traffic to Park Corner over Chitten Hill through well-established fields. The two slightly curving stretches are totally unlike those south of the river, and another feature is the sharp change of direction at the water. By contrast, what on general layout looks like the older road makes a much smaller re-alignment just south of the river and continues north of it as Green Lane (only recently abandoned). It is important to note that the parish boundary between Morden and Lytchett Matravers formed the east margin of this lane in two straight stretches as far as Scutt's Gate (2c). The latter is the name of the cottage standing where the Roman line was crossed by the road from Lytchett Minster, a late turnpike and now the A35. Northward from Scutt's Gate the parish boundary runs straight again, and it is clear that Green Lane must once have continued on the west side, thus perpetuating a third length of the Roman line up from the river. These stretches of road-cum-parish boundary (2a–b–c–d) are all three of closely similar length, each of about 400 m. The third reaches the south-west corner of the plantation of Rough Bulbury, which forms part of what seems to be an ancient land-holding of post-Roman date, including the hillfort of Bulbury itself. At Rough Bulbury, the parish boundary continues north as its western side, but visibly curvilinear and of clearly different inspiration. However, the third stretch of straight parish boundary commemorating the old road makes a distinct angular change of alignment (2d) for some 20 m before it meets the ditch and bank of the plantation. There is enough parish bank seen on the ground here and on large-scale maps to indicate that the new alignment is pointing towards the hillfort of Bulbury, some 750 m distant north-east. Inside the coppiced plantation of Rough Bulbury, and just north of the first crossing on the main north-south woodland path, tractor weight has shown up what may be evidence of a former transverse hollow-way, otherwise invisible in the undergrowth. The line projected from the south-west corner of the plantation through this spot would bring us to the central west side of Bulbury, where a gateway might be expected.

How trustworthy is the conclusion that the road traced from Sandford was a

Roman military construction and that it was designed to link Wareham and Bulbury? There is certainly no doubt that a well-laid out road led from Sandford to Sherford, and then to Rough Bulbury south-west of the hillfort. Given the evidence that this cambered road in straight stretches was of earlier than eighteenth century date, is it likely to have been built by other than Roman hands? Years ago, even Collingwood could have hesitated, in view of the uncertainty of a road that in those days could be accorded no apparent destination. For one thing, hillforts belonged to the Iron Age and, for another, Roman roads in Dorset were expressly stated to owe nothing to the military phase. But, fortified by the knowledge that such roads were apparently built to Hod Hill, Flower's Barrow and Woodbury at that early date, the present course will make sense if the weight of the facts favours communication with Bulbury.

How, then, to explain the precise route taken between Sandford and the hillfort? A direct line, as the crow flies, would have had two disadvantages. It would have required, first, to cross further high ground in the centre of Gore Heath and, more importantly, to tackle the obstacle presented by the ill-drained lower ground north of the river, known by the revealing name of *Slepe* ('slippery muddy place').[2] While it was probable that a ford had existed at Sherford in Iron Age times, it is also likely that the Roman course, carefully laid in three equal lengths to reach the south bank, was designed to skirt the margin of the unfavourable terrain around Slepe.

Bulbury has been so heavily ploughed at stages in the past that its configuration is difficult to decipher today. Happily, Cunnington in the nineteenth century[3] made a reliable record that it had four entrances, two of which, on north and south, appeared to be later than the Iron Age in their simpler construction. Thus, with four gateways, this hillfort may well have been better converted to Roman purposes than others in Dorset that may have possessed Roman garrisons. The Iron Age gates were considered insufficient or inconveniently placed, so the newcomers were obliged to create extra means of movement in and out of their converted fort. Did Bulbury thereby assume a perimeter pattern closer to the accepted Roman standard?

(I) Cold Harbour to Woolsbarrow

This road was a branch from the main route to Woodbury and its course, in the direction of Woolsbarrow, can be first picked up close to the southern apex of Triangle Plantation (Chapter 5F). This is the beginning of a straight stretch of 1.6 km that takes the observer by an established bridleway to within a short distance of the hillfort. It will have often attracted attention in the past without its true antiquity being examined. Distractions have been caused by the continuation of this line after Roman times: southward (discussed in Appendix 32) and northward (discussed below).

The agger can be seen as a firm, low ridge, 4 m wide and 0.2 m or so high, forming the eastern edge of Triangle Plantation (Appendix 34). It has long separated this woodland from former heath or poor farmland to the east, where there is now for some distance a belt of land serving a BP pipeline. The feature can in no way be confused with the kind of turf boundary-bank, associated, for example, with medieval enclosures, elsewhere on the wastes north of Wareham. In respect of dimensions, the Roman road to Woodbury, on the other side of the Plantation, is similar in width, but with a bolder profile. Beyond the north corner of the wood (1a), the ridge emerges for some 170 m as a gorse-covered barrier of full width, between bridlepath and pasture to the west.[1] It then continues past a new farm-building and a pond for a further 70 m as a more disturbed feature, though still distinct. A ditch and the bank of a recent enclosure (not marked on

Ordnance Survey in 1890) next enter the picture (1b). The ditch has been cut into the western half of the agger, with the 'new' bank thrown up on the eastern side. After another 200 m, approaching the water-course that flows from Stroud Bridge, the trace of the old road disappears in peaty soil and rushes. The creation of the pipeline in 1988 involved earth-moving to improve natural drainage, so disturbing a band of terrain that the stream is no longer forded as in the nineteenth century. A little way beyond the new footbridge, the Roman line reappears, again used to bound an enclosure, an older one this time named 'Old Ram', and once again with a massive ditch cut into the western half of the agger.

At the north-eastern end of this second wood, visible evidence of the Roman line peters out as it reaches a boundary stone, engraved '1817' (1c). This marked the meeting of three parish boundaries, of which two from west and south-east retain their banks. The third continues, but there is no parish-bank in this case and the boundary must have followed the road-ridge. Was this at one time a more obvious feature in the landscape ahead than it now appears?

The course certainly becomes identifiable again as such for the next 70 m or so beyond the stone, as a low gravelly ridge precisely midway between two wide-flanking banks also of little height. A short distance further, on reaching more open heath, the Roman course, much abraded, crosses a spot where another streamlet used to be forded, but which has been subjected to modern 'improvement' (1d). The track (once a more recognizable boundary) then rises gradually for another 50 m on a wide course amid heath and young trees. It shows as an irregular band of grassy sward and bare patches, created by the movement of mechanized transport. Nevertheless there are indications, particularly at first, close to the ford (where the parish boundary starts to run north along this imprecisely marked line) that some firmer material of ancient date must await confirmation.

At the top of the rise, this broad track over open ground is succeeded, at the passage of the electricity overhead power cables, by an even broader band of ground (1e). This has been kept as a typical fire-break, since modern afforestation began on either side. There has been massive disturbance here where another recently improved track crosses from east to west.

This fire-break line now comprises, for 250 m northwards, a substantial modern gravelled vehicle-track on its east and a low cambered strip on its west. The latter, probably the older route, has every appearance of a residual heathland feature, but grassy now and robbed of much of its native flora. It should represent the old parish boundary, and the question arises: When the boundary was agreed in early days, what line was being followed, an alignment that was already visible in the shape of this well-established track or one that had been laid out for that purpose? After 250 m, the modern gravelled track leaves the straight fire-break and swings north-west, running athwart the apparent older route (f). The latter does not seem, however, to continue as such towards the north, although the fire-break remains the same width in that direction. The first Ordnance Survey 25-inch maps show the parish boundary from here northward as 'undefined' and slightly off the original straight course, implying that there had indeed been a 'defined' feature, in the shape of a track or low ridge to follow up to that point.

Indeed, the old track that we have been following has continued absolutely straight from its branch with the Wareham–Woodbury road, a distance of 1.6 km, with excellent suggestions of antiquity for the stretch past Triangle Plantation and beyond. On the lie of the ground, this was a suitable point from which to reach the col that gave access to Woolsbarrow, now only just over 300 m away, for, to the west, before the re-alignment, the ground falls away sharply into a dell. A narrow, modernized vehicle-track, spared the forestry ridging, climbs steadily towards the hillfort in two short stretches. The single gateway that it is heading for was the only entry physically possible into this well-defended stronghold on its prominent knoll. The last stretch of the present route curves markedly in the last dozen metres, leaving undisturbed a straight fragment of the earlier road. This short length, shrouded in gorse, is perceptible as a distinct chord of the arc, with a recognizable camber 3 m wide. There is no reason whatsoever to suppose that this remnant could be of recent origin. In appearance and alignment it must represent the remains of a properly constructed road into this small hillfort. Just beyond, we reach the actual access into Woolsbarrow. The most recent comment on this important feature recalls that made on other Dorset hillforts: 'A *modern* trackway obscures the original form of the entrance.'[2] The Iron Age entry has certainly been massively altered in the past. Significantly, the route thus created lines up with the last stretch of the road as represented by the surviving length of cambered ridge. A separate trackway from the east and north-east curves up and round the slope into the entry and should represent the original Iron Age access. It certainly preceded the present 'modern' access, which, *prima facie*, is claimed to be the work of the Roman army.

(J) Hod Hill to Rawlsbury

The course of this road well illustrates what might be called 'a Romanized native track', a term often used in the past but seldom explained. For some of the way this road certainly took advantage of what seems to have been an existing ridgeway. From the surviving evidence of Roman construction still visible in a number of places, there seems no need to propose a separate category in a case like this. On the other hand, it has always been difficult to prove the genuine prehistoric antiquity of such long-distance routes following the crest of high ground. Long ago, Crawford reminded us of the possibility that 'the Romans converted parts of the Cotswold ridgeway into the Foss-way'.[1] He was, of course, arguing from the example of an accepted Roman road that was preceded in places by a 'natural' trackway. In the present example the reverse process will propose that what many will claim as an accepted and obvious ridgeway remains, in its surviving form hereabouts, a Roman creation. The view has been that in Britain made-up roads constructed over a distance were non-existent even as late as Iron Age times. But Roman engineers introduced elements that have become hallmarks of their work: a layout in straight lengths; and a build-up involving a cambered cross-section. These straight lengths could be relatively short where the terrain and pre-existing usage combined to determine the optimum route. The course described has not been tested by excavated cross-sections, so the purist will still withhold judgement. However, the visible remains from the Bell Hill sector alone provide first-hand evidence that road-builders of the Roman army were at work on these mid-Dorset heights.

During the occupation of the Roman fort at Hod Hill, this route began at what has been called its Water-gate, otherwise Hanford Gate, at the extreme north-west corner of both the native stronghold and its Roman successor. Richmond explained this causewayed entrance through the native defences basically as an access for water-supply from the Stour, whose flow today at its nearest point passes less than 100 m away as the crow flies. His plans show that the outwork (Richmond 1968, Vol. II,7 and fig. 4B) was also given a causeway. A made road (which he calls indifferently both 'roadway' and 'trackway'), some 50 m long, is clearly marked running between the two causeways and on to what he called the shoulder of the spur. The Roman course indeed continued downhill, basically parallel to the Stour. It is traceable today as slightly broken ground with scrubby

5J.1–4 Roman road from Hod Hill to Rawlsbury

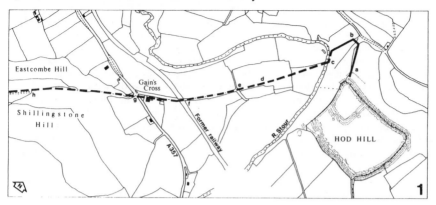

5J.1 Hod Hill to Rawlsbury: The Stour

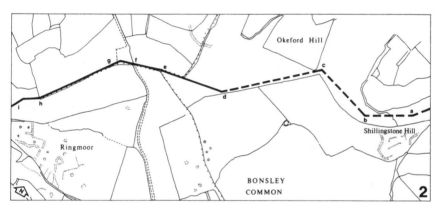

5J.2 Hod Hill to Rawlsbury: Bonsley Common

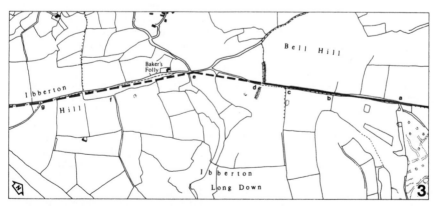

5J.3 Hod Hill to Rawlsbury: Bell Hill

trees (1a), partly followed by the modern field boundary. The track shows on an early air vertical as two straight alignments, before the growth of present ground cover. There is a very sharp prohibitive slope on the west, clearly determining the route as Richmond stated.

At the bottom of the decline, the Roman course swung back towards the river from a north-westerly to a south-westerly direction. At what we would call a hairpin bend to head towards the river, there has obviously been at some time in the past a massive build-up of chalky material, now cloaked by the formation on it of lighter brown soil. The following straight stretch (1b) to the water is flanked and emphasized on the side away from Hod Hill by a substantial bank. The feature, presumably medieval, separates Nutcombe Wood from the course which here has been eroded into a muddy hollow-way, cutting through the foot of the slope. For some distance this erosion has destroyed the original Roman metalling, but a length of good cambered ridge (4 m wide) shows up after some 200 m, when the lane, no longer entrenched, starts to swing away from the bank. The ridge is soon buried in deep humus towards the present wooded edge of the Stour on the high outer curve of an incised meander.

If the alignment had continued from here it would have had to cross not only the main river, but also what is now a short cut-off backwater. There are indications of a descent on the west down to a cleft in the bank, which would have provided the access to water that Richmond spoke of when he described the angle-gate of the Roman fort. However, the course taken to traverse the Stour seems to have turned the opposite way, close to the line of the present path, to reach a point (1c) opposite a significant old hedge-line on the other bank.

The width of the river and the height of the verges (assuming minimum change since antiquity) suggest the necessity of a bridge at this river-crossing, but there is no certain clue to what might have happened. On the other side of the water, the first 40 m of the hedge-line mentioned above took up the course that we now find once bisected the great meander taken by the Stour.[2] The alignment goes on invisibly over arable for 60 m more to reach a disused gate giving access through a massive hedge-bank. This is an interesting point for a minor change of direction, for older maps reveal that we are entering a well-defined rectangular field-system (Appendix 17), which had adopted the Roman road as its central division. Unfortunately, all field boundaries within have now been destroyed, but 80 m of recorded hedge-line once continued the Roman route south-westward from the gate. The presence of an old causewayed road pre-dating the enclosure fields is suggested by a published photograph taken from Hod Hill high up to the east. An incised linear feature, possibly a buried ditch or a slight hollow-way, can be seen in the pasture going north-east from the butt-end of the present Hodway Lane (1e–d).[3]

From that point, for some 200 m, the present gravelled farm-track, today favoured by anglers, is accompanied on the north-west by a wide border with a ditch and hedge beyond. The verge stands on the probable line of the Roman road and comes to end westward, when the old course is crossed by the existing track. Both re-align (1f) slightly on the rising slope, a little short of the former railway bridge that spanned the cutting, now refilled. This is the beginning of a stretch of about 800 m, obliquely climbing Shillingstone Hill. The line almost certainly runs immediately south-east of upper Hodway Lane which diverts slightly. Several cottages and farm buildings are set well back from the lane, leaving a faint ridge visible in places alongside its southern edge.

This alignment passes along the sharp and dangerous crest well known to the motorist on his way to and from Shillingstone. A good stony ridge takes up the story inside the first field-gate (1g) south of the lane that continues to rise beyond the modern A351 road.

From this point, the route we shall follow has long been suspected to have served the people of the Iron Age and earlier,[4] but its use by the Roman army was only a surmise, based on the proximity of the fort on Hod Hill. It is soon increasingly obvious to the observant walker that the lane was originally terraced with deliberation into the steep northern face of the hill. The shelving is mainly bordered on the hazardous outer side by a substantial bank, certainly a medieval feature as we see it now, but suggesting (by comparison with Bare Cross, Church Knowle) that it started as a Roman feature. The bank rests on the edge of material dug from the inner hillslope where several quarry-pits can be seen at intervals. For nearly 400 m the ground falling away from the road is taken up today by Eastcombe Wood, and the climbing track appears to be following several short, but distinctive alignments before the bank, clearly acting as the wood-boundary, departs westward, away from the road. A little higher than this point we reach the end of the steep climb of 1:8 engineered in the scarp slope. Here there are still signs of a low, outer marginal bank, certainly not that of Eastcombe Wood. The terrain is flatter, though still rising, the gradient now averaging 1:16. Where another track branches southward to the left, a wide clearing for vehicles has been created (1h). Nevertheless the story of the probable Roman route can now be deciphered partly from present indications on the ground, partly from recent documentary sources. Mixed woodland continues to grow on both sides, although the higher ground on the south-east was still open pasture until not long ago. It is interesting that the next stretch seems to have acted as a boundary to 'Celtic' fields on the south-east, and the nearest of these respected the line of the road.[5] The old track has been widened by machine cutting into the slope, but it is clear that the way was already terraced on the lower northern side: the sharp edge of older road-materials shows on early aerial views and on the first Ordnance Survey 25-inch map. The road, as revealed in this way, runs west-south-west for 150 m, then re-aligns (2a) towards the south-west over a distance of 650 m in two further short stretches, the first of which is commemorated by a substantial bank (2a–b). The course, slowly climbing, again becomes the lower verge of the modern widened vehicle-track, and eventually reaches close to the top of the crest at a height of some 212 m.

To keep to the higher ground and avoid a descent ahead, the course now re-aligns sharply (2c) for 250 m before resuming its generally westerly direction. Along this stretch there are good signs of an agger, now bordered by woodland on the west, with the modern track on the south-east quite separate and parallel, but grassy and obviously not the post-Roman route. Older large-scale maps establish that the public right of way wandered off-line hereabouts and was severely ploughed during and after the Second World War, an action which curiously enough has restored the priority of the Roman course.

The Roman road now (2d) regains direction westwards, passing through twentieth-century wood for 250 m as a disturbed linear feature on the north flank of a wide vehicular access and fire-break. The traces of an agger then continue on alignment as the metalled camber of a hedged lane, the north side of which now forms the southern boundary of Okeford Fitzpaine parish (2e).

The course of the Roman road has now reached an area where testimony to its age and construction become very plain to the observant eye. The short straight alignments are visible enough as such on the ground, but since they appear deceptively sinuous or rounded on maps, their telltale origin is disguised. Along the top of Okeford Hill and Bell Hill, in one way or another, the old road has determined the southern boundary of Okeford Fitzpaine parish.

The survival of a chalk and flint agger, often independently of the existing lane, forms a vital clue here. West of the south-east angle of the boundary, as far as the present Okeford–Turnworth carriageway, the agger remains a positive feature around 4 m wide. For all that distance the earliest 25-inch Ordnance Survey map (1902) gives the parish boundary as the *centre* of the road (CR). But today, nearly ninety years later, for the western half of that stretch, the centre of that agger is occupied by a hedge. As happens so often, the lane has shifted to the margin. Where the agger reaches the Okeford road (2f), erosion has exposed its base material of heavy flints overlain by chalk, conclusively proving its earlier date at this point of intersection. West of the modern road, parish boundary and Roman course have continued their centuries-old relationship, though the agger is usually less obvious. Again, the parish boundary has been perpetuated by a hedge on the south of the track, although the early Ordnance Survey map established its line in the *middle* of a known public thoroughfare. The course thus passes south of the Okeford Hill car-park, but north of the modern existing bridleway, where a belt of scrub lies along the line. Over a short distance, beyond the stile from the car-park (2g), the course, having crossed to the south, re-aligns twice to form a straight stretch south-westward of 500 m. The old road either runs in the verge between cart-track to the north and hedge-bank to the south or is buried under the bank itself (a substantial parish boundary). At the end of this straight (2h), the hedge moves to the north side of the track for 200 m with the agger forming the edge of the arable. Thus the succession, taken approximately south-north, reveals: (i) Roman road (ii) track (iii) bank. The agger here is definitely not a creation of the modern plough, since on the next alignment of similar length the ridge has visibly crossed the track to give the sequence south–north: (i) track (ii) Roman road (iii) bank.

The Roman course now reaches a remarkable stretch of some 1.2 km along the crest of Bell Hill. At the angle of re-alignment (3a) directly south-west, the modern track crosses the Roman course and the parish line. It is seemingly a recent creation on what was virgin soil and presents a serious obstacle of water and mud most of the year. For the first third of the stretch then, the profile, south-east to north-west, shows (i) parish bank (ii) slight ditch (iii) low Roman ridge (iv) track. A strip of brambles and undergrowth usually extends over features i, ii and iii. Beyond the gate leading into the Ringmoor Iron Age and Romano-British settlement, for the second third of the stretch, a hollow-way can now be distinguished between the parish bank/ditch and the road-ridge. For the final third of the stretch, the Roman road is well defined where the vegetation is less obstructive. The profile is best seen just past the second gate (3b) at a grassy clearance marked by an oak-tree: (south-east to north-west): (i) parish-bank (ii) ditch (iii) shallow hollow-way (iv) cambered road 5 m wide (v) side-ditch and up-cast, making a sharp edge. The linear features were recorded by the nineteenth-century Ordnance surveyors without appreciation of the historic differences involved.

At the end of this stretch the Roman course is again shrouded in thick vegetation before it is once more crossed (3c) by the present-day track which here regains the route of the hollow-way that had developed alongside. This point sees the junction of three parishes: Okeford Fitzpaine, Turnworth and Ibberton. The boundary we have been concerned with (separating Okeford and Turnworth) continues straight onward for 170 m as a hedge-bank only, separating Okeford and Ibberton. Noticeably, it is in line with the Roman road (no longer visible as such), rather than with the Okeford–Turnworth boundary-bank on its south-east. This slight adjustment, noted by the Ordnance surveyors from the earliest days, supports the primacy of the presumed Roman line in pre-dating parish boundaries.

The course of the road, now shared by the existing track, passes transversely through a cross-dyke, which has helped to create the angle in the Okeford boundary (3d). There is an interesting relationship awaiting solution here: it seems likely that the builders of the dyke respected either the Roman road or its native predecessor. Now in Ibberton parish, this slightly descending slope off the high ridge reveals nothing today on land that has been subject to the plough. In compensation, the long Bell Hill boundary is aimed at the spot where two modern roads from Belchalwell Street and Ibberton climb the steep scarp to join the old ridge-road. The *prima facie* evidence is that the alignment is continued for 160 m beyond this junction by the made-up road and that the angle for the next stretch occurs almost at the Baker's Folly inn (3e). This stretch runs for 1 km along the edge of Ibberton Hill, the present road more or less sitting on the old course. The latter seems to be confirmed by the fact that an open space conserving old downland (3f) yields no positive sign of a ridge.

We now reach that part of the high ground called Woolland Hill. It appears at first glance as if the modern road is curving round in an un-Roman manner. However, as is evident from the large-scale map and in places from the ground itself, the Roman road was laid in three straight lengths as far as the triangle of space distinguished as the site of Bulbarrow (4a–b–c–d).

The relationship of the early road to the parish boundary, which has now come up from the west, is most revealing for the length 4a–b, recorded in a Saxon land-charter of 833.[6] At first, the Roman course runs, clad in hawthorns, between parish bank and the modern road. In the strip of ground can be spotted the sites of army huts, once carefully concealed, for the observers and gunners stationed on this magnificent viewpoint. Beyond these modern monuments of war, halfway along to the junction with the road from Milton Abbas, one can glimpse the camber of the old road surviving where the present carriageway slants even further away. Now, as far as the road junction, the parish bank has been set midway on the agger, as is made clear, near the end of this alignment, where it has been chopped through for a gateway (4b). Here the narrow turf-bank was set on the flint camber of the original road, 3 m wide. It is flanked by slight linear depressions, either the edges of the camber or side-ditches.

On the south side of the four-way road-junction, the agger is independently clear, 3 m wide in grass. For a short distance a hedge-bank does not ride on top, while the converging parish boundaries are no longer closely involved. Beyond the next branch-road (this time from Ansty), the Roman course continued the ridgeway route for more than 500 m, from 4b to 4c. Today it is associated with the old laid hedge, growing on it or beside it. A slight re-adjustment of angle midway was required to avoid a cleft in the hill-slope. Then, in the triangular ground at Bulbarrow, at the start of the next stretch (4c–d) the early course has been traceable for some 50 m as a distinct ridge in rough scrub. However, much of the ground is now enclosed by a bank and planted with trees. The faint ridge is interrupted by a further lane from Ansty, after which the existence of the Roman course is supported by the behaviour of the existing road. Its straight hedge and built-up verge (a new feature) on the south side continue the alignment for 400 m. There is no hedge-line on the north and, until enclosure, the surface profile here from south to north would have shown hedge-bank, agger and medieval road in succession. The hedge-corner (4d) is reached as the ground begins to descend in the direction of Rawlsbury Camp, which commands the spur at the lower end of the high ground. At this point, the modern/medieval road that has been commemorating the ridgeway parts company and heads for Stoke Wake via the slope flanking the hillfort on its north. The Roman road re-aligns at the hedge-end for the penultimate time, and its course is soon betrayed by an intermittent slight ridge on an original fragment of grassy down.

After 150 m, at the narrowest part of the col, there is a steep fall to the south and the Roman access skirts the edge of a cross-ridge dyke (which might in its original form have been an outer defence work). What shows clearly here is a cart-track, cut into the slope and flanked by a substantial flint ridge. Which was the actual road? Here and closer to Rawlsbury this incised way looks to be a deliberate creation rather than the result of wear-and-tear. This has the hallmark of a Roman military work similar to the terraced climb at Church Knowle (Chapters 5, 8D).

From there a further re-aligned stretch of 150 m runs to the hillfort defences on the edge of the steep drop by way of a well-cut vehicle track, flanked by the same flint border, 2–3 m wide. Close to the Iron Age entrance, terraced tracks climb to join the causeway from what must have been the lower farmland of the hillfort community. However, the relationship of terracing to the presumed Roman access remains unknown without excavation. There has been uncertainty, too, about interpreting the Iron Age entrance itself into which they lead: 'The precise form is difficult to determine because of disturbance.'[7] Can it be that, here, as at certain other hillforts, the reference to post-Iron Age 'disturbance' simply points to Roman military reconstruction (Chapter 8E)?

(K) Lake Farm towards Winchester

There has long been uncertainty about this road since its existence was first suggested some sixty years ago. Colonel Drew, who came across the promising length of agger at Park Farm, just east of Wimborne, was supported in his identification by O.G.S. Crawford, a notable authority in the field. Although this feature has since been scheduled as an ancient monument, its Roman origin and purpose have not been generally agreed.[1] Had the fortress at Lake Farm been recognized a little sooner, that would certainly have removed the puzzle about the purpose of this road leading from the New Forest. As far as this writer is concerned, the knowledge that several roads radiated westwards from Lake has made it as certain as any forecast can be in archaeology that the fortress must also have had a land communication with the east. That expectation did not of itself verify any possible course on the ground, but it has acted as an incentive to complete the system of early roads that served the Lake fortress.

The road is here picked up after it had crossed the Stour from the base at Lake. How it did so has not yet been resolved, but the Park Farm alignment (1a–b) lines up with a point just east of Canford Bridge. To reach a possible Roman bridge raised at that spot, most of this first stretch running along the southern bank of the river probably aligned with the longitudinal axis of the fortress as at present confirmed, that is, west–north–west to east–south–east. In that case, it is unlikely that the construction of first a railway, then a bypass, will have left much trace on the ground, except close to the fortress. Buried metalling there may still be on the flats, awaiting discovery on either side of the Stour. There is no problem, however, once we reach the Park Farm alignment. This is firmly delineated by a hedge-line south-west of the farm-buildings and then north-eastwards by the scheduled agger, 4 m wide, for a distance of some 400 m in all. A little further on, the ridge used to be observable 50 m south of the bend in the neighbouring Ringwood Road (until recently part of the A31 trunk road). Houses have been erected on the line, but it could be traced in the rear garden of 'Mile Oak' (1c). For the next 1000 m, on the same alignment, even buried details will have been destroyed by buildings and a new roundabout. However, beyond the

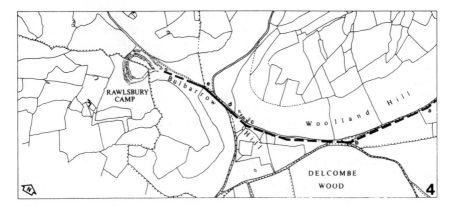

5J.4 Hod Hill to Rawlsbury: Rawlsbury

5K.1–4 Roman road from Lake Farm towards Winchester

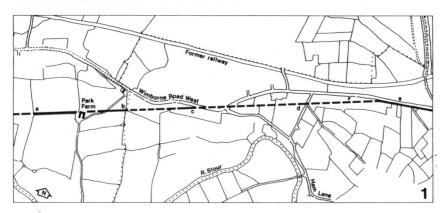

5K.1 Lake Farm towards Winchester: Park Farm

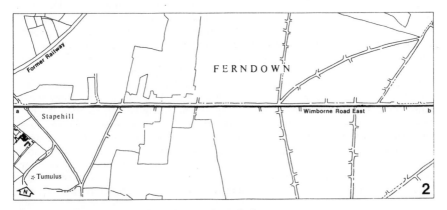

5K.2 Lake Farm towards Winchester: Stapehill

roundabout, at the north-west end of Fox Lane, a bungalow (no. 180, 'Kozee Korner') is plainly set on a broad ridge whose position cannot be explained by former cultivation (1d). The aim of this alignment is the top of Stapehill (1e), precisely at the start of the 3 km straight to Trickett's Cross. While this would be an ideal point of re-alignment for a Roman surveyor, what evidence can be adduced that this straight length ahead to the Cross (2a–b–3a) is basically older than turnpike days? The facts must be closely examined, because a similar straight reaches Trickett's Cross running from Poole to Ringwood. This is a case where documentary sources and older maps must replace the retrieval of information directly from the ground.

Ringwood Road from Stapehill to Trickett's Cross seems to have passed over heathland, always notable for its scarcity of settlement. Diversions created by property-owners were rare in such a landscape and over the centuries a Roman road might be expected to maintain a reasonably original course as the 'King's Highway'. If both ends of the road can be reliably dated 'pre-turnpike', with no reason for deviation between them, the case for a Roman antecedent is strengthened. The contrary argument will apply to the other Ringwood Road from Longham to Trickett's Cross, where, as a Roman build is not suspected, we might anticipate a purely turnpike line, the straightness of which was an eighteenth-century creation (Appendix 33).

Sometimes obvious clues seem to have been missed in the past. The Enclosure map for Hampreston, 1813, makes it plain that the turnpike line nowhere crossed a pre-existing field-boundary. A road that had been deliberately straightened by the eighteenth-century engineers would have revealed at least one example of such a boundary continuing on both sides of the new carriageway. On the other hand, the fact that all such boundaries start at the turnpike might seems to argue that the field-system was entirely post-1760. Indeed, the fields alongside, except for a couple at the western end, were late enclosures, as they were not subject to ecclesiastical tithes. But, more tellingly, the by-roads traversing the heathland all exhibit elbows or deviations where they cross the turnpike line. Thus it is difficult to see all these routes as having been created post-1760, and, on that evidence alone, they were apparently observing a long-existing straight road that was taken over for the turnpike. As so often happened, portions of surviving bank and ditch on the south had come to act as a boundary, more or less over the original Roman agger. The medieval road that became a turnpike and then a modern thoroughfare ran alongside and parallel on the north. Taylor's map of Dorset (1765) appears to confirm that the 'new' turnpike, then only half a dozen years old, was itself replacing an existing road. We should note that as it passed westward from the top of Stapehill, the medieval successor to the Roman road (called Wimborne Road West) was ultimately attracted towards the growing settlement at Wimborne, its course wandering typically to and fro.

At the Stapehill end of the straight to Trickett's Cross, a few cottages standing beside the beginning of the alignment are probably of eighteenth-century date, contemporary with or later than the start of the turnpike. While they do not necessarily support a pre-turnpike line, there are various field boundaries associated with them that can only have developed earlier. Thus, a few dwellings, subject to tithe in 1840 (and so, presumably, for a long period before) butted on to the end of the straight from Trickett's Cross. There is good reason for thinking that, apart from evidence from other points along the course we are following, the western end of the Stapehill–Trickett's Cross stretch overlies a pre-turnpike road.

The position is certainly more revealing in the vicinity of Trickett's Cross itself

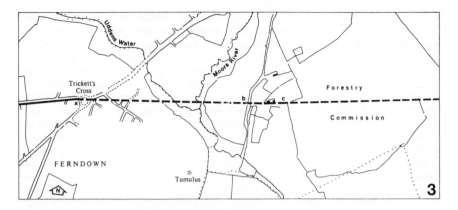

5K.3 Lake Farm towards Winchester: Trickett's Cross

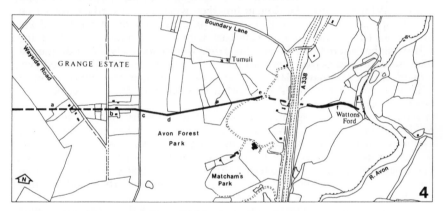

5K.4 Lake Farm towards Winchester: Avon Forest Park

and requires close examination (with further discussion of post-Roman communications in Appendix 33). The Roman line that reaches here from Stapehill has been running along the southern margin of the turnpike. A century ago, the last 800 m, which became the parish boundary between Hampreston and West Parley, were marked by a row of trees, a type of planting often found along an older boundary feature. At the Cross itself (now a roundabout, but the name is certainly recent), the Roman alignment changed by 8 degrees to an easterly direction, ultimately aiming at Watton's Ford across the Avon in Hampshire. Somewhere to the east, on the lower ground beside two streams, lay the site of St Leonard's Chapel, the Farm and Manor of Rushton and, possibly, the Domesday hamlet of *Langeford*, an earlier name suggested for the same settlement. The growth of Ringwood, and farming activities on the banks of the Moors river and Uddens Water, eventually diverted travellers two ways from the Roman line to pass over the river at St Leonard's Bridge and Palmer's Ford (Appendix 33). Beyond the river-flats and the old county boundary, the re-aligned Roman road can be traced as the fragment of an old hollow-way (3b), which was crossed at right angles by the later medieval route coming from the north at this point towards Palmer's Ford. The Roman line then went on eastwards, betrayed on older maps as a wide drove (3c), clearly on course for the Avon ford 3 km further on. The creation of a caravan park with a tarmacadam access from the A31 trunk has altered details, but this drove was deliberately based on the old road, so as to run between enclosures won from the waste by the medieval farmers of the St Leonard's lands. As far as the Avon river, the course is now in what was, until a few years ago, within the county of Hampshire, but now belongs to Dorset.

The next part of the alignment crosses 1.6 km of forestry land and then large residential plots adjoining Wayfield Road. This stretch has not been closely examined on the ground. To judge by what lies further east, there may be residual evidence to detect, but the traces are likely to be rare and inconclusive. There has been the obvious modern disturbance, particularly from afforestation ridging, while the Ordnance Survey maps do not show property boundaries that might point to re-use of the Roman line.

Fortunately, a little further on, after Foxbury Road (4a), the track of the Roman road becomes unusually traceable and fully complements Colonel Drew's discovery on Park Farm towards the other end of the this road. Just west of the point where the alignment from Trickett's Cross can be estimated to reach Foxbury Road,the terrain has been farmed and nothing positive is visible. Then, immediately east of Foxbury Road, the boundary between two holdings of several acres has been based on the Roman line and yields important information. The grounds of 'Castle Mead' on the north and 'Foxbury Glen' on the south are at first separated by 30 m of gorse covered ridge, 5 m wide, 0.3 m high and topped by a small independent turf-bank. Past the bungalow on the north, the small bank continues by itself and is marked by a line of pine trees, while the ridge of the road, after being flattened around 'Castle Mead' itself, becomes perceptible again in rough ground. It runs parallel to, and north of, the boundary-bank and then, beyond a barn, is also picked out by a line of pines planted on it, like those on the field-bank alongside, probably fifty years ago. The low narrow bank dividing the properties goes on to reach the tarmac of the Ministry of Defence military road that connects Barnsfield Heath to the south with Boundary Lane. However, the ridge of the Roman road (as the telltale pines come to an end) re-aligns to run due east some 30 m short of the military road. With a change of angle of 6 degrees it passes under the field-bank and then visibly across the grass in the corner of the field on the south

(Ordnance Survey parcel 0046). The reason for this change of line will soon be apparent.

Reaching the eastern side of the military road (5b), we are now on the open heathland of the Avon Forest Park (South Block). In the park, the course of the Roman agger has been plotted by eight cross-profiles (Appendix 34) for the next 600 m (Appendix 35).

It now becomes clear that this brief change of line was to enable the Roman engineers to keep their road to an even gradient. Skirting the spur of higher ground (now largely occupied by Ordnance Survey parcel 3575), the road-material is visible in the sides of a recently cut open drain. The line then re-directs east-north-east in gorse and heather as a slight terrace visible in the surface profile. After another angular adjustment, the road shows as an impressive agger 6 m wide and 0.3 m high (5d). This feature merges into the north edge of Ordnance Survey parcel 6761. This is a relatively modern boundary, but gives every indication of having been laid out along a visible ridge in the heath. South of the isolated modern house, 'Pine Copse', the line re-adjusts once more and traces can be picked out in further heath as the course aims for the gap in the hilly terrain bordering the Avon valley. West of the busy A338, in dense rhododendron shrubbery, there is nothing easily visible to substantiate the route. However, between the angle of re-alignment (5e) in the gap and the river the course basically followed the track shown on ealier Ordnance Survey maps as a typical series of short straights. To the east of the A338, there are indeed good indications in relatively unspoilt terrain, not long emerged from heathland. The river is reached in three stretches, each about 150 m long. In the second of these (5f), the agger runs alongside on the north of the present flat gravel track. The age of the ridge is demonstrated where the overlying black heath-humus is still intact. For the third stretch to the river (5g), the course of the Roman road is again traceable on the south of the gravel track.

Watton's Ford was an important historic crossing-place of the Avon, and its role in the suspected Roman road from the Wimborne area has been taken as highly probable. On the other bank we are in Hampshire, so the course of this road will not be pursued here.[2] However, from there onward, via Vales Moor and Picket Plain, various indications of the road occur on its way to the area of Stoney Cross and eventually, Winchester.

(L) Dorchester to Eggardon, Waddon and the West

From Dorchester to Two Gates, just east of the great hillfort of Eggardon, the present vehicular road has long been recognized as following a Roman predecessor. For 14 km the course keeps to the high ridge in a series of distinctive short alignments, and one factor emphasizing its antiquity is a coincidence with parish boundaries over that distance. From Two Gates it has been stated that 'the metalled (i.e. "post-Roman") road turns north-west towards Eggardon and the Roman road continues west as a track.'[1] Only *one* Roman road was signified at this critical point. Certainly a well-defined agger can be traced westward of the modern road and its structure has been examined by an archaeological section cut athwart the line.[2] This has been the generally accepted route leading towards Exeter, but establishing it precisely further along the coast to the mouth of the Axe has always proved a difficult task. That course did not offer the kind of terrain that was normally favoured by Roman army engineers, as it involved a series of steep ascents and descents. It was completely different in character from the preceding 14 km from Dorchester and lacked the tactical military advantages of the northern route of point 2 below.

It will be argued that:

1. the Roman road from Dorchester to Two Gates was a military construction, probably based on a prehistoric ridgeway;
2. the same early road, keeping to the ridge, was continued onward to the north and north-west to create a link with the Roman fort at Waddon Hill and later with distant Exeter;
3. a short branch was probably built to link with the Iron Age entrance-road into Eggardon;
4. the Roman road recognized as continuing westward from Two Gates was a later coastal route between Dorchester and Exeter.

The acceptance of these four statements depends largely on the proof of the second. Certainly, as a logically surveyed possibility for a link between Dorchester and Dumnonian territory, the northern loop along the ridgeway round the Marshwood Vale must always have seemed a better initial choice than the hills and dales of the southern route skirting the sea. That northern track enjoyed positive advantages: the terrain was always firm ground and not subject to flash floods; visibility was such that surprise attack could be forestalled; and since it was already in some service as a native highway, movement by Britons could be controlled. Importantly, the northern route ultimately passed close to Pilsdon Pen, the strongest hillfort in the western lands of the Durotriges, and there were two others, Lambert's Castle and Coney's Castle, not far away. Nevertheless, to fit in with military progress, this road was probably built in two, or even three, stages.

(a) Dorchester to Two Gates

When this well-known road reaches the higher ridge west of Dorchester its course, as closely followed by the present narrow tarmac road, proceeds in several stretches with well-defined angular bends. These re-alignments, forced to some extent by the terrain, involve changes of 45 to 50 degrees. Their precision and coincidence with parish boundaries for a long distance have pointed to a military layout unmistakably of Roman origin. It must have seemed curious to many that the same criteria did not betoken Roman roads leading to Eggardon and continuing north-west of Two Gates.

(b) Two Gates to Waddon Hill

The course to Waddon Hill from Two Gates runs for 6.4 km in very similar fashion to the previous stretch from Dorchester. Short alignments zigzag their way along what is in generally fairly level high terrain, with steep descents on each flank limiting the exact line. Basically, the existing metalled road is built on or closely beside the original Roman road. However, whilst there are series of straight stretches, some coinciding with parish boundaries, there are also un-Roman fragments with an irregular course, which do not immediately yield confirmatory surface evidence close at hand. These unpromising sectors must, in the past, have deterred claims that the road from Dorchester did indeed pass this way. Today the heights are no longer the sole province of sheep; intensive arable farming has often destroyed or seriously lowered the remains of an agger. All the same, where Roman and modern/medieval roads temporarily part company and divert or run side by side, portions of the causeway may still persist.

From Two Gates north-westward, the Roman course follows the present metalled road in two short lengths as far as the tumuli east of Eggardon, with the parish boundary of West Compton and Litton Cheney running beside its wide north verge (1a–b–c). The existing road next turns due north to go a little way beyond the south-west angle of Toller Porcorum parish (1c and 2a). The

114

5L.1–6,2A Roman road, Two Gates to Waddon Hill

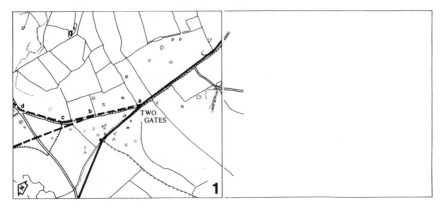

5L.1 Two Gates to Waddon Hill: Two Gates

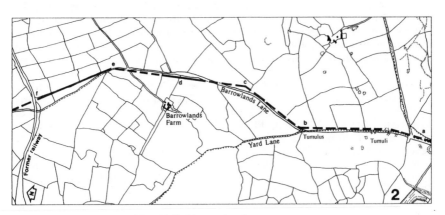

5L.2 Two Gates to Waddon Hill: Barrowlands

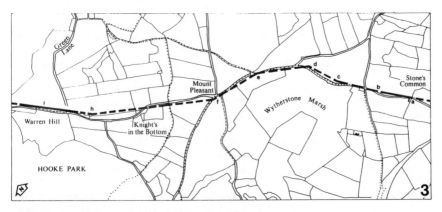

5L.3 Two Gates to Waddon Hill: Mount Pleasant

boundary of West Compton moves away north-east off-line, a slight deviation that has left a triangle of waste ground. For 1.6 km, to the entrance of Barrowlands Farm, the two roads almost coincide in three further straight stretches (2a–b–c–e), with the Toller parish boundary co-existing only with the first of these. Before the farm entrance, the straight 300 m of this third part of Barrowlands Lane is maintained to the south by 200 m of the east side of Higher Barrowlands Wood, with evidence of the residual agger (2d).

After the Barrowlands entrance, the line starts downhill towards the only stream gap in this ridge course, once utilized by the branch railway from Maiden Newton to Bridport. This is a new alignment (2e–3c) of 1500 m to Stone's Common across the little valley, beginning with the deeply incised modern road. The latter gradually diverts westward, so that, at the top of the slope, there is a good view of a substantial causeway, up to 4 m wide, keeping on the line to the east and forming a straight field boundary down as far as the stream (2f). This boundary significantly formed the end of the medieval furlong-fields of Toller Porcorum. Between that point on the stream and where the nineteenth-century road was crossed by the railway, the water used to be forded. Thus two stages of diversion from the Roman road can be traced towards the west.

North of the stream and beyond the old railway track, the land is rising again, but the Roman line has disappeared under arable until it is rejoined higher up, on Stone's Common, by the metalled road swinging back on to its original course. For a little distance, parallel to the east, the older agger is visible on the edge of Stone's Common. It has large trees disposed along it, and runs along well above the present thoroughfare, which has briefly curved away again, incised by long usage into ground level. At the Clift Lane crossroads the Toller parish boundary and existing carriageway pick up the course. They all run together for two parts of three stretches (3c–d–e–f) that keep a level course round the low ground of Witherston Marsh. At Mount Pleasant, some 30 m south-west of the road-junction to the farm, the ridge is visible just south-east of the hedge and then is revealed where the road asphalt rises up and over the older line. The Roman course must then continue undetectably across arable, the North Poorton road and further arable. On the slope down to the quaintly named Knight's in the Bottom, it is rejoined briefly by the modern metalled road that is normally its successor. A straight hedge takes the old line across this deep dell, while the later medieval/modern road curves away and around to swing back at the high ground once more, where the cottage known as Hunter's Lodge has been built close beside the original track (3h). We are now on Warren Hill, and the two roads run side by side for more than 300 m, the old causeway being mostly very visible on the north-east, despite ploughing, 3 m wide and 0.25 m high (3i).

The next alignment (4a–b) begins shortly before the turning to Hooke, but there is little by way of evidence beyond the behaviour of the present road, which at the beginning and end of this stretch is probably precisely set on the Roman line. Round this corner of Hooke Park, the middle portion deviates a little, possibly because of the steep slope of the dell. Originally, the Roman course may have kept straight here by means of terracing now lost through erosion. A short length of the Mapperton–Hooke parish boundary coincides with the third part of this alignment before dropping away down towards Toller Whelme.

At this point the Roman road takes a new direction along the high ground (4b–6d), aimed almost due west at the site of the Roman fort on Waddon Hill more than 5.6 km distant. For the first 1.6 km, as far as Hackthorn Hill, the slightly wandering course of the metalled road is closely related. There is a significant detail halfway along, at the top of Dimstone Hill, where the

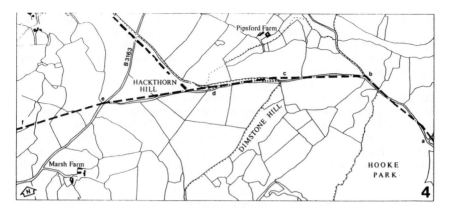

5L.4 Two Gates to Waddon Hill: Hackthorn Hill

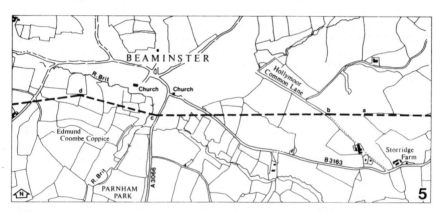

5L.5 Two Gates to Waddon Hill: Beaminster

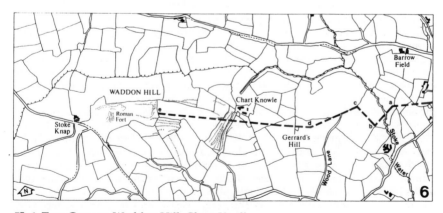

5L.6 Two Gates to Waddon Hill: Chart Knolle

Mapperton–Toller Whelme parish boundary crosses the ridge from north to south. Some 50 m of prominent causeway meet the boundary angle from the east, running north of the road and well inside the hedge-line (4c).

A little further and we pass an area of pits where, it will be claimed, a later Roman road branched to the north-west, continuing along the ridge. The course towards Waddon must be assumed to have been followed closely on its southern flank by the modern lane until it reaches the T-junction with the B3163 to Beaminster. There was an adjustment of 10 degrees towards Waddon Hill at this fine viewpoint (4e), close to the summit of Hackthorn Hill. Beyond the junction, the ground to be followed falls away rapidly down towards the river Brit and the evidence for the Roman road depends largely on field-boundaries. North of Storridge Farm, for 800 m (4f–5b), three such boundaries continue the line which is also followed by a long-acknowledged footpath. The third hedge (5a–b) has now been grubbed out, but it is noteworthy that where it met Hollymoor Common Lane the latter ends, suggesting that the Roman road and the lane had once provided a continuous thoroughfare.

The presumed Roman course has now dropped into the intensively cultivated field-system of medieval Beaminster. Nothing by way of substantiation is to be seen on the surface until the Brit is reached. The precise point on the east bank at which the crossing of the water was made is almost certainly opposite (5c) a low, but prominent spur from the high ground south of Beaminster town, unnamed on large-scale maps, but crowned by Edmund Coombes Coppice. The crossing, whether effected by a ford or a bridge, was still exactly on the alignment of the previous 4 km, but once on the spur a slight deviation was clearly demanded to avoid the steepest part of Coppice hill. The path of this deviation is marked by a broad strip of terracing (5d) which can be traced running contourwise midway down the northern slope. It is a feature that might involve some later element of lynchet formation, but it must certainly be older than the massive field banks than lie athwart the line at its eastern end. A number of Romano-British finds around this hill indicate that, after the departure of the army, the road served a civil settlement of some kind in contact with Dorchester. North and north-west of the hill the military road presumably swung back onto its original line, but there is no surface sign on Green's Cross farm.

At the Stoke Water the course is precisely back on the line from Hackthorn Hill 4 km away. Fortunately, on the east bank, the antiquity of the crossing (by footbridge and formerly ford) is established by a deep hollow-way (6a) running a short way downslope from the north-east and older than the present field-system.

On the other bank, the road-engineers faced the climb of Gerrard's Hill, with a gradient soon exceeding 1:4. Despite disturbance of the flat ground beside the stream, it is clear that the problem was tackled by a zigzag to the south. The first leg was formed by a build-up of soil and, higher up, by terracing into the rise as far as the turn. Thus the present path 150 m long up the steep slope was lengthened in two stretches to 250 m, with a corresponding easing of the ascent. For another 150 m the path and Roman course climb with a hedge-line as far as the end of Wood Lane. After that point a footpath, marked on Ordnance Survey, appears to have followed the course almost to the top of Gerrard's Hill. Thence there was a re-alignment aimed directly at the Roman fort on Waddon Hill. However, it is likely that the course deviated slightly north to utilize the col on which Chart Knolle (or Knowle) House stands. Hill-top erosion and long-term human activity have made recovery of the remainder of the line as far as the fort difficult without excavation in the right place.

This last alignment, north along the ridge west from Chart Knolle, receives marginal support from a discovery reported in 1959 on the hillside due north of the Waddon fort and a little way down the slope. This was a wide scatter of tesserae, showing that a Romano-British building lay there, of sufficient substance to require communication eastward with the Beaminster settlement and with Durnovaria.

(c) The Road to the West
As far as a point on the ridge south of Toller Whelme, this road was, of course, the one described above which was first designed to communicate from the east with the outlying fort at Waddon Hill. To understand where a second road branched off we should look south-west of Toller at the triangle of land forming Hackthorn Hill (5L.4d). That area is framed on the south by the Roman road/modern road towards Waddon, on the north-west by the Beaminster–Toller Down road and, finally, on the north-east by the Mapperton–Toller Whelme parish boundary. Most of that boundary, to the apex of the triangle at Dirty Gate, takes up the alignment of the Roman road to the west. The gap between the Waddon road and the southern end of this stretch of boundary was once filled by a bridleway and a field angle (1890 O.S.) that represented the junction. Where Roman road and green lane and/or boundary coincide the original layout is betrayed for some way by the series of short alignments 400–800 m long. After the first (400 m) to the south of Dirty Gate, there are three more running to the west of Higher Langdon, measuring 400 m, 800 m and 400 m successively. The last of these alignments shows up as a good agger at the top of the rise, immediately south-west of, and parallel to, the stretch of green lane west of Higher Langdon.

After this point, the writer has not made the detailed examination of the potential course of this road that he would have liked. That must be left to the local worker in the future. There is every likelihood that the evidence that leads past Higher Langdon will continue to emerge here and there following the track of what must have been an older ridgeway (Chapter 5M, following).

(d) Two Gates to Eggardon (fig. 5L.1–2A : proposed Roman courses omitted on 2A to allow evidence of parish boundaries)
In general terms it must always have looked as if the Roman road west from Dorchester was running to Eggardon and not simply following the chalk ridge on the way to Exeter. This possibility is now strengthened by the first stretch of the Roman course to Waddon past Two Gates. To reach Eggardon, all that was needed was a slight re-alignment and a projection of some 400 m to reach the south-west entry of the hillfort (a–c). There are, however, no hints of such a direct line from any documentary or photographic source and the terrain, well farmed as it may be today, would surely have yielded some trace. However, alternatively, the military road may be revealed by further parish boundries. On this traditional Dorset downland, for centuries given over to grass, boundaries normally followed existing linear features rather than a bank and ditch specially dug for the purpose. Their message cannot be lightly ignored. In the present example, the behaviour of a boundary between Two Gates and Eggardon may throw light on Roman battle tactics at the approach to what was a formidable obstacle in the path of the Second Legion.

At the end of the first short length of the Roman road towards Waddon, north-west from Two Gates (5L.1) a further straight parish boundary (between Askerswell and Powerstock) begins this possible branch to Eggardon (a). It diverts by 50 degrees to run direct south-west for some 200m. On the way, the local top spot-height of 252 m is passed, somewhat higher than the interior of the hillfort only 400 m away. This would have been the ideal position from which to direct the assault on Eggardon, with an overall view of the surrounding

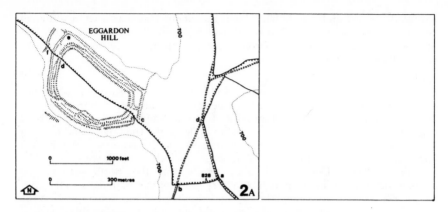

5L.2A Eggardon area, showing probable Roman military road

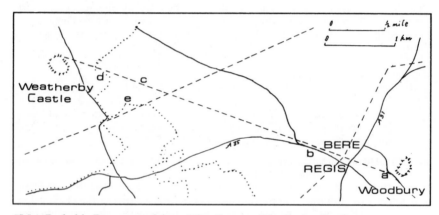

5M.1 Probable Roman road from Woodbury to Weatherby Castle

countryside. A little downhill the boundary hedge-bank joins at a right angle what was arguably the course of a major Iron Age trackway (b). This ran contourwise into the hillfort (c) from the south where it is commemorated by the present road from Askerswell (e–b–d). From that angle to Eggardon, the trackway has been provided in the past with a substantial agger, concealed on the upper side by soil-creep, but showing a clear edge on the downhill side, with a separate field-bank.

The course of this branch can be proposed only tentatively as a Roman road-link into Eggardon and requires explanation and testing by the spade. Until substantial excavation takes place at and around that site (an unlikely event in the economic climate), we cannot be sure, here any more than at other hillforts, whether the natives surrendered without a struggle or fought. Nor can we know for certain which of the Durotrigian strongholds were given a temporary Roman holding force. But, as argued in this book, there is a high degree of probability of the latter event where a road of ostensibly Roman build demonstrably formed a connection. Eggardon must have been a strong candidate for such treatment.

Until established by excavation, the existence of this military link-road may be regarded as merely speculative. What, then, to sum up, are the reasons strengthening the case? Firstly, from the outskirts of Dorchester to this point, seven straight lengths of the accepted Roman road have been followed by parish boundaries. It is not difficult to see this eighth length of boundary as of Roman origin, particularly since it passes close to the high point in the district, a detail of tactical significance in movements to and from the hillfort, before and after battle. Secondly, this slight diversion to the south-west took the shortest route to control the Durotrigian trackway at a comfortable distance from Eggardon. Thirdly, the entrance road (b-c) shows signs of a well-structured build-up that in no way should be typical of the Iron Age occupants. Fourthly and lastly, in the light of what happened at other hillforts, the control, at least temporarily, of Eggardon and its commanding position must have been essential to the security of the garrison at Waddon Hill.

(M) Other Roads ?

It would be surprising if the military roads constructed by the Roman army in Dorset were still everywhere equally traceable. The reasons why some stretches of road vanish and others can still be discerned also operate in the case of Roman roads elsewhere, but conditions in this county are distinctive. Dorset has always been an essentially farming county, with wide areas of light soil on downland or heath.

Roads that had only transitory use in leading to hillforts, and passed over thin soils subject to later tillage, could have disappeared long ago. This is the case with the early roads on the chalklands, where only locally fortunate circumstances (like use as a boundary) may have conserved part of the original build-up. There the Roman army did not find it necessary to slot the base material of their roads into a special depression. By contrast, some of the best remaining evidence comes from the sandy heaths, although there, too, the pressures of afforestation and building developments have, more recently, destroyed stretches of early road. Curiously enough, in some cases, parts of these roads, whatever the bedrock, remained in use right through to medieval or even modern times, as shown by regular resurfacing seen in sections, or by their incorporation in the routes of today. The many examples of reasonable survival other than as a modern road can be picked out in the descriptions given in 5A to 5L above. The principal reasons for survival are those time-honoured in the investigation of Roman roads:

- a medieval hollow-way evolved beside the original agger, which remains intact, more or less as it was when last remetalled;
- the Roman road served as boundary for estate, field or parish;
- the area continued as pasture, rough grazing or undeveloped heathland, undisturbed by modern plough.

It is certain that the road network created by the legion was even more extensive than has been described in Part II. There is work here for local groups or keen individuals, prepared to spend time and energy on mapwork and in the field. The road from Hill View to the Corfe Castle gap (Chapter 5E) and on to Purbeck is a case in point. Of the roads listed below that the legion may have constructed, there is indirect evidence in particular for numbers 1, 2 and 3, which, unlike those already listed, appear to lack only unmistakeable surface traces of surviving agger. What is required in the case of these further probable roads is confirmation by the spade at a spot where the early metalling has received the protection of soil cover.

1. Was the military road from Wareham to Woodbury continued to the hillfort known as Weatherby Castle? There is no positive sight of an agger along the probable route to be outlined, although the disappearance of most surface traces could be ascribed partly to the growth of Bere Regis village, partly to the intensive arable farming of the chalklands. But numerous clues point to such an early road. The post-Iron Age entrance at Weatherby reinforces the likelihood that this hillfort was subject to the same treatment as many other hillforts in Dorset.

Weatherby Castle lies 4.8 km west-north-west of Woodbury, and is one half larger in area with more elaborate defences. We cannot be surprised if its central position in the chalkland belt, precisely midway between Badbury–Spetisbury and Maiden Castle–Poundbury, should have invited special attention from the Roman commander both before and after its capture. Given a military road from Wareham to Woodbury, there seems no reason for it not to have continued to Weatherby, with the latter such a strong candidate for a temporary Roman garrison. Whereas the Roman road from Wareham to Woodbury passed for most of its length over heath unfavourable to farming and so preserved from ploughing, the probable route to Weatherby on chalk was always subject to the hazards of cultivation. It probably had a slighter construction than the later Roman road from Dorchester to Badbury Rings, which has been so razed in places north of Bere Regis that it too has completely vanished locally, both on the ground and in air photographs.

The indications are that the suggested military road from Woodbury to Weatherby was able to aim at a direct line almost from the south-west gate of the former to the north ('post-Iron Age') gate of the latter. At the start, Cow Drove, the old turnpiked lane, runs from the Iron Age gate for 100 m in a westerly direction, before bending sharply north. The south side of this lane probably conceals the Roman road under a wide, flat bank, that does not seem to have originated merely as a boundary to this part of Hove Wood. A separate ridge emerges from under the bank near the bend in the lane just mentioned, and appears to be the abandoned start of an old descent in zigzag form. This descent, turning sharply in a south-westerly direction, has to avoid on the west and north-west a deep area of swallow-holes within the wood. There are enclosure banks at the top of the slope that delimit an old way down. The second part of the zigzag, closer to the foot of the steep slope, is in the form of parallel clefts or hollow-ways now pointing west. This was an access (5M.1a) between Woodbury and Bere village that had long service and (possible Roman origins apart) formed the logically shortest link in medieval times when the Fair enjoyed its heyday. The

122

route had declined or even fallen out of use by the time that the turnpike from Wareham was created, which adopted the circuitous Cow Drove as the only possible vehicular route. Villagers on foot were using a path off the original direct line that survived, in its turn, until the construction of the bypass. When these double hollow-ways reach the lower edge of the wood, the track is blocked by a substantial field-bank of later build, and then signs are lost in the arable beyond.

The direct visual line from Woodbury to Weatherbury would have been soon rejoined by the zigzag, after which it passed parallel to Blind Lane following a low crest of ground, and then entered the village proper north of the junction of West Street and North Street. Inside Bere Regis, the two halves of West Street suggest an origin earlier than medieval times and a special relationship to the proposed direct line. The western stretch is straight, the eastern slightly curving, both measuring about 320 m. There is a spur of higher ground on the north side, called Barrow Hill, which plays a part in the story. Its slope was sufficient obstacle to a Roman alignment to require slight terracing if the straight course was to be maintained. There are indications of such a terraced edge north of the eastern stretch of West Street, traceable in back gardens or yards, before the straight western stretch of the street coincides with the line. It cannot be that this edge results from earlier house-platforms, since it gradually approaches and merges with the western stretch of West Street, nor does it bear any immediate relation to property boundaries. Somewhere just west of Day's Lane, the course of this Roman road must have intersected with that from Lake to Dorchester, laid out only a little later.[1] The straight western stretch of West Street (5M.1b) once lay outside the medieval buildings of the village, as shown by the name Butt Lane, a road branching from the junction of the two stretches. There is another pointer to the antiquity of this western half of West Street. The road from Shitterton comes uphill to join it at its far end, and on the face of things, this link is likely to have existed from the early medieval origins of both these adjoining settlements. Since Shitterton, like Bere, dates from before Domesday, the straight alignment of the west of West Street is also at least as old as that historic document.

From West Street onward, there are no visible or documentary clues for 2.4 km to substantiate the line for the Roman road. The new bypass (not marked on the plan) soon bars the way of the road running to Roke and Milborne St Andrew. This, in medieval times, would have been one of a number of tracks (including the residual Roman road) spreading out over the downland from Bere. The Roman line projected from West Street descended a shallow valley to cross two small chalk streams, then climbed a steady slope to a height of just over 91 m between Roke and Weatherby. The two hillforts are just intervisible (Woodbury–106 m and Weatherby–99 m) over this intervening highest ground, and it is here that the next clue to the vanished Roman alignment can be picked up. On this well-ploughed chalk upland the track of the later Roman road from Dorchester to Badbury has also disappeared, but some 300 m west-north-west of the point where the two courses presumably intersected the earlier road is betrayed by a zigzag in the medieval lane (at 5M.1c) running from Ashley Barn on the south-west and following the parish boundary for part of the way (5M.1e). Precisely the same type of phenomenon can be seen at Ashley Barn itself, where again a medieval road briefly follows the line of a Roman road, in that case the one from Dorchester. These examples are pre-enclosure features, belonging to a time when a slight earthwork like a Roman agger could still be distinctive on the downland. On the hilltop occurs the only redirection of the alignment from Woodbury, a slight deviation of 5 degrees towards the north-west corner of Weatherby Castle. Across further arable and a minor road, we reach the point where an ancient terraced way can be traced with difficulty leading up the slope to an unnoticed post-Iron Age gap in the outer defences of the hillfort. From there it is a short distance to another post-Iron Age entry into Weatherby Castle of a type that we can now begin to associate with the Second Legion (Chapter 8E).

2. Given the construction of roads to far more distant places, communications must also have been required from Lake towards two neighbouring hillforts. To reach Spetisbury (where there are strong indications of Roman activity (see Chapter 8E) a road is suggested by a green lane and old boundaries associated with Moorcourt Farm and Newton Farm at Sturminster Marshall.[2]

3. Dudsbury could have had access from Lake by a branch from east of Park Farm along the line of Ham Lane (B3073) towards Longham, a road whose basic straightness dates to well before the time of enclosures. The alignment appears to be picked up by the old embanked field-boundary on the hilltop just south of Hillamsland Farm,[3] halfway between Longham and Dudsbury.[4] Hengistbury, however, continued in native occupation, so that an existing valley track running inland would not have been upgraded by the Roman engineers.

4. Westward of Waddon Hill and Pilsdon Pen, a road must have been constructed to Exeter, before the military site at Lake was finally replaced. Years back, traces of a branch from the Roman road to Waddon (5L) were visible going on along the ridge high to the east of Beaminster. It then presumably swept round on the upland to pass over Horn Hill towards Pilsdon Pen. This looks very much like a romanized prehistoric way of much greater tactical value to the Second Legion than the up-and-down coastal road built later, which would have been only marginally shorter. It will have passed significantly close to two hillforts, Lambert's Castle and Coney's Castle.

5. There is every reason to think that the Roman army must have required links north-westward across the Blackmore Vale, to reach South Cadbury and Ham Hill. Both hillforts lie outside the modern county, but within Durotrigian territory; both, on the evidence, held a Roman garrison of some kind. A military road running up the Stour valley would seem a logical extension of the link from Badbury Rings to Hod Hill, having South Cadbury as its immediate destination. It is a little less easy to postulate a parallel early road through the middle of the Vale from the end of the high ground at Rawlsbury, but the lie of the land continues to favour such a route in the direction of Sherborne. This is an under-examined area of Dorset, and the presence of important villas at Hinton St Mary and Fifehead Neville makes it certain that good roads existed later in the Roman period, and they could well have had military beginnings.

6

Where Was the Fort at Dorchester?

In the 1960s the quickening pace of development in Dorchester was causing concern in local archaeological circles. In order to cope with the steady call for excavation, the county society revived the Dorchester Excavation Committee, first created to deal with the pre-war discoveries in Colliton Park. One particular objective was to locate, if possible, the early Roman military site which, from every indication, lay somewhere inside the town of Durnovaria and formed its origin. Finds datable to the conquest years – pottery, military equipment and a scattering of coins – had turned up at various points within and without the ancient walls.[1] The nodal position enjoyed by Dorchester in respect of the road-system did not necessarily strengthen the case for the Roman fort, since not one of the routes then recognized was proven to have been created in the mid-first century A.D. Considerable excavation has taken place in areas threatened by new building, with some notable discoveries that include the public baths of the Roman town. But, despite all this work since 1968, there has been no claim of positive evidence for the siting of the early fort. The south-west corner of the 'Walls' and the nearby interior of the civil settlement proved a disappointment, with no signs of major activity there before the second century A.D. Yet that area, with its excellent right-angled defences, had been thought likely to conceal proof of the long-sought military presence. The matter seemed intractable. This chapter will seek to solve the problem. As a direct result of tracing the early Roman roads into Dorchester from Lake Farm and from Wareham, and re-assessing details of past excavations and discoveries, a strong argument can be made for the location and size of the missing fort.

If we consider the topography of Dorchester as the Roman surveyor might have seen it, the most suitable position for a military site would be in the area aptly named Top o' Town. Here the land reaches a height of 78 m, compared with the corners at the north-west (58 m), south-west (64 m) and south-east (63 m), while the bottom of High East Street lies at only 54 m. It is true that this elevated terrain, within the later town-circuit, would accommodate only a relatively small fort, but a substantial semi-permanent base has been ruled out by negative results from local excavations. Significant, too, is the evidence from the major early sites at Lake Farm[2] and Exeter,[3] which now makes Dorchester an unlikely candidate. In Dorset, two well-excavated Roman forts are sited on hill-tops, at Waddon and Hod. 'The favourite location [for such an auxiliary fort] was undoubtedly at the end of a spur or on a small plateau with falling ground on three or four sides, at the confluence of two streams or a river with a tributary, commanding extensive views along both valleys ... '.[4] Although a Top o' Town fort would have had its outlook along the Frome valley partly blocked by the prominence of Poundbury, its tactical advantage close to that hillfort is obvious, while there was a clear view northward along the Cerne valley and an uninterrupted sighting of Maiden Castle about 3 km away.

These situational factors have not been given the attention they deserve in the search for the Roman station inside Dorchester. The area at issue is now almost entirely covered by buildings, roads and a car-park, such that, apart from the 1961–63 excavations to be discussed below,[5] and some work on a lesser scale, there is little chance of resolving matters in the foreseeable future by further trenching. It is as well to remind ourselves of the kind of ground evidence that might be concealed, traces of which may already have been unwittingly recorded: the defence-system, comprising a ditch or ditches and the remains of a rampart; camp-roads; building foundations probably showing as slots and post-holes for timber structures; pits and gullies of various kinds and purposes. These features, listed in order of importance, would be acceptable help towards a solution. Associated finds of military equipment, coins or pottery may be sparse just where they could be vital, so that dating of some early levels may depend on later superimposed deposits. The Colliton Park excavations of the 1930s concentrated on the lower ground which was then to have County Hall built upon it, a little way removed from Top o' Town proper. Nevertheless, it is surprising that only recently has re-examination of the material from those days revealed scattered finds of military type and date which could have come from an early and unsuspected military site not far away.[6] What turns out, however, to be most informative is a fresh look at certain of the discoveries made in the 1960s on the library site at the top of the slope.

The work on the library site revealed, from west to east, the tail-end of the Roman town-rampart, two 'roads' and several buildings, together with ovens and pits. In general, the dating of these placed them in the second century or later, but one 'road' was thought to belong to the first century. It is with this earlier feature, described as Road 1 in the final report, that we should begin a re-examination of the evidence, made possible by the detailed plans and section-drawings.

What is striking about Road 1 (6.2f and 6.3b) is that it was laid in the western part of 'a wide, shallow cut into the natural chalk ... Flints were pushed into the surface over the whole area.' This reinforcement of flints extended not only across the width of the cut or depression, but also westward, where it was covered by other significant layers, the last being the tail of the later earth town-rampart. Some unusual aspects of Road 1 have been further discussed since the publication of the Colliton Park report:[7]

(a) it does not conform to the known elements of the Roman street-grid but apparently curves sharply eastwards in a defined arc;
(b) it was laid on natural chalk, which had been stripped of its turf and topsoil covering;
(c) it was of first century construction and, despite the lack of firm dating evidence, the latter part of that century was favoured;
(d) the wide cut, perhaps intended for a very wide road, is considered 'an unusual method' of road-foundation in Roman Dorchester.

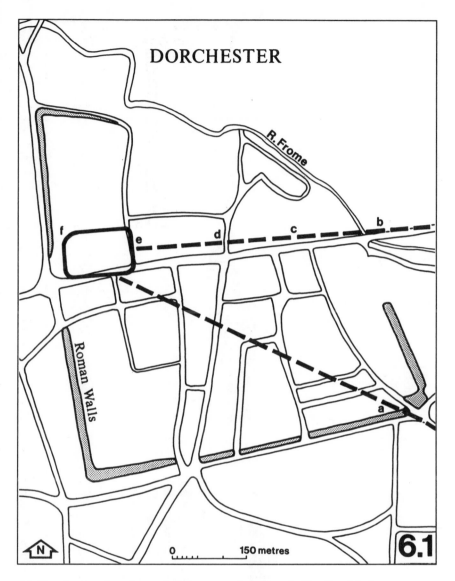

DORCHESTER

R. Frome

f
e
d
c
b

Roman Walls

a

N

0   150 metres

6.1

6.1 Dorchester, showing early Roman roads and probable site of fort

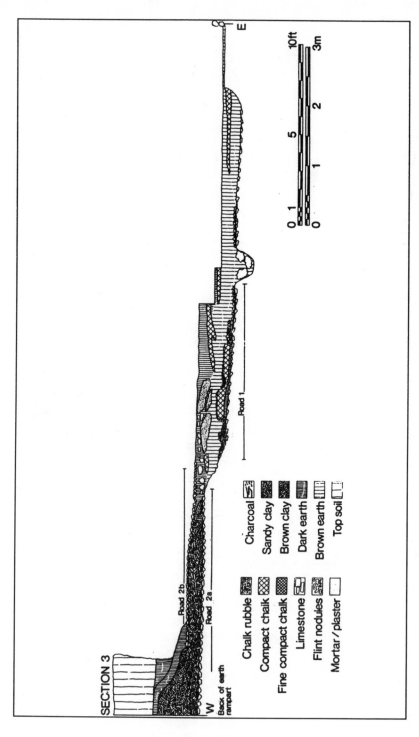

6.2 Section 3, Colliton Park 1961–3. 'Road 1' is proposed as the *via sagularis* of the fort and 'Road 2a' as the remnants of a rampart.

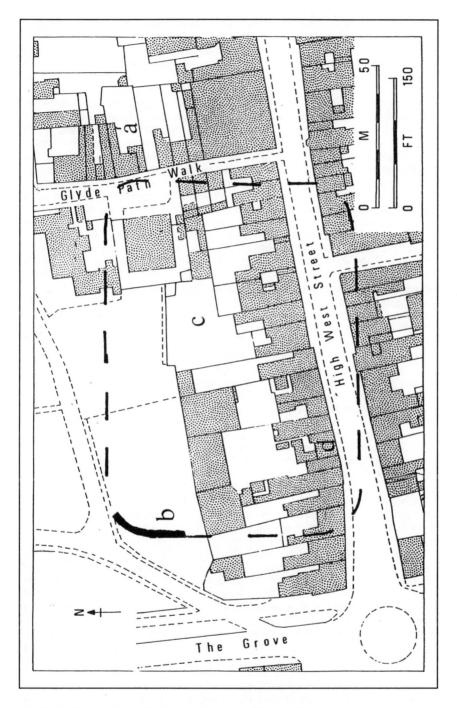

6.3 Probable location of fort in north-west of Dorchester

To these points may be added the flint reinforcement laid into the cut and extending westward, which emphasizes a large-scale effort in planned development that took place in early Dorchester. All this is acceptable, but when we look at the conclusions on discoveries immediately west of Road 1, it can be argued that the evidence from the sections has been misread. 'Road 2a' cannot be a road at all on the facts presented. Its surface is said to have been composed simply of the flint reinforcement on natural chalk, which to the east, within the cut, merely formed a prepared base for a much narrower Road 1, built of chalk lumps and surfaced with gravel. If Section 3 of the final report is inspected, it will be seen that 'Road 2a' was carefully covered by 'sandy clay' (shown as 'brown clay' in the section) for a width of around 4 m and a maximum thickness of 25 cm. This deposit ended at the west edge of the cut in which Road 1 was set and there was no explanation for it by the original excavators or by later commentators. It is not thought to be a build-up for Road 2b, since the flint metalling of the latter is independent of it and is stratigraphically later than Road 1.

These problems can be resolved if we consider Road 1 as the *via sagularis* or perimeter road inside the long-sought Dorchester fort, laid in the cleared *intervallum*. That mysterious 'sandy clay' would then be nothing more than the remnants of the demolished rampart. The curving behaviour of Road 1 as it turned eastward following the north-west corner of the fort (supported by examination of the plans and sections) shows that the wide cut of the *intervallum* was beginning to turn also.[8] If the sandy clay deposit does not appear to follow round the curve, there is nevertheless a sign of a charcoaly slope on that side (Section 1) and the section-drawing stops just where the sandy clay could begin. The description of this deposit fits that of typical rampart material of turf and topsoil derived from stripping the ground down to natural chalk. This stripping procedure involved a wide belt forming the circuit of a Roman fort, and it is curious that its importance in the initial construction of earth-and-timber defence-systems has not been emphasized in discussions of Roman military techniques.[9] Indeed, in the present case, the removal of the topsoil and some chalk to create the belt was carefully recorded, but what remained unexplained was not only *why* the cut was made, but also *where* the spoil went thereafter.

If we estimate the stripped belt as measuring 11.25 m from the east side of the cut to the west edge of the 'sandy clay' where it is dipping down just beyond Section 3, and give the original turf and topsoil a depth of 0.3 m, a figure is reached of 3.3 m for the height of material available for building the rampart from this source. If we add to this potential height a possible width of 4.4 m for the rampart-base, estimated from the profile of the sandy clay in section, we reach dimensions for the defence-work which fit what would be expected at a fort in this period. The question arises: What of the chalk spoil from the actual cut and from the external ditch or ditches beyond the rampart? It has been pointed out, in respect of the reconstructed Roman fort at Baginton, that 'the spoil removed from both ditches would be sufficient to provide the core for a rampart *only one third* of the 3.6 m estimated height'.[10] In this area the defences skirted the top of slopes running downward on all sides, especially to west and north. It is more likely, therefore, that the chalk from the ditches was used to increase the effective depth of the latter by creating counterscarp banks. Further turves would have been available from the zone occupied by the ditches and probably served to revet the rampart on its outer face, so enlarging its basal width to something like 5 m. As regards the cut, some of the material removed here went back as build-up for that *intervallum* road, but not before the bare chalk, hazardously slippery in wet weather, had been reinforced by a surfacing of rammed flints, which also extended west beyond the cut to form a cobbled foundation for the rampart (a similar road-base has been noted close to the Iwerne river at Lazerton, Chapter 5B).

There was little by way of small finds from the 1961–63 excavations to establish that this was indeed the interior of a fort as such. However, there were some useful clues. Scraps of mid-first century samian ware (unusual at that time on a purely civil site), and two Claudian coins of the imitation type regarded as military issues, were found in pits of second-century date and must have come from disturbed earlier levels. An important point to resolve is the signficance of two coins, one of Domitian (A.D. 81–96) and one of Trajan (A.D. 103–117), found *within* the layer of sandy clay. This might suggest the time after which the latter was laid down, but these coins must be intrusive. The deposit in which they came to light was only 25 cm thick at maximum when Road 2b and what seems to be the tail of the civil rampart were built upon it. The sandy clay was so thin that it must have been liable to have surface finds trodden into it, in the period before those events took place. For comparison, we may note that a coin of A.D. 141 was located in the flints of Road 1 (the suggested *via sagularis*), but the excavators took it simply to give a date *before* which (but not *when* or *after* which) that road was constructed.

Some other finds from the 1961–63 excavations may act as pointers to an early military presence close by. Thus, an artillery bolt-head of iron must be relevant when recently identified finds from a little further north are taken into account. Although such weaponry often occurs on later military sites elsewhere, a large group of bolts in Dorset has come from the Claudian fort at Hod Hill. Of special interest are the 200 or so hob-nails from Roman sandals that were found associated with the uncovered 13.5 m length of Road 1. This statistic represents a density of 15 hob-nails per linear metre. We can hardly be thinking of a cobbler's chance loss, so there was clearly considerable movement on foot at an early stage in the life of Dorchester. It is logical to suppose that the wearers of this characteristic footgear were more likely then to have been Roman soldiers than romanized Britons.

Possibly as significant as any of the material described so far is the group of half a dozen brooches of first-century date. The concentration of these finds in the area of Building 1, together with early coins and early samian has been observed, but not the relevance of the find-spots of similar brooches from the excavations at Hod Hill. At the latter site, of seven brooches, four came from the foundation trenches in the barrack-blocks and the other three, found in native huts, were considered strays 'from the occupation of the Roman fort'.[11] If we leave aside the range of brooches from Maiden Castle of like date[12] (where direct connection with the Roman army may be suspected but is not proven,[13] all the signs in this corner of Dorchester are for ascribing these brooches, together with the coins and samian, to a military, not a civil, context.

There is ample evidence, therefore, for believing that the early Roman fort in Dorchester lies unrecognized at Top o' Town. While military finds and mid-first-century pottery have occurred at various spots in the town, only here do early features of definite military purpose combine with datable finds in a location suitable for a fort not of major size. Do the early roads, described in Chapter 5, support that location, as their final alignments reach Dorchester? Their importance is paramount, since they should independently indicate its siting and orientation.

The Roman road from Lake Farm reached the Dorchester area on the proven alignment from Kingston Maurward–Stinsford (5C.11 and 6.1). It was heading for Top o' Town, the highest point in what became Durnovaria, and that is where we should look for evidence of the early fort.

131

If we assume that the north-west corner of the early fort (fig. 6.2) lies just west of the present County Library in Colliton Park, the final alignment appears to be aiming for the mid-point of the east side of the fort. Here *porta decumana* might be expected, since normally the rear of the fort faced away from the enemy. However, for the reason explained below, this was probably the main entry, the *porta praetoria*. Can the line of these eastern defences be suggested, and are there positive clues to lend support?

The construction of Roman forts had settled by the mid-first century to normal proportions of 3:2 for length to width, although these figures would always be flexible from site to site.[14] Now, the north side of what is taken to be the *via sagularis*, when projected eastwards, apparently runs parallel to, and some 50 m north of, the projected Stinsford alignment. Thus the east side of the fort might be expected to measure 100 m and, by proportion, the north side should be some 150 m long. On this basis, the western ditch or ditches should lie under the western rampart line of Durnovaria and the eastern almost aligned with the southern length of Glyde Path Road.

An indication of the possible eastern defence-ditch(es) is suggested by re-examination of details from discoveries in the garden of no. 37 (6.1e and 6.3a) made in 1959.[15] Here, below fragments of mosaic and plain tesselated floor, natural chalk was found to be sloping downward towards the west, becoming eventually too deep for further check at around 1 m below the mosaic. This gradient was against the normal slope of the ground, which descends gently eastwards. There was clearly at this point a man-made feature of some size, back-filled with artefact-free soil. Could this indeed be a defensive ditch around the fort? The location would fit the suggested perimeter and the depression appears considerably older than the mosaic, itself dated to the fourth century. If the question arises why no better trace of the perimeter ditch(es) has yet been exposed, the answer is not far to seek. Most of the course of the defence-system as proposed is now inaccessible under buildings or roadways and, even west of the County Library (for the short distance where further investigation might be possible), it is well buried under the later rampart. The observant eye may have noticed that, north of the libarary, the road-surfacing has cracked, sunk and undergone repair, a process created, not by modern service-trenching, but by a deep ancient linear feature of some kind, precisely where the fort-ditch should be expected.

Two further excavations within the area suggested as the interior of the fort require comment, although their evidence is non-committal in terms of military origins. The long trench in the garden (6.3c) of Wadham House[16] showed that, if this was the fort interior, turf and topsoil had not been stripped in the mid-first century and this would fit normal military procedure. A short length of wall-footing was of early date, but not aligned with the suggested fort perimeter. A little to the west, when Merchant's Garage (6.3d) was demolished,[17] rescue excavation noted early building slots, but of insufficient length to be claimed as military.

We next need to turn to the entry into in Dorchester of the early Roman road from Wareham. There is now further evidence discussed in Chapter 5G, for its course coinciding with Alington Avenue (pre-1988) from the Mount Pleasant junction as far as the railway bridge. Here a branch was apparently aimed towards the south gate of Durnovaria, but the original road went onward to follow Icen way to Gallows Hill. From that spot, the pre-rampart road of early origin at Culliford House[18] took the final stretch down a slight combe into what is now central Dorchester and then up to Top o' Town. If the thoughts expressed about the siting of the fort are correct (6.1a), this road appears to aim at where we might expect the south gate of the fort and supports its proposed width and configuration. Thus, can we locate with some confidence the approximate position of two of the fort-gateways? Were these all? A third can be thought distinctly likely on the north side. This would have led down to the river and, indeed, the odd finds, previously mentioned, from the Colliton Park excavations before the Second World War, indicate some military activity on this slope. As regards a gateway in the fourth side, facing west, it is very possible that this early fort, like that inside Hod Hill, had only three gates, since the roads to the west and north-west, undoubtedly of military origin, appear to link with the fort's southern side. If the analogy with Hod continues, then the entry from Lake Farm became the *via praetoria* of the fort.

To summarize so far. The case for locating the early Roman fort in Dorchester at Top o' Town is fourfold.

First, widespread excavation has eliminated any possibility of a semi-permanent military base approaching the size of the civil settlement of Durnovaria.

Second, the Top o' Town site is the most advantageous in the district from the tactical angle.

Third, the early roads from east and south-east focus unerringly on that elevated part of Dorchester.

Fourth, in 1961–63, excavation revealed the north-west corner of the fort, in the shape of what is claimed here to be the *intervallum* road, the *via sagularis*, and remains of the early rampart alongside.

From the information that has been outlined, the dimensions of the fort can be estimated. The ditch-perimeter ran from just north of the County Library, under Colliton House, then sweeping round east of Glyde Path Road (Shire Lane) to turn again on the south side of High West Street. Hardy's statue stands where the south-west ditch corner must be expected. The area of the fort-interior would thus come to 1.5 hectares (3.7 acres) so that the Dorchester fort was smaller than that at Hod Hill, but larger than that at Waddon. It has long been thought that, as they progressed westward, the Roman forces had to be spread out more thinly on the ground than had been anticipated, and the notion is now supported by the behaviour of the road-network in East Dorset. The pilum shafts and further artillery or ballista bolts from Colliton Park close by were legionary equipment, but it is likely that the garrison, as at Hod and Waddon, also included an auxiliary detachment.

It remains to comment on the Roman roads approaching Dorchester from an easterly and a southerly direction. The roads from Badbury Rings, Wareham and Weymouth (Radipole) all appear to observe the circuit of the civil settlement post-dating the fort. The Badbury road which joins that from Lake just outside the east gate of the Roman town belongs to the civil phase, with little sign of long and sustained use, at any rate between Durnovaria and Badbury. The road from Wareham, as already pointed out, makes a slight change of direction before taking up the Culliford House line that ran towards the fort. This angle could have arisen as a purely visual adjustment of line by the Roman engineer. But such an explanation seems to be ruled out by the similar angle of the road from Radipole where it enters the town. This road is surely early, and at that point lacks a plausible reason for visual re-alignment. A reason why the roads behave as they do can be established from clues in excavation reports.

West of the entry of the Weymouth road where it passes through the Roman civil perimeter, what may be a trench-laid road was recorded in 1955 and further seen in later excavations.[19] It was 3 m wide, of a construction similar to that of Road 1 in Colliton Park, where the 'trench' was twice as broad as the metalled way. This discovery was for long considered a possible *intervallum* road to a major fort, since it was stratigraphically earlier than the civil rampart. Indeed, in the full section cut across the Roman defence-line in 1969–70, this probable road was associated with a wide primary bank. The bank was laid on the original ground-surface of turf soil and did not appear to qualify as the remnants of a fort-rampart. The earliness of these features was further demonstrated in the section by the formation of a thin turf cover over it before the later rampart was built in the second century.

The civil circuit of Durnovaria coincides with all these facts if it is assumed to have followed the boundary of a previous fort-zone, the *territorium*, outside the fort reserved for the use of the military. It would be consistent, too, with Roman planning that the same boundary marked the perimeter of the original marching-camp used by the large force assembled for the initial campaign in central Dorset. Both these considerations now merit closer examination since, singly or doubly, they widen the setting for the fort at Top o' Town.

It is accepted that a semi-permanent camp had to make use of space outside the defended area reserved for basic quarters. Such extra space was needed for exercise, parades, rubbish pits, probably a bath-house, even allotments for fresh vegetables. An annexe to a fort, acting as a wagon-station, has often been identified, but less is known about broader zones of dependent land. There has been discussion in recent years of the problem, with the suggestion that shortfalls in distances between towns as recorded in Roman itineraries were the result of measurements from the edges of town-zones rather than from town-centres.[20] The town-zones in question are assumed to be larger than the suggested Dorchester zone. The latter would have covered only some 30 hectares (75 acres), but the distance of 400 m to the east and south-east entries of the roads from Lake and Wareham looks like the distance to be expected between fort and zone-boundary. A comparison with the Roman fort at Hod inside the setting of its hillfort is suddenly revealing.[21] The location of that military site in the far corner of the native interior strongly hints at a fort-zone, which small clues tell us may have been used for training auxiliary cavalry. Both there and at Dorchester, the Roman positions were located on the highest ground in the north-west of the available area, closest to potential attack.

An initial marching-camp will always be difficult to prove, since the later civil ditches could have destroyed the slight defences involved. The primary bank recorded in 1969, and suspected elsewhere, appeared too wide for such a purpose, and yet too simple to have carried the rampart-walk of a typical fort. However, as an enclosure bank skirted by an external ditch, it would have had a straightforward role as a definite boundary to what is proposed as the fort-zone.

134

7

A Military Post at Wareham?

As regards Roman origins, Wareham has always been something of a mystery compared with the county town at Dorchester. In the latter case, the civil settlement has never forgotten its early status, thanks to profuse structural and other finds, allied to documentary sources which confirm its Latin name. It is true that, if its military beginning has not recently been in doubt, the whereabouts and size of the Dorchester fort have proved a difficult problem to solve. Wareham, however, has posed problems of a different order. Its earthen 'Walls', and neat layout within, were long regarded as Saxon and excavation has gone far to support that view. There were always some people, nevertheless, who thought the street pattern had a Roman look about it, for odd sherds and coins of those days occasionally turn up in the town. But specific evidence, such as building remains, has been conspicuously absent, and G.S. Williams, in 1944, had positively no doubt that 'Wareham was not a Roman town'.[1] Ten years later, R.A.H. Farrar concluded simply that one had 'an impression of widespread occupation in the Roman period ... based on some pre-Roman settlement ... in the north-west quarter'.[2] Furthermore, Wareham would have derived considerable importance, he thought, from its position at the head of Poole Harbour, within easy reach of the local industries involving pottery, shale and stone. The series of samian sherds stored at the church of Lady St Mary could well be re-examined 'in the light of modern knowledge'. After thirty years that fresh look at the pottery adds significantly to our understanding of the origins of Wareham, although due attention must be paid to the new finds from Ower not far away.[3] Recently, D.A. Hinton considered the existence of a Roman town as such unlikely, but the north and south causeways and the road west towards Dorchester 'could have been in use at a very early date'.[4]

We have seen in Chapter 5 that Wareham lay at the focal point of a road network which was linked with the Roman military base at Lake, near Wimborne (fig. 7.1), and, if we look ahead to Chapter 9, it apparently represented an important phase in the invasion campaign. The behaviour of those roads alone strongly suggests that the land between the mouths of the Frome and the Piddle was occupied by a military post, a possibility never seriously under

135

consideration in the recent past. The fact that three of the roads from Wareham can be demonstrated to have led to hillforts is a further telling point in the argument. But the lesson drawn from the newly identified roads is only part of the story. We need to look at the strategic advantages of a military site at Wareham that would have attracted the Roman command in advance of the invasion, and then review the local evidence, particularly the pottery referred to above.

There are sound general reasons why we should expect the Roman army to have established a unit of some kind between the rivers at Wareham. In the first place, there can be little doubt that the site was strategically vital to the Romans, once they were established in East Dorset. Not only was it the lowest bridging point of the Frome and Piddle, almost at the tidal limit, but it also provided the sole access from inland into the Isle of Purbeck, whose isolation was completed to the west by the soggy ground at Luckford Lake. In addition, this passage at Wareham also controlled the route westwards up the Frome valley, which was to be of great importance to Roman tactical progress in that direction and is well illustrated by the construction of the road to Dorchester. It will not have escaped notice, either, that the Wareham site was conveniently distant, on average, about 8 km, as the crow flies, from each of the four hillforts that had to be confronted in that area.

Mentioned by Farrar, there were other advantages of the site, which came to be developed in the post-campaign situation, and these are discussed in Chapter 9. Certainly the early exploitation of Purbeck marble, and the rapid development of the local pottery industry in response to army requirements, must have increased the potential of Wareham as a road-centre and as a small port. No question, then, there were compelling general reasons for setting up a Roman military station at Wareham as soon as operatively possible. What then has been discovered to support the notion of this early activity and locate it within the town?

Throughout the western and northern interior within the Walls, Roman finds are mainly later than the military period of the mid-first century. In that area the soil overburden, though deep, has not been sufficient to prevent various exposures of the subsoil, but none of these has revealed any sign of gullies, pits or ditches that might have fitted into a military context. In the south-east quarter matters are different. The church of Lady St Mary has a collection of Roman and medieval potsherds, mainly unprovenanced, but almost certainly derived from grave-digging in the nineteenth century. Among the material are thirteen fragments of samian ware. The recent re-appraisal of the latter by Dr Grace Simpson (Appendix 14) confirms the existence of two groups, one early, the other a little later, and adds some important precision. Six sherds belong to the second century A.D., when Roman Wareham was a relatively modest civil settlement and can be ignored here, but the other seven all date before the mid 80s.

Before considering these earlier sherds, we should note the present state of the ground from which they seem to have come. As noted above, the soil within the Walls is everywhere very black and usually 1 m deep – a good 'garden' tilth underlain by gravelly bedrock. However, the soil is much deeper in the cemetery east of the church, where the graves, though nearly 2 m down, do not nowadays reach the bottom of the black deposit. In one part of the cemetery, it appears that the Victorian sexton dug deeper graves for the poor, to allow more than one burial per location. While this procedure would presumably have penetrated the subsoil, only the top of any Roman features could have been randomly touched. Modern service-trenches are absent from this area; it is not surprising, therefore, that we should still be dependent on the observant eyes of last century.

Of the seven samian sherds in the earlier group from the cemetery area, three are fragments of the decorated form Dragendorff 29. Two of these (A4 and A5) can now be reliably dated to the years A.D. 43-60 and, interestingly, may be the work of Gaulish potters represented among the finds from the Roman military sites at Hod Hill and Lake Farm. Decorated samian of that relatively short space of time is not only eminently datable, but also possesses another more indefinable quality. 'Like Roman bronze coins, decorated *sigillata* shows a distinct, though not, of course, exclusive tendency ... to concentrate on areas ... of specifically Roman occupation. It was in fact characteristically the pottery of the Roman conquerors.'[5] Now, until recently, this view of the position in Colchester during Claudian and early Neronian times was reflected generally in Dorset, with pottery finds of that type apparently occurring only in the vicinity of Roman military sites like Lake Farm, Hod Hill and so on. The unexpected finds of continental imported pottery, pre-invasions and post-invasion in date, at Ower, on the south shore of Poole Harbour, add a new dimension to the situation. They did not appear to have reached any pre-Roman settlement, if any, in Wareham, nor is there evidence for such imports having reached native settlements in quantity. However, the post-invasion samian at Ower, contemporary with that from Wareham, entered Poole Harbour only when the area was under Roman military control.

It is customary for such sites to be finally confirmed by the discovery of metalwork that can be attributed with a fair degree of certainty to Roman soldiery. Given the depth of soil in the cemetery area, it is not surprising if no such finds appear to have emerged in the past inside the town. However, one object recorded as found 'near' Wareham may indeed have had a military origin. This was part of the handle of a bronze *patera*, now on display at the Dorset County Museum. Typically, a *patera* was nothing more or less than a soldier's mess-tin or skillet. Fragments of five other such bronze handles can be traced in Dorset: four from Hod Hill and the other from an early level in Dorchester,[6] not far from the probable site of the fort. In isolation, as an inexplicable stray in the Wareham area, this find would not evoke comment, but it may now be regarded as another clue to add to evidence for the military site.

It is relevant to point out the evidence for the alignments of Roman roads within Wareham (Chapter 5D and 5G). The western entry from the direction of Dorchester appears to be aimed at the north end of the bridge that must have been built over the Frome. But it might also, by projection, have arrived at the west gate of a small fort in the area later occupied by a monastic settlement and Lady St Mary Church. Similarly, if the probable line of the Roman road preceding North Street is also projected, the two roads would have met in the middle of what is now Church Green, arguably at what could have been the west gate to the fort. On this basis, the Saxon church was built on the site of the first-century Roman military site, a not altogether surprising circumstance. This was always likely to have been an important part of the town, for the quay on the Frome close by remained for many centuries the trading centre for the region, until replaced by medieval Poole.

The case for the Roman military station at Wareham must at present rest on the details offered above. Essentially it depends on the behaviour of the early roads as described, strengthened by a few finds of distinctive character. For some towns elsewhere, this has been all that was needed to claim such an origin and there is no reason why we should regard Wareham any differently. As at Dorchester, for a long time ahead, it is unlikely that test-excavation will be possible to establish the matter conclusively. But it cannot be a bad thing to leave some historical problems for future generations to ponder and pursue.

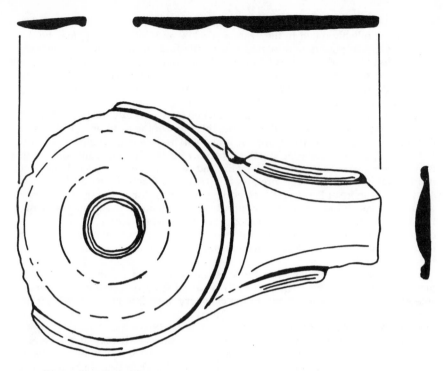

7.1a Patera handle from Wareham (Dorset County Museum drawn by Teresa Hall)

7.1b Military patera from Gloucester (drawn by Teresa Hall)

8

Other Signs of the Roman Army in Dorset?

In Victorian times, it was not uncommon for the local antiquary to explain the origin of earthworks on the slenderest of evidence. Barrows, for example, were trenched in an afternoon, not to prove that they were burial mounds, nor to establish factual material on which to date them, but rather to lift and display the grave-goods of a mysterious prehistoric race. The variety of bumps and ridges that could still be seen on downland and heath evoked little interest if the spade brought out little by way of unbroken artefacts. It was to be a little time before the detailed recording of General Pitt-Rivers in Cranborne Chase made an impact on our approach to the unwritten past.

By contrast, today, the advance of stratigraphy has meant that earthworks do not need to be the subject of hit-and-miss theories. Thus it is often possible to date a particular example because of its similarity in build and setting to others that have been methodically examined. However, where there are strong doubts because of unusual features, the only recourse may be to test by means of a trial-trench. Even then, the results depend on the chance that stratified datable material will be recovered in the right context. In all the sites that will be described, their connection with the Roman military occupation of Dorset stems partly from visible constructional features, and partly from their relationship to what have been claimed as early Roman roads in Chapter 5. The evidence in each case will not be found negligible and in due course may lead to the proper identification of these historic sites, and their conservation, where not already secured.

(A) **Earthworks at Candy's Farm, Corfe Mullen: a signal-station?**
It is only in recent years that groups of earthworks east of Candy's Farm, Corfe Mullen, have been given attention. They are not all easy to decipher on the ground, and certainly, without excavation, will not meet with universal acceptance as to their interpretation. One slight earthwork, more noticeable in conditions of drought, is a stretch, plus a zigzag or dogleg, of the Roman road from Lake towards Dorchester (fig. 5C.1). A second group comprises house-platforms with other features, clearly of medieval type, and lying further east, closer to Wimborne Road.[1] Between these lies a third area of earthworks on and

around a spur on the north-facing slope (SY 99399880), some 450 m west-south-west of the Roman fortress at Lake Farm. At the foot of the spur, bedrock is composed of a narrow belt of London Clay, while the spur itself projects from an equally narrow parallel belt of plateau gravel. A first look at the terrain suggests that features of several periods are involved here. The case will be made that these represent the remains of a Roman fortlet of some kind, modified and partly overlaid by medieval farming activity. Was this a signal-station? Despite the recent demotion and even denial of such installations (of which more below), it is hardly credible that the Roman army was devoid, under all circumstances, of recourse to visual communication. If an example is to be sought and tested dating to the Claudian period, this possibility at Candy's Farm should be considered.

The plan of the earthworks as they now appear is based on a number of traverses surveyed with a dumpy-level.

The earlier earthworks
On top of the spur it appears that the ground was levelled to create a flat squarish emplacement. This area, measuring 30 m east-west by 25 m north-south, was then, it is claimed, enclosed by a rectilinear bank, then an inner ditch, surrounded by a second bank and an outer ditch. Not all these features are immediately recognizable at first sight today. The remains of the innermost bank or rampart are visible only along the north side, with an entrance gap 5 m wide midway between the curving north-west and north-east corners. Flanking this rampart line on the north side, there are signs of the filled inner ditch, interrupted by the entrance causeway leading up to the entrance gap. This inner ditch can no longer be seen to any degree on the east, though an eroded depression on the slope of the north-east corner is probably connected. On the west, its line is commemorated by the re-cut ditch of the later north-south field boundary discussed below, and, on the south, by the devious course of the cattle-walk. The berm and associated bank are not now separately distinguishable, and indeed that may have originally been the intention. Material thrown inwards when the outermost ditch was dug may well have been used on three sides of this prominent spur in order to create a shelf on the berm rather than a bank as such. By far the best defined feature of the complex is the outer ditch, skirting the north foot of the spur, then rounding the north-east corner and running along the eastern foot. To the north-west and south-east, the curving corners can be discerned and have been confirmed by survey. The west and south sides and the south-west corner have been well buried by later farming operations extending over a long period of time.

It was an important feature of the early earthworks that they were located beside the Roman road that passed on the north at the foot of the spur, and led from Lake Farm ultimately to Dorchester.

The later earthworks
The key to deciphering the history of the various earthwork features is the north-south field boundary mentioned above. From Candy's Lane to the spur, where there is the present gateway between the two fields, an immense depth of soil has built up in the west field, so as to form a positive lynchet with a maximum height of 1.25 m, flanked on its eastern side by a small ditch (re-scoured at intervals). North of the gate separating these fields, 2979 (west) and 4781 (east), this lynchet gradually becomes less marked as it runs just west of the flattened top of the spur, though the accompanying ditch has been deeply re-cut. The lynchet soon curves round westwards, but the field-boundary continues north as a gravel bank now built of spoil from its flanking ditch, which has been dug through the

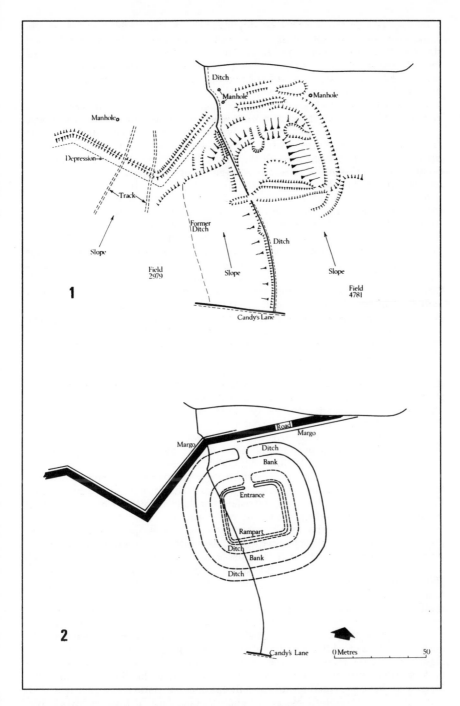

8A.1 Earthworks and the suggested signal station, Candy's Farm, Corfe Mullen

berm between the inner and outer ditches of the earlier earthwork. This gravel bank, surmounted by substantial oak trees, was probably created during the final stage of the cultivation that produced the lynchet. In its last stretch northward the field-boundary loses the gravel bank at the point where it crosses the buried line of the earlier outer ditch, and then straightens again on the other side of the disturbed course of the Roman road.

The story of the field-boundary can be established with reasonable certainty. It began as a land demarcation at a time when the inner ditch of the rectilinear earthwork was still visible and the west alignment of that ditch could be extended southward to the predecessor of Candy's Lane and northward to the furrow which must have marked the partly filled outer ditch, beyond which point the Roman road had remained in local service. Modern re-use of the ditch, most recently to take drainage from Candy's Lane, cannot disguise its antiquity.

After this field division had taken place, other features developed. The squarish flat top of the spur bears traces of a shallow scoop, 12 m long and 7 m wide, possibly the site of a building. This is bounded on its south by a low secondary bank, forming an edge to the shallow hollow-way of cattle-walk which provides access between the two fields. This depression turns sharply as it reaches the south-east corner of the earlier outer ditch. At that point a lynchet-like edge continues the line and runs on eastward as far as the Wimborne Road. One and a half metres high above the somewhat levelled ground to its north, this feature cannot be fully explained as resulting from post-Roman farming activities. A further disturbance, noted above, just outside the north-east corner of the spur-platform, probably started as part of the filled inner ditch. Finally, at the northern foot of the spur, there is a small bank parallel with the alignment of the Roman road passing here just to the north from its junction with the Poole Harbour road to the east. This was apparently a hedge-bank lying over and along the original outer ditch. It lies close to trenching carried out for sewage pipes in the 1960s, an operation that has not made it easier to understand surface details.

A Roman signal-station?

The significance of the earlier earthworks as described can be confirmed only by excavation. But, given the interpretation offered by the writer, they may be claimed to bear the mark of Roman military engineering, not so surprising a thought considering the closeness of the fortress at Lake Farm. The two features that can best be picked out are the flattened top of the spur and the precise line of the mostly buried outer ditch, traceable for half its perimeter course. The dimensions, though symmetrical, do not form an exact square, but if the intention was to use the lie of the ground to best purpose, the result was apparently successful. What emerges in view here is a rectilinear enclosure, defended by a pair of ditches. As a signal-station this can be given close parallel in the West Country. Thus the inner fortlet on the top of the spur had an area of 780 square metres, which compares with 750 square metres for the fortlets at Martinhoe and Old Burrow in North Devon.[2] These fortlets also possessed a double-ditch systems, but in addition were surrounded by a wide outer enclosure with its own ditch and bank. The pattern is repeated on a number of possible signal-stations, well recorded in the North of England.[3] Such a wider enclosure was arguably superfluous in the present case, since the post was so close to the Lake fortress. It is probable that the fortress lay within a military zone or *territorium*, and excavations along the Roman road heading west towards Dorchester have provided useful clues that this signal-station, if such it was, had been sited at the western margin of such a zone. East of this earthwork, the evidence, albeit from one cross-trench only, demonstrated the existence of a side-

142

walk or *margo* on the *south* side of the Roman road running from the road-junction south of the fortress. But, from at least two excavations west of the earthwork, the *margo* was detectable on the *north* side. Further, the unusual zigzag in the road just west may have bearing on the siting of the earthworks. We can add that the entrance to the fortlet gave access on to the road to the west. Thus, if we accept the probability of this fortlet, it is reasonable to infer that the military squad coming on duty from the fortress walked along the south footpath lying within the *territorium*, the boundary of which ran along the road in this area. Further west, beyond the signal-station, the sidewalk, now on the north, would have served for foot-patrols or the armed escort accompanying a supply-train, the north-west being the hostile quarter. As against Martinhoe and Old Burrow, the absence of an outer enclosure, if correctly interpreted, strengthens the case that this change of routine occurred at the edge of a military zone. Such an outer enclosure must have acted as a mini-military zone in locations where the post was isolated and vulnerable, but this example at Candy's Farm was not so placed.

What would have been the role of this suggested signal-station? The position selected by the Roman camp-prefect was on a high spur close to, but well above, the fortress. It offered an excellent view across the Stour valley to Badbury Rings, 5 km away, where, on current indications, the invaders placed a small unit on watch after the early battles. There was also a sighting of Keynston Down, with its small signal-post, half the distance of 18 km to Hod Hill. It has been generally taken that there were two methods of sending messages from such locations – by smoke-fires and by semaphore. At Candy's Farm, the task would basically have been the reception of signals in the event of emergency. Its main function was probably to hold a watching brief, ready to receive warnings or urgent calls for aid. An outlying garrison like that at Hod Hill could ask for and expect reinforcements with only a few hours delay.

In conclusion, it must be emphasized that the problem of identifying a particular site as a Roman signal-station has not been resolved with certainty even among the many recognized Roman military sites in the North of England.[4] There is a recent view that even the existence of signal-stations as single-role installations has been, to put it bluntly, an imaginative exercise on the part of archaeologists.[5] If we consider Martinhoe and Old Burrow, these fortlets, by their very situation, certainly must be judged to have served as outposts on the watch for incursions from South Wales. The Candy's Farm site, if verified, was well placed to survey the Stour valley in a manner impossible for those on guard down at the Lake Farm fortress, even if they were standing on rampart-walks. How signals reached them or were sent out, whether on foot, horseback or by smoke or semaphore, are not points to elaborate until the Candy's Farm earthworks have been confirmed by excavation.

(B) Two Earthworks at East Holton: Roman forts?

The earthworks to be described lie in a part of Dorset very close to one of the busiest roads in the south-east of the county, yet their siting has made them more or less inaccessible to the public for many years. Other factors must have played a part in the failure to consider them as genuine antiquities. In particular, through shape and function they resembled fields won relatively recently from the heathland. It occasionally happens that unrecorded earthworks can be given a reasonable identification without immediate need to excavate. This goes for many ploughed-out monuments visible only as soil marks on air views. In this respect, one thinks of round barrows with their distinctive circular ditches and Roman forts and camps of characteristic geometrical shape. If the enclosures on

Holton Heath had shown up as soil features, there would have been little hesitation in suggesting that they were of Roman military origin. Fortunately, both earthworks, though both to some extent altered or damaged, still survive for close inspection and so can speak for themselves in constructional detail and general location.

Enclosure A

The first earthwork, centred approximately at SY 95959170, lies on private land 400 m north of Holton Farm, at a height of 8 m above sea-level. Until very recent times, the area was open heathland set on a bedrock of Bagshot sands. The present vegetation cover is a natural growth of pine with some holly and laurel. Additionally, for half the year, the ground features in question are well screened by bracken. Thus the view in all directions from that spot is now restricted compared with the distant and not so distant past. The waters of Lytchett Bay and the Wareham Channel must once have been visible to the north-east, east and south-east, a fact no doubt of significance in the location of the earthwork and, as we shall see, of the second one, too.

The configuration of the enclosure is almost square and, from details on the Ordnance Survey 1:2500 plan, the dimensions are as follows: north-west side – 80 m; north-east side – 80 m; south-east side – 76 m; south-west side – 75 m, giving an area of 0.6 hectares (1.48 acres). These measurements are based on a perimeter composed of a bank and an outer ditch and it can be assumed that the Ordnance surveyors' single line on the map was tracing the top of the bank. This is low and uniform, with an aspect of antiquity lacking in most other similar features on the heathland. It is 3.5 m wide and stands 0.4 to 0.6 m above the middle of the ditch, which averages 2 m wide. What is especially important about these perimeter details is their deliberate rounding at each of the four corners, which all remain intact. The earthwork was clearly a unitary construction, built at one and the same time, and the shape of the corners formed an essential element. Unfortunately, Ordnance Survey plans do not show gateways to ordinary fields, but there must obviously have been at least one original entry. On the ground it can be argued that there was such a gap midway along the south-west side, but damage has occurred through the driving of a wide fire-break through the pine-trees and the earthwork, action which has left intact only the northern half of this possible gateway. On inspection the gap appears to have been closed at some time by a narrower turf bank, with a causeway left to replace the ditch. Inside the enclosure, the ground, where not disturbed by the fire-break, looks to have been levelled rather than ploughed, though judgement is impeded by thick humus and the dense vegetative cover.

On the evidence, the enclosure has no special relevance to the medieval and later history of East Holton Farm. It lies isolated from the field system associated with the latter and is not marked on the 1843 tithe map. While it was recorded on the first edition of the six-inch Ordnance Survey map (as a field, not an earthwork), when the heathland was still dominant, and on large-scale maps since, it did not appear on the first series of the 1:25 000 maps, only to be shown on the second. The point must immediately be made that the bank and ditch of this earthwork involved considerable effort in its building, and a different method from the turf barrier and shallow ditch typical of the normal heath enclosures. We may infer from the scale of the perimeter features that they represent a demolished rampart, fronted by a substantial ditch. The rounded corners provide a strong hint that this was a Roman military layout. The symmetry of the enclosure, almost a square, allied to the straightness of its sides, reinforces that view. A walk round the top of the bank (not everywhere an easy

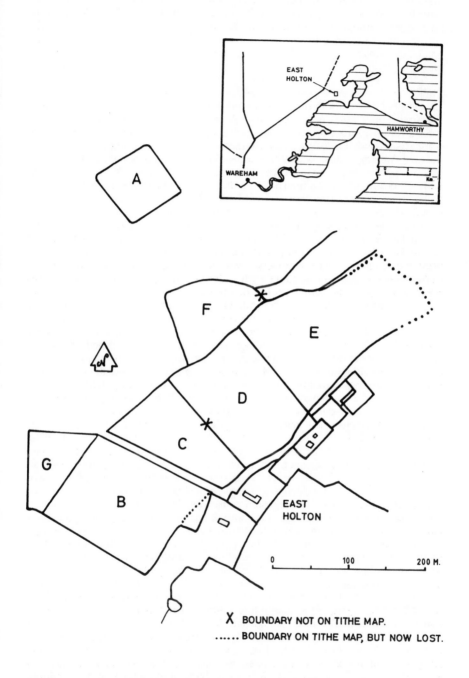

8B.1 Location of suggested forts (A and B), East Holton

task) makes it clear that there is no sign of an original entrance except that already noted as possible midway in the south-west side. This discounts the chance of a similar gap midway in the opposite north-east side, where the construction of the fire-break has flattened the ground. Against that, a Roman fort of this small size might have had gateways to the number of four, three or one, but hardly two opposing.

Enclosure B

This is sited 400 m south of the earthwork just described. In contrast, it presents the first appearance of a hedged field under permanent grass. While its configuration approaches a rectangle rather than a square, it makes an interesting comparison with Enclosure A in having adjacent angles of 82 and 98 degrees, those of A being almost exactly the same. The dimensions of its four sides are as follows: north-west – 130 m; north-east – 155 m; south-east – 132.5 m; and south-west – 158.5 m, giving an internal area of 2 hectares (4.9 acres). It is not at once obvious on the ground that the bank that limits the enclosure (and which provided the statistics given) is older than the ones around the various fields to the east. The north-east side looks very like an ordinary hedge-bank, if a little wider. This is not surprising, since the feature along the edge of the road to East Holton has been subject to modern disturbance. The other three boundaries each present a different aspect: south-east – very low and grassy and almost flattened in places; south-west – wider and with a look of antiquity like Enclosure A; and north west – here the outer profile of the bank and beyond has been almost buried by humus from old woodland. This bank appears everywhere to have measured 3–4 m in width. This enclosure, like A, seems basically to have had a single outer ditch, so filled that its original width is concealed, save at the west corner. Here the ditch cuts deep into gently rising ground, and both it and the bank display a rounded shape, while its breadth of 2 m looks impressive. Along the north-east side the tarmac road is flanked by re-cut drainage ditches, but the south-east external line of the earthwork offers some interesting details. There is a suggestion of a causewayed entrance midway, although a slight bank and a small ditch (of later date?) continue the main perimeter line across its neck. In recent times, the enclosure has had field-gates inserted at each end of this south-east side, which would explain the abandonment of a central entry. Another problem arises in that the causeway looks as if it might have passed between double ditches along this side, which would have replaced the single ditch so well defined at the west corner. Two lines of trees are recorded on early Ordnance Survey maps (which might explain the linear depressions) but they are also shown as crossing the suggested causeway. The interior of Enclosure B is relatively flat and, while under grass now, it has been arable for long periods in the past. The soil is dark and even to at least 0.4 m depth, and within the rounded south corner bank of the enclosure lies as much as 1 m higher than outside. This accumulation represents a long period of farming and contrasts with the shallower, lighter soil in the later fields east of the tarmac road.

It has been suggested above that Enclosures A and B not only have certain affinities in construction, but both present an air of considerable age, which might point to a common Roman military origin. The isolation of the first means that we have difficulty in trying to date it in relation to other features in the landscape. Certainly it was not being used for farming and was indistinguishable from heath at the time of the tithe map. That is not enough to reinforce its case for being a Roman fortlet, despite the close resemblance of the enclosure perimeter to such an original. There is, as we shall see, support in its actual location, but this argument applies equally to enclosure B. It is important, then, to establish, if possible, that the latter was in existence earlier than the medieval period, Holton being recorded in Domesday.

The pattern of the field-system north and west of Holton Farm today is not difficult to decipher when nineteenth-century map evidence is taken into account. If we look at the block represented by CDE and ignore the divisions between which are irrelevant long-term, we can see that it developed from the straight edge of the road running from the north-west along the north-east side of Enclosure B. This block was an extension based on B, with C offset slightly at the start, and formed a band of arable using the width of a 'short' furlong identical to the longer dimension of the enclosure. Incidentally, these fields, B, C, D and so on, appear to be referred to as 'closes' in 1564.[1] The sinuous north-west and south-east sides of CDE contrast strikingly with the straight counterparts of B. On the face of things, therefore, the field we have been calling Enclosure B was the start of the system under discussion. This view is supported by facts already noted, namely the depth of soil within B and the aspect of those parts of bank and ditch that best remind us of their original state.

The Domesday entry for *Holtone* is brief but useful. William of Braose held half a hide and land for half a plough with a value of ten shillings. What is interesting here is not the fact that William as manorial lord farmed directly, but rather the apparent area of arable that was his concern. There are indications that in this part of England the commissioners worked on the basis of a geld-hide standing at 40 acres (16 hectares). In the case of a simple return like this, with no mention of meadow, woodland, mill or tenants, for a place like Holton, set remotely on uninviting heath, it is likely that the figure of hideage reasonably reflects the only real asset, the arable acreage. Given then, 20 acres as the area of tilled land in 1086, we find that B, C, D and E cover just over 18 acres. The correspondence is close enough to further the thought that Enclosure B had been created long before the late eleventh century, if, by that time, what is clearly a later field-pattern had already evolved eastwards as C, D and E. There is no real doubt, for the record, that the Domesday entry referred to this particular area at what has come to be called East Holton. Here we have Holton Farm and, south of Enclosure B, a traditional village pond, whereas West Holton, now virtually destroyed by the railway and the one-time Cordite Factory, was a peripheral settlement, its closeness to the shore pointing to a greater interest in the sea.

One obstacle to accepting A and B as Roman military works without excavation would until recently have been set by their possession in each case of only a single gateway.[2] Such first-century examples certainly existed (e.g. at Cappuck),[3] but they were unusual enough to pose a problem. However, thanks mainly to aerial photography, an increased number of these small forts or fortlets has been recognized. Besides the one entrance, a basic feature is the small area (0.5 hectare, 1.2 acres) though a double size is known. Most are in Scotland and belong to the second century, but roadside fortlets may be more common in the Province than has been realized.

These two suggested Roman forts require proof by test-excavation, but it is likely that they were in service successively, a point that will emerge as we consider their siting and the role they would have played in the invasion. Both lay only 3 km distant from the landing beach used by the Roman army on the Hamworthy peninsula. They enjoyed a clear view (today slightly obscured by trees) of the shore on the west side of the landfall and could also oversee the waters to the west and north-west, from which direction raiding parties might be feared. Bulbury, the nearest hillfort, was only 5 km away, with Woolsbarrow a little further at 6.5 km. It is an interesting comment on Roman campaigning tactics that a distance of 5 km also separated the fortress at Lake Farm from its first major opponent, Badbury Rings. There is every reason to think that a military unit stationed on Holton Heath would have seemed logical and necessary to the Roman commander when planning the operation at Hamworthy.

From the point of view of function, the argument that Enclosure B came first would fit the circumstances of the landing, with access from the direction of the beach. It was large enough to accommodate an auxiliary infantry cohort of 1000 men, capable of resisting any sudden native attack or threat to the temporary port. By contrast, Enclosure A had its suggested gateway looking towards Wareham, along the road that was newly built over the heath from upper Corfe Mullen and Lake Farm. It held one quarter of the number of troops and acted as a police post, having by that time only a secondary interest in the harbour.

One detail remains to be considered, and is of special interest in a Roman context if, as suggested here, it is of contemporary build. This takes the form of a further enclosure, G, polygonal in shape, added to the north-west side of Enclosure B. It has almost one quarter the area of the larger with a similar residual bank and ditch that also have a look of considerable antiquity. The terrain within G, covered by scattered trees and heath, never seems to have been arable like B to the south. There is no question that it is of different date and construction from a more recent enclosure F to the east, with which a map may suggest resemblence. Given the identification of B as a Roman fort, there is no difficulty in interpreting G as an annexe, a military area attached to a fort and devoted to vehicles, draught animals and extra storage. If a similar structure is sought in our region, the Roman fort seen on air photographs at Crab Farm, Shapwick, appears to have an annexe affixed to its short side as here. Its size is proportionately the same in relation to a fort slightly larger than Enclosure B.

(C) Roman Bridge Abutments at Turners Puddle?

South of Turners Puddle Church, the Roman road from Lake Farm to Dorchester crosses the Piddle and begins a long alignment from that river towards the south-west (fig. 5C.7b and SY 82989327). The Piddle is here divided into two channels negotiated today by fords and footbridge. However, at the main water-course to the south, the careful observer at this isolated spot cannot miss the remains of an earlier construction in the shape of long mounds on either bank. These, it will be claimed, were abutments built for a bridge. What is the evidence for this feature and for its date?

The river Trent or Piddle pursues hereabouts a slow, somewhat meandering main course through wet meadows, and its normal width is only 3 m or so, shallow enough for wading knee-deep. However, after rain in winter, the situation worsens and footbridges are certainly a local necessity. The surviving fords must be something of a rarity in Dorset these days, since they have not been turned into concrete water-splashes. Passage nowadays through the streams seems limited, however, to tractors and horses.

It is important that we can identify at this spot, with reasonable certainty, the lost place-name *Streteford* in the medieval Barrow Hundred (Appendix 15). While the first element *strete* offers a strong presumption that the area is indeed associated with a Roman road, the second element suggests that in Saxon times either the bridge had fallen completely into disuse or it had not then been built. On the other hand, this place-name, first recorded in the fourteenth century, needs to be compared with a documented entry for 1473: *prat' iuxta Longbrigge* ('the meadow next to Longbridge' – Mills 1977). The meadow can be seen from the tithe map to be that immediately south of the present ford and bridge remains. Basically, a place-name like *Streteford* should go back to a time when the Roman road was still a recognizable feature in the local landscape, even though its earliest surviving record is only a century or two previous to that for *Longbrigge*. These references to ford and bridge at different times are problems best discussed after considering the ground details.

The case for a bridge abutment on the north bank of the river is straightforward. A ridge, some 8 m long and 3 m broad, stretches back from the site of the ford in a south-west to north-east alignment. On that side the ford-track from the south, having crossed that alignment in mid-stream, emerges from the water to become the old lane that runs towards the church. Close to the river on the north bank, the ridge is masked in a small thicket, but it can be seen extending into the corner of the adjacent field. There is enough visible to check that it lines up with a similar feature on the south bank. There, significantly, the track out of the ford has developed on the opposite flank of the south ridge or abutment. The ford, as a way to the church, is demonstrably later than the suggested bridge. The subsequent lateral erosion on the south ridge has worn into it, with results that have been a little destructive, but also revealing. This south abutment is seen to be capped by 0.2 m of topsoil overlying a thin layer of gravel, which in turn forms a surface to a consolidated deposit of chalk about 0.1 m thick. The chalk rests on compacted flints of large size, set apparently on the original sloping bank of the river. Notably, the chalk stratum is absolutely level and ends sharply before it reaches the edge of the stony build-up above the water's edge. There is no question that the chalk can have been laid to serve a ford rather than a bridge, a possibility ruled out by its horizontality. It was provided with a very solid base and surfaced with gravel. The topsoil over that gravel must have taken a long time to accumulate, since it has formed in an elevated position and survived the occasional wear and tear occasioned by closeness to a ford.

The details exposed by erosion to the ridge on the south side strongly suggest that the remains on each side of the river are those of abutments for a bridge. Each abutment would have been constructed by piling heavy flints on the sloping river bank behind a timber revetment. The sharp edge of the chalk layer clearly marks the site of such a wooden framework, probably in the shape of a transverse horizontal beam supported on vertical posts. These then carried the bridge-span over the water to a similar erection on the other side (fig. 8C.2). The chalk was used with a topping of gravel to form the road surface leading on to the bridge.

What has been described is a basic type of structure commonly built for local use from Roman times onward. Without prejudging the matter of date at this point, it is interesting that a construction of this kind was identified at Fishbourne and attributed to the military phase in the first century or at the beginning of the subsequent civil period:

> At the stream-crossing a timber bridge was provided. It was a simple affair based on two flanking rows of oak piles, nine inches in diameter, rammed into the ground on either side of the main stream-channel to serve as revetments, behind which the rubble and gravel of the causeway were piled. On top of each row of timbers a single horizontal beam would have been placed to serve as a base for the thick planks which would have spanned the eleven-foot gap between the rows. The bridge itself was quite narrow, barely 10 ft wide, but a ford was provided by the side of it, perhaps to allow livestock and wheeled traffic to pass while pedestrians could walk more comfortably across the bridge.[1]

Are there grounds for suspecting that the first bridge built here, for which the abutments were intended, was the work of the Roman army? Against that view must be set the name *Longbrigge*, recorded in 1473 and as recently as 1791, and

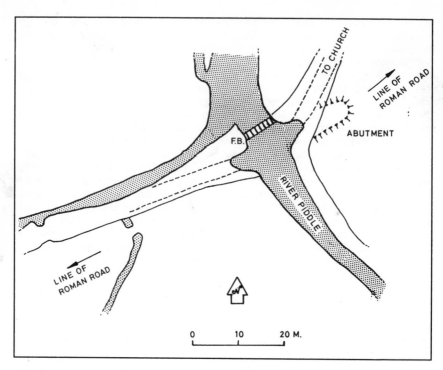

8C.1 Turners Puddle (not to scale)

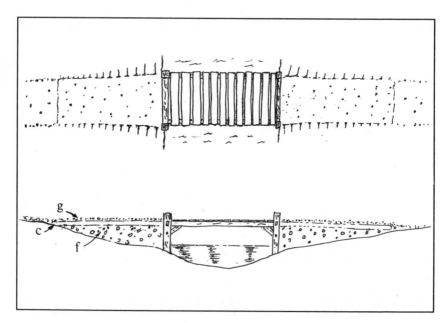

8C.2 Plan of bridge abutments, Turners Puddle

150

also commemorated on the 1840 tithe map as *Long bridge mead*, which lay due south of the disued bridging point. However, a survey of the Frampton Estate in 1801, gives only a *foot*-bridge thereabouts from Throop, and its modern successor spans the river at about the same spot, west of the abutments in question. The width and substance of the southern abutment, too, suggest that the original bridge was designed to take vehicles. It is important, as we have seen above, that the ford taking the road from Throop to the church crosses the Piddle *transversely* between the abutments, so that if the *Longbrigge* was a structure at this point, the bridge must have fallen into disrepair before that route developed for the ford. Most likely, the late medieval name was applied to a footbridge such as exists today, a necessary installation when villagers from the south of the parish had to come to church over a stream too deep for stepping-stones. Furthermore, we must remember that there was a second water-course to cross, immediately south of the church. This channel of the Piddle is wide here and was possibly once used for a mill. As it, too, was provided with a footbridge, the two bridges in combination probably gave rise to the term *long*-bridge. This second stream, where it was crossed by the Roman road a little way to the east, seems in earlier times to have been small enough to ford. By contrast, the bridge abutments over the main stream-bed were deliberately aligned to accommodate that stretch of Roman road from Damer Hill before it turns towards Throop and Affpuddle Heath. They are therefore older than the lane that curves away across the line of the former bridge and towards the church.

There is a case, then, for thinking that the abutments are earlier than the *streteford* name, which for more than one reason must be of pre-Norman origin. Given the other factors – alignment with the Roman road, depth of soil on the abutments, comparison with the Fishbourne bridge, implications of the medieval *long*bridge – it is arguable that at this remote place we can still see remains of a bridge constructed by the engineers of the Second Legion Augusta in the first century A.D. As so often when dealing with earthworks, the answer can come ultimately only from excavation.

(D) Bare Cross, Church Knowle: Roman terraced road and cutting?

The engineering work that carried the Roman military road from Wareham up on to the Purbeck ridge is an important link in reconstructing the Roman campaign in East Dorset. By taking into account other similar activities in the area, it is possible to appreciate something of the physical effort and time scale involved.

The earthworks comprise a cutting through the ridge to which access from the north was gained by way of a terraced road and an associated feature that will be interpreted as a *margo* or side-walk (fig. 8D.1 and SY 93068213). The cutting was carved through the sharp spine of the high ground where Upper Chalk and Middle Chalk meet. It measures 18 m maximum in width, narrowing to 2 m for the track. The depth of rock removed is some 4 m centrally and the sides slope uniformly at 30 degrees. These slopes are almost exactly at the gradient recommended by modern practice, ensuring a basic angle of rest after construction. Downland turf forms readily on these Purbeck hilltops, aided over the centuries by sheep grazing, so that what we see now is not very different from the original appearance. There is no sign of major soil-slip and the vehicle track has been kept clear by occasional use, though for some time past it has been supplanted, except for walkers, by the wider road from the south that makes a sharp hairpin bend to the west. The metalled track at the base of the cutting is broad enough for vehicles passing in only one direction at a time, a revealing detail when we come to consider the terraced stretch and the purpose of the whole scheme.

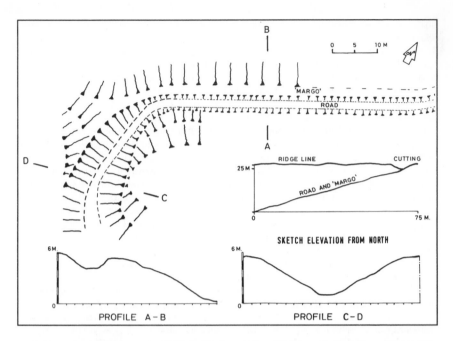

8D.1 Plan and profiles of terraced road and cutting, Bare Cross, Church Knowle. For the sketch elevation, horizontal scale differs from the vertical.

8D.2 Terraced Roman road, Bare Cross, Church Knowle, looking south

152

When the Roman road from Wareham reached the foot of the Purbeck Hills there were two choices for climbing and moving in the direction of the Flower's Barrow hillfort. The first was to go westwards up the dry valley between Stonehill Down and Ridgeway Hill, a tactically disadvantageous route out of keeping with military thought. The second, the one chosen, was steeper by far and involved substantial engineering work, including the cutting at the top. But this ascent was more immediately rewarding, since the col at which it was aiming, between Ridgeway Hill and Knowle Hill, was the lowest local access to the spine of the Purbeck ridge. The terracing by which the climb is made measures some 110 m in two straight lengths of equal dimension, with a minimal re-alignment centrally. The lower first stretch is aligned with the faint traces of an edge noted in the field to the east. It has suffered some disturbance from the construction of a Victorian tramway down the slope, but retains an even width of just over 5 m, now mainly turf-covered.

Halfway up the steady gradient of 1:4, where there is the slight change of alignment, the terraced way divides longitudinally into two separate strips that maintain their clear identities for the rest of the ascent (fig. 8D.2). The inner strip gradually drops below the level of the outer and in due course leads into the cutting at the crest. There is no problem in interpreting this as a carefully engineered vehicular track, built, along with the cutting, to a precise plan. The outer strip, as we now see it, is a flat-topped bank that rises to an average height of 1 m above the inner road. When the latter curves to enter the cutting, this outer strip goes onward to merge into the downland slope to the north-west and west. Further down the slope from this outer bank, a break in the ground can be seen indicating that there has been a substantial build-up of extra soil. Thus, while the inner track was created with a relatively slight removal of soil and bedrock on its inner side, the mass of spoil used to support the outer raised bank could have come only from a nearby source, in this case the cutting. The total impression given is of a co-ordinated effort executed (one may well say) with military precision. The origin and purpose of this Purbeck feature must always have been something of a mystery, particularly in terms of explaining that outer bank.

Seen in the context of the Roman road from Wareham to Flower's Barrow, does this terraced road with its outer bank and its cutting make good sense? Can the bank have been the type of side-walk or *margo* identified at several points, for example, at the start of the military road from Lake to Dorchester? It cannot have formed merely a reinforced verge, for the lower stretch deliberately included in its width the strip that higher up was to become the raised bank. It would seem unnecessary to have included there such a reinforced edge, unless it was serving as a *margo*. The objection will be offered that this may well have been a path for foot-passengers, but Roman? Why Roman military? Could it not have been a later addition to the scheme? In general terms, the terraced road and the cutting, as explained elsewhere, can only be explained as joining the causewayed road from Wareham with the causewayed road from Flower's Barrow and so of similar purpose and date. But in detail, apart from the visual fact that the *margo* was always part of the whole construction, a provision like this for those on foot was not normally provided on roads throughout history, except under certain conditions. Military waggons or a train of pack-animals moving in hostile country would have required at least part of their escort walking or riding *beside* them. A scene on Trajan's Column depicts just such a state of affairs. If we visualize what seems to have been intended in the present case, the *margo* enabled the armed escort to remain at the side of the supply-train and then to reach the hill-top *above* the cutting, a vital point of vantage in anticipating an attack.

(E) Dorset Hillforts: causeways and cuttings

Hitherto only one hillfort in Dorset has exhibited examples of Roman military engineering which have had general acceptance as to their origin. Apart from that obvious case at Hod Hill, little enthusiasm has emerged to explain the so-called 'Roman' entrance at Badbury Rings. The reason was simply a lack of direct evidence attributing its construction to the Roman army. It has been assumed that an entry into a hillfort that was clearly later than the Iron Age could have been cut at any time in the last two thousand years. Why, then, was the Badbury example thought to be probably of Roman build? The time is ripe, in the light of the new information presented elsewhere in Part II, to reconsider this problem and others in the same class. 'The stationing of garrisons in the commanding positions offered by hillforts can hardly strike us as surprising. More surprising is the fact that until recently Hod Hill has seemed to be such an exceptional site in this regard.'[1]

Given this general view by Malcolm Todd after his work at Hembury in Devon and the evidence of the early roads in Dorset, it is possible now to identify those hillforts that in this writer's view received the attention of the Roman army. The hallmark seems to be an engineering technique straightforward in its application: a passage chopped through the native rampart, with side-slopes at the angle of rest, and the spoil used to create a new causewayed entrance over the accompanying ditch. The object might have been one of three: to make an access of a Roman type for a military unit stationed within; to demilitarize a native stronghold;[2] or to create a line of communication through the hillfort in the shape of a road. The distinction between the first two of these aims might be difficult to establish without putting a spade into the ground. But it is important that, in a number of cases, a road was demonstrably built to link with a particular hillfort. This circumstance must point to the presence of a Roman garrison and as a corollary should make us suspect such a garrison where only the engineered gap can be seen and the probable early road has left little trace on the surface.

In this category, we may place not only Hod Hill (we can now add a road-access to the known Roman fort), but also Flower's Barrow, Bulbury, Woolsbarrow, Woodbury and Rawlsbury. A second category depends on the proof of an early military road, basically a matter for the programme of excavation: Weatherby Castle, Spetisbury, Dudsbury, Pilsdon (a road westward from Waddon?) and, probably, Lambert's Castle (associated with the early road presumed to skirt Marshwood Vale on the north). In both these groups, the hillforts exhibit engineering work of the type described above, whether a road-connection has been proven or remains merely probable.

The following hillforts were all linked to early military roads, a fact implying that they held Roman garrisons:

1. Hod Hill

The Romans drove two entries across the Iron Age defences, the Water-Gate and the Ashfield Gate. In one important respect, the former is not typical of our series, since it clearly formed one of the gateways to the Roman fort itself. Though the Water-Gate involved a causeway across the defensive ditch, the cutting through the inner rampart had to allow for the construction of later timberwork, so that instead of slopes on each side at the angle of rest as in an open cutting, vertical faces were dug, now hidden by the scree from two thousand years of erosion. This is not to say that the Romans did not construct gate-structures at the entrance gaps to be described. It is unlikely, but we do not know, because they have not been examined for this information.

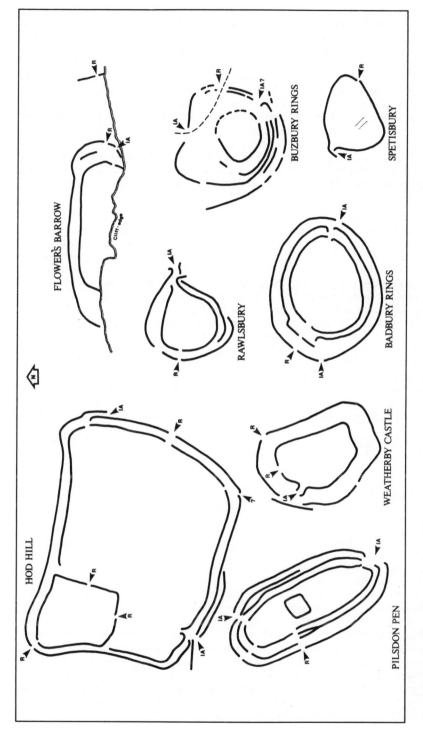

8E.1 Hillforts in Dorset with probable Roman entries (R = Roman. IA = Iron Age).

The Ashfield Gate must, therefore, be regarded as the model for the series. In his report on the excavations of the 1950s, Sir Ian Richmond maintained that at first the Romans used the native entrance, the Steepleton Gate, in the north-east corner for access to their own camp, until they constructed the Ashfield Gate midway in the east side: ' ... a sharply outlined cutting with sides sloping to the angle of rest, sliced through the main rampart and ... the outer counterscarp mound'.[3] He noted 'corresponding with the cutting, two causeways in line, each 20 feet wide [that] filled the native ditches. ...' He was able to demonstrate the existence of a third causeway laid across the quarry pits within. No sealed evidence was found to prove the contemporaneity of cutting and causeways with the Roman military presence in the hillfort, but the general circumstances put the case beyond doubt as far as Richmond was concerned. The discovery that the early road from Lake was directed at this entry past Ash and Lazerton has simply reinforced the argument.

2. Flower's Barrow
The causewayed road that led from Wareham and Stoborough and climbed on to the Purbeck Hills was aimed from its inception at this hillfort. In addition to its formidable defences of at least two phases, Flower's Barrow possessed an outwork formed of a linear bank and ditch designed to block the way from the east along the high, narrow ridge on which it was set. The Roman road from Wareham passes through this outwork by means of a causeway and a cutting and goes on to cross the outer (but not the inner) defence-line of the hillfort in similar fashion. The first of these features is, on the face of things, older than the parish boundary between Tyneham and West Lulworth, which wanders off southward after following the Roman alignment a little way from the east. The second feature, by contrast, has always been regarded as later than the Iron Age gateway close by, but, in company with the first, has remained unexplained. There seems a possibility that the flat space between outwork and hillfort was chosen as the site for a Roman camp rather than the interior of the stronghold. The cuttings and causeways on each side would then have acted as gateways to a military area defined to north and south by naturally steep slopes. The area thus available would have come to 2.3 hectares (5.3 acres), a size that, to judge by Hod Hill and Crab Farm,[4] was convenient for the type of major military unit being outposted during the invasion of Dorset. In this way, the invaders would have taken full advantage of this vital vocation, with its sweeping views over the inner vale and hills of Purbeck and also, more importantly, over the Frome valley, as far as the hillforts of Woolsbarrow and Woodbury, some 14 km away.

3. Rawlsbury
Rawlsbury has been described as a strongly defended bivallate hillfort. It lies some 10 km south-west of Hod Hill, its site on the chalk escarpment overlooking the valley of the Develish brook. Rawlsbury provides a typical cutting of the kind under discussion, with the warning that applies to some of the others, namely the absence of direct excavated evidence placing responsibility on the Roman army. There are two existing entrances, of which the one from the east is in the native tradition with a passage through an elaborate system of banks and ditches. The other entrance, on the west, comprises a straight approach through gaps in the rampart and causeways over the ditches. It is interesting that the parish boundary between Stoke Wake and Woolland follows the line of the western entrance and then, after wandering across the interior of the hillfort, passes over the defences, so ignoring the eastern gateway. By implication, the western gateway was already in existence when parish boundaries were finalized, but later than the Iron Age occupation. This dating bracket may seem

too broad to be significantly helpful. However, comparison can be made with the causeway and gap through the outwork at Flower's Barrow, where a parish boundary behaves in a similar manner and there is positive association with a Roman military road. In the case of Rawlsbury, why was this new access sited on the opposite side to the romanized ridgeway from the Roman fort at Hod Hill? The reason is not far to seek, given the need, as the campaign developed, to control further hillforts to the north, north-west and south-west. Banbury, Dungeon Hill and Nettlecombe Tout, in that order, await the test of the spade, but there is no reason to think that they were not actively defended against the Roman invader. They have been too eroded to make it possible even to surmise their re-use by the legion.

4. Buzbury Rings

The Roman military road from Badbury Rings to Hod Hill was obliged by narrowing high terrain to pass through this minor hillfort, otherwise described as 'an enclosed Iron Age and Romano-British settlement'. On its approach from the east the route was blocked by two substantial banks, separated by a median ditch. The obstacle was dealt with in the usual manner, the banks being razed and the spoil used to create a wide causeway between. As with similar works elsewhere, the neatly sloped cuttings form a distinctive hallmark of Roman precision, while the impressive causeway, fully 10 m broad, combines with the residual banks on each side to present golfers with an approach and hazards of an original nature. However, unlike others in this list, the Buzbury causeway was not an entrance, but served basically as a thoroughfare. The continuation of the Roman road westwards, re-emerging from the enclosure, seems to have taken advantage of an existing Iron Age entrance, if the contours of the outer native circuit are any guide.

5. Bulbury

Only excavation could test whether Warne, the Dorset antiquary, was right in seeing this hillfort endowed with four entrances at the four points of the compass. These features are now finally ploughed flat, but there is no reason seriously to doubt Warne's observations, and the existence of an early road leading towards this stronghold from Sandford and Wareham does make it probable that two at least of these gateways were the work of the Roman military.

6. Woodbury

The Roman road to Wareham to the hillfort remains the main reason for suspecting that a Roman military unit was briefly garrisoned here. The south gateway to which it led appears to have been widened since antiquity, probably in connection with the famous medieval fair and the even earlier chapel (not to mention the present farm complex within). There are altogether five other entries at present traceable into the hillfort, some of which are considered secondary.

7. Woolsbarrow

This hillfort is so sited on a flat-topped knoll that only one entrance has been feasible. Originally the approach was effected by a peripheral rising track on the south-east, which was protected at the actual gateway by an out-turned bank and probably a ditch. Ground evidence shows that the Roman road from the south was cut straight through this defence work.

The following have as yet no proven link with an early military road though the evidence should still be recoverable.

8. Badbury Rings

The entrance into the hillfort normally used by visitors passes through the outer defence circuit (ditch and rampart) by means of causeway and cutting. This is the first part of the gateway tentatively identified as Roman, which continues through the barbican ditch and rampart in the same manner. Both these gaps were contrived to line up with the original western gateway. The neat and positive construction of this secondary entrance, with its similarities to the Ashfield Gate, supports the notion of a Roman build. More importantly, perhaps, this entrance, by cutting through the barbican that protected the inner native gate, was obviously post-Iron Age, while the straight, firm cut through *two* lines was hardly the random work of a few individuals. However, Badbury has not yet been shown to have held a Roman military unit, although it would have enjoyed good inter-visibility with the suggested signal-station close to the Lake base, across the Stour valley. Badbury is also in a different category from the majority of the examples that follow: no evidence can be offered as yet for an early road leading into the hillfort through the post-Iron Age entry. There is the likelihood that if the Roman fort at Crab Farm, 1.6 km to the south-west, was of the invasion period rather than of the time of Boudicca, it did possess a road-link to Badbury. The fort lay athwart the line of the Badbury–Dorchester road, which on the airphotographs is seen to be later, since its metalling crosses the fort's defences.[5] That does not rule out a first road linking this fort to Badbury and the important roads to the north.

9. Eggardon

Eggardon was one of the major hillforts of the Dorset tribe, with multivallate defences of great strength and a level interior covering 8 hectares (20 acres). It could be expected to have had the same treatment at the hands of the invaders as many other strongholds, namely, capture followed by the stationing of a Roman military unit, which carried out alterations to the earthworks still discernible today. The fact that the long-accepted Roman road west from Dorchester reached so close to Eggardon may have seemed a coincidence based on the siting of the hillfort at an angle in the chalk ridge. But, in the light of current knowledge, the truth must surely prove otherwise. The spot enjoyed too obvious a strategic advantage, 11 km from Waddon and 14 from Dorchester, to have been left vacant by the Roman army.

At the north-west end of the hillfort, the final Iron-Age entry (2A.d) involved a gateway through the inner rampart and ditch. This was followed by a protected diversion northwards to reach an outer gap (2A.e) which passed between the second and third lines of defence through an enclosure or 'barbican' (cf. Badbury Rings, above). There is, however, another series of gaps passing straight through the outer defences from the inner gateway (2A.f). This 'post-Iron Age' construction involved both a cutting and a causeway over a ditch. The gap is narrow, just sufficient for a vehicle perhaps, and recalling the suggested Roman 'postern' at Spetisbury (below).

The south-east gateway (much disturbed over the years, otherwise basically retaining its Iron Age layout), is linked to the other entrance by the parish boundary more or less bisecting the hillfort. There are interesting problems here which only excavation might resolve. Why does the boundary, running in two straight lengths, so closely resemble a genuine low agger, 3 m wide and 0.3 m high, instead of a bank and ditch, constructed for the purpose? Is this the 'central' track as authoratively described, with the 'modern' one beside it?[6] 'Why does it line up with the ends of the inner ramparts instead of the centre of the gateways? Were the secondary gaps cut out to ease this layout of the medieval boundary or did they belong to an earlier period? By analogy with what has been demonstrated elsewhere, the latter details, at least, look like Roman work.

10. Pilsdon Pen

This hillfort was the largest in the western territory of the Durotriges and the nearest to the Roman fort at Waddon, only 3 km east. Pilsdon might well have been expected to reveal details of the type of engineering work under discussion that could be ascribed with any confidence to the Roman army. There are four entrances, of which two, at the south-east and north extremities, are so related to the defences as to make it certain they are Iron Age creations. But the two others, at the north-west corner and midway along the west side, represent major efforts that do not look to have been designed by the original inhabitants. Both involve straight cuts and causeways into the enclosure, and the western one in particular has been excavated. It was served by a carefully cobbled surface leading within towards the small square earthwork that forms a prominent, but unexplained, feature in the interior. The perimeters of this earthwork were said[7] to consist of a palisade set in a bank of soil and flanked by a slight external ditch. Certain Roman military details like a gateway centrally placed in one or more sides seem to be lacking and the apparent signs of rectangular buildings within are now confidently thought to be the work of rabbits.[8] Was the earthwork simply a crude medieval warren? However, the discovery of two ballista bolts must be regarded as a direct pointer to the Roman presence. Pilsdon was just out of sight of the Roman fort at Waddon and there are two further hillforts to watch not far away, Lambert's Castle and Coney's Castle. Given the small size of this suggested military site 0.2 hectares ($^1/_2$ acre) within Pilsdon, could it not have held a warning beacon ready for firing such as is depicted in the scroll at the foot of Trajan's Column?

11. Weatherby Castle

Like Rawlsbury, this hillfort has two distinct and contrasting entrances. One is typically Iron Age in character, with its slanting course through the double line of defences, a feature of the gateway being the out-turned inner rampart. This access runs in from the south-west, but some 60 m to the north-east; the second entry from a point almost due north involves 'a broad gap ... certainly not original' formed by cuttings through the inner rampart and a causeway over its ditch. Unlike the first entrance, the second has its corresponding gap in the outer defence line not, as at Badbury Rings, for example, immediately in line northward, but further to the north-east where the outer eastern rampart sharply terminates. Thick vegetation makes it difficult to check how access was gained up the slope at this point, but it is pointed out elsewhere that there are hints of an early road leading from the direction of Woodbury towards this particular entry gap. The inner and outer parts of the second entry, like others in this series at other hillforts, involved considerable labour. It is difficult to see a rural re-use after Iron Age and Roman times making this second entry necessary, when the original gateway was not far away. There is no tradition for a fair or similar local gathering in Weatherby to explain the need for extra access, as is arguably the case at Woodbury.

12. Poundbury

It appears that the eastern entrance was furnished with lateral ditches and that the Iron Age ditch was deepened at the same time by the digging of a fastigate channel typical of Roman military work. In Victorian days, the County Museum exhibited iron objects like ballista bolts and a sword from the same area. While only the sword is now traceable, the finds suggest that, after it had been captured by assault, the hillfort was used by the Roman army. These events would fit into the period immediately before and after the campaign against the local hillforts, including Maiden Castle, Poundbury (area 5.5 hectares, 13.5 acres) provided the

Roman command with a larger temporary camp than the fort (estimated area 1.5 hectares, 3.7 acres) that came to be built not far away as the origin of Dorchester.

13. Spetisbury

This has always been a puzzling earthwork and, it will be submitted, a much misunderstood one. The humpy nature of the single rampart, added to the curiously flat-bottomed ditch of great width, for long stimulated the conclusion that Spetisbury was an unfinished hillfort, apparently abandoned on the approach of the Roman army. But limited excavation in 1958,[9] showed the ditch as almost certainly of a normal V-shape, with a massive backfilling of chalk lumps. No reason was offered, but what surely happened here was that an effort was made to nullify the ditch as a defensive feature. The configuration of the denuded Iron Age entrance suggests that there may once have been a counterscarp bank on the other side which at some time or another was razed flat. While parts of the rampart were also apparently flung back into the ditch, so as to interrupt its continuity, that source was manifestly insufficient to explain the depth and evenness of the present ditch-fill. When and why did these circumstances take place? We should remember, too, the burials exposed in the nineteenth century by the railway builders, which now seem to offer new problems of interpretation.[10]

Once the Second Legion set up a base only 8 km away, on the same bank of the Stour, Spetisbury had to be eliminated as a threat before the river could be crossed for the attack on Badbury and the advance on Hod Hill. Even after its defences had been neutralised, Spetisbury presumably required temporary occupation by a Roman unit, as in the case of many Dorset hillforts. What is the evidence?

As in the case of various other hillforts, Spetisbury displays an access that is acceptably post-Iron Age. That one small gap is still traceable on the south-east sector of the rampart perimeter. This zone of the hillfort has suffered in particular from the tread of cattle, yet it is still possible to see that the sloping sides of this entry were carefully cut to the important angle of rest, 30 degrees. The gap, whenever dug, was intended to be limited to men on foot or pack-animals. It is only 5 m wide at present parapet height, narrowing down to 0.7 m centrally. The cut goes down 1.4 m into the Iron Age rampart without reaching to the pre-rampart surface.[11] A terraced path was created on the outer slope to lead down at an angle to the great ditch – on the evidence, after it had been partly refilled. Was a small causeway constructed here before that operation? The ditch is certainly rather shallower here than elsewhere, but decipherment of the ground is masked by cattle-tread. Indeed a second false gap is being created by the movement of docile, but weighty cows. Massive trees growing on the outer ditch-lip (the only place on the hilltop where there are trees) may mark the spot where the small climb to the outside ground level (0.75 m) could have occurred. This was the nearest point of entry into Spetisbury from the direction of Lake Farm. Beyond the trees, there are indeed signs of possible early stony road-metalling brought up by animal-burrowing in a band of grassy sward. Can there have been a short-stay Roman presence inside, and was their non-vehicular access, a kind of postern-gate? An answer may be assisted within the hillfort itself.

The interior of Spetisbury slopes markedly down to the north-east towards the Stour, so that the flattest ground and the best tactical site for a Roman unit would have been on the higher south-west quarter. Slight earthworks (shown simply as two parallel edges) have been recorded here in the past, with hints that they were connected to the medieval field-system of Charlton Magna.[12] As seen today, the story on the ground is a little more complicated and certainly more enlightening.

Area 1 comprises a platform some 36 m long and 7 m wide with a relatively level surface standing 0.2 to 0.4 m above the grass on three sides. The south-west side abuts a long shallow depression beyond which there is another distinct edge about 0.3 m high (a lynchet 'riser', if this were a lynchet) and around 36 m long. Area 2 has this edge as its north-east side. Its south-east side continues for perhaps 15 m the alignment of the end of Area 1, before the slight slope fades out. The north-west side can also be traced as a slight edge for a shorter distance. The terrain has presumably been lightly ploughed in bygone days and it has undergone the constant movement of animals grazing. It is clear that, lying at the top of a descent, Area 1 was once deliberately platformed, even if time has eroded its sharp edges into bevelled slopes. There can be no accident about its dimensions which translate into imperial terms of 118 and 23 feet. Of the legionary barracks at Hod Hill, Richmond wrote: 'all six measure over-all 118 by 20 to 25 feet'.[13] If a Roman barrack had once stood on Area 1, with a view towards the Stour and Badbury, it cannot be chance, either, that Area 2, on the flatter top of the ground, has the same long dimension with a width at least enough for more than one similar building.

Three points about the barrack building in Area 1, ultimately require to be tested by excavation: (a) its reduced size, as at Hod Hill, reflects the relative shortage of troops for garrison purposes in the first years of the Roman conquest; (b) a timber hut means that the unit here presumably over-wintered rather than merely camped for the campaigning season; (c) the barrack was parallel to the alignment of the suspected road arriving from Lake via the postern-gap already described (a circular proof, but nevertheless worth noting).

14. Other hillforts

(a) There can be few hillforts in the area of the Durotrigian tribe that do not possess gaps in their defences apparently later than the Iron Age and so capable of qualifying as creations of the Roman army during its short, but active, sojourn in Dorset. Those listed above offer reasons for being so considered, and others whose case will not be argued here include: Chalbury, an extra ramped entrance at its lower end; Dudsbury, two later entrances cut through the defences; Chilcombe; three recorded entrances.

(b) Two major hillforts in South Dorset, Maiden Castle and Abbotsbury Castle, require separate consideration. Both must have been doughty opponents to the Roman army, but their story after capture does not appear to have involved the provision of new causewayed entrances, as in examples listed above. Yet both offer hints that the army may well have been active within their respective perimeters.

Maiden Castle does not possess entrances other than those at the eastern and western extremities, the first being the site of the so-called war cemetery, where the British buried their dead. The excavations of the 1930s brought to light samian pottery of mainly pre-Flavian types. Wheeler explained this as debris from the continuation in residence of the Iron Age people, until they moved into Durnovaria, when the military finally left the area. It has been suggested, however,[14] that these scraps came from a Roman military unit stationed within Maiden Castle after its seizure. Interestingly, the provision of an early metalled road leading through the eastern gateway is offered as further support to the theory.[15] It may be added, too, that there had been increasing evidence for the growth of a Durotrigian township on the lower ground north of Maiden Castle, with dating material that places its occupation between the capture of the hillfort and the founding of civil Durnovaria. With its former inhabitants so close by, Maiden Castle can hardly have been left empty at this stage and a Roman police-post seems very likely. The creation of any extra causewayed entrance for this small garrison across the mighty defences of Maiden Castle would not have been justified by the size of the unit or its location. It would have been in sight of the Roman fort at Top o'Town, Dorchester, only 2.4 km away.

There has long been a suspicion that a small squarish earthwork inside Abbotsbury Castle was a Roman signal station of some kind. After recent excavation, doubt has been cast on this notion, several reasons being offered.[16] No structures could be identified within, while the one entrance was off-centre in the east side and lacked lateral gateposts. The pottery evidence was uncertain, but could give the earthwork a date between Iron Age and late Roman. If Abbotsbury, like Maiden Castle, acted as a police-post, the military personnel would have been quartered elsewhere than in this small enclosure. The latter might then have served simply to hold the signal-pyre and a guard. A gate would not have been required for a small enclosure guarded by a sentry actually *within* a military camp.

What, then, to sum up, are the reasons to support numbers 1 to 13 above as exhibiting evidence of Roman work? In several cases, a newly identified road leading through a post-Iron Age rampart gap is confirmation enough. The example at Buzbury Rings served the passage of a Roman road from Badbury Rings, while the gaps at Flower's Barrow are intrinsically tied into the early road from Wareham. At Hod Hill, the Ashfield Gate, even before its examination by Sir Ian Richmond, was suspected of being Roman in origin. It is useful to note that excavating a section does not necessarily provide the answer to the dating problem. Thus Richmond found by simply digging that the creation of the Ashfield entry took place *after* the Iron Age quarry pits had been dug, but there was no sealed entrance in the causeway material to establish firmly that the Roman army was responsible. In general terms, the precise construction of the Ashfield Gate was contrasted with the sinuosities of the Home Gate, the other post-Iron Age entry, leading from the village of Stourpaine and probably therefore of unplanned medieval build. In all the cases quoted it is indeed the similarities in construction and setting that underlie the claim to a Roman origin, a claim substantially supported where there is association with an early road.

By identifying the Roman presence at so many Durotrigian hillforts it is now possible to further our understanding of the strategy behind the campaign in Dorset. In most cases, particularly where a road-link is demonstrated, we should be considering that the objective was the posting of a temporary garrison rather than simply an effort to render the stronghold more difficult to defend.

9

The Roman Campaign in Dorset: movements and timing

In Part II an outline has been given of new discoveries relating to the presence of the Roman army in Dorset. Where they arise mainly from the writer's own investigations, the facts will no doubt take time to be assimilated by those engaged in similar studies. Until recently the operations of the invading forces in the west and south-west have lacked clarity simply because the information was still in the ground, unexcavated, or on the surface, unrecorded. But there has been progress both in Devon (the territory of the Dumnonii) and, as it is here claimed, in Central and East Dorset (the territory of the Durotriges). It is possible, therefore, to venture some positive conclusions on the conduct of the campaign in Dorset and of the pacification that followed. In advance, there are certain premises in the argument that need to be stated.

First, we must take it that the further west or north-west a fort lay, the later was the date of the initial occupation. This may seem obvious but it has required demonstration by the dating of finds from Waddon and Hod. Furthermore, a recent view[1] proposes that the fortress at Lake started as late as A.D. 48 at the very time that Waddon replaced Hod Hill. However, unless and until proven otherwise, if we follow the road-pattern detailed in Chapter 5, the fortress at Lake must logically have been founded earlier than the outlying fort at Hod Hill, even if the difference is only a matter of a few weeks. Given this westward movement of the Roman forces, the emerging facts will be shown to fit into the coherent picture of a stage-by-stage progress rather than of the lightening war favoured in the past by most authorities. There is a corollary in respect of road communications. Any road linking eastern and western forts is in effect later than either of these establishments and the implication is that both were functional when the road was built.

Second, on historical grounds and the archeological evidence, the time scale of the military base in Dorset must lie within the period A.D. 43 to 61 or soon after these starting or terminal dates. As regards the first, there are reasons for placing the arrival of the Second Augustan Legion in Dorset no earlier than 44 or even 45,[2] if time has to be allowed for the part played by Vespasian elsewhere in South Britain. He has long been assumed to have taken a leading role in a campaign in the south-east of Britain, through Kent to London. However, a case has also been

9.1 Stages of the Roman movement through Dorset, as suggested by the layout of the early roads (see also Fig 1.1)

made (Hind 1989) that the main landing of the Roman forces took place at harbours in Hampshire and Sussex. Thence, it is thought, they pushed inland north-west and north-east from a storage-base at Fishbourne. This theory has the merit of fitting into the discovery of the road-link between Lake farm towards Winchester. Was this the direction of an initial thrust by the Second Legion on land from the Hampshire Basin? Certainly, coast-wise, as a preliminary to tackling the problem of the West Country, the Isle of Wight was secured, as the Roman historian Suetonius reminds us. No doubt there was a landing at Southampton, the future *Clausentum*. There is general agreement that the military phase in Dorset ended with the Boudiccan revolt in 60–61 and its aftermath; the local impact will be discussed later. A critical date for our purposes is the estimate of A.D. 60 or so for the construction of the milirary base at Exeter,[3] since that event presumably took place when its predecessor at Lake was finally evacuated.[4]

Third, it is not unreasonable to assume that, from the moment of their arrival in Dorset, the Second Legion and its auxiliaries, working from a base at Lake, near Wimborne, had been set a major objective: to conquer and then pacify in the first place one particular tribe, namely the Durotriges of greater Dorset. Long ago, Richmond thought that the Roman plan in Britain, so far as it could be detected, was 'to deal with the tribes piecemeal'[5] and there is support for this view of Roman policy from what happened when the legion finally moved its headquarters westward. The city of Exeter in Devon, as its later civil name implies (*Isca*, of the Dumnonian tribe), was an early military foundation in the extreme south-east of that tribal area sometime after the mid 50s. In the same way, the base at Lake, similarly placed in respect of the Durotriges, seems to have been intended to deal with a specifically tribal territory. The difficulty remains: which was the other British tribe subjugated by Vespasian's forces? The Roman general seems to have been back in Italy by the time of the advance into Devon around A.D. 50. Did Lake Farm also serve as headquarters for operations to the north-east in Hampshire and Wiltshire, the lands of the mysterious Belgae, whose capital was Winchester (*Venta Belgarum*)?

Fourth and lastly, the system of military roads now shown to survive in Dorset must have been closely linked to the stages of the campaign against the Durotriges as well as suggesting garrisons in the hillforts to which they led. It always used to be thought that such roads basically followed the initial routes taken by the Roman army as it moved against an enemy. With the modern emphasis on the need for material proof that view has been somewhat in abeyance, though tacitly accepted for some roads and by some archaeologists. However, now there is every reason, in the face of the new facts, that such was the case in this county. Both the destinations of these roads and their pattern on the ground will therefore underlie much of the argument that follows.

Given the above provisos, the fourth of which formed the basis of Chapter 5, the attempt will be made to trace the Roman campaign through Dorset and to suggest the timing of the operation. Four main stages appear to stand out, distinguished by geography, logistics and above all, the layout of these early roads.

Stage I

The first question to be asked has been touched on above and will probably never find a completely satisfactory answer: How did the advance-guard of the Roman army first arrive in Dorset? Was it by landing at Hamworthy or was there a forced march from the direction of the Test valley along the line of the road built to connect Lake with the east? We can be certain only that the opening events of the campaign in the West Country were the result of the most careful advance-planning on the part of the Roman command. That, at any rate, we may conclude from the location of the first military sites. It is likely, on the grounds of distance overland and the evidence from Poole Harbour, that the main supplies for the legion and its auxiliaries came by water. If one object of the Lake Farm site was to cut off Hengisbury and the lower Stour valley, that was best supported by the landing at Hamworthy. It is of great interest that, for the years before the invasion, excavation has revealed close trading contacts between Poole Harbour and Gaul, and possibly further afield (Chapters 1 and 10). This was presumably the means by which Romans learnt of the best place on the Dorset coast for a safe landing by a large body of men.

The Hamworthy peninsula lay only 8 km south of the inland base to be set up at Lake and its choice ensured a successful start. It has indeed often been said that land-and-sea 'combined' operations did not form part of the regular routine of the Roman army, but what took place in this region of Britain during the Claudian invasion makes a different story. The original landings in Kent and possibly in Sussex had left a fleet of craft available and we can trace their use in the discoveries of early Roman finds along the South Coast. These suggest a series of small ports or anchorages: Fishbourne (where military structures of importance have come to light), Hamworthy, Radipole (Weymouth), and Topsham (Exeter). To this list may be added the mention by Suetonius of the capture of the Isle of Wight.

As in the case of any peninsula, the key to the situation at Hamworthy lay in the control of the narrow neck of ground, 800 m wide, linking with the mainland. Only by that route could an invading force make its way into tribal territory and later maintain a supply-line to its units in the newly conquered interior. The nearest native hillfort that might have represented trouble for the Romans was sited at Bulbury, only 5 km to the north-west, across easy country. Though not the largest of the Dorset strongholds, it must have been embattled and ready to harass the invader. The earthworks on Holton Heath (Chapter 8B) require to be finally proven by the spade, but appear authentic and in the right place. An auxiliary force stationed there was ideally placed to keep an effective watch on the access to the Hamworthy peninsula and its landing facilities.

Hamworthy soon saw the typical build-up of men and supplies of every kind that has characterized large-scale invasions all through history, although in most cases unrecorded. This unloading and deployment will have occurred at the same time as the construction of the first Holton Heath fort, Earthwork B. However, there was no point in the main contingent waiting on the peninsula, virtually hemmed in, and little time could have been lost before it was on its way to the site selected for the base-camp at Lake.

That spot beside the Stour enjoyed important advantages. A major force once entrenched there controlled the river gap in the narrow forest belt that separated chalklands from heath and it effectively cut off Hengistbury and Dudsbury from other tribal strongholds upstream. Furthermore, the Lake site lay on well-drained valley gravel and was protected by the waters of the Stour against the first serious adversary along the middle course of that river, namely the hillfort at Badbury Rings, only 5 km away. That was an easy march for an army stationed ready for assault; both distance and setting represent typical Roman military thinking, paralleled on occasion during Caesar's campaigns in Gaul.[6]

It is hardly likely that the attack on the Stour hillforts could have taken place until adequate stocks, especially of food, had been brought to Lake from the harbour. Grain and animals were not forthcoming in quantity from native sources until troops moved further inland and could to some extent live off the countryside. We would therefore expect that one of the first tasks of the camp prefect would have been to organize communications between sea and base. Several exposures in Corfe Mullen tell us that a first road from the harbour appears to have been laid out merely wide enough for single carts to move along in one direction. No other of the military roads identified was as narrow as this first phase from Poole Harbour. The next road-surfacing thereabouts, not long after, was twice as broad and flanked by a margo or side-walk. Only when this base-camp was securely linked to its port could the Roman commander have safely started to reduce the hillforts in the Stour valley.

A key battle undoubtedly developed at Badbury, which commanded the natural gateway into the chalk heartlands of Dorset through the gap already mentioned close to Lake. As a preliminary, the Romans had to neutralize the lesser hillfort of Spetisbury, 8 km upstream from Lake, but threateningly placed on the same bank of the river. It could not have been left in view of Badbury and unscathed, while Roman forces were engaged across the Stour. The fact that military buildings were apparently erected inside Spetisbury points to over-wintering from one campaigning season to the next, a stay that could have extended to at least one year. As at Hod Hill, the component units of the garrison were below strength, if the size of the probable barrack building inside Spetisbury is a guide. The famous mass burials at Spetisbury are not easily explained. They fit better into the post-Boudiccan situation, discussed later, although the badly recorded finds of weaponry still present difficulties.[7]

Badbury's later importance in the Roman period (when it became known as *Vindocladia* has always been attributed to the system of roads which came to be constructed with the hillfort close to their junction. Do these lines of communication intersecting in this way throw light on the conduct of the Roman invasion itself? The situation is further complicated by the discovery of the early military road to Hod. It has long been known that major Roman roads led to Old Sarum and to Bath from the fork north of the hillfort where the route from Poole Harbour branched into two. Now the fact that there was a road to Hod Hill turns a bifurcation into a trifurcation. Adding to the problem of sequence, the road to Dorchester itself forks from the Old Sarum road north of the hillfort and its behaviour in crossing the Bath and Hod roads has been thought to indicate a later construction than the Bath road.[8] Only the road from Lake to Badbury and then onward to Hod Hill is certainly of military origin. What then was the origin of the other two running north-west and north? Were they built by the military or under the later civilian administration?

There is agreement that the road towards Old Sarum was constructed to run straight to or from the junction at Badbury, so that the branch towards Dorchester is recognizable as a later addition built, it would appear, when the military sites at Hod Hill and, possibly, at Lake had been given up. The two angles at the Badbury trifurcation are exactly equal, which suggests that the three roads were surveyed and laid out by the same engineers, if not precisely at the same time.

If the Sarum road is seen therefore as the work originally of the Roman army, we are left with the implication that the massive hillfort at Old Sarum itself held a Roman garrison in the early phase of the campaign westward. Did this road linking with Old Sarum follow the path of a first thrust by the invaders northward from the Lake base or southward from old Sarum itself? The latter circumstance would have meant that part of Vespasian's forces had moved overland from the Southampton-Winchester area and originally from the port-facility at Chichester. If a Roman force had moved north, however, this route must be a much more likely way inland that the suggested alternative up the Avon valley to the east.[9]

There is thus a further tactical possibility that can be only briefly considered, as it takes us beyond the modern county, although still within the borders of the Durotrigian tribe. If Old Sarum was the site of a temporary Roman military presence, on the inference that the road from Badbury is early, then the known Roman road from Old Sarum towards Cold Kitchen Hill 26 km to the west and beyond may also reveal the direction of early movement by the Roman army. The major bases at Lake and then at Exeter seem in each case to have been established for the specific purpose of defeating one particular tribe. If the Old Sarum–Cold Kitchen Hill road had a military origin, it was laid out almost exactly through the strip of country that separated the Durotriges from the people to the north, the Atrebates. Such a manoeuvre by the Roman command would have effectively isolated the Dorset tribe and may be regarded as part of Stage II, after the Stour valley had been secured as far as Hod Hill.

The fall of the native stronghold at Badbury will almost certainly have been accompanied by the rapid seizure of the hillfort at Dudsbury and the capitulation of the promontory-settlement at Hengistbury, both cut off downstream. This was probably the moment in the campaign when the Roman army pierced a new entry into Badbury Rings on the western side. This implies not only that the inhabitants were forcibly ejected, but also that a Roman military unit was installed within. It is difficult otherwise to see the purpose of the reconstructed entry, which was one of the first in the series of similar engineering works in Dorset, described in Chapter 8E.

What would have been the special role of this early Roman outpost at Badbury? Five kilometres south across the valley, the remains of an earthwork on Candy's Farm have been interpreted as those of a signal-station serving the Lake base. The location was ideal to link with a Roman unit inside Badbury whose task could have been twofold: to keep watch and ward on a hostile countryside, and to be ready to pass signals across and along the Stour valley, with inter-visibility a vital factor in these precautions. It is generally accepted that the Roman army placed reliance on an efficient signalling-system to give early warning of threats to their forces. The case here is reinforced by the discovery of the probable fortlet-cum-signal-station on Keynston Down, 5 km west from Badbury and precisely midway along the 18 km separating Lake from Hod.

The 2.4 hectare site at Crab Farm[10] may have been constructed at this early point. However, until tested by excavation, its date must remain uncertain, although a Boudiccan connection is probable. However, its location, close to Badbury and with Spetisbury in sight across the river, might fit a highly volatile situation after operations in the immediate area, but before movement west or north-west.

Further up the Stour valley, the next major obstacle was provided by the twin hillforts at Hambledon and Hod Hill, of which the latter was the senior partner. It is true that there was an enclosed settlement at Buzbury Rings on the way. This has usually been denied the status of a hillfort proper and its siting and defences can have presented little problem, except later to obstruct the construction of a road.

At Hod Hill the installation of a Roman garrison inside the native stronghold was carried out with greater foresight than at other hillforts, since only there do we find anything like a defence perimeter organized in classical style. The nature and size of the garrison are important, as it was uncharacteristically made up of less than half a legionary cohort and half an auxiliary cavalry regiment. Did this arrangement mean that the Romans were hard pressed to find sufficient troops for these duties? Could it imply, too, that an auxiliary unit, normally posted on its own in an outlying fort, needed strengthening by the presence of legionaries?

The procedure may indicate indeed that, by the end of Stage I, the Roman army had reached its immediate limit in manpower, supplies and communications. The invaders now effectively held the Stour valley for some 40 km from Hengistbury to Hod Hill and it cannot have been a coincidence that the Lake fortress was sited midway between each of those important native sites. Such precision seems to be the result of choice rather than coincidence and supports the view that control of this long Stour valley tract was indeed the set objective of the Roman command in this opening phase.

It is probable, therefore, that, in order to consolidate the military position of the close of Stage I, the construction was completed of the following roads: Hamworthy–Lake (Phase 2 of that road, to judge by the section at East End), Lake–Badbury, and Badbury–Hod Hill. Those from Badbury to Old Sarum and from Badbury towards Bath were, it is suggested, the work of Stage II, a little later. There is also the road that ran from Lake towards Winchester, an early necessity for communication with that part of Britain already under Roman control. Roads connecting with Spetisbury and Dudsbury seem likely and while there is some indirect evidence for both, excavated proof is needed. Until, and even after, the completion of the first roads, we can expect a respite before progress westward was resumed.

The question arises: How long did these activities last, stage by stage across Dorset? Account must be taken of the various operations in this first stage: the landing of large numbers of men and animals with stores, creating a massive transport problem; the construction of camps and forts, temporary or semi-permanent; a variety of confrontations with the native Dorset folk in the open or besieged in hillforts; and, as a particular legacy that we can still trace relatively easily, the survey and laying out of the basic roads. The length of time required to subdue hillforts is discussed in Stage IV below, but, with eight major native sites in the Stour valley, something like three to four days each or one month overall seems to set a high standard on Roman efficiency.

Fresh research shows that both the quantity and the quality of timber required for camp buildings and fortifications have been under-estimated. The availability of this vital material, therefore, particularly where local timber was insufficient or unsuitable, obviously posed problems of timing and transport. It has been argued that the Roman army always brought in its train a supply of timber that had already been carpentered.[11] Moving the heavy beams needed for gateways and towers must have demanded good communications, first by sea, and then by adequately surfaced roads. In South-East Dorset, during this first stage, Vespasian's men laid down a minimum of 32 km of road that we can justifiably call military. To create this length of road, a recently suggested schedule would indicate that a minimum fortnight's work was required by a substantial body of men.[12]

It is difficult to fit all the activities of this initial phase into less than two months. Since the campaigning season before modern times did not normally cover more than the best six months of the year from April to September, the effort of the Roman invaders to obtain a firm foot-hold in Dorset could well have required half the period available. How far this kind of estimate can be trusted will be seen when the Roman campaign has been traced across Dorset and the timing set against the limited, but significant excavated evidence.

An important problem remains. How did the Roman command dispose the forces it had available? The original Lake fortress (whether of 12 or 16 hectares) was constructed on a smaller scale than a legionary headquarters of later days. In a conquered region the auxiliary infantry and cavalry were normally assigned to the smaller outlying forts. In Chapter 4, one view was noted that present evidence is insufficient to prove that legions were being fragmented in the first century in order to strengthen auxiliary detachments. However, Richmond's conclusion that the Roman camp within the native stronghold at Hod Hill held a mixed garrison of auxiliaries and legionaries makes us suspect now that this measure was repeated at other hillforts. Richmond estimated the total number of Roman soldiers within Hod Hill, combatant and non-combatant, as 718. On this basis, in order to place temporary garrisons in, say, eight hillforts, it would have required more than half the strength of Vespasian's combined army of some 10 000 legionaries and auxiliaries. A substantial mobile reserve had to be kept at Lake, so that the temporary garrisoning of hillforts in the early part of the campaign seriously held up the rate of advance against the Dorset tribe.

Stage II

If the period of two to three months suggested for the first stage approximates to what actually happened, then the next stage could have fitted into the second half of the first operational season. It is possible that into this second stage could be fitted the activities of a Roman force originating from Lake and operating in what is now South Wiltshire to tackle the hillforts of that area which archaeological finds tell us lay in Durotrigian territory. The early movement of Roman units in the direction of the Mendips and Bath (and, of course, South Cadbury and Ham Hill) must likewise be assumed, both from Lake and, as argued above, from Old Sarum. It is true that over the whole of Cranborne Chase north of Badbury only the odd discoveries give a hint of the Roman military presence and those finds were not necessarily related to the actual invasion campaign. However, Mendip silver-lead was apparently being exploited by A.D. 49 and the nearest route to the Continent led to Poole Harbour.

The Roman command had now to complete the control of Poole Harbour and the south-eastern Durotrigian lands, including the Isle of Purbeck. At the same time, it is likely, as outlined above, that the isolation of the Dorset tribe was ensured by a force moving westward from Old Sarum, and soon constructing its own roads in support. The key to developments westward from Lake lay in establishing a force at Wareham beside the lowest bridging-point of the two rivers, close to the tidal limit. This task must have been aided by water-transport from Hamworthy and overland by cover from the small fort on Holton Heath, distant some 5 km and 8 km respectively.

Roads have been shown to lead from Wareham to Woodbury and probably onward to Weatherby Castle; from Wareham to Bulbury, and, strikingly, from Wareham to Flower's Barrow. By virtue of their destinations they must be of military origin and possess double interest. In the first place, as they led to hillforts, they were presumably constructed along the routes taken by the Roman forces when moving into action. Then, the very existence of these roads means that they were built to serve temporary garrisons stationed within the hillforts, in accordance with the Roman policy long demonstrated at Hod Hill. Both Flower's Barrow and Woodbury enjoyed panoramic views of tactical value extending across the lower heathland in the direction of Wareham and as far as Bulbury and Woolsbarrow.

The reduction of the hillforts in the operational area which had Wareham at its centre marked an important phase for the Roman army. Wareham was ideally placed as a local supply base and retained its role when the army pushed on westward. There is no way of telling whether a successful assault on one hillfort led to the rapid surrender of others that thereby became isolated or had weaker defences, but such might have been the case here. However, we leave the realm of speculation with the positive evidence for the roads leading to all five hillforts, with the strong implication that a military detachment was stationed within each of the latter. With communications again the priority, in this phase of the campaign some 48 km of road came to be laid out, representing, once more, two to three weeks effort by a large work-force. This road-network soon included a branch towards the Corfe Castle gap from Hill View on the road to Flower's Barrow, the latter route remaining at this time the chief Roman line of communication in Purbeck. The five hillforts dealt with in this part of Dorset are comparable in number to the six that fell previously in the Stour valley and support the idea that a similar time-scale of two to three months might have been required.

If the identification of the two Roman forts on Holton Heath is correct, then it would seem logical that towards the end of this stage the smaller (A) replaced the larger (B). The initial landings have been safely carried out, more troops could be dispatched further west into Dorset. However, there was still a watch to be kept on the waters of Poole Harbour, with supplies now coming ashore at two places, while the road connecting the base at Lake with the post at Wareham was vital enough to require special patrolling duties.

It is suggested, therefore, that the first season of the Dorset campaign saw the army entrenched in its base at Lake Farm, controlling the main Stour valley and the lower basin of the Frome-Piddle. Of ten or so hillforts, more than half are known to have had roads built to them and must have held military units. These were not necessarily all of the size proposed for Hod Hill. Not included in this total are the northernmost hillforts of the Durotriges, sited just beyond the bounds of the modern county. They may have been dealt with by the Roman force based at Old Sarum and driving westward in the direction of Ilchester. The movement of this wing of the advance is strongly suggested by discoveries at two outlying Durotrigian strongholds. The footings of Roman military buildings have been discovered at South Cadbury, although the grisly massacre at the north-east gate is now thought to belong to the Boudiccan revolt. In the nineteenth century, quarrying at the other Somerset site on Ham Hill led to many finds of legionary and auxiliary equipment.

Stage III
It is possible, then, that the legion resumed operations against the Durotrigians in the second season of its arrival in Dorset, after it had over-wintered in the south-east of the tribal area. The hillforts tackled in this next move forward seem to fall into three groups, a view emphasized by the terrain and by the likely tactical deployment of Roman forces. In the case of the first group (A) the evidence is largely inferential, but groups B and C are backed by the knowledge that military roads can now be traced that reliably followed the initial thrusts:

(A) In the north of the modern county, there are hillforts at Mistlebury Wood and Penbury Knoll, which could well have been the targets of a Roman force advancing along Ackling Dyke from the direction of Badbury. This Roman road, as it survives today, is massively built up; this is not an original feature, but the result of re-metalling added at various periods. The only spot where the Dyke re-aligns in the course of many kilometres across Cranborne Chase is on Harley Down, equidistant from the two hillforts above (5.5 km from each). There is clear evidence that Mistlebury was never completed as a hillfort, but, as with many other similar sites, it has not been tested by systematic excavation.

A third hillfort, Bussey Stool Camp, may also have been reached about this time by the Roman army from Bradbury, working along the line of what was to become the road to Bath passing alongside.

171

(B) In Central Dorset, the secure fort established at Hod Hill in the first season became, in the second, a base for local operations. There were four Durotrigian hillforts lying in a generally western location from Hod: Banbury, Rawlsbury, Dungeon Hill and Nettlecombe Tout. It is impossible without digging to be sure that all of these were still occupied by tribesfolk in the mid-first century A.D. and so resisted the Roman invaders. Certainly the indications are that Rawlsbury came in that category. The military road replacing the ancient ridgeway from Hod to Rawlsbury is a pointer to what happened. It first led simply from the Water-Gate to the Stour, then was continued as an up-graded 'romanized' way to Rawlsbury, following the path taken by the original invasion force. To the knowledge that Rawlsbury was the destination of that road can be added the fact that its causewayed western gateway gives every appearance of Roman build. Furthermore, in general terms, the central position of Rawlsbury, amid the native strongholds of Group B, goes far to explain why a Roman unit should have been located here at this stage in the campaign.

(C) In South Dorset, the key to the further progress of the Roman campaign was to lie with the fort at Dorchester. There will be no quarrel with the view that it was set up after the capture of Maiden Castle and Poundbury. There is no reason why Poundbury itself, having succumbed, should not have served the Romans first as a marching-camp. The entrances to the hillfort, five in number, may include some created by the Roman military.[13] If the fort at Dorchester possessed the layout that has been outlined, then, as elsewhere, the expectation is that the roads leading to it from Lake and from Wareham followed the army's lines of approach from the east. The road from Lake via Stinsford was aligned, it has been argued, along the longitudinal axis of the fort at Top o' Town, whereas the other road from Wareham apparently arrived at a side-gate. Not unexpectedly, therefore, this arrangement would show it was through the main gate at the fort, the *porta praetoria*, that the road passed, communicating with headquarters. That road from Lake must confirm the route taken by the bulk of the forces destined to operate in the Dorchester area. The march of 32 km from the base at Lake, while not unusual when circumstances required, was probably broken by a marching-camp halfway or nearer Dorchester. Such a site might be sought at Stinsford, only 5 km from the major target at Maiden Castle and, as at Lake, protected by the course of a river. The role of Wareham was no doubt to furnish supplies and, if need be, reinforcements from a landing-place one third of the way nearer than Lake.

It is significant that the road that was soon built from Lake to Dorchester passed close to the earlier road-link from Wareham to Woodbury and even crossed the extension that may have led on to Weatherby Castle and was no longer in use. The implication here is that Roman units were quartered at those two hillforts only for the period between two campaigning seasons. This possibility supports the thinking that seems to have lain behind Roman military strategy, namely that troops should be moved onward as soon as a tribal district was regarded as sufficiently pacified.

What were the immediate objectives of the Roman forces that had reached the Dorchester area? There can be little doubt that this was the moment of truth for the defenders of Maiden Castle, the largest and most formidable of all the Durotrigian strongholds. But its fall, so dramatically revealed in the famous excavation of the 1930s, must have been accompanied by successful attacks on two others not far away, Poundbury and Chalbury. It is true that, despite excavation at and around Poundbury, little light has been thrown on events there at the time of the legion's arrival, although the native settlement extended from the hillfort down the slope and towards the site where the Dorchester fort came to be built. However, in Iron Age times the three hillforts enjoyed a mutual inter-visibility that an enemy no doubt had to take into account when engaged in hostilities.

There have been sufficient early discoveries at Radipole, Weymouth, to confirm that it had port facilities contemporary with the Roman military advance. Such would be a logical continuation of the land-and-sea policy last demonstrated in Poole Harbour. Hamworthy, Wareham and Radipole were the only military ports utilized by the legion along the Durotrigian coastline. In each case, as illustrated at Fishbourne, the preparations must have been considerable by way of moorings, landing-stages, and warehousing in addition to defence-works and barrack-buildings and would be carried out in the knowledge that the harbourage had to serve for at least one over-wintering period.

In this central southern area of Dorset, the reduction of three hillforts, the establishment of a forward post and a harbour were followed by the construction of important road-arteries running back from the Dorchester fort in its support towards Radipole (10 km), Wareham (24 km) and Lake Farm (34 km), giving a total of some 68 km. If we add the probable 32 km built in the other two areas of Stage II, at least 100 km had to be laid out, an undertaking that might have taken two months or so. The adaptation of existing native routes would have helped, but the importance of the Roman military road as such cannot be over-emphasized to ensure control after conquest.

If we now try to estimate the timing of Stage III, the triple thrust into North, Central and South Dorset may well have taken a month, allowance being made both for the preparations and for the immediate aftermath. To that should be added the two months for new roads. It is hardly necessary to recall that a road is not serviceable until completed, so that no further westward movement was possible for a minimum of three months. By then half the campaigning season would have passed. In any case, the Roman troops must have needed a respite at this point, with around ten hillforts to be occupied or demilitarized in some shape or form. A newly conquered people required a constant watch and the farmers in particular had to be persuaded to go back to their crops and animals, following the old adage of turning swords into ploughshares. The renewal of local activities, too, like marketing and pottery-making, would certainly be encouraged, not only between native and native, but also between native and Roman. The Roman army was now in the heartland of the Durotrigian tribe, and a further period of time possibly elapsed for police work against resisters and for deals with those Britons ready to collaborate. Then, with the autumn weather ahead, there could be little thought of further progress westward during that second year in Dorset.

Stage IV

In further campaigning the northern wing of the Roman advance will have continued progress through the Durotrigian territory that now lies in Wiltshire and Somerset. Its progress is therefore outside the present work, but we should recall the evidence for Roman garrisons of some kind inside the hillforts at South Cadbury and Ham Hill. The 'romanized' trackway which has been considered to have linked Old Sarum with Ilchester some 64 km west requires to be examined and substantiated, but it probably indicates, certainly in part, the supply-route that was soon brought up to standard, similar to that built westwards from Lake and then from Dorchester further south in the tribal area.

Within the bounds of the modern county, the Roman units stationed in the centre, with their local base at Hod Hill, may not have been moved forward at least for a couple of years. Occupation at Hod seems to have lasted no more than five to seven years, possibly as little as three or four, without the fort being reduced in size. It is not difficult to find reasons why the invasion thrust should have been temporarily halted in this area. The next hillfort to the north-west, at Milborne Wick in Somerset, was 16 km distant on the other side of the forested Blackmore Vale. When it came to the movement of large bodies of men, the terrain of the open chalklands further south presented an easier problem. There, well-documented Roman roads stretch away from Dorchester towards the west and north-west. The latter, connecting with Ilchester, must be of military origin, but arguably later in build than the first invasion thrusts, for the nearest major Durotrigian position lay just over 32 km away at Ham Hill, in South Somerset. On geographical grounds, that site was almost certainly an objective of the northern Roman advance outlined above.

By contrast, beyond Maiden Castle, for the 32 km westward from Dorchester as far as the river Axe (probably the tribal boundary) there extended a strip of country which was controlled by half a dozen hillforts. These included formidable or well-placed strongholds like Abbotsbury, Eggardon and Pilsdon Pen. It is not surprising, therefore, that the recognized Roman road running from Dorchester almost to Eggardon should here be claimed as a military construction, the work of the legion. Like some other early Roman roads in Dorset, it must have been part of a pre-existing native ridgeway. There has never been any dispute that this older way in prehistoric times continued to follow the high ground north-east of Eggardon, whence it swept round in a great arc to the north of the Marshwood Vale. Yet, strangely, there has been no positive quest in the past for the evidence of a Roman road superseding the older track on this obvious route. It was certainly followed by the army in the first instance in order to effect the subjection first of Eggardon and then of Pilsdon Pen.

The establishment of Roman routes (soon to be roads) from Dorchester to Radipole and from Dorchester to Eggardon completed the control of the Durotrigian zone that included Maiden Castle and Abbotsbury Castle and was limited on the south by the coast. Possibly, Abbotsbury, being so close to the sea, fell as the result of a combined land-and-sea operation. However, this hillfort may not have offered a sustained resistance, for the preoccupation of the Romans with native opposition seems to have centred further west, beyond Eggardon. There are no positive clues to suggest how Eggardon fell to the Second Legion, but it was ideally placed, we have seen, as a police post. It is not impossible that initially the bulk of the Roman forces continued along the ridgeway as far as Hackthorn Hill. From here, they apparently took an almost direct line to Waddon, dropping down to the lower ground of the Beaminster valley before climbing Gerrard's Hill to reach Waddon. Their fort on Waddon Hill and the road claimed to lead to it from the east seem together to provide insight into the invaders' tactics in more difficult terrain than that met earlier in Dorset. There was, indeed, evidence from the excavations at Waddon for an initial tented phase with slighter defences, suggesting this kind of role in the westward advance before timber buildings were erected and stronger defences constructed.

Waddon Hill cannot have furnished attractive quarters to soldiers from a warmer clime, but the narrow ridge on which it was poised had its advantages. North and south there were steep slopes, making deep defensive ditches unnecessary on those sides. Further west along the ridge and only 3 km away, the landscape was dominated by the highest hillfort in Dorset at Pilsdon Pen. Perhaps the most significant feature of the Waddon siting was the access from the east, across the Beaminster valley from Hackthorn Hill and then up Gerrard's Hill. Approach along this route was completely concealed from the distant watchers at Pilsdon, a visual advantage that also operated for the actual location of the Roman fort. If, in order to reach Pilsdon, the Roman troops had exclusively used the ancient trackway following the ridge round the north of Beaminster, they would have easily reached the gap controlled by the defenders of that hillfort, but their movements would have been visible for several kilometres. A double attack may indeed have taken place, with the strength of the force from the direction of Waddon remaining unknown until the last moment. After the capture of Pilsdon and the ejection of its inhabitants, there is evidence, not unlike circumstances at Hod, that the Romans installed a small military post of some kind within, access to which was improved by the creation of an extra causewayed entrance. There are indications from the behaviour of existing lanes and parish boundaries that the Romans created a metalled road from Waddon to Pilsdon along the north crest of the high ground, but fieldwork is required to substantiate the point. From the Waddon base and its Pilsdon outpost, the campaign was renewed against the group of Durotrigian centres of resistance left to be subdued as far as the Axe river-line.

Thus at Waddon as at Hod, there was, after the opening battles, it seems, the intention to establish Roman power within a radius of some 10 km in areas previously under the sway of a number of native hillforts in West and Central Dorset. To cope with an essentially similar military situation, the military fort at Waddon occupied an area one-third smaller than Hod. Other things being equal, this should mean a smaller garrison, although Webster expressed the view that both forts probably held the same number of legionaries and auxiliaries in the same number of barrack buildings. At Waddon Hill, because of destruction by quarrying in the past, the point cannot now be checked. However, Webster's estimate remains valid and supports the view that Waddon replaced Hod in a new advanced position during a general movement forward in the province. This manoeuvre, the argument goes, stemmed from the new policy set up in A.D. 47–48 by the second Roman governor, Ostorius Scapula. Confronted by the opposition of Caratacus in South Wales, Scapula placed the Roman army on the offensive. The excavated finds from both those Dorset forts do, indeed, point to the years A.D. 48–50 as a critical period in that re-deployment of forces in the region. How far does the close dating fit into the timing of the campaign in the Durotrigian territory, as we have been pursuing it?

During Stage IV, in West Dorset and the Axminster area of Devon, the Roman fort at Waddon was the local centre of operations, when around a dozen native strongholds found themselves the object of unwelcome attention by the legion. It may again seem speculative to reckon how long all this might have taken, although it is not difficult to arrive at a minimum number of days in which this part of the campaign might have been accomplished. Certainly, hillforts could hardly have fallen at the rate of one every day, for example. Even an average of only three days for each hillfort would represent over one month's active service without any respite. To this has to be added the time spent in bringing up to standard a minimum of 32 km of road from Dorchester to Waddon alone, a matter of at least a fortnight. We can exclude, at this point in the Roman advance, the work involved a little later in continuing the ridgeway road past Hackthorn Hill so that it developed into the main communication with Exeter. Thus we arrive at six weeks as the least time that can be allowed for the West Dorset campaign and its necessary aftermath and, given the terrain and the distance now from the main base at Lake Farm, that period looks an under-estimate. We should think of three months or half a season's campaigning as the probability. For the rest of that season consolidation was enforced by the nature of the terrain and by the closeness of a fresh tribal territory, beyond the river Axe.

175

When the stages detailed above are taken into account, then, on reasonably conservative figures, the Second Augustan Legion took three years *minimum* to move across Dorset and so complete the conquest of the native tribe. The view has been offered that entry into Dorset probably did not occur until A.D. 45, which means that the semi-permanent camp at Waddon Hill was not constructed, *at the earliest*, before the latter part of 47. This dating is not far removed from Webster's estimate of 48–50 and can overlap, should, for example, one of the stages in the campaign across Dorset require an extra season.

If the legion needed three to four years to cover the 64 km from Poole Harbour to the Axe, that hardly suggests that the Dorset tribe was easily subjugated. Certainly, the rapid campaign previously suggested by many does not fit the facts. Vespasian could not have been back in Rome by A.D. 44 if the Durotriges were one of the two powerful tribes he overcame. Equally, all the recent evidence from Devon has already forced views to change. No longer is it believed that the Romans had established control as far as Exeter before A.D. 47.[14] More realistically, we have been told, to quote only one view: 'These campaigns ... almost certainly extended over several seasons .'[15] The discoveries described in Part II of this book provide the substance to back that revised statement and allow Dorset to enter recorded history against a background of facts reflecting what actually happened.

Finally, it is interesting by comparison to read what the historian Tacitus said about Vespasian's successful battles in Judea against the Jews in A.D. 67 and 68: 'Good luck, a distinguished record and excellent subordinates enabled him within the space of two summers to plant his victorious flag throughout the whole of the flat country and in all the cities except Jerusalem.'[16] In the 60s the opposing forces were larger than here in central southern Britain, but the area involved was more extensive and the Jews must have been more sophisticated warriors than the Durotriges. If Tacitus implies that three seasons of campaigning, not two, were anticipated in Judea, that highlights the unexpected length of the operations in Dorset and its environs.

PART III
Of People and Places

10
Ptolemy's Isca

The most notable contribution to the geography of classical times came from the astronomer and mathematician, Ptolemy of Alexandria. His main work, compiled towards the middle of the second century A.D. lists nearly 10 000 places within and without the Roman Empire. For each named location Ptolemy provided details of its latitude and longitude that he had received from various sources. The first statistic was based on the notion of a smaller globe than actually exists (hence Columbus later thought he would reach India, not America) and the second took as its origin of zero degrees one of the Canary Islands, the furthest point west known in Ptolemy's day. Despite obvious shortcomings, the information made it possible to create a tolerable map of the known world. Britain, as seen by Ptolemy, was one of the subjects of a comprehensive work, *The Place-Names of Roman Britain*, 1979. It must long remain the major source of reference, but the siting and meaning of some place-names will always present problems.

Some twenty years ago the writer put forward new evidence concerning the location of two important sites in southern Britain listed by Ptolemy. The case appeared to gain some support at the time and, it will be argued below, has been strengthened by subsequent archaeological work. The 1979 study, however, made no mention of these suggestions and received some oblique criticism for not doing so. It is unlikely that those with access to that work and an interest in the early history of Dorset will also be aware of the note published in 1968.[1] The opportunity, then, is taken here to reprint the substance of the argument with its two illustrations updated and then to add some further observations in the light of fresh thought and research:

> The discovery of a Roman military establishment of some size near Wimborne in Dorset might have been forecast long ago, if the clues provided by Ptolemy of Alexandria had been read differently. This is the contention which it is hoped to substantiate in this note.
>
> First, we may compare Ptolemy's information[2] for the towns of Central Southern Britain with their actual geographic locations. To the known towns have been added: Exeter; the Iron Age hillfort at Maiden Castle; the

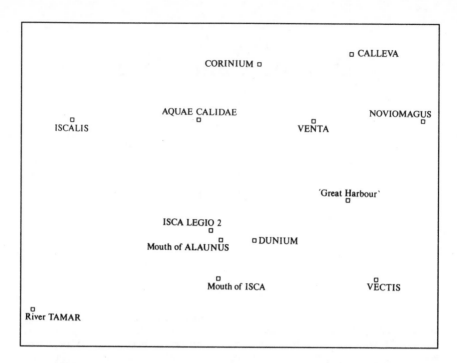

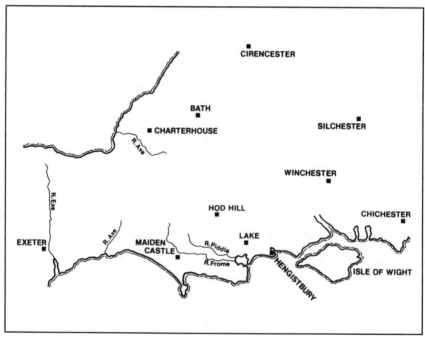

10.1–2 Central Southern Britain – Ptolemy's place-names and their location

Wimborne fort; and the Iron Age and Romano-British settlement at Hengisbury Head. We need to examine relative positions, Ptolemeian and modern. It can immediately be seen that the Wimborne fort is very close indeed to where ISCA LEGIO II AUGUSTA was placed by Ptolemy's figures. Exeter, normally, but unsatisfactorily located with *this* ISCA, is far more displaced from its putative Roman equivalent than any other town shown. Thus Ptolemy's CALLEVA, though more to the north than it should be, forms a triangle with VENTA and ISCA that is geometrically similar to the slightly smaller triangle Silchester–Winchester–Wimborne. We may also compare the two triangles AQUAE CALIDAE–CORINIUM–ISCA and Bath–Cirencester–Wimborne. So far, so good. But what about DUNIUM? If DUNIUM is Maiden Castle, we are back to having to accept Exeter as Ptolemy's ISCA. But a further glance at the maps provides a second candidate for identification with Ptolemy's DUNIUM, namely Hengistbury. If the case I have been arguing that ISCA and Wimborne are one is sound cartographically speaking, then Hengistbury as DUNIUM must greatly strengthen the issue. The similarity of ISCA–DUNIUM and Wimborne–Hengistbury is striking. By the same token, the pair Exeter–Maiden Castle are not only disproportionately sited in relation to all the other towns, but also too far distant from one another. What now is the archaeological evidence to support the contention that Ptolemy's ISCA was at Lake, Wimborne, and his DUNIUM at Hengistbury Head?

Regarding the site at Lake, it will be sufficient at this stage if we accept that Ptolemy's information referred to a military station there, whether or not it was actually called ISCA. In other words, by the time Ptolemy compiled his statistics (somewhere around AD 130, it is thought), confusion in name there may have been indeed, since by then LEGIO II AGUSUTA had been established at ISCA SILURUM for 50 years. But the confusion may have been between that ISCA (Caerleon) and the Wimborne fort ('ISCA' or not), with ISCA DUMNONIORUM adding to the trouble. It is not impossible that Isca with its Celtic meaning of 'water' or 'river' should have been the name of the Wimborne fort too, or perhaps *first*. For the military site there seems ideally placed close to an old bend of the Stour (Celtic 'powerful'), which finally reaches the sea by Hengistbury ... [The note here explained the importance of the Lake Farm site, then relatively unknown, and continued] ... The crux of the argument lies in the identification of Dunium with Hengistbury. In his report on the monumental dig at Maiden Castle, Wheeler supported the view, long held by antiquaries in the 18th and 19th centuries, that Maiden Castle was Dunium, one of the few named sites in pre-Roman Britain. He cautiously added in a footnote: 'This "agreement" is roughly relative to the position of known sites named by Ptolemy and is not of course absolute.' What claims has Hengistbury? As a trading port with widespread connexions, Hengisbury must have been well known before the Roman Conquest. Coin-distribution maps emphasise the importance to the Durotriges of the Stour Valley route with Hengisbury at its mouth. While the Maiden Castle excavation produced but 15 coins of pre-Roman date, that at Hengistbury yielded more than 3,000 and the settlement may have been minting its own type of cast coin. The pottery at Hengistbury is every bit as Durotrigian as that at Maiden Castle. The area of settlement at Hengistbury as revealed by excavation only is comparable to the whole of the interior of the hillfort. There was no end to occupation at Hengistbury as occurred soon after the Conquest at Maiden Castle,[3] for Roman coins and pottery continue into the second century and beyond. Hengistbury might seem to suffer the disadvantage that it ought to be a hillfort in a land of hillforts. But Ptolemy referred only to the 'town of Dunium'. It was not necessarily the capital (Wheeler's use of 'chef-lieu' suggested this). All we need ask ourselves is whether, on the evidence, Hengistbury could be Ptolemy's Dunium. I subject that this was the case and so, in turn, that Ptolemy's ISCA, was a direct allusion to, if not a name for, the newly identified military site at Lake, near Wimborne.

With the interval of time, the above note requires comment and addition, although its concluding words will be shown to retain their message. First, one important reference was unfortunately omitted. Although in 1943 Wheeler had given further credence to the equation 'DUNIUM = Maiden Castle', Rivet (1958) had later put forward a new idea: 'DUNIUM = Hod Hill'. His view, as then available, must be quoted in full: 'Ptolemy attributes only one *polis* [city] to them (i.e. the Durotriges), DUNIUM. This name, which suggests a hillfort, does not occur in any of the later authorities and has been thought to refer to Maiden Castle, but since Ptolemy normally lists only Roman or romanised places it might perhaps be better applied to the early Roman fort built inside the native stronghold at Hod Hill.' Rivet has further emphasized the apparent 'uniqueness' of that siting as strengthening its identification with DUNIUM.[4]

Rivet's view was a reasonable assumption when it was made, but its basis must now be held untenable. As things stand it is no longer the case that Hod Hill was the only hillfort in Dorset to have held a Roman garrison, and it was occupied for a shorter time than the much larger base at Lake Farm. The second of his facts was plain enough in 1979 when *The Place-Names of Roman Britain* was published. Yet, surprisingly, in that important standard work, Lake as a possibility known to Ptolemy was omitted, and Hod included. As it happens, Rivet and Smith did provide information indirectly furthering the argument put forward by the writer in 1968.

First, they made it clear that Ptolemy was using details of places in southern Britain that mostly seemed ' ... to date from Claudio-Neronian times or at latest early Flavian times'. In the earlier part of that period the site at Lake was still operational as a major legionary base. Exeter, however, does not seem to have fully superseded Lake before A.D. 60. Ptolemy could, therefore, have been using co-ordinates applicable to either location, though the one in Dorset better fits the argument.

Second, Rivet and Smith provided a map and a table comparing distances from London, actual and Ptolemeian, in respect of places identified in Ptolemy. Hengistbury-DUNIUM can be shown thereby to lie a little nearer the estimated Ptolemeian distance from London than Hod-DUNIUM (in Roman miles: Ptolemy's DUNIUM: 105, Hod Hill: 112, Hengistbury: 100). This may be splitting hairs, but the point has to be made. Out of thirty-six place-names listed in the table, Hengistbury-DUNIUM takes second place in accuracy and this would be right for a south-coast harbour long known to continental sea-captains.

Third, a most interesting identification is that of another place, ISCALIS, which lay, according to Ptolemy, somewhere west of AQUAE CALIDAE (Bath). This, thought Rivet and Smith, could well have been the name of the early Roman fort and lead-mining settlement at Charterhouse-on-Mendip. The name ISCALIS is taken to mean 'place on the ISCA river', a notion difficult to accept, since the site is 5 km from the Somerset river Axe (= ISCA) flowing into the Bristol Channel. This writer's suggestion is that the name was formed ISCA + ALIS on the analogy of QUALIS ('of what kind') and TALIS ('of such a kind'), so that it meant 'place that belonged to or was associated with ISCA'. Significantly Mendip lead was probably being mined from the area of Charterhouse as early as A.D. 49, on the indirect evidence of a stamp on what now seems to be a plaque rather than an ingot.[5] The mining was certainly being carried out in the mid 50s under the control of the Second Augustan Legion, directed, therefore, from Lake, which, as pointed out in the note above, credibly had the name ISCA in some way attached to the site. It is not acceptable that Exeter received its ISCA name *after* ISCALIS had been established for some time. This hardly seems a likely procedure, offering a major military site a name so close to that of its subsidiary, which had borne the name for some years already. The reverse more plausibly represents the actual circumstances: that is, a major military site could have given its name, suitably modified, to a minor fort dependent on it, a process that would also fit the early Roman activity at Charterhouse.

If the ideas so far presented additional to those of 1968 have any force, there is a case that the Lake site did indeed possess the name ISCA from its foundation. The original name was then carried onward to successive legionary bases: ISCA–Exeter and ISCA–Caerleon. The objection will be made that ISCA (British, meaning 'water') was the name of the rivers both at Exeter (modern 'Exe') and at Caerleon (modern 'Usk'). How then could the original base at Lake have been termed ISCA when the local river-name derives from a British word meaning 'powerful' in the present form 'Stour'. The explanation may be simple. In the English language today, we possess several common nouns or generic terms like 'river', 'stream', 'brook' and so on indicating varieties of water-course. The British language spoken from the time the legions arrived seems to have had similar closely related common nouns, of which ISCA and ABONA (modern 'Avon') are notable examples. But there are other modern river-names in the West Country which are derived from pre-Roman British *adjectives*. Besides 'Stour' above, there are 'Frome' (= 'fair, fine'), 'Brue' (= 'brisk') and 'Tamar' (= 'dark'). Such adjectives would in the first place have been associated with a second word, one of the British nouns for 'river'. Thus a new Roman military site could have found itself adopting one of these two elements for the place-name. Given the choice in the first instance of the simple common noun for 'river', it is not difficult to see why, in succeeding waterside sitings closely resembling each other, the name 'ISCA ' should have been retained.

There is in Ptolemy's *Geography* further circumstantial evidence (which the writer was not bold enough to submit in 1968) leading towards the same answer to the same question: Was it indeed Lake Farm that was pinpointed and named by Ptolemy's informant as the original location of the Second Legion in the West Country? Noticeably, Ptolemy's ISCA was placed almost exactly at the mid-point of the coast-line of southern Britain, between the Lizard (DAMNONIUM or OCRINUM) and the cliffs of Dover (CANTIUM promontory). Can it be coincidental that Lake Farm and Poole Harbour to the south are also situated at the mid-point of southern England? Again, not far away, Ptolemy's placing of St Catherine's Point on the Isle of Wight was extremely accurate, and this goes also for the siting of the mouth of the Tamar at Plymouth. If the Romans had reasonably accurate charts for any part of the British Isles it must surely have been the south coast.

What, then, of two rivers ALAUNUS and ISCA whose mouths Ptolemy located south of ISCA LEGIO II AUGUSTA? Much thought over the years has been devoted to their identification. Sited so near to the major southern Roman base, they cannot have been too far adrift from reality. Yet, if this ISCA was the Exe south of Exeter, the unknown river ALAUNUS runs impossibly athwart its course. A better solution can be found south of Lake in Poole Harbour, with its key role before and after the actual Roman invasion. The two Dorset rivers, Frome and Piddle, flowing into the harbour from the west would fit the situation. 'Frome' with an adjectival origin would have abandoned its ISCA. 'Piddle' is, however, a Germanic word of later Saxon introduction, having lost in its turn all trace of any British element, which could have been the missing ALAUNUS. Wareham, a focal point of early roads, lay between the mouths of these rivers, which must have been known to Roman navigators and chart-makers. The point is emphasized by the discovery that Poole Harbour had shipping contacts with Gaul in the years before the invasion, as well as at an earlier date. It has been noted that 'from Poole Harbour the rivers Frome and Piddle would have provided trade access routes to West Dorset'.[6]

11
Some Roman Personalities

It is a major defect in re-creating the drama of Romano-British days purely in terms of archaeological discovery that the human actors almost always remain shadowy figures without a name. This is particularly the case in Dorset, where, apart from the early military period, three and a half centuries were to pass leaving not a single positive link with a recorded historical event or personality. The few inscribed tombstones tell us little more than that certain individuals existed: Carinus, 'a Roman citizen', and his family at Dorchester; an officer of the Twentieth Legion, buried in the Cerne valley; a Romano-Briton at Tarrant Hinton, commemorated in the mid-third century. Villa excavations in Dorset have provided a fund of information on basic everyday living, but the estate owners will for ever be anonymous ghosts lacking the substance that posterity can attribute to beings of flesh and blood. We are luckier in what can be gleaned from the early Roman campaign in Dorset and its aftermath. Three Romans at least can be identified by name whose careers will have involved them in the military operations in various ways.

Before looking at these individuals, we should note the reluctance sometimes expressed by archaeologists to associate specific discoveries with documented events. After the Roman invasion, Britain entered the annals of history and thenceforward the temptation sometimes arises to link what is revealed in the ground with the scanty list of events and people known from Latin writings. That reluctance on the part of archaeologists is understandable, since it is easy on thin evidence to make far-reaching claims. However, there must surely be degrees of certainty and uncertainty. Nobody can dispute, for example, that well-dated charred deposits in Colchester and London are indeed relics of the Boudiccan revolt recorded by Tacitus and others. In the present case, for Dorset, we have a similar overwhelming probability that Lake Farm was the temporary headquarters of the most prestigious of the three Roman soldiers mentioned above, Titus Flavius Vespasianus, commander of the Second Legion Augusta and later in life, somewhat unexpectedly, emperor in his turn.

Suetonius gives a full portrait of Vespasian in his imperial role and he was undoubtedly one of the more acceptable Roman emperors: a bluff character of

11.1 Vespasian – a bust from Carthage (British Museum)

rustic origins and a disciplinarian with a sense of humour and a love of fairplay. His strong, square features have been faithfully rendered, it would seem, in a well-known bust that has survived the centuries. The details of his character and life-style do not require repetition here. We learn little specific about the man himself at the time of the invasion, when he was in his thirty-third year. Although of recent senatorial rank, it is interesting that Vespasian apparently owed his command of the legion to the support of an energetic freedman, Narcissus, enjoying a position of trust in the Claudian administration.

Another Latin historian, Cassius Dio, adds further details to the outline of Vespasian's part in the campaign as provided by Suetonius. At the battle to control the crossing of the Medway, following the first landings in Kent, Vespasian and his brother, acting as his second-in-command, reached the other bank and set up a bridge-head, critical to the success of the operation. Since Vespasian's promotion in charge of the Second Legion had begun at Strasburg in eastern Gaul, it is to be presumed that the same body of men was with him at the Medway. The information is important, since this involvement must have delayed the transfer of both legate and legion to Dorset, and is one reason why, in Chapter 9, that event was ascribed to the year 44 or even 45 rather than 43, as so often quoted.

We can be sure from the evidence in the county that the Durotriges of Dorset formed one of the two tribes defeated by Vespasian's generalship. Was the other tribe the Atrebates of Wiltshire and Hampshire or the Dumnonii of Devon and Cornwall? The latter folk in the far south-west seem ruled out, for the Romans did not appear at the hillfort of Hembury (north of Honiton) and the major base at Exeter before the 50s,[1] by which time (A.D. 51) Vespasian had been given a consulship in Rome. However that may be, his successful campaigning in Britain certainly brought him the award by the Roman Senate of honours known as *triumphalia ornamenta*. It has long been thought that Vespasian was one of those so decorated when Claudius returned to Italy from his brief visit to Britain late in 43 or early in 44. However, for that period of time, there is, it seems, an absence of solid proof that Vespasian gave up his command to return to Rome, whereas 'for a later date such as 46 or 47, there exists historical evidence, scanty and complicated though it may be'.[2] The revised timing of Vespasian's active service in Britain, as suggested, fits what has been proposed in Chapter 9: 'If Petilius' campaign extended over three seasons, it seems more probable that Vespasian's occupied three, those of 44, 45 and 46, than barely more than part of one.[3]

Vespasian, as legionary legate, was responsible overall for the safety and strategic employment of a large number of men, some ten thousand legionaries and auxiliaries. After the second-in-command, a senior tribune (his brother, said Cassius Dio), the third rank was an officer known as the camp prefect, *praefectus castrorum*. The man holding this important post had to organize all the basic engineering work, building and supplies required by the army units in question and his duties included the construction of roads. Significantly, the network of communications created in Dorset and traced in Chapter 5 was the particular contribution of Vespasian's camp prefect towards the happy final outcome of the hostilities against the Durotriges. We are fortunate in that it is possible, again with no need for reluctance in the statement, for the officer who fulfilled this task in Dorset to be identified. What is more, his background and career can be traced and throw light on the type of Roman staff officer who faced and solved very practical problems in the county nearly two thousand years ago.[4]

The facts come from an inscribed memorial stone, found in the nineteenth century, not here in Britain, but in far-away Turkey. The inscription reads as follows:

P.ANICIO
P.F.SER.MAXI
MO.PRAEFECTO
CN.DOMITI
AHENOBAR
BI.P.P.LEG.XII.FVLM.PRAEF
CASTROR.LEG.II.AVG.IN
BRITANNIA.PRAEF.EXER
CITV.QVI.EST.IN.AEGYPTO
DONATO.AB.IMP.DONIS
MILITARIBVS.OB.EXPEDI
TIONEM.HONORATO
CORON.MVRALII.ET
HASTA.PVRA.OB.BELLVM.
BRITANNIC.CIVITAS
ALEXANDR.QVAE.EST
IN.AEGYPTO.H.C   ILS2696

A free translation goes like this:

To Publius Anicius Maximus, son of Publius of the Sergian tribe, prefect to
Gnaeus Domitius Ahenobarbus, first centurion of the Twelfth Legion
Fulminata (The Thunderer), camp-prefect in Britain of the Second Legion
Augusta (The Emperor's Own), prefect of the army garrisoned in Egypt,
decorated by the Emperor for his campaign services and awarded the Mural
Crown and the Unsullied Spear for his part in the British War, the city of
Alexandria in Egypt (has dedicated this stone) in his honour.

This inscription came to light at a town today called Yalvac, 225 km south-west of
Ankara. It was known in ancient times as Antioch of Pisidia to distinguish it from
the more famous Antioch further east, situated in what was then the Roman
province of Syria. Roman practice makes it certain that such a stone as this could
have been raised only at a man's *origo* or birthplace. So here we have a
commemorative tablet erected in the middle of Asia Minor by the city council of
Alexandria to honour a person whose career literally spanned the Roman world
from its north-west frontier in Dorset to the mouth of the Nile. In detail, his story
has much of historical interest.

As in the case of later British examples like *Col*chester and Lin*coln*, (whose
modern names remind us of the fact), Pisidian Antioch was the site of a Roman
colony established by Augustus in 25 B.C. The army veterans who settled there
were Italian ex-legionaries who, as a reward for long service, were given land in a
new colony. They were assigned collectively to a Roman voting tribe, the *Sergia*.
So the paternal grandfather of Maximus might have been one of the original
settlers at Antioch. In the present case, the association was with the Sergia tribe.
The name of the *gens* or clan – Anicius, and of the family – Maximus, could well
have replaced names of barbarian or non-Latin origin. A little later, there is a
record in Asia Minor of a governor of Bithynia called Anicius Maximus, probably
a relative, even, maybe, the grandson of our Maximus. In the later Roman
Empire, the family of the Anicii were to become even more prosperous and
influential.

The inscription goes on to state that Maximus was sometime 'prefect of Gnaeus
Domitius Ahenobarbus'. Now, the leading municipal figures in a Roman town
were the *duoviri* or 'two men', similar to the two consuls who were annually

elected to govern the Roman republic. Occasionally notable Romans, members of or close to the imperial family, were elected to office by the town council, anxious perhaps to obtain the good offices of someone influential at Rome rather than hoping the offer to be accepted. When the high personage agreed, though unable to serve in person, he would name a replacement or ask for one to be named. With *praefectus* in its proper sense of 'someone acting for another', it is apparent that this was the way Maximus obtained office in his native town. Ahenobarbus, belonging to a well-known Roman family, was the father of the emperor Nero and died in A.D. 40 at the age of forty. Nero was only three in that year and inherited one third of his father's estate. However, the emperor Gaius Caligula, who was also named in the will, not only took everything, according to Suetonius, but also banished Nero's mother, Agrippina. Later, when Claudius succeeded Caligula, Nero had his inheritance restored. Apart from its general interest, then, this link with Nero's father also indicates when Maximus is likely to have served in Antioch as magistrate. It was probably in A.D. 32 that Ahenobarbus married into the imperial family; he may have been offered a magistracy by a provincial town after that, but possibly at an earlier time if he had a local connection with the town. A closer date for Maximus' year of office may emerge as we examine his life as a Roman officer.

In this respect, the key entry on the inscription is the double reference to Britain. The new information about the activities of the Second Legion in Dorset soon after A.D. 43 needs to be related to Maximus and the post he held. First, however, what was he doing earlier in his military career, one year having been spent, we know, as magistrate at Antioch?

Maximus is named as *p.p.* or *primus pilus* (first javelin) of the Twelfth Legion Fulminata – otherwise the first centurion of the sixty-odd who were the regular officers commissioned to take day-to-day control of the 5000 legionaries. That legion was apparently then stationed in Syria, but to have reached this respectable staff-rank, Maximus must already have had a long period of service elsewhere. If he had begun in the ranks he might have been something like twenty years of age in A.D. 13, while if he had received a direct commission, his army career could have started at thirty in A.D. 23 or so. His early service was most likely in eastern legions, ending with his appointment in the Fulminata.

His promotion and transfer from that legion to the Second stationed in Strasburg probably took place by A.D. 39 when he was about forty-five. It is thought that his first major decoration was awarded by the emperor Gaius Caligula and this would fit events in that year. The campaign (*expeditionem*) would have involved action against German tribes across the Rhine or perhaps against rebels in Gaul. As a reasonable assumption, therefore, it was between 32 and 39, before he left the eastern Mediterranean, that Maximus obtained special leave to act as twin-magistrate in his native Antioch. After 39, Maximus must have been busy not only with operations from the frontier fortress at Strasburg, but also with preparations for the invasion of Britain, initiated by Caligula, and then effected by Claudius.

What were the kinds of duty undertaken by Maximus as camp-prefect of the Second Legion? A quotation (in an eighteenth-century translation) from the *Epitoma Rei Militaris* by the later Roman writer Vegetiius gives a good idea:

The praefect of the camp ... had a post of no small importance. The position of the camp, the direction of the enrenchments, the inspection of the tents or huts of the soldiers were within his province. His authority extended over the sick and the physicians who had care of them; he regulated the expenses relative thereto. He had charge of providing carriages, mules and the proper tools for sawing and cutting wood, digging ditches, raising parapets, sinking wells and bringing water into the camp. He likewise had the care of furnishing the troops with wood and straw, as well as the rams, *onagri, ballistae,* and all the other engines of war under his direction. This post was always conferred on an officer of great skill, experience and long service and who consequently was capable of instructing others in those branches of the profession in which he had distinguished himself.

There are also references in Tacitus to a military detachment busy with roads and bridges and in the charge of the prefect of the camp. Not all these functions would leave indelible traces in the ground to remind us of the prefect's efficiency, but the range covered does include many items still traceable to spade and trowel. As we have seen, the siting of camps, their defence systems, the supply of water and road communications were all essential to the process of conquest and pacification. All the same, these activities in Dorset cannot be considered the principal explanation for the decorations that Maximus received in 'the British war'. While his organization skills have left their mark still visible in Dorset soil, we must not deny him credit for setting a personal example in battle-operations. The *corona muralis* was a real crown, representing a wall, and was, at least originally, made of gold. As its name indicates, it was intended to go to the first man over the enemy wall. However, Maximus was about fifty in A.D. 43, so we might think of the *corona* as a general issue to senior officers in the victorious legion, when Claudius held his triumph the following year. The *hasta pura,* a full-sized spear of silver or gold, often accompanied a crown, rather like a bar to a modern British medal, except that it was awarded apparently on the same occasion.[5]

We do not know how long Maximus was posted in Dorset. It was proposed in Chapter 9 that the campaign against the Durotriges took two, possibly three, seasons to complete. Therefore, with this objective achieved, his term of duty ended. Is it a coincidence that in one recent view mentioned above, Vespasian may also be considered to have served in Britain until 46 or 47 at least? A victorious legion could be expected to have been led by a team who worked well in partnership and was split only at the end of the task in hand.

We have noted a natural disinclination among archaeologists to associate specific earthworks or excavated remains with known historical events, unless there is clear-cut proof. The reluctance is even stronger when it comes to named individuals. However, in Dorset, the timing of the Roman campaign and the succinct details provided by historian and inscriptional mason must provide a different backcloth against which to view the forts and roads. Certainly, Vespasian has always been recognized as the G.O.C. of the local Roman forces. But it is surely time for Publius Anicius Maximus to receive equal recognition as what we might call his quartermaster-general, the third in command in the legion and the man most directly responsible for the ground evidence still recoverable nearly two thousand years later?

At any rate, in his day, Maximus found that recognition and went on to serve with even loftier rank elsewhere in the empire. As it happens, there was a third Roman officer from the Second Legion, whom we can positively associate by name with Dorset during the military occupation. He held exactly the same post as Maximus, but had a very different fate. This was Poenius Postumus, who fell on his sword at the time of the Boudiccan revolt, beset by the dishonour that he thought he had brought to his fellows. The scanty details are later discussed in their historical setting. If we cannot be certain whether Poenius was in Dorset or Devon, or even elsewhere, when he took his life, the event illustrates how keenly the concept of personal disgrace could be felt in the Ancient World. Did he, as *felo de se*, receive due cremation, and was the resting place of his ashes commemorated by a tablet yet to come to light?

A final Roman personality who should be mentioned as a probable visitor to Dorset during the initial military period involving Vespasian is the governor of the new Roman province, Aulus Plautius. His was the direct responsibility for the successful prosecution of the subjugation of lowland Britain. It is impossible to think that for the three to four years of his governorship he did not leave his headquarters, presumably at Colchester, in order to inspect the regions recently brought into the Roman orbit. Certainly, Claudius rated him so highly that the emperor went forward to meet him on his return to Rome so as to present his decorations in person.

PART IV

The Military Phase in Dorset

12
An Uneasy Peace

The most intractable task in archaeology is trying to bring back to life the human relationships, social, political or religious, from the material remains of a lost past. Mostly the matters are too complex to be in any way even adequately explained by sherds of pottery, coins or scraps of metal or stone, the residual debris recovered from most excavations. Occasionally, however, light may well be cast on known historical circumstances by discoveries from the ground. The fifteen years or so of Roman military presence in Dorset have left no certain trace in written record, although the confrontation of Roman legionary and Durotrigian tribesman must have proved a time of challenge and intrigue. Yet the very shortness of that period may help us to understand what happened. Archaeology can demonstrate that in that brief spell there were major changes in local responsibility, production and marketing. Can we reasonably infer native reactions to these events? The answer must surely be yes, provided the experiences in so-called 'occupied' countries through the centuries can be invoked to reinforce evidence which in itself may not seem to have a story to tell.

The invasion of a foreign territory and its subsequent integration into the political structure of the conqueror have predictably always divided the newly subject people into three broad groups. At one extreme, there are the elements in the native population who continue to oppose the newcomers in every way open to them. This will include those who prefer the doubtful fruits of a struggle for independence to the assured safety of what they regard as dependent servitude. At the other extreme we find people prepared to work with the invader and even to welcome him, given the right terms – in the modern world they are looked upon as either 'realists' or 'collaborators', according to the standpoint of the individual. These stark hues of black and white at the margins, as in all human situations, shade off to greys of all kinds in the central mass of the folk living in the occupied territory. The Second World War and events in many countries since have made us familiar with the problems lying behind words like 'resistance', 'outlaws', 'freedom fighters', 'extremists' and so on. Pressures and loyalties of clan and family become exacerbated by threats and fears of exposure. Many would choose the compliance of the Vicar of Bray and prefer a quiet settled life to the blandishments of openly declared attitudes. But, as events develop, people are forced to adopt one extreme or another, albeit unwillingly and temporarily.

All these circumstances were familiar to everyone living in the periphery of the classical world, whether inside lands freshly incorporated in the empire or just outside in one of the barbarian tribes, conscious of the menace of Rome. The familiar concept of 'divide and rule' associated with Roman power found concrete expression on the grand scale in the creation of client-kingdoms of friendly peoples bound by treaty. In Britain after the Claudian invasion, history and archaeology combine to present notable examples of such Roman policy and of its reception by some Britons. Thus Cogidubnus, king of the Sussex tribe now known as the Regni, appears to have helped the Romans at the time of the invasion. He is known to us partly through an approving mention by Tacitus, partly through an inscribed stone found long ago at Chichester, and there has been much speculation about his exact position in the Roman world. Whatever that might have been, his main contribution to the success of the invasion in the South was probably to ensure the use of the base and port at Fishbourne, near Chichester. This action placed his people on a friendly footing with Rome, as against the evident hostility further along the south coast when the invader reached Dorset.

There is strong evidence, as we have seen, for the wholesale forced evacuation of hillforts in Durotrigian territory (i.e. 'Greater Dorset') after the Roman conquest, if only in those cases where the newcomers installed temporary garrisons. In general, we can but guess at the place held by an Iron Age hillfort in the life of the tribesfolk. It was no doubt degrading enough for the chieftain and his family and immediate followers to be turned out of their ancestral home. The hostile feelings of the vanquished towards the victors must have intensified where the invaders set up a military station inside what had been for generations a respected native stronghold and a local ceremonial centre. Thus, at Hod Hill, the inhabitations suffered the double ignominy of seeing their principal hut peppered with ballista-bolts and then having to withdraw completely for the installation of a major Roman fort. At Maiden Castle, it is probable that the dispossessed were allowed to re-build their village on the low ground to the north of the hillfort. They were in full view of their ancient fortress, which was to retain their esteem through the Roman period. Outside South Cadbury, the Durotrigian hillfort now in Somerset, a similar hamlet was constructed by the native folk after their defeat by the Roman army. There can be no doubt that the Roman command, from the beginning, was ready to show the Durotrigian folk that the conqueror could be generous in his attitude towards a courageous foe. Otherwise how to explain the 'war cemetery' at Maiden Castle, where the native dead were able to be buried by the survivors with traditional rites on the scene of their defeat? As we shall see, episode contrasts with massacres at hillforts that the legion carried out on a different occasion and for different reasons.

It is obvious that the Roman invasion would have created life-long antagonism and a desire for revenge among some elements of the local tribe. These feelings required a full generation to dispel, but would have been nurtured to support activities in the immediate aftermath. Thus one class of extremists was established, strongly anti-Roman. In the early years of Roman rule, British resistance in general found a leader in the legendary figure of Caratacus, who rallied support among tribes still beyond the conquered territory, particularly in Wales. In A.D. 47 the counter-measures taken by the second Roman governor Ostorius Scapula included the disarming of native Britons within the new province. This understandable procedure instigated a first revolt by the Iceni of East Anglia, who 'had voluntarily acceded to the Roman side'. It would be interesting to know whether or not that rising involved the local tribesmen in any way. Probably not directly, for, by contrast, they had just been fighting a hard and unsuccessful series of battles against the Second Legion.

Indeed archaeology tells us that some of the Durotrigian tribe very soon co-operated with the new masters, to the extent at any rate of producing goods and foodstuffs, probably by way of trade rather than as a result of coercion. The best example of this development comes in the shape of pottery, a common find in excavations, but in this case a revealing one.

Pottery was one essential item that did not always travel well in a military supply-train, whether land- or sea-borne, and in its coarse every-day form it was heavy and fragile. While the soldier had his bronze mess-tin for active campaigning purposes, in a semi-permanent camp requirements were more elaborate. At table, officers could use better quality imported ware, soon brought in by traders from Gaul, but there was always a high demand for kitchen vessels of barrack-room standard. Probably the commonest sherds found in excavation at Lake Farm have come from vessels of coarse Durotrigian ware, easily identifiable in a number of ways as the product of local potters. These included a type of bead-rim bowl, similar to those vessels which strikingly accompanied the native burials in the war cemetery at Maiden Castle. These vessels were often used in cooking, as shown by traces of fire around their base. The urgency of the military demand for such comparatively low-grade pottery has been further demonstrated by the discovery at Corfe Mullen, near the Lake base, of kilns,[1] operating around A.D. 50 for the supply of the Roman army. This site did not confine its activities to turning and firing jars and bowls of local Iron Age inspiration. There was also a considerable output of romanized wares, notably jugs and flagons in a characteristic whitish clay, intended for table use by all ranks of the Roman forces. Yet another recognizable product was a mortar for pounding food, an everyday culinary utensil in the Mediterranean world, and definitely not of Iron Age origin.

How precisely these romanized innovations were introduced is not certain. The native potters may have copied examples given to them or they may have learnt from someone familiar with Roman tastes who had been brought in specially from the continent or from the more sophisticated tribal areas of south-east Britain. What the finer wares do certainly demonstrate is co-operation with the new arrivals by some members of the Durotrigian tribe. Duress may have played its part at the start, but that would not explain the surprising growth of the local pottery industry as a supply source for the army in subsequent years. Dorset black-burnished ware ('BB1' to distinguish it from 'BB2', a similar ware from somewhere in eastern England) came to be manufactured in quantity on the south shore of Poole Harbour and it was used at all the military sites in Dorset. It continued to be supplied to the units long after they had left this tribal area. Such assiduity by the local pottery workers can be explained only by the fact that it was well worth their trouble. But another kind of trouble could always have threatened from the opposition of fellow tribesmen clinging to hopes of regaining their old freedom. Indeed the closeness of the Corfe Mullen kiln to the Lake fortress suggests its operators may have enjoyed some degree of Roman protection.

The durability of potsherds as evidence in the ground tends to make us forget in what quantity other vital materials must have reached the Roman garrisons in Dorset from Durotrigian craftsmen and farmers, either willing or perhaps forced to trade with the newcomers. Although the legionary ranks could rely on soldiers who were also smiths or carpenters, basic materials like timber, crude iron, leather and corn had soon to be obtained locally. Some of these do not leave much by way of archaeological evidence, although, despite that, their source can sometimes be traced. It is interesting that two military sites in Dorset (Hod and Waddon) have yielded fishbones of cod, while one (Waddon) has shown that wrasse was consumed. The latter species in particular is caught off British shores. To these we can add oysters, a dish prized, it would seem, by the legionary commander at Hod outside whose kitchen a pile of shells accumulated. Again at Waddon Hill, two different species of oyster have been identified, as well as the common cockle. What is significant about such saltwater food is that native fishermen and merchants were almost certainly involved, implying further groups of tribesmen who co-operated with the newcomers.

From Dorset sites, sufficient bones of domesticated animals – sheep, cattle, pig – have been recovered to establish the reality of contacts between the Roman army and the native peasantry. Were these contacts made in the course of marketing and bulk-buying or when supplies were simply sequestrated, possibly in the form called taxation? It is difficult to say. The farmer, unlike the fisherman, had little mobility and could not easily avoid unwelcome demands by the new masters.

The same problem of human relations between conquerors and conquered comes up in the matter of corn supplies. Cereals were a vital commodity in the everyday diet of the Roman solider, and the chalklands of southern Britain a source of abundant harvests. There are references to this type of situation across the Channel in Caesar's *Gallic War*, as, for example, when the Romans were settling down to the siege of Avaricum (Bourges): 'To maintain a supply of corn he [Caesar] kept importuning the Boii and the Aedui; but the Aedui were lukewarm and gave little help, while the Boii, a small and feeble tribe, had only slender resources, which were quickly exhausted.'[2] These were circumstances easily transferable from Gaul to Britain only a century later. Fragments of military 'donkey-mills' of Pompeian type have been found both at Hamworthy and Corfe Mullen, not far from Lake, and underline the importance of this product to the Roman commissariat. Corn brought across the Channel from Gaul would have travelled in the husk rather than as flour. While such a mill cannot confirm the source of the grain, it is possible that, when the eastern half of Dorset with its cornlands had yielded to the imperial standard, the Roman command was able to obtain at least some supplies. Nevertheless feeding an extra 10 000 men (not to mention the transport animals) must have over-stretched matters in the tribal area so that imports from Gaul or from friendly tribes in eastern Britain probably continued for some time. Whatever the case, even if the tribe had had a corn surplus for export before the invasion, the Durotriges would not have been happy to cope with these foreign mouths and one can only guess at the tensions created.

Thus there are very sound reasons for suspecting divisions within the ranks of the local tribe as soon as the Roman army began to organize supplies, whether of food or of raw materials. If we lack the authentic comment of Caesar's words in Gaul, the archaeological evidence in Dorset is hardly mute, so long as we accept the relevance of human parallels in different countries and in different centuries.

During the military phase in Dorset, the new roads, built to connect army units, were probably followed only by natives trading with the Roman garrisons. It was only after the departure of the legion and the growth of town-life and later of villa-estates that the roads were to see sustained use, depending on their convenience for civil purposes.

There were Roman garrisons in this area for fifteen to twenty years. Excavation tells us that Hod Hill was apparently occupied by a combined army detachment from the beginning until the early 50s, while activity at Waddon was understandably a little later, from around 50 to 60. Richmond attributed the end of the Roman occupation of Hod Hill to a serious fire. He ruled out that it had to do with demolition and thought accident a more likely cause than hostile action. It is indeed possible only very indirectly to link Dorset with what happened elsewhere in Britain as tersely recorded by the Roman historian Tacitus. The early revolt led by Caratacus, during the late 40s and early 50s, must have had at least sympathetic support from the Durotriges, but, centred as it was in Wales and the borders, to establish local connections of any kind will never be easy. We may note in passing that the ambivalent British attitude towards Rome is well illustrated by what happened to Caratacus. After his final defeat, he sought refuge with the Brigantes, a tribe of the Pennine region, but was handed over to the Romans by the Brigantian queen, Cartimandua. To his undoing, she no doubt wished to cultivate their friendship and possibly stave off invasion.

Before the mid 50s A.D. , sufficient confidence was felt in the pacification of the Dorset tribe for the Roman command to be ready to push on westward and north-westward from Dorset. An inscribed lead ingot[3] from Northern France makes it probable that as early as 49 the mineral was being exploited in the Mendip Hills on behalf of the Second Augustan Legion. There are various other indications beyond Dorset of such a movement. Thus a signal station was established at Old Burrow on the North Devon coast, apparently to keep an eye on the Bristol Channel and insurgent tribes over in South Wales. In Central Devon, Roman Forts of various sizes are now known at North Tawton, Okehampton, Bury Barton and several other places. Nevertheless, the main base of the Second Legion seems to have remained at Lake Farm until after 55 and probably as late as 60–61. A small force probably stayed even a little longer at lake, but its abandonment as the legion's headquarters was the occasion for the construction of a new base at Exeter in the territory of the Dumnonian tribe in Devon, clearly a development of great importance.

The precise date when that first fortress was set up at Exeter will probably always remain a matter of some uncertainty,[4] but on present evidence the move seems to have occurred by 60 and probably late in the governorship of Didius Gallus (52–57). However, the creation of the Exeter base was not without further and even enhanced economic involvement with Dorset. The continued dependence of the army on its original pottery supplies is significant: 'the majority of the coarse wares used by the legion were produced by the black-burnished ware industry of South-East Dorset.'[5] Indeed, those Durotrigian potters went on obtaining contracts from Roman quartermasters for many years, sending their products as far as South Wales and, ultimately, even up to Hadrian's Wall when that was built. There was a renewal of such contracts in the North during the fourth century, so that the impact of the Second Legion on aspects of life in that part of Dorset was long-lasting.

One of the most interesting discoveries in excavations at Exeter has been the great suite of legionary baths, where most notably 'considerable quantities of Purbeck marble from South-East Dorset were employed for internal decorative features.'[6] The use of this material in Roman times for inscriptions, mortaria and building details has long been known, but the Exeter finds are among the earliest dated examples yet. Certainly there are baths awaiting discovery at Lake Farm and there can be little doubt that the narrow seam of Purbeck marble was being exploited soon after A.D. 50 in the vicinity of Wilkswood Farm, near Langton Matravers. The early military roads in Purbeck gave easy communication with Wareham, which probably acted as the entrepôt for the expanding trade in this newly prized material. The signs are that crude blocks of the stone intended for buildings were transported to be finally worked at their point of use. No doubt, by labouring in the quarries, the local natives would have been happy to act as casual workers to supplement their subsistence as peasant farmers. But perhaps some Durotrigian recalcitrants had to act as forced labour in a chain-gang.

The early military presence in the Isle of Purbeck also had repercussions on the production of another local mineral. This was Kimmeridge shale, hard and black when first extracted from the ground, but deteriorating to a flaky brown after long exposure to the elements. Part of a tall vase of shale, turned on the wheel, was found at Lake in 1981, possibly an example of the army trading with the tribesmen. But shale made good tesserae for flooring, which also reached the Exeter base, along with other articles of the same material.

The first years under Roman military rule cannot have proved particularly easy for the Durotrigian people. There is still much to learn about the material contacts between the tribe and the legion during the military phase. While new opportunities, it is true, had brought profitable livelihoods to some, especially those living in Purbeck, the old animosities must have rankled with many other members of the tribe. Roman units were eventually leaving the hillforts, but it is unlikely that the leading tribesmen were allowed to return to their old strongholds and sanctuaries.

One of the remaining mysteries centres on the dwellings of the Durotrigian people. Sometime in the later first century, the typical Iron Age round hut came to be replaced for many folk by rectangular timber-framed huts. The change has been noted and reliably dated to the 70s at places as far apart as Studland and Uplyme, near Lyme Regis. This was after the departure of the last units of the military from Dorset, yet it is tempting to see in this development the impact made by the orderly barrack buildings of the Roman army on local Britons. While appreciating the advantages of wide, settled markets in the civil zone of the new Roman province, they can hardly have failed to have noticed the greater convenience of the rectangular plan as a framework for everyday living. Yet during the relatively short military occupation, it is likely that the old way of living continued more or less unchanged for the majority of the tribe. Circumstances were otherwise for those turned out of hillforts. North of Maiden Castle, on the low ground, a settlement is known (Bowen and Farrar 1970) involving a rectilinear layout of plots and, almost certainly, dwellings. Dated to the mid-first century A.D., the site may be regarded as a 'plantation' of the former inhabitants of the neighbouring hillfort, built therefore under Roman direction.

13
Dorset and the Boudiccan Revolt

The Boudiccan revolt is generally dated to A.D. 60–61 and is well recorded in two works by Tacitus. A number of factors contributed to the discontent that lay behind the rising: loss of independence, taxation in payment for foreign innovations, and highhanded behaviour by some Romans, especially in the territory of the Iceni in East Anglia, home of the Boudiccan royal line. Additional encouragement came from the absence of the governor Suetonius Paulinus and a substantial part of the military forces, who were campaigning against the Druids in North Wales. The full story outside Dorset has been told:[1] the defeat of part of the Ninth Legion, the sack of Roman towns, including London, and the final victory of a re-assembled Roman army. Our concern here will be to assess the involvement in the rebellion of the Second Legion and of the Britons in its military zone.

Tacitus refers to a general rising, but we do not know for certain if the Durotriges of Greater Dorset or their tribal neighbours took a direct part, whether by engaging in local attacks or by sending a contingent to join Boudicca's warrior forces. Their original resistance to the invasion and Roman policy in respect of the hillforts suggests that some of the Durotriges at least would have supported Caratacus and now were ready to heed a summons from Boudicca. However, there are clues from Tacitus and from excavations that combine to throw light on a situation otherwise plunged in gloom.

The best-known incident linking the Second Legion to the Boudiccan disaster (as it seemed to Romans within and without Britain) was the suicide of its camp commandant, Poenius Postumus. We have only bare, tantalizing details of what happened after the defeat of Boudicca: 'He fell on his sword when he heard of the honours won by the Fourteenth and Twentieth – for he had robbed his own men of a like distinction and disobeyed his commander's order, in defiance of army regulations.' This is reliable documentary evidence from which it has been possible to draw various inferences, some acceptable, others debatable. In the first place, Poenius probably had failed to send troops to join the punitive expedition that quelled the British revolt. As an experienced soldier, in the line of P. Anicius Maximus, a notable predecessor (Chapter 11), why did he not comply with a military order of utmost urgency from the governor of the province himself? The reason usually offered is that Poenius thought that the West Country was also ready to rise against the Romans and he could not hold the territory with a depleted force. Whatever the circumstances, in Roman eyes he had sinned and was presented with the only course apparently open in those days to a ranking officer. How far does the archaeological record explain his dilemma and the potential threat he faced?

On the most recent evidence the headquarters of the Second Legion were being transferred from Lake in Dorset to Exeter in Devon sometime in the late 50s, possibly in A.D. 60. Significantly, perhaps, as already noted,[2] there is a view that 'moves from one permanent base to another were often gradual as sections of the new fortress were built.' The situation, then, could well have caught Poenius with his forces stretched between two visibly hostile tribes and with his command-structure based in two centres. Had he moved his forces as requested, then possibly the Roman positions in Dorset and Devon could have crumbled, threatening the outcome of the Roman fight back. Unheroic as it seemed, his decision may well have saved the day for Rome.

Further archaeological discoveries in at least two places bring the conclusion that some elements of the Durotrigian tribe did indeed prepare for action. This threat appears to have met fearful retribution before or after the defeat of the Boudiccan rebels. One case arises from an interpretation of facts different from that normally argued. At Spetisbury in 1857, the main ditch of the hillfort was cut through to make a railway cutting, revealing in the process the remains of around eighty bodies. The find has always been taken to denote a mass burial of Durotrigian dead. Dating this event has stemmed largely from the identification of surviving weaponry as being of Iron Age type. As it is now thought that some of the material and so some of the burials were Saxon,[3] the railway navvies apparently dug up finds from more than one period. However, in general, the original assumption that the human remains were mostly of first-century date seems tenable enough. There is further supporting evidence in the shape of a fragment of what is reliably thought to be the edge-binding for a Roman shield. This certainly points to the presence of a legionary or auxiliary force when most of the burials took place. But at what moment precisely did that grim event occur? It is usually blamed on the invading Roman army of the mid 40s A.D., the circumstance being compared to the 'war cemetery' at Maiden Castle. But at the latter hillfort, the British warriors were allowed to bury their own fallen kith and kin, placing beside them the customary ritual offerings of food. If the Romans had previously carried out the slaughter at Spetisbury to ensure easy victories thereafter, would they have reversed that policy after the determined defence of Maiden Castle? The happening at Spetisbury looks more like revenge exacted for a wrong done. Fortunately there is a compelling parallel with better dating from elsewhere in the tribal territory, just outside the modern county of Dorset.

South Cadbury, a large Durotrigian hillfort in Somerset, 8 km north of Sherborne, was the scene of extensive excavations in the 1960s and one important discovery throws light on our problem.[4] It was revealed that a considerable number of men, women and children, thirty or so in all, had been massacred in the south-west gateway and left there unburied. Brooches and the bulk of the pottery scraps made it certain that these were people of the Durotrigian tribe, but the vital question remained: When were they killed? Final reconsideration of all the dating evidence is that the event most likely to have been responsible was the Boudiccan revolt and its aftermath. The horrific circumstances at South Cadbury contrast strikingly with the orderliness of the ceremonial at Maiden Castle, but they do furnish an exact comparison with the slaughter at Spetisbury.

Is it possible to infer what happened locally in 60–61? Did trouble start when a number of hillforts were re-occupied by rebellious native groups? By the end of the 50s, the only major military stations in Dorset were likely to have been at Lake (a reduced garrison, now that Exeter was coming into service), Wareham and Dorchester, all with links between the sea and inland areas and along the South Coast. There were probably no Romans left inside hillforts for the key Roman fort inside Hod Hill had been disused since the early 50s. A limited protest of this kind might have been inspired by some Durotrigian leaders, members of a tribe known for its independent attitude. Such isolated challenges to Roman authority certainly provided no obstace to disciplined Roman counter-measures. However, these protests would represent a potential for creating further pockets of trouble that might cut off the Second Augustan Legion and its auxiliaries, now that many units had advanced into Devon and Somerset. If we allow time for the re-occupation of hillforts and for news of Boudicca's defeat to reach legionary headquarters (wherever that was by then) the shame of Poenius Postumus can be guessed. The acting Roman commander was having to quell petty centres of discontent, just at the moment when the historic action he had chosen not to join had taken place elsewhere. His suicide must have stunned his men and their feelings may be read in the ferocity of what they did at Spetisbury and South Cadbury.

There is one military camp set up by the Roman army in Dorset that could possibly be connected, not with the invasion, but with the threat of a Boudiccan uprising in 60–61. That is the 2.4 hectare (6 acre) fort at Crab Farm (noted in Chapter 9), 1.6 km west-south-west of Badbury Rings. It was discovered from the air in 1976 and is dated at present by surface finds, which appear to be a little later than the early campaigning phase. The site is only 5 km from the main base at Lake across the river, almost too near for the advancing forces of the mid 40s to have required such an encampment. It was ideally placed to block co-operation between the hillforts at Badbury and Spetisbury, an advantage that could also have served, of course, both in the original invasion and in the 60s. The answer to the problem still lies in the ground.

It is a reasonable assumption that the movement back into Durotrigian hillforts, if it took place, was the work of those who had earlier lived in them and enjoyed the privileges attached thereto, whether as rulers or retinue. But the majority of tribesmen were humble farmers, who, as far as can be made out from excavations, had continued their traditional way of life little changed since the invasion. Are there no clues telling us how they reacted to the Boudiccan call and the subsequent retaliation by the Romans? Information that may be helpful here has emerged from the large-scale excavations on two Durotrigian farming settlements at Tollard Royal and Gussage All Saints.[5] To these can be added scattered results from other sites, mainly dug for their Romano-British interest.[6] Characteristic of some Iron Age occupation sites were two ditched enclosures, one within the other. The smaller of these served domestic huts, while the larger was intended for general farm purposes. What is interesting is that at most of the locations the inner enclosure at least was given up and its ditch filled back early in the Roman period, whereupon the peasant farmer rebuilt his dwelling a little way off. The new position for his hut or huts may have remained inside the outer circuit, but that too seems, where identified and tested, to have gone out of use at the same time. Although there is some uncertainty about dating, these events occurred in the period following the arrival of the legion. Why then did some Durotrigian farmers appear simultaneously to have abandoned a traditional way of life inside a defended homestead? Can we see here the hand of Rome – a co-ordinated action enforced from above? It would be logical that all should be taught a lesson. The ultimate penalty was reserved for the tribal chiefs, and a less harsh reminder for the workaday majority that embattled independence was a thing of the past.

The turmoil of the Boudiccan disaster – a lesson to both Britons and Romans – must have been followed in Dorset by a period during which the army detachments still stationed there continued to be on watch. How long will remain a matter of guesswork, even if there were further excavation, for example, at Lake Farm. Refinements in dating finds take time to develop and may never be precise enough for the purpose. The increasing number of forts and camps being found by aerial photography in Devon and Cornwall, tell the story of a slow, steady advance from Durotrigian lands into Dumnonia, probably beginning by the early 50s. In the middle 60s, a fort was established inside Cornwall at Nanstallon, and by then we may think that the last legionary or auxiliary cavalryman had left Dorset. A chastened tribe was ready to adopt Roman ways, and the cantonal capital was soon to be founded at Dorchester, where full advantage could be taken of the roads built by the newcomers.

CONCLUSION

14
The Legacy of the Second Legion to Dorset

The discoveries described in Part II have by no means in all cases been vindicated by test-excavations. While it can be claimed that the authenticity of important stretches of the road-pattern is well supported by sections, no doubt some students of Roman Britain will still reserve judgement in other cases. In addition, the other earthworks ascribed to the military may arouse controversy, even if their existence is intimately connected with the roads. What can now be recognized is that the Second Legion Augusta and its auxiliary forces were actively campaigning in Dorset for a longer period than previously thought. This increase from a few months to several years may look trifling against a backcloth of twenty centuries, but it fills a significant gap in our understanding of the Claudian invasion in southern Britain. We now need to ask to what extent that brief presence of some fifteen years or so left its imprint on later developments in the county. The question is not an idle one, for parts of the military roads are still in service, one way or another. Again, when we look at Dorset towns, two at least, the most important historically, both with long pedigrees, can trace their origin back to the arrival of the Roman army.

The road-pattern leading into Dorchester has always been accepted as basically Roman. High West and High East Streets certainly formed one axis for a route into and through the town, despite the recent view that the road north of the Frome from Badbury reached the East Gate at an angle. But the Badbury road has been shown to have suffered little sustained wear, and a major result of the present investigation has been to restore as Roman the line we know was created by the legion from Stinsford through Grey's Bridge to the foot of High East Street.

There has also been agreement in the past that Durnovaria, like many other towns in the British province, began as a military establishment of some kind. Nevertheless the size and location of that early fort remained, as we have seen, a mystery. The argument in Chapter 6 has hopefully provided the evidence for clearing up those two essential details. In any case, there has never been any real doubt that the town-site of Dorchester was the creation of the Second Legion Augusta, developed and enlarged under the later *civitas* council. It is unlikely that there was any interval between the two administrations, for the local system of military roads leading from the surrounding countryside would already have encouraged a native market, replacing the function of nearby hillforts and also serving the Roman garrison. If Dorchester wants to look for a founder, there is no need to go further than Vespasian or his camp prefect, honoured in Asia Minor (Chapter 11). The suggestion has been made in Chapter 6 that the civil settlement of Durnovaria came to occupy the area formerly devoted to the military zone outside the fort. In that respect, the bounds of Saxon and medieval Dorchester within the walls, the heart of the traditional town, were dictated by a Roman officer in the mid-first century.

Wareham, like Dorchester, has been shown to lie at the centre of a distinctively Roman pattern of roads, often suspected, but never seriously checked until now. Some Victorian antiquaries indeed went so far as to assert that the street network within the walls was based on a pre-existing Roman camp. They would hardly have questioned the belief that the roads leading directly into Wareham had an essentially Roman look about them. Then came a period when the real origin of Wareham was placed no earlier than Saxon times. Thus a more unexpected outcome of present investigations is the revival of the claim that a Roman garrison was stationed on the ground between the rivers. As we have seen, modern excavated proof is lacking, although the probable site is far smaller than was suggested in the nineteenth century. It is possible that this favourable locality had seen even earlier settlement, whereas at Dorchester, the closeness of the Poundbury hillfort meant that the military site was what we could call a 'green-field' choice made by the Romans. However, there have never been discoveries at Wareham of sophisticated buildings of stone and tile such as graced Dorchester in its heyday between the second and fourth centuries. On the other hand, the system of roads bequeathed to the surrounding district by the Roman army meant that Wareham was able to continue a modest role as a market and small port. It is true that the only tangible finds of the later Roman period comprise scattered potsherds and the occasional coin. But the regional trade in objects of shale and stone from Purbeck point to the continued importance of the military choice of site. It must be significant that the inscribed memorial stones of seventh to eighth century date[1] came from the vicinity of Lady St Mary. These finds on the probable site of the first-century fort establish that there was a settlement of romanized Celts who were living at the focus of roads still surviving in part today. In the eighth century, Saxon Wareham took over Roman points of entry at north and south when the great earthen walls were raised, even if the route on the west was then moved away from the original course to Dorchester. Abbot's Quay, however, remains to commemorate the Roman line. If evidence of continuity from those early days is sought, the block of properties containing Holy Trinity Church may well represent a nucleus of late Roman or post-Roman buildings still discernible when the Walls were built in the ninth century. Elsewhere inside Wareham, only North Street and possibly South Street are close to their Roman counterparts.

Another Dorset town that indirectly at least must owe its origin to the road-builders of the Roman army is Beaminster. The road from Dorchester to Waddon ran, it is claimed, along the north slope of the unnamed hill (crowned by Edmund Coombes Coppice) south of the medieval centre in which the church stands. If we judge by a relatively small number of finds in the past, that hill was a focus for settlement in Roman times, after the army moved on. The road provided an invaluable link with the provincial capital at Dorchester. Probably, in the seventh or eighth century, it came to form the southern boundary of the monastic estate. The place-name may point to the existence of that early land-grant rather than to the otherwise unknown founder of the town.[2]

It must be the case that the first settlement at Wimborne drew advantage from its relationship to local military roads. The foundation of the double monastery in 720 by the sister of the king of Wessex underlines the existence of good communicatons to link it with the outside world. From the east, the Roman road from the Winchester direction needed only a short diversion to serve the new establishment. From the south-west, the Roman roads from Wareham and Hamworthy in combination diverted near Lake Farm towards a river-crossing which was tackled later by the present seventeenth-century Julians bridge. Like Wimborne, Wareham had a nunnery before the ninth century and was the burial-place of Saxon royalty, so that an identifiable road-link between these two places in those days is no surprise.

Another Dorset settlement that, like Wimborne, seems to have grown up at a spot favourably served by the early roads is Bere Regis. It lay at the junction of the Lake–Dorchester road and the strongly presumptive road to Weatherby Castle. Again resembling Wimborne, the village has not yet produced evidence of occupation in the Roman period, either at the time of, or after, the military phase. Its origin as a town should be ascribed to Saxon times. It is therefore relevant that the 'hundred of Bere' was in existence before the Norman Conquest. Hundred courts generally met at a spot accessible to all the tithings, an important detail for both respresentatives and suitors. 'Hill-tops, fords, cross-roads were marked out as inevitably for such moots as the market town is today for agricultural reunions.'[3] The Bere Hundred once included Pallington, 6.5 km away beside the Frome, from which the only direct access could have been along the Roman road across Affpuddle Heath and through 'Streteford' at Turners Puddle. Not all hundred moots at crossroads developed into towns; a notable exception was Badbury. But Bere probably also continued to serve as a local market that, once a year, it was convenient to hold in Woodbury hillfort nearby.

To a very great extent both Dorchester and Wareham owed their continued regional importance after Roman times to the road systems laid out in the mid-first century. There must, of course, have been additional reasons which owe nothing to the Second Legion, otherwise we should expect similar townships, for example, at Badbury Rings and, in particular, close to Lake Farm, near Wimborne. How, then, can we assess the role of the legion's roads in the later history of Dorset?

Certainly, if we consider the 350 years of Roman rule that followed the departure of the army, the original military roads made a vital contribution to the prosperity of the region. Excavation on every Roman site in Dorset indirectly supports the statement. The goods traded on even the humblest of peasant farms came in variety from home and abroad. Their presence implies movement by road. Time and our climate have allowed only the durable to survive, such as pottery, objects of glass and metal, and those of purely mineral origin like stone tiles and shale. We can only guess at the mass of woven goods, and those of wood, leather, straw that have perished in the soil. The oyster shells found on many sites suggest the work of travelling hawkers, still a feature of the countryside in Hardy's Wessex. Up near Hadrian's Wall, the fortunate preservation of a soldier's correspondence at Vindolanda demonstrates the use of maintained roads for the movement of mail. Villas and humble farms alike had to have their links to the network of military roads. It is likely that the important fourth-century villas at Hinton St Mary and Fifehead Neville lay close to Hod Hill and Rawlsbury respectively. At the same time it is obvious that places at a road-nexus, like Dorchester, Wareham and Badbury Rings, being eminently accessible, must have become local or regional markets.

After Roman times, the complete network of roads gradually tended, with the passage of centuries, to break down into purely neighbourhood routes or mere property boundaries, before sometimes vanishing altogether. It has been suggested that Roman roads remained in use well into Saxon and Norman times, often being followed by invading armies. The descent on Wessex by the Danes in 874 is a case in point: according to the Anglo-Saxon Chronicle, they moved rapidly from Cambridge to Wareham and only for the last few kilometres from Corfe Mullen was this great host considered not to be following known Roman roads or long-distance trackways. Now that gap can be filled by the branch-road from East End, Corfe Mullen to Wareham. The further movement of the same body of men from Wareham to Dorchester and then to Exeter illustrates this later use of roads first intended for Roman military traffic.

Additionally, the relative importance of a Roman road in later times may well be gauged by the number of settlements that have grown up beside or athwart it. Some of these may have had Roman origins, but it is certain that such villages, with early churches sited close to the road, confirm its continued service before and during the Saxon period. Thus the military road from Lake Farm to Dorchester passes through five villages with their parish church sited in this way: Corfe Mullen, Bere Regis, Turners Puddle, Tincleton and Stinsford. It is now possible to understand the present setting of Stinsford Church. Today, it lies isolated at the end of a lane that is a blind alley for vehicles. Yet it once lay beside a busy highway that saw continuous service until the park at Kingston Maurward was created around 1700. Remarkably, too, the final alignment into the town saw the three Dorchester parish churches sited alongside, underlining the importance of the road well after the Roman period. As it happens, the Eggardon–Axminster Roman road, of uncertain course and post-military layout, also traverses several villages with old churches. One of the medieval routes from Exeter to London passed that way through Bridport and Dorchester and then onward, principally following Roman military roads via Stinsford and Tincleton to Bere Regis, Wimborne and Ringwood. This was almost certainly one of the itineraries taken by the Norman kings in their perambulations through this part of England.

Perhaps a less tangible association of post-Roman settlement with the Roman roads of Dorset is presented by the place-name KINGSTON, which has drawn attention in the past and is again the subject of research.[4] Seven examples of the name occur in the county and one just outside.

PLACE	LOCATION
1. Kingston Lacy	On Lake–Badbury Roman road.
2. Kingston Maurward	On Lake–Dorchester Roman road.
3. Kingston Russell	1.2 km S. of Dorchester–Eggardon Roman road.
4. Winterborne Kingston	On Dorchester–Badbury Roman road.
5. Kingston (S. of Ringwood)	On Lake–New Forest Roman road.
6. Kingston (Purbeck)	? On Roman road into Purbeck.
7. Kingston (Haselbury Bryan)	? On Roman road through Blackmore Vale
8. Kington (sic W. of Gillingham)	? On Roman road towards S. Cadbury and Ham Hill.

Of the above, four lie on Roman roads that originated with the military and one (no. 4) on a road deemed later. The two (nos 7 and 8) in the north of the county suggest where signs of early Roman communication might be sought. Movement in a medieval world not known for its road-building may explain the siting of KINGSTON settlements. Were they basically local centres for royal tax-collection?

The Roman road from East End, Corfe Mullen, to Wareham was connected meaningfully with the village of Lytchett Minster. It can be seen from the tithe map of 1836 that the medieval field-system took the shape of an elliptic rectangle, some 60 hectares (150 acres) or so in area (fig. 14.1). The line of the Roman road as described in Chapter 5D formed a median to the enclosed land.[5] It is likely that the arable, divided two-fold by that road at Lytchett Minster, reflected the two-field system of cultivation recorded in some parts of medieval Dorset.[6]

The Roman road from Dorchester to Wareham retained its identity as the through route between the two towns until the eve of the Norman Conquest at least. Both places had mints and both were linked by journeys recorded in the Anglo-Saxon Chronicle, as in the case of the Danish invasions, mentioned above. Stokeford, at the passage of the Frome 5 km west of Wareham, is a place-name known already in the thirteenth century, so that the river-crossing had continued in use until then. A bridge at Wool was mentioned in 1343, making it likely that at that date the 'Stoke Ford' had been superseded for major traffic by the deviation that still forms the road looping over Stokeford Heath.

Why did some stretches of an early military road disappear, while others survived into present use? Some answers have been put forward in Chapter 5. It commonly happens that, for one reason or another, a divergence took place. Often this alternative track is not too far away; study and excavation may show that it was a deliberate act by the occupant of the land. Thus, west of the Old Mill at Corfe Mullen, a sharp and awkward bend on one of the county's busiest main roads (A31) was a relatively late development at the close of the medieval period. Until that time, the Roman road had continued straight from Mill Street and had undergone substantial re-metalling before that short stretch was abandoned. When the turnpike engineers of the eighteenth century improved the carriageway from Poole to Blandford, they had to adopt at that spot a feature that caused little difficulty to horse-drawn traffic, but is potentially lethal today.

This deviation at Corfe Mullen was minor and could have brought little profit to the farmer or land-owner. But there are examples of other deviations, which were clearly intended to keep public movement away from a residence or a farmstead. The great loop in the same Roman road as it approached Dorchester seems to have arisen from the creation of the park at Kingston Maurward. Closer to Corfe Mullen, Charborough Park presents notable examples of diversions occurring in the sixteenth and nineteenth centuries. But, on open downland, disuse of the old road may have resulted from the slow development of parallel tracks and it was the route most convenient for local travellers that prevailed. This can be noted on Bloxworth Down, where the present trunk road (A31) pursues an erratic course north of the Roman line.

The growth of a settlement in post-Roman times has led, curiously enough, in some places, to the decay and final abandonment of the original line. The Roman road from Wareham to Dorchester passes directly through Wool and played a part in the growth of the early village, which was recorded before Domesday. As noted above, the road fell out of favour when the stone bridge came to be built over the Frome, giving a route that led either to Bere Regis or to Wareham. A little distance to the west, the track of the ancient road through the fields and over the stream at East Burton was replaced by a medieval road that took a wide sweep around the southern perimeter of the village.

Other examples of deviations minor and major will be noted as the interested reader traces the course of the Roman military roads. Each has its own story to tell of man and landscape since Britain was part of the Roman Empire. As a contrast, it is relevant to ask why certain lengths of the system should have so survived that they have long been recognized for what they are. In some cases, they run over remote downland or heath that has been cultivated in modern times only and there has been no competition from neighbouring tracks. The Dorchester–Old Sarum Roman road is often in service as a parish boundary, which indicates it was passing not *through*, but *between* local settlements when the boundary was adopted. Without this administrative recognition, its track could have vanished from sight, as has happened in the vale west of Tolpuddle. It is remarkable that in the 47 km from Dorchester to Woodyates, this well-recorded Roman road of mixed military and civil origin traverses only two sizeable settlements that can be called villages, namely, Winterborne Kingston and Shapwick. That is strange, since it is the best known in this region of England, often possessing a prominent agger and long straight alignments, always recognizably Roman features. Excavation has shown, indeed, that, as a route leading from Dorchester to Badbury, it bore very few signs of wear or repair, quite different from the condition of the road that passed by Stinsford Church. North of Badbury Rings it has always retained local importance, and stretches there that have fallen out of use were still being trodden until the eighteenth century and the advent of competing turnpikes. Dorchester's communications with the east, however, always depended on the two Roman roads created by the Second Legion: towards Bere Regis and Corfe Mullen on the one hand, and towards Wareham on the other. Precisely because these roads had such a variety of use or disuse in subsequent centuries, their course became a matter of decipherment as against the stark evidence of lonely Ackling Dyke.

What then has been the contribution of the Second Legion Augusta to the history and landscape of medieval and modern Dorset? We can point to the foundation of two major towns and a system of roads that has in many places retained importance and directly and indirectly led to the origin of a number of smaller settlements. This element is less impressive, no doubt, than in districts of the North where the army was so much longer in garrison, but it is considerably larger than seemed possible in the recent past. Furthermore, this review would be incomplete without looking at the other activities of the Roman army that have left their mark still traceable today, minor though it may be.

As we have seen, the invaders contrived various cuttings and causeways, usually to gain access to and from hillforts, and some of these may still be serving a modern purpose. The Roman entry into Badbury Rings, for example, is walked each year by thousands at that popular spot. Not far away, at Buzbury Rings, golfers carefully aim along and through Roman features that needed no adaptation to become a fairway after long service as part of what was known as Wimborne Way. Hillforts were always remote places after their final abandonment and the later use of a Roman access was strictly limited to the local farmers. Thus the north entry to Weatherby Castle created by the legion obviously proved convenient to the villagers of Milborne St Andrew, as it still does to the estate.

Time and the hand of man have dealt harshly with other earthworks that we may attribute to the Roman armed forces. On departure from a fort, the normal military routine was to fill back perimeter ditches with the rampart material. This operation was so thoroughly carried out at Lake Farm that the land almost at once reverted to arable. However, in remote areas the defences of smaller forts seem to have been spared complete levelling. If the Roman fort at Hod Hill survived in good shape until the ninteenth century, it was probably because the site was given over to pasture until being ploughed only a generation or two ago.

By contrast, of the earthworks on Holton Heath, which have a strong case to be Roman, one at least had been converted into a 'close' at an early date and still forms part of the East Holton field-system.

In later Roman times the town of Durnovaria appears to have turned Maumsbury Rings into an amphitheatre by using the shelving and access created by the Second Legion. These changes in the Rings were not thereafter of consequence in history until the Civil War of the seventeenth century, when Maumsbury became a gun-emplacement defending Dorchester. Even then the Parliamentary artillerymen owed more to the constructional work of the original Neolithic builders than to the Roman soldiery.

As the twentieth century nears its close, the county of Dorset is being more and more subjected to large-scale housing developments that not long ago would have been called small towns. Old highways are being rendered obsolete by new roads and bypasses after having served for generations. Nevertheless, with difficulty, we can trace back to the Second Legion two towns and a network of roads in every stage of repair and disrepair. These contributions to the landscape must seem minor in comparison, but they were the first marks of a civilized way of life that distinguished the Roman Empire from the barbaric lands beyond. They may rightly take a modest place in the Dorset heritage.

APPENDICES
(a) Excavated sections or part-sections in Corfe Mullen

Appendix 15
East End 1977

In 1977, Wimborne Road, Corfe Mullen, was widened at East End in the area where it crossed the former railway track. To aid the demolition of the bridge and the filling-in of the old cutting, an access eastwards from the modern road was carved by machine into the north slope. It was this exposure that revealed the information to be described. The hitherto accepted course of the Roman road from Hamworthy passed west of the bridge, but the facts now proved otherwise: the course lay some 21.86 m to the east.

The site (SY 99529845 and fig. 5D.1b) lies at a height of 48.8 m O.D. on the north side of the Sleight Terrace, which comprises a hill-capping of glacial gravels overlying Bagshot sands of Tertiary date. It was the latter softer bedrock that predominated at this precise spot, so that it was easy to pick out the large gravel flints, brought for constructional purposes from the nearby terrace. On first examination it seemed that the machine might have disturbed and dispersed everything to a greater depth than the Roman metalling. However, besides observing the section-face it was possible to trace the lowest road-material in plan along a narrow band about 1 m wide. This threw light on Phases 1 and 2 in addition to revealing an unexpected post-setting.

The Section
After the cleaning of the section-face, the road was seen to be occupying a shallow depression scooped into the slope of the old surface, which had a gradient of 1 : 12 to the east. The mass of the road-material, composed of layers of flints and smaller stones mixed with darker soil, stood out against the natural yellow-orange sand. While the actual surfaces of successive phases of build and, on the western side, their side-ditches, were perceptible, the stony metalling of each constructional period was mostly homogeneous. The section-drawing emphasizes the junction-lines in the stratification, with the key indicating the phases to which these lines refer. Road widths given take into account the angle of the road alignment to the face of the section.

Phase 1
This consisted of a narrow causeway, some 2.4 m wide, made up of a 23 cm thickness of flint and gravel, lying between side-ditches each 60 cm wide. The

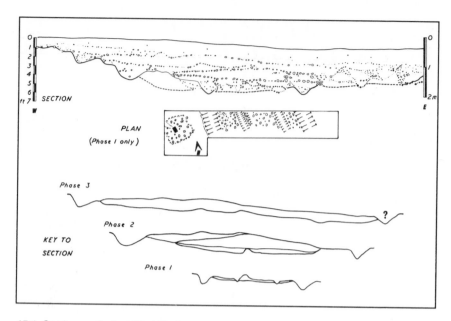

15.1 Section and plan, East End

15.2 East End – Phase 2 side-ditch and road metalling, from west. Stones of post-setting between. Imperial scale.

15.3 Post-setting beside Roman road at East End, from south

infilling of these ditches derived mainly from the metalling thrown down for the succeeding phase, but the western one contained additionally some patches of grey clay. Visible in the road surface were two parallel ruts, with inner edges about 1 m apart and outer edges about 1.5 m apart, pointing to a wheel gauge of around 1.35 m. A ridge of heavy stones lined the inner edge of the western route, as though gouged out of the metalling by wheel movement. Between the western rut and the western side-ditch a band of laid orange-coloured gravel suggested differential surfacing for that strip of the road, possibly to serve those on foot (a *margo*). The natural sand on which this first road was built had been disturbed down to a depth of 23 cm. The bottom of this disturbed layer is shown on the section by a discontinuous line. The disturbance may have been created partly by the tread of the road-makers as they sunk in the soft subsoil, partly by topsoil removal and ground levelling along the projected line of the road.

An intriguing discovery was made to the west of the western side-ditch. Striations in the sand and associated lines of small stones were observed dipping down towards the east, showing that what at first sight looked to be natural sand had been dug out and replaced before the ditch was cut. Alongside the early road there emerged a massive build-up of heavy flints, forming a cairn-like support for a post, around which excavated sand had been thrown back. The base of the cairn was roughly square and tapered to take a rectangular post measuring 15 cm by 10 cm. An irregular grooved depression leading from the north-west corner of the post-socket was probably a demolition slot created when the post was taken out. The post-hole had its longer axis parallel with the road alignment. Its depth was 35 cm and it noticeably widened towards the top, suggesting that the timber had been rocked to and fro in the process of removal. The probable function of this unusual structure is discussed below. It is shown as a Phase 1 feature, but it is possible that it was constructed later in that phase to accompany the wider Phase 2 road.

Phase 2

When the Phase 1 road was widened, a base course of loose stones, gravel and soil, some 15 cm thick, was laid over the original side-ditches and road-surface. Over the eastern side-ditch there was set a more massive foundation of large flints (some as long as 14 cm) to a depth of 30 cm. This formed the eastern edge of the remaining build-up for the Phase 2 carriageway, which was then laid over the base course and comprised heavy flints (up to 10 cm long) in stony, gravelly soil. On the surface of this low Phase 2 causeway it was possible to see many small particles of grit less than 2.5 mm in diameter, presumably the result of heavy wear by iron-shod wheels. The new road-surface was twice as wide as before, some 4.9 m. On each side the sandy subsoil, already disturbed in Phase 1, was levelled to leave 1 m verges, beyond which the new side-ditches were dug. The eastern one was slight, 60 cm wide and half as much deep. The western was a little wider and its filling stood out clearly in plan as far as it could be exposed. After some use, a further layer of stony metalling was laid across the western sandy verge and the accompanying side-ditch. This layer is regarded as road-widening for Phase 2 rather than a base course for Phase 3 because its upper surface bore slight traces of rutting with a stony central ridge similar to Phase 1. The road was thus broadened to some 7.3 m. It is just possible that the eastern verge and ditch were included in the wider carriageway, but the information, observable only in section, was inconclusive.

Phase 3

A further layer of stone and gravel, up to 30 cm thick was deposited over the Phase 2 road to provide a final width of some 9 m or so. A western side-ditch, of like dimensions to that in Phase 2, was cut, but this time immediately adjacent to the edge of the new build-up. While this ditch, dug entirely in natural sand, was readily discernible with its filling of small stones, the exact placing of the other side-ditch (if such there was) proved difficult to trace in section only. Once again, there were suggestions of slight rutting on the western third of this road-surface, which was horizontal in cross-section and so presented greater stability to vehicles than the pronounced camber of the eastern two-thirds.

A further and final use of the road may be indicated by a stony layer running from the rutted ridge just mentioned to a point beyond the western side-ditch of Phase 3. At this stage, before it was abandoned for a line further west, the road appeared to have been an unditched track about 3.9 m wide.

Discussion
(1) *The Post alongside the Phase 1 Road*
Like the road with which it was associated, this unusual feature must be of Roman military origin. From the constructional point of view, one would expect the base of a significant post erected by Roman engineers to have been set in a pit and held securely by the rammed infilling. Such a pit was often 1.2 m square, as at Hod Hill and Longthorpe. Here a depression was scooped in the sandy subsoil and the post set in a cairn, which was then covered with the excavated material. Nevertheless, the structure had an essentially military look. The cairn was square with a base smaller in area than that of the pits just mentioned, but wholly in keeping with a smaller post of squared timber and carefully aligned lenthwise with the road. Relating the size and depth of the socket to the probable height of the post, we can estimate that it is unlikely to have stood higher than about 2.7 m if in a framework with other posts or more than 1.8 to 2.1 m if in isolation. It was not possible to seek further posts to the north on either side of Phase 1 road, while any to the south would already have been destroyed one way or another.

Soon after the investigation, the writer considered the following notions as to the purpose of this post:

(a) In association with other posts unidentified, was this post part of:
  – a gate or barrier
  – a timber building
  – a post-and-rail fence?
(b) If used singly, did this post serve:
  – to mark a special location
  – to give general information?

The conclusion reached at that time (1978) was for a single post. Since then, the branch road to Wareham has been identified, starting from just south of this spot, and is highly relevant in any explaination. The writer's original thoughts are here quoted, before the new facts are taken into account:

> The notion that the post was a single, isolated one appears more in keeping with the cairn-construction. The implication would then be that it carried a sign. Was this of general import, the name of the military base, for example, or was it more closely connected with the actual location, as in the case of a milestone (milepost) or a land boundary? These two functions might well coincide. The post stood 0.428 of a Roman mile from the edge of the defence-works of the base at Lake Farm to the north and 6.44 Roman miles from the possible landing-place at Hamworthy where the road may have reached the shore (SZ 006902).

Could it be argued that a distance of perhaps 0.43 of a Roman mile represented the width at this point of a military zone surrounding the Lake fortress? Pits indicating military activity had been found in the area south of the fortress. If the zone has ended at the site of our post, it would have excluded the site of the kilns where native potters were producing Durotrigian and romanized wares, as well as the possible cemetery near Cogdean Elms (RCHM, *Dorset*, Vol. II, 600-1). It was thus possible that the post had marked the edge of the military *territorium* from which, under campaign conditions, native Britons would have been barred. The same spot might also have marked the sixth mile from Poole Harbour. However, the fact that the discovery is now known to lie at the one-time junction of roads to Poole Harbour and to Wareham makes it highly probable that this was the site of a simple finger-post. It has been pointed out regarding Roman roads in general that 'understandably painted wooden signposts have disappeared' (Chevallier 1976, p. 52). This post-hole may best be seen as the setting for such a timber traffic-sign, arguably the earliest recorded in the British Isles.

Appendix 16
Lake Farm 1981

During the winter of 1980–81, massive ground clearance in advance of the Wimborne bypass offered an opportunity for examining the Roman road from Poole Harbour south of the Lake Farm military base. Close to the junction of Wimborne Road and Willett Road a broad swathe of soil was removed in field 6900, thus exposing the Roman alignment as a gravel strip. An area (A), 14 m by 8 m, was cleaned up over that gravel line with the help of local volunteer labour (SY 99669892 and fig. 5D.1a). This enabled a section-trench to be cut along the north side of that area to test the construction of the road. Smaller clearances (B, C and D) were later made close to Willett Road. Part of the top of the Roman agger, belonging to the civilian period, had been destroyed by the machine, but the story of the military phase remained to be examined and interpreted. From a check on the precise line of the road, its course was seen to have been slightly re-aligned a little way north on the other side of the Chillwater Brook, so changing from a north-easterly to a north-north-easterly track. It is of interest that at this spot and for a number of metres either way, uphill and downhill, the bedrock is grey London Clay. Thus the stony material for constructing the road had to be brought a short distance either from the valley gravels below or, more likely, it would seem, from the plateau gravels above.

As at East End, only 500 m or so up the hill (Appendix 15), two phases of early road were identified. The first phase of heavy yellow gravel was 2.5 m wide, laid directly on the grey clay, with a 1 m *margo* of finer red gravel on the east. A side-ditch on the west was flanked on its far side by a bank of gravel, which may have served for repairs to the road-surface. In the second phase, the road was buit up to a height of 0.5 m and its width extended eastwards to some 4 m overall, so covering the *margo*. The western side-ditch was widened and deepened 1 m wide and 0.5 m deep), while a small side-ditch was dug 10 m away to the east. The third phase of the road spread over the earlier ditches and measured up to 9 m wide. Any clues to the height of the final agger and to the number of times it was re-metalled or repaired had been removed by machine. The material of the first two phases yielded almost no finds and it was only in this third build-up of road that residual finds occurred in quantity. Notably, too, the western edge of the Phase 3 metalling was beginning to curve westwards in the south-west corner of

16.1 Location map, Wimborne Road re-alignment, 1981

Area A, but examination of this possible branch-road could not be finished. Later it was shown that this was indeed the beginning of a Roman road of great significance (Chapter 5C).

The smaller clearances B and C were sited just south of Willett Road as it then was. They identified what appeared to be a gravel footpath, with a well-cut ditch on its north, which was proceeding eastward from the Roman road, almost at right angles. There had been evidently some need for communication on foot, via the road, between the fort and a point south of the brook. One wonders whether that might have been the location of the military bath-house. The brook provided the water-supply to the interior of the fort and could have served a bath-establishment. It must be noted that scraps of brick among finds from the excavation may have come from a building resistant to heat.

16.2 Wimborne bypass – exposure of road

Appendix 17
Whitehall House 1982

There was no visible trace of a ridge in this field, but the location for the trench (SY 97639847 and fig. 5C.1f) was based on the slight re-alignment noted in Higher Russell's Copse and observable during drought south of Court Farm bungalow. The section-trench 7 m by 1 m, proved long enough to span the expected line, but too short to resolve what subsequently in other cuts (this was the first) were thought to be significant constructional features. These omitted details included the full width of the belt of ground originally stripped to make the road and the dimensions of a probable *margo* or side-walk on the north. The site is close to the valley bottom of the river Stour and bedrock consists of loose sandy gravel with large flints, overlying chalk a little way below. The zone intended for the road must indeed have had topsoil removed, for the basic foundation of large flints and sand, up to 30 cm thick and 2.5 m wide, had been deposited directly on this underlying valley gravel to form a gently cambered base. This central course of flints was given a surfacing of fine gravel 20 cm thick. Some renewal of material had taken place and there were indications of further laid gravel on the north side, taking the road-width to 3.75 m, but details were uncertain. A shallow grooved depression, 15 cm broad and as much deep, ran in the south of this cleared zone, exactly parallel with the causewayed road. While this depression might have been a small side-ditch, it could equally well have formed one of a pair of wheel-ruts off the line of the road, with its companion beyond the trench. It should be noted that the natural valley gravel ran down from south to north in the section-trench, dropping 40 cm in 7 m. At its north side a 50 cm thickness of mixed gravel had been laid against, and beyond, the causeway. On the evidence from other investigations of this road in Corfe Mullen, this could be part of a *margo* built up to give a level track commensurate with the original cambered ridge.

During its later history the road was worn down midway to its original foundation over a strip of 2 m, and in this disturbed band an early medieval sherd was found. Thereafter, the surface deteriorated to a succession of stony ridges more like farm-tracks or field boundaries. The last of these disappeared under worked topsoil that accumulated centrally to a depth of 30 cm.

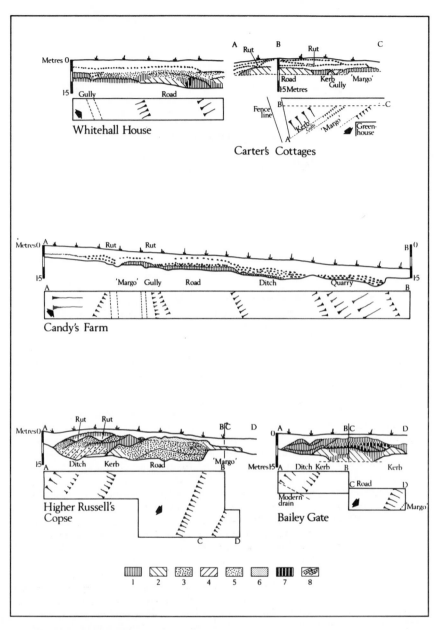

17.1 Sections from five sites in Corfe Mullen

Key:
1: loose gravel and flints
2: packed gravel and flints
3: redeposited stony subsoil
4: sandy silt
5: dirty gravel
6: grey clay, some stone
7: soil formation
8: gravel interface, isolated flints

Appendix 18
Higher Russell's Copse 1982–3

In this copse the ridge was sectioned a little east of the spot where it makes a slight re-alignment. The section-trench, 8 m by 1.25 m (ST 97989847 and fig. 5C.1e) was later widened over its northern half and then extended northward. The evidence may be summed up as follows:

Stage 1 A cambered road was constructed with a south verge and side-ditch and a north *margo* or side-walk; Iron Age or early Roman sherds (small finds 13) were stratified in the make-up, which was set in a wide depression cut down to the subsoil.

Stage 2 The centre of the original road came to act as a land-boundary; the northern side of that road and the side-walk fell out of use and accumulated undisturbed black humus. The southern side of the road continued in service, while the verge and side-ditch became steadily silted up.

Stage 3 The southern band of road received further gravel and flint metallings which stretched almost half-way across the silted up verge and side-ditch. A late feature in this stage was a slight gravel bank which separated the abandoned northern strip from the surviving road and reinforced the notion of an age-old function of the Stage 1 road as a boundary.

Stage 4 A period ensued with a succession of blackish, gritty and stony surfaces over the southern side, the last of which was distinguished by two substantial parallel wheel-ruts, some 1.25 m apart. A sherd from early in this stage (small find 4) could be dated to the twelfth century or thereabouts.

Stage 5 A well-laid stony surface with a good camber formed the last of the series which, from Stage 2 onward, occupied the southern side of the earliest road and its verge and side-ditch. This latest road also had a side-ditch on the south below which two twelfth–thirteenth century sherds were found (small finds 5). A fragment of brick (small find 8), possibly fifteenth–sixteenth century in date, formed part of the top road material.

In detail:

Stage 1: The Original Road Construction and Dating
The bedrock in Higher Russell's Copse consists of a reddish ochre clayey sand

18.2 Excavation of Roman road, Higher Russell's Copse, 1983, looking north

with striations of gravelly stones, part of the Reading Beds. In the copse itself this was overlain by a subsoil of leached greyish clayey sand, above which an extremely black layer formed the topsoil. The manner in which the road was built appears to have been as follows:

First, topsoil and bedrock were removed to a depth of about 0.5 m over a band 6.5 m wide. Second, a retaining kerb was formed for the southern edge of the agger (finally 4.25 m wide) by laying a bed of single heavy flints on top of which was piled a line of gravel 1 m wide at base and almost 0.5 m high. Third, the intervening depression, 4 m in breadth, was partly refilled with mixed sandy loam and some stones (presumably topsoil and bedrock which had been initially removed). This foundation material formed a median ridge or *spina*. Fourth, on either side of the ridge, a further deposit was thrown in, composed of soft orange loam mixed with some grey clay (turves ?), gravel and fragments of charcoal. Fifth, this was covered in turn by re-deposited gravelly and clayey bedrock, packed to provide a perceptible camber, still surviving on the north, but much disturbed by later wear on the south. As an element in the fifth part of the build-up, the surface was given a coating of grey clay about 5 cm thick. This finish was apparently applied in two layers under drying weather conditions, but once consolidated and hardened to fine cement, it would have resisted wear and drained easily. The sixth step was the creation of a *margo* or side-walk on the north flank. Heavy flints and then gravel were laid on a strip of the old undisturbed ground-level to give the feature a width of 1.5 m. Seventh and finally, the bounds of the road were confirmed by a deepening of the outer verge 0.5 m beyond the kerb for a slight side-ditch and a scooping away of the topsoil beyond the north side of the *margo*.

The causeway of the original road between kerb edge and *margo* edge was thus established here as 4.25 m wide. Its date of construction in general terms must coincide with the military occupation at Lake Farm, since the stretch through High Russell's Copse forms part of the Roman road shown to link Lake Farm with Dorchester. In addition, there was independent support from the excavation itself. Sherds of native ('Durotrigian') ware occurred within the road material (small finds 6 and 13), while a fragment of second-century samian (small find 14) was found lodged in what would have been the last visible trace of the *margo*.

Stages 2–5: The Later History of the Road

The road retained some use in the post-conquest years of the Roman period as suggested by the sherd of samian ware (a find indicating that there is an undiscovered settlement not far away). The south verge and side-ditch silted up after an initial accumulation of gravelly material deriving from the nearby road-surface, which came to accept traffic on its southern half only. This strongly suggests that from early times the road was also serving as a land boundary. It must be meaningful that the dark humus of vegetable origin characteristic today of the Copse seems to have formed also over the northern half of the road after that boundary came to be observed. On the south, at least two metallings of gravel encroached over the silted-up verge and side-ditch, providing a track only 1.25 m wide, enough for a pack-horse, perhaps, or foot-passengers. The last of these metallings was associated with a small hedge-bank running along the line of the original road, but sited almost over the south kerb of that road, by then well buried. The development of wheel-ruts showed that the vehicles were now passing over the Roman verge and side-ditch below. This rutted road had a camber and its own small south side-ditch in which was discovered twelfth-century pottery. At a time when the ruts had become filled with black soil, the last event in the life of the road took place with the laying of substantial metalling, mainly of heavy flints and up to 25 cm thick, to make a good cambered surface 2 m wide. The age-old land division was still being observed along the north edge of this late medieval way.

No account can be given of the role played by the massive bank that lies between the south end of the section trench and the A31 trunk road. It runs for some distance parallel with the Roman/medieval course and the modern road to the south, which was a late turnpike creation of 1841.

Appendix 19
Bailey Gate Level Crossing 1982

This excavation took place close to the old railway track, south of the cottage formerly used by the crossing-gate keeper (SY 96999848 and fig. 5C.1g). To the east, in the grounds of the Wessex Water Laboratory, a faint ridge is visible, apparently continuing the alignment established at Higher Russell's Copse and Whitehall House. There is a degree of uncertainty, since the terrain has been affected by the installation of piping. Given the proximity of fences and huts, it was found expedient to dig two staggered trenches so as to provide a cross-section of the buried agger that came to light in the first trench. Bedrock here consists of gravel overlaid by reddish loam.

The sequence of events by which the original road was constructed proved decipherable as follows:

(1) Topsoil and turves were cleared over a strip wide enough to encompass the actual road, its side-ditch on the south and the apparent *margo* on the north;

(2) Within this strip a shallow trough was cut into bedrock;

(3) Within this trough again, a narrower depression was cut, some 2.75 m wide, in which to key the road-material only;

(4) Heavy flints and gravel were packed centrally into this depression to a maximum depth of 0.75 m in order to form a 'backbone' or *spina* with the profile of an inverted 'V';

(5) Loose spoil, including turves, was packed into the gaps between the edge of the depression and the *spina*, the turves showing as stone-free bands of grey soil;

(6) Heavy flints and gravel were laid along the north and south edges of the depression to form 'kerbs' with similar profiles in section (i.e. an inverted 'V');

(7) Further gravel was laid between the crests of the kerbs to complete a gently cambered surface 3 m wide;

(8) A shallow flat-bottomed side-ditch, up to 1 m wide and 0.3 m deep was left on the south, between the edge of the wide trough (no. 2 above) and the south kerb;

(9) A *margo* was apparently constructed on the north side with a base of flints and a topping of gravel, but only its edge was discernible in the northernmost of the two staggered trenches.

After its first period of use, the original road-surface became covered with brown silty soil. It probably remained as a grassy track, by which time the side-ditch had mainly filled with stony material. Later, renewal of the surface took place a number of times, so maintaining a road-width similar to the original. The final well-gravelled surface was accompanied, it seems, by a small side-ditch built against it on the south. However, a modern pipe-trench made it impossible to check this detail. There was also a lack of datable finds for these early phases. After the gravel road became disused, 10 to 12 cm of brown arable soil accumulated before there was evidence (fragments of coal and iron, Victorian china) of nearby railway construction around 1860.

Two important points emerged from this cross-section. The road had a remarkable revival of use, presumably in medieval times, with the later buried camber well preserved at this spot. Then, at some time before the turnpike was built around 1760, the awkward deviation occurred that makes this spot on the A31 a distinct hazard to today's motorists.

Appendix 20
Candy's Farm 1983

In 1981 rescue excavation on the Roman road from Poole Harbour took place south-south-west of the Roman military site at Lake Farm. Where investigated the road was seen to possess a widening curve westward from its western edge, but time did not allow that particular detail to be followed up. However, not long afterward, this tantalizing evidence for a branch-road of some kind required to be tested. In particular, was it related to the line of Roman road whose course apparently ran through lower Corfe Mullen? To answer this question, a section-trench was cut in 1983 only 20 m west of the suspected junction, but this time on the land of neighbouring Candy's Farm (SY 99629893 and fig. 5C.1e). The trench, measuring 15 m by 1.25 m, was sufficient to span a wide belt of linear features, which included the expected branch-road. Associated Roman pottery, mostly of the military period, threw useful light on the sequence of events.

Natural bedrock here consists of London and Reading Beds. To the east, in 1981, only a short distance away, grey clay predominated, but here the subsoil comprised orange sand and clay with some gravelly stones. If we ignore the ridge of stony arable soil which developed later over the early road, then the basic details that emerged all belonged to the Roman military period. Before any constructional work proper took place, the original topsoil, 15–20 cm deep, had been removed down to bedrock over an east-west strip of ground 9 m wide on a gradient of 1:16 sloping to the north. Then, from south to north, the following features had been incorporated in this strip:

(1) *A band of fine gravel*, some 1.5 m wide and up to 10 cm thick, converging to run parallel to the line of roadway (no.3 below). It had been laid over two grooves or ruts worn into bedrock. The southern of these grooves, uphill, had been carefully packed with heavy flints, later partly robbed out or disturbed. The layer of gravel ended against that flint line, which formed a kind of revetting edge, but extended over and beyond the northern groove, this being devoid of special packing. The band of gravel is best regarded as a *margo* or side-walk, but there are details, in particular the two grooves or ruts, that will be further discussed below.

(2) *A shallow gully*, forming a distinct division between *margo* to south and roadway to north; the convergence of the former towards the latter meant that the gully narrowed from east to west.

(3) *A central belt of stony metalling*, 3.25 m wide and 25 cm thick, which made up the branch roadway on its expected track; it had been laid directly upon bedrock and in places a thin grey deposit was seen underlying it and possibly resulting from bracken or similar vegetative material used as a key. The surface had no camber, but was relatively flat, resting on a slight basic shelf giving drainage northwards. There were occasional traces of yellow gravel on the top metalling and broken fragments of burnt heathstone occurred either in the first material or in early repairs.

(4) *A wide, shallow gully*, being the rest of the stip cleared down to bedrock and left as a feature fully 3 m broad.

(5) *A depression*, 0.5 m deep at best and 4 m wide, having a shallow southern slope, up towards the previous gully (4) and with a steep northern edge. Bedrock here consisted of a mixed clayey sand with lenses of gravel which would have provided the right kind of material for the roadway. The depression may have served such a purpose, either originally or for repairs.

On the surface of the road and *margo* there was a considerable scatter of potsherds belonging to the mid-first century A.D. (including samian, amphora, mortarium). While these finds immediately post-dated the structures, the soil a little higher contained samples of Oxford ware typical of the later Roman period.

What is the explanation for the channels provisionally called grooves or ruts in feature (1) above? It seems best to regard these as wheel-ruts, created by a laden cart, which was swinging round from a southerly departure-point so as to run in a westerly direction beside and parallel to the roadway. As the cart moved along, material could have been thrust off on to either road-surface or *margo*. In the latter case it looks as though the parallel ruts served as a useful guide to the breadth of the feature. The heavier metalling required on this sticky band of London and Reading Beds could be obtained either from the valley gravels nearer the Stour or from the plateau gravels higher up. The latter source was obviously more convenient for usage half-way down the slope, so that it is likely that flint and gravel were quarried on the hilltop, near the known pottery-kilns.

Appendix 21
Carter's Cottages 1984

Behind no. 2 Carter's Cottages, Candy's Lane, it was noticed that work to create a garden patio had begun to cut into the northern edge of the well-defined ridge marking the line of the Roman road (cf. plate 5C.12 for the view in the garden just to the east). The opportunity was taken to examine that part of the road which was to be removed (SY 99079876 and fig. 5C.1c).

The width of the road could not be determined, but other constructional details appeared to confirm various of the findings elsewhere in Corfe Mullen: at Higher Russell's Copse, Whitehall House, and Bailey Gate level-crossing and (for the Roman road to Wareham) at Cogdean:

(1) The initial build-up of flint and gravel had been laid in a shallow trough cut into bedrock (gritty clayey sand, London and Reading Beds) and based on a central *spina* of firm material.

(2) North of the roadway, a gravelled strip 90 cm wide could be interpreted as a *margo* or side-walk.

It is interesting that at this point (allowing for the lack of a complete cross-section) a *margo* was identified on the north side and this was also true for the other sections to the *west* in lower Corfe Mullen.

Early dating evidence was scanty, but the rim of a flanged bowl in hard grey ware, possibly of third-century date, came from the surface of the *margo*.

Appendix 22
Cogdean, Corfe Mullen, 1987

A large-scale building development began in October 1988 at upper Corfe Mullen between Higher Merley Road and Higher Blandford Road. This area had already been prospected for indications of the Roman road from the Lake base to Wareham and good visible clues had been observed in the shape of various ridges, old hedges and banks as described elsewhere. The projected works included a major local link road which would give a more direct route from upper Corfe Mullen towards Wimborne. Its planned course crossed that of the anticipated Roman road and would, it was hoped, provide important confirmation for the latter. Topsoil stripping for the new road was carried out by machine and the trench crossed the expected line of the Roman road in the middle of former pasture, where all surface trace had disappeared, giving exposure of the sandy gravel bedrock over a width of 8 m. This revealed precisely on alignment a band of very dark soil flanked on its east by a slightly prominent band of compacted gravel, each feature being several metres wide. At this stage there were only hints of a second dark line parallel to the first by way of another side-ditch. With the kind co-operation of the civil engineers concerned, a special trench was cut close by machine, across the line of the Roman road (SY 99139775 and fig. 5D.2a), but not quite at a right angle. This was dug deep enough to establish conclusively its main details, but a high water-table made it impossible to clear completely to the bottom of the original foundation material. The trench immediately proved its worth by revealing that there was indeed a well-defined east side-ditch and, parallel to that and forming part of the road-construction, a narrower gully. Both were filled with the dark humic soil which characterized the west side-ditch.

The road was built by first digging a furrow at least 10 m wide and probably 0.75 m deep into the fine sandy gravel which easily gets waterlogged even in this hilly position. Two retaining kerbs of compacted heavy gravel were laid within this strip, nearer its eastern side, parallel and 5 m apart, and these formed the frame for the road. Then, a *spina* of similar heavy gravel was constructed down the central line between the kerbs, in order to ensure the final camber. The next stage was to throw back subsoil and topsoil (grey patches represented odd turves) that had been removed from the furrow and pack it down evenly between the kerbs and over the spine.

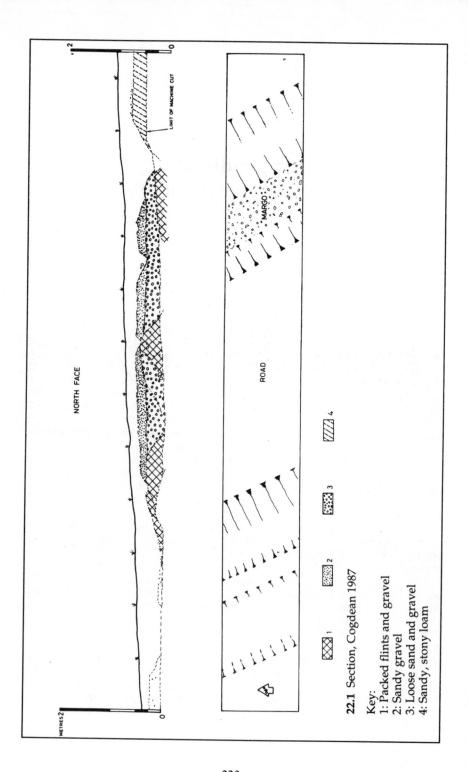

22.1 Section, Cogdean 1987

Key:
1: Packed flints and gravel
2: Sandy gravel
3: Loose sand and gravel
4: Sandy, stony loam

Although this stretch of road is in good condition, unworn by much later use or disturbed by re-metalling, the final surfacing created by the Roman engineers is a little uncertain, simply because of centuries of exposure. However, the harder stonier top to the road seems to have had a covering of lighter clay as a kind of cement, visibly seeping down into the upper layer of surface material, along with discoloration of the gravel due to wear and tear. This would have been similar to the 'cemented' surface of the Roman military road exposed in Higher Russell's Copse, Court Farm. The gully, clearly seen on both section-faces, had been cut into the final road-surface, providing a band 1 m wide next to the east ditch. This can be interpreted as a *margo* or footpath beside the actual road, which thereby was left with a working breadth of 4 m.

There was no positive signs of long-standing wear on the road. A thin layer of gravel and sand spilled on to the lower fill of the west ditch from the edge of the surfacing. It belonged to the last period of use in which the road was involved, a long time ago, judging by the depth of undisturbed black soil above, but not otherwise datable. The hedge-line and footpath passing to the west of this spot show that the local route deviated from the Roman line before the late medieval field-system came into existence.

There were no finds of early date, a not unexpected result of a machine-trench cut straight down to bedrock at short notice.

22.2 Section of Roman road from Lake Farm to Wareham, Cogdean, Corfe Mullen 1987, looking north

(b) Other excavated sections

Appendix 23
Preston Cottages, Tarrant Rushton 1968

Trenches were cut on either side of, and at right angles to, Preston Lane (ST 94200500 and fig. 5B.2b) which was suspected of following the first re-alignment of the Badbury to Hod Hill Roman road first suggested by Codrington. Topsoil was shallow, varying from 25 cm to 32 cm over natural chalk, but a little deeper on the north-west of the lane. There the sloping ground was barren for the length of the 7.5 m cut, except for one unexpected object found deep on bedrock, namely an iron disc-nail of the type K24 at Hod Hill (Brailsford 1962, Plate XII). If this distinctive artefact was of the same date, then it was an interesting pointer to the close passage of the Roman army.

The second trench, 9 m long, on the south-east, traversed promisingly a band of crumbly chalk already visible on the surface of the arable and parallel with the lane. The band proved to be of redeposited chalk, 20 cm thick and 4.9 m wide, carefully laid on light brown soil barely 10 cm thick and somewhat disturbed by the plough. The chalk band began just north-west of the barbed-wire fence with its edge further marked by very large flints. Inside the fence a sinkage in the chalk layer was noted 1.3 m wide. It was identified later as the filled trench of a drain leading from the Tarrant Rushton airfield (1939–45) down towards the Tarrant stream. Alongside the edge of the chalk band furthest from the lane the natural chalk was flat and then, after 2 m, the bedrock showed a pronounced edge to an area where disturbance by scoops suggested quarrying had occurred.

Subsequent work elsewhere has supported the view that the chalk band represents the Badbury–Hod Roman road. On firm, well-drained downland the Roman engineers did not always deem it necessary to key the base material into a foundation trench. The ground was cleared of vegetation and a minimum of topsoil removed. Chalk was quarried from land just away from the road and laid to form a slight camber, on which flint and gravel, thinly strewn, formed a wearing surface.

Appendix 24
Badbury Rings 1968

This trench, 18.3 m long and 90 cm wide, was dug north of the Rings (fig. 5B.1b), parallel to and 19.8 m west of the axis of the Dorchester–Sarum Roman road (ST 96390331 and fig. 5B.1b). The object was to test the alignment of the suspected road towards Hod Hill, long suggested by the straight parish boundary between Shapwick and Pamphill.

Topsoil here was extremely thin, no more than 15–20 cm over the natural chalk. The land was then still being tilled, with the plough biting into bedrock, so that there seemed little chance of recovering worthwhile evidence. However, a belt of scattered loose chalk and flint soon came into view in precisely the anticipated position, underlain by patches of darker soil over the natural chalk. There was no obvious sign of this feature on the undug surface, perhaps not surprisingly as the total thickness of the material was never more than 15 cm, often less. If the siting of this belt fitted the line of the expected road, its width of 4.9 m proved also to be the same as that seen in other sections cut across it elsewhere. The only other detail of note in this exploratory trench was a shallow ditch, virtually parallel and 3 m to the north. It had apparently been refilled (deliberately?) with chalk and soil, when a narrow groove was cut into it, not exactly on the same alignment as ditch and road. This ditch could well have been a boundary to the road when it was in use and the groove could represent fencing, but the relative dating of these details was impossible to determine.

Two small soundings were cut closer to the Dorchester–Sarum road. One off the line of the Hod road, showed the side-ditch of the Sarum road as 1 m wide at the top, then narrowing centrally to a spade-slot. The other sounding tested the point where that side-ditch met the Hod road, but traces of the latter were confined to chalk fragments vaguely in the right place. Certainly the plough was encroaching in those days too close to the agger of the Sarum road. It may also be noted that in the later nineteenth century turves destined for Bournemouth were lifted in quantity from north of the Rings, which would further explain the shallowness of the present topsoil. A section across the massive build-up of the road to Sarum ought to be more revealing.

In 1985, in Long Plantation to the north-west of Badbury Rings, the East Dorset Antiquarian Society cut three cross-sections across the parish boundary continuation of this road. In two places, the parish bank and ditch were found to lie north of an older alignment of residual chalk fragments and flint. It was greatly disturbed, but very similar to the exposure nearer the Rings, described above. The third trench was dug at the eastern end of the Plantation and revealed that the parish bank (now invisible at surface) had been bult over a slight ditch lying north of a well-preserved flint and chalk road 3m wide.

24.1 Badbury 1968. Early road seen as dark band, from south

Appendix 25
Lazerton Farm, Stourpaine 1972–3 and 1986

The long ridge that formed the manorial boundary recorded by Drew was first investigated in 1972 and 1973 (Field, 1973). It lies west of the house at a right angle to the Iwerne river and is aligned directly with the Ashfield Gate on Hod Hill. The linear feature at the base of the ridge was then reported simply as an 'ancient causeway', but the later evidence from close by (described below) and from elsewhere establish its origin as Roman military. The restoration of the Lazerton ponds and of their water inlet from the river brought an opportunity in 1985 for the newly formed East Dorset Antiquarian Society to check the ridge west of the length that had since been scheduled as an ancient monument.

The section-trench was dug close to the point where the inlet or channel had apparently been cut through the ridge certainly before the later eighteenth century (ST 86261041 and fig. 5E.5d). Fortunately, removal of the overburden had not penetrated to the earliest levels. As the Roman road reached the lower ground of the river-flat, it was made slightly more prominent as a positive causeway. This fact became apparent on the west face of the section-trench. Although still dealing with a bedrock of chalk, Roman engineers here adopted methods similar to those noted elsewhere on less stable terrain. Their procedure was as follows:

(1) A shallow scoop was carved into the natural chalk at maximum 30 cm deep centrally over a strip some 6 m wide;
(2) Large flints were inserted into the base of the scoop and cemented in place with puddled chalk; particularly large specimens were rammed along the north edge of the scoop, which was to become the north edge also of the road build-up (cf. Road 1, Colliton Park, 1961–3, Chapter 6);
(3) A small bank of heavy flints was laid towards the south side of the scoop to form a 'kerb' for the road-material proper, so giving the road-base a definable width of 4 m;
(4) Fragmentary chalk and probably some soil were thrown back as the main base of the road; there was no obvious central spina; probably the rammed chalk was considered firm enough to hold the camber, as on other stretches of road laid on chalk;
(5) A final wearing surface of smaller stone and flint was strewn over the bed of chalk fragments.

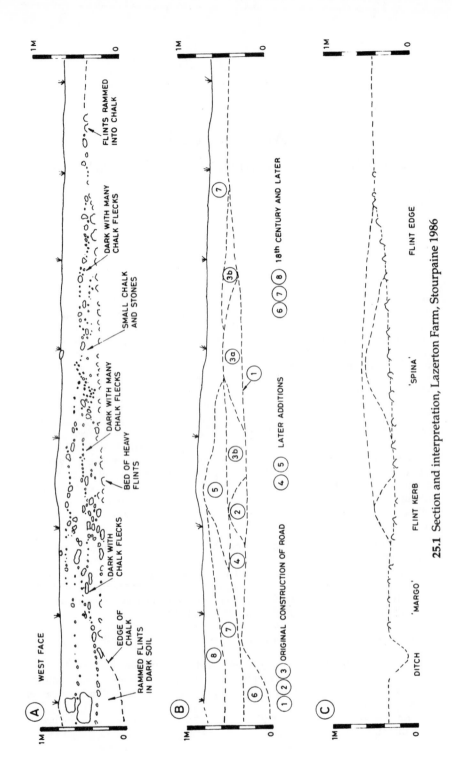

25.1 Section and interpretation, Lazerton Farm, Stourpaine 1986

A

WEST FACE

FLINTS RAMMED INTO CHALK

DARK WITH MANY CHALK FLECKS

SMALL CHALK AND STONES

DARK WITH MANY CHALK FLECKS

BED OF HEAVY FLINTS

DARK WITH CHALK FLECKS

EDGE OF CHALK

RAMMED FLINTS IN DARK SOIL

B

① ② ③ ORIGINAL CONSTRUCTION OF ROAD

④ ⑤ LATER ADDITIONS

⑥ ⑦ ⑧ 18th CENTURY AND LATER

C

DITCH 'MARGO' FLINT KERB 'SPINA' FLINT EDGE

234

It is possible that a side-ditch was also provided south of the flint kerb, but the feature noted could have been of later date.

Components 4 and 5 were much disturbed, possibly by root action after abandonment. A thick layer of humus had accumulated over the original road before a further build-up occurred.

Appendix 26
Castle Close, Wareham 1987

In October, 1988, the construction of a tennis court in the gardens of Castle Close, Wareham, led to the exposure of part of the Roman road that had connected Dorchester and Wareham before Alfred's Walls were built. It was found that the south-east corner of the newly levelled layout had cut into gently sloping ground, so revealing what appeared to be layers of metalling. The site (SY 92168718 and fig. 5G.1a) lies precisely on the alignment for which the evidence is discussed in Chapter 5G, some 10 m west of the garage, with the house beyond. The area could be expected to have suffered interference long ago from the building of the Norman castle and this was confirmed by the evidence.

The section available for examination consisted of two vertical soil-faces making a right-angle in the corner of the future playing area. On the eastern face appeared the edge of part of a cambered road. Its basis was a scooped depression into which layered soil, gravel, pebbles, and finally heavy stone had been successively placed. A first central deposit of yellow gravel could not be fully examined any deeper, but it might have formed part of the central *spina* (layer 'a') on which the camber was built. In the angle of the excavated cut, the topmost stony stratum (layer 'h') reached a thickness of 0.4 m. On the southern face the bands of heavy stone and pebbles forming road-material rose to continue the camber. These renewals of metalling clearly took place over a long period and were followed by an accumulation of soil, discussed below. Finally, well before the present, most of the road was sharply chopped off on the west at an angle of 45 degrees. The latter event can be seen as part of the process of shaping the castle-mound, probably in the early twelfth century. The unusual angled section revealed about half the camber of the road, which would have had a width of some 4 m overall.

An important detail in its own right was the typical black soil of Wareham that had accumulated evenly from the ground level of the original road until the present. As in the case of the burials and roads at Northport (*Proceedings* **110** [1988] pp. 152–4), the relative depths of features were in harmony with the interpretation of past events. Three critical layers can be isolated with their covering of soil:

26.1a, b Sections, Castle Close, Wareham 1987

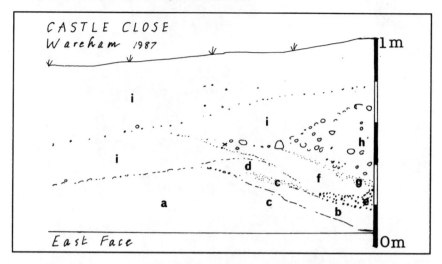

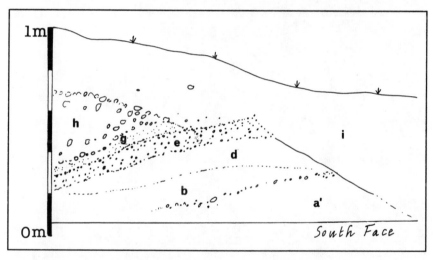

Key:
a: Natural gravel, undisturbed, yellowish-orange in colour.
a^1 Similar gravel, but with stonier top surface, possibly redeposited material for a *spina*.
b: Dark mixed loamy soil.
c: Yellowish, sandy.
d: Dark brown soil.
e: Pebbles and small stones.
f: Medium brown soil.
g: Small stones and sandy, pale colour.
h: Large flints.
i: Black humic soil, typical of Wareham.

26.2 Exposure of part of Roman road from Wareham to Dorchester, Castle Close, Wareham 1987. (viewed from north).

(1) Original Roman level to Saxon disuse of road = approx. 800 years represented by 25 cm of soil cover = *3.1 cm per century;*
(2) Saxon disuse of road to the present = approx. 1200 years represented by 40 cm of soil cover = *3.3 cm per century;*
(3) Norman scarping to the present = approx. 900 years represented by 37 cm of soil cover = *3.8 cm per century.*

An inch a century (2.54 cm) has often been quoted as an average for the formation of soil on an open lowland site in Britain, so that the above figures seem about right for ground inside Wareham never likely to have had intense cultivation.

The construction of the tennis court has removed part of the scarped edge of the circular platform that formed the emplacement for the Norman castle (depicted in RCHM, Vol. II, Part 2, p. 323). In compensation, it has provided confirmation of the Roman road from Dorchester whose alignment towards Abbot's Quay was interrupted by the West Wall and its great ditch.

Appendix 27
Stoborough Heath, Arne 1987

In June 1988 a strip of the low earthwork forming the suspected Roman road on Stoborough Heath was cleared of scrub in advance of the new bypass. A team from the Trust for Wessex Archaeology was given the opportunity to dig a cross-section by hand (SY 92626535 and fig. 5E.2a). The full details will be given by the Trust elsewhere, but it is possible to summarize here the way in which the feature was built.

First, after the removal of the overlying black humic heathsoil from the belt of ground in question, a wide scoop of almost the same width was made into the subsoil of sticky clayey sand. A side-ditch was dug on the west and re-dug later at least once. On to the centre of the scoop the topsoil was spread out, probably including heather and scrubby vegetation, to form an unusual base for the road. On top of this, the mixed subsoil was replaced in a gentle camber (around 4 m wide) for the road proper, being packed down and beaten to form a surface of what can be called *terre battue* rather than *pisé*. To the east of the camber it appears that a narrow strip of the scoop (about 1.5 m wide) was covered by coarse dry sand from a little way off, in order to create a *margo* or side-walk.

Some details of the linear feature probably derive from its survival as a local boundary after disuse. However, the feature betrays intrinsically the construction of what must be claimed as a typical example of a Claudian military road happily lacking later repair. The scoop into subsoil has been a regular hallmark of sections cut by the writer in Dorset. The use of heather, bracken or brushwood has been noted in sections of the Mamworthy to Lake Roman road, while the creation of a hard, beaten road-surface of mainly clayey soil was an important detail, in particular, at Higher Russell's Copse, Corfe Mullen (Appendix 18). This technique is known on the Continent (Chevallier 1976, p.92) and was probably more common than has been realized. Undoubtedly this was a way of building a campaign road very quickly to keep an outpost in touch with its base. A well-defined road was needed to enable relief troops and supplies to move in mist, fog or darkness over unfamiliar terrain.

Appendix 28
Butcher's Close Stinsford 1988

(The following is reprinted from *Proceedings* 110 [1988])

In June 1988, a trench was dug by machine in the grounds of the Dorset College of Horticulture and Agriculture at Stinsford, west of Dorchester. The object was to establish whether in fact the long ridge previously noted concealed the line of a Roman road leading into Dorchester from the east and ultimately originating from Lake Farm, near Wimborne. The section-trench, 13.5 m long and 1.5 m wide, was completed by hand in respect of the last 1.5 m, as the JCB had to avoid a stone wall which unexpectedly came to light towards the southern end of the cut.

At the point excavated (SY 71239102) the ridge lies on the southern slope of the field known as Butcher's Close, immediately east of the church and the former vicarage. Bedrock was reached at approximately 1.25 m and comprised, not Upper Chalk as indicated by the geological map, but Plateau Gravel with a surfacing of fine clayey loam. The excavation revealed, precisely on the line expected, a sequence of road-building that had taken place over a long period of time.

The first activity on this site had been to scoop into bedrock a shallow depression some 5 m wide, in which to key the foundation of the early road. Large flints were rammed into the despression and reinforced with heavy gravel to create lateral kerbs and a central spine. On this skeletal framework looser material (undifferentiated bedrock) had been thrown back and topped by packed ochre loam, relatively stone-free, and a final stony metalling. Seen in section, the camber of this original road made a very distinguishable deposit colourwise, and it contrasted with the variety of dirty stony layers which continued the story of the road thereafter. On the south this early road possessed a round-bottomed side-ditch, at maximum 50 cm wide and 25 cm deep, the south side of which was the edge of the depression, while the north formed one of the gravel kerbs. The ditch-fill was a blackish stony soil, devoid of finds, although a sherd of early medieval type came from a high level over it. South of the ditch, large flints had been packed into the original natural loam, making a band half the width of a probable *margo* that would have been 1 m broad. The cambered surface of this early road had apparently been broadened on the north from 3.5 m to some 5 m, so that in that direction the metalling spilt over the original cut edge of the depression. Over this early road, layers of banded, dirty, stony metalling 15 cm thick were seen to have accumulated uniformly before a new road-strip, also 5 m wide, was laid out further north. The south edge of this second road rested against the last metalling of the first. However, in this second case, the stony metalling, which gradually built up to a thickness of 80 cm, was mixed with blackish soil and, while lines of material did occur, there was also much disturbance.

Thus the road had undergone two main phases and a multitude of re-metallings before it fell out of use. The evidence is that this abandonment could have been as late as the seventeenth century. It is most significant that even at that time the line of the original south ditch was clearly serving as a property boundary on the edge of a wide lane. Unexpectedly, this notable fact was emphasized by two successive linear foundations for single walls which were constructed precisely over each other and over the dark final fill of the ditch. Wall 1 (the earlier) consisted of a single layer, averaging 40 cm wide, of flat slabs of hard chalk or limestone, but without any positive sign in the short length uncovered of what the superstructure might have been. Wall 2 (the later), 50 cm wide, lay over it, separated by a thin layer of dark soil, and was built of roughly two courses of similar stone with a rubble infill.

Machine-trenching undoubtedly saves time and labour, but its cost can only be truly measured in the loss of the odd find that would have suggested when a particular road surface was laid down. Thus the dating of the early road, and of the phases and rebuild that followed, was limited to the obvious fact that they preceded the latest wall. It was only in association with this ultimate feature, and directly below it, that datable material finds came to light. Pieces of medieval brick occurred in the layer of soil in which the final wall had been embedded, while the infill of that wall yielded two substantial fragments of medieval window, showing that a building of that period had been available for robbing in the vicinity.

The limited work in Kingston Maurward Park has given solid proof of an early road, constructed on the same principles that have been noted elsewhere in these investigations as characteristic of Roman military thinking. If regarded as a 'litmus test' to confirm the final stretch of Roman road from Lake that led into Dorchester via a river-crossing at Grey's bridge, then the object has been achieved. To conclude, it must be said that, from surface features in the pasture, Butcher's Close gives every promise that large-scale excavation would reveal in some detail the story of this road in relation to the medieval remains of Stinsford and so, indirectly, its importance to Dorchester, so close at hand.

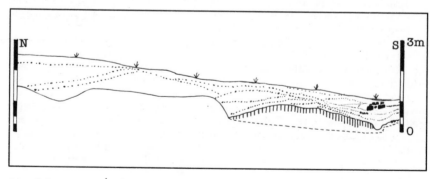

28.1 Schematized section, Stinsford 1988

242

28.2 Section of Roman road from Lake to Dorchester at Stinsford, 1988, looking north-west

28.3 Roman road from Lake to Dorchester at Stinsford, 1988. South edge and side-ditch with late medieval wall-footings above, looking east.

(c) Other information

Appendix 29
A Lost Place-Name

Place-names containing the Anglo-Saxon word *street* in its various forms have usually been shown to have a close association with the presumed course of a Roman road. A significant example is Stratford, spelt as such or in alternatives such as STRETFORD, STREFFORD or TRAFFORD. The matter was put forcibly by Ekwall: 'All the Stratfords are on Roman roads.' His argument was based on being able to associate these place-names with roads whose existence was already archaeologically accepted. If the converse is true (and there seems no reason why it should not be), a Roman road may be expected at a river-crossing which can on other grounds be ascribed one of the above place-names. If the archaeological evidence for the road is strong, then, in the spirit of Ekwall's dictum, the addition of the name appears to make that case incontrovertible.

The *Dorset Lay Subsidy Rolls* of 1327 and 1332 list details of a certain STRETFORD tithing situated in the Barrow Hundred, the whereabouts of which has remained a mystery. The other tithings were all hamlets that can be located today: Affpuddle, Bryantspuddle, Turners Puddle, Shitterton and Worgret. All these lie in the area immediately south of Bere Regis, so that STRETFORD should be found in the same vicinity. Can it be satisfactorily demonstrated that the name of the missing tithing alluded to a *Roman* road crossing the river Piddle?

In his *Place-Names of Dorset*, Part 1, p.275, A.D. Mills discusses the problem of locating STRETFORD in relation to other documentary references where the name is combined with HYDE (LA HYDE CUM STRAFFORD 1316 and HIDE STRATFORD 1696), the latter being a late name for the whole tithing. The location of HYDE (Hyde House, Higher and Lower Hyde House, etc.) in the south-east corner of Bere Regis parish (some 5 km south-east of Turners Puddle church) leads him to suppose that the ford giving its name to STRETFORD 'was no doubt on the River Piddle or Trent, perhaps where it is crossed near Hyde House by the Bloxworth–Wool road, which may then be the *straet* referred to' (loc. cit.). This view discounts his earlier suggestion in *Dorset Lay Subsidy Roll of 1332*, p.10, f.n.2, that STRETFORD may be an error for the nearby place-name SNATFORD, shown by him in *Place-Names of Dorset*, Part 1, p.276, to have well attested early spellings and to be of quite different origin.

One clue to the answer may reside in the family name Alderham or smilar which occurs frequently in Turners Puddle records from 1244 onward. The 1327 Roll lists a William Alresham as a tax-payer in the missing Stretford tithing. He belonged to a local family of standing since, in 1327 and 1332, a relative, John Alresham, acted as one of the two tax-assessors for the whole Barrow Hundred of over 100 tax-payers. William, then, was probably living at the family holding, for the name is linked to both *Allerhams Coppice* and *Buckshill Coppice*, which lie only 0.8 km south-east of the ford in question at Turners Puddle (*Place-Names of Dorset*, Part 1, pp.295–6). There is no problem, then, in directly associating a one-time hamlet (possibly itself called Allerham) south of the Piddle ford with the name STRETFORD and with the course of the Roman road from Lake Farm to Dorchester.

One difficulty remains that the patient etymologist must try to explain. In the 1774 map of the county created by Bayley for Hutchins's *History of Dorset*, Hyde is shown only 1.6 km east of the ford, hardly a cartographical error, since John Hutchins was Rector of Wareham not far away and must have known the local district as well as anywhere. David Mills has suggested to the writer an explanation fitting place-name analysis to the archaeological case that Stretford was south of Turners Puddle church. His words are here quoted in full:

(1) it must be signficant that the Hyde-Stretford tithing was in Barrow Hundred, unlike most of Bere Regis, but like Turners Puddle itself;
(2) if there was a connection between the two places still in 1696 (HIDE STRATFORD), is it possible that Hutchins places Hyde where he does in 1774 because he still knew about such a connection? In other words, he labels the northern part of the tithing (which had earlier been the Stretford) by the more familiar name of the whole tithing.

Appendix 30
Samian Pottery from Wareham
by Thomas May, C. D. Drew and Grace Simpson
with drawings by Teresa Hall

The ancient burial ground within which stands Lady St Mary's Church beside the ford, now bridged, across the river Frome, may have been where all these sherds were found. However, only nos A11 and A12 are marked as having come from the cemetery. Mr Norman Field has pointed out to the third-named writer that the earliest Dr.29, nos A4 and A5, in the styles of Aquitanus and Senicio respectively, are matched at early military sites in Dorset: at Hod Hill, which Sir Ian Richmond stated was not occupied after A.D. 51 (on coin evidence), and at the legionary site at Lake Farm, where the name-stamp of the potter Licinus is also recorded, whose work is known at the Waddon Hill fort. Wareham would be a most suitable place for an early Roman fort. The churchyard is on an elevated site alongside the river. A small area in front of the west end of the church is open ground and might well be worth excavating in case Roman remains could be found there. The three contributors to this report have each usually (but see A6) come to similar conclusions about the attributions of sherds to individual pottery and about the dating of the thirteen sherds. Colonel Drew recorded Thomas May's notes in a handwritten account with small drawings of the sherds and R.A.H. Farrar refers to them in *Proceedings* **76** (1954), p. 82.

Illustrated
The original numbering as marked on the thirteen sherds (A1, A2, etc.) is shown in brackets. Sherds A2, A6 and A8 have not been illustrated here, and the stamps only of A1 and A7:

1. (A3)   Dr.29, a late example of this South Gaulish form. Small leaf-tips decorate the soffit. The bowl-maker's name is lost and only the two letters OF for *officina* or workshop survive (number 5 below). *c.* A.D. 65–80.

2. (A4)   Dr.29, on which only the detail of the frieze is clear. The style is like that of Aquitanus, see *Knorr* (1919) Taf.8A, but with different motifs. See also *Knorr* (1952) Taf.3A and 4D, also *Hermet* (1934) pl. 36,43. Note the small beads below the central moulding. *c.* A.D. 43–60.

3. (A5)   Dr.29. Below the central moulding are alternate small panels with three poppy-heads in the upper part of a saltire design, and a narrow leafy

246

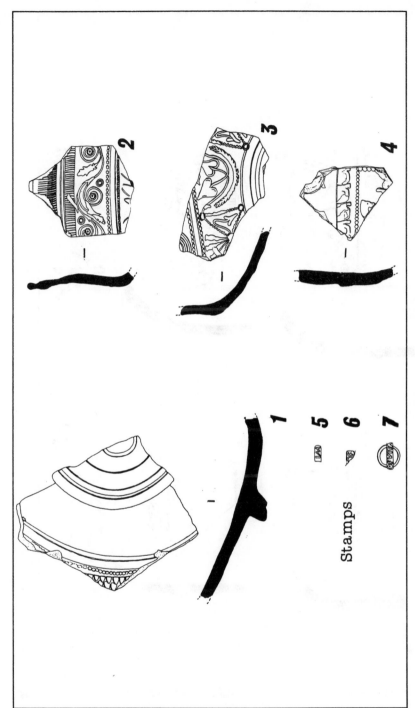

30.1a Samian pottery from Wareham

247

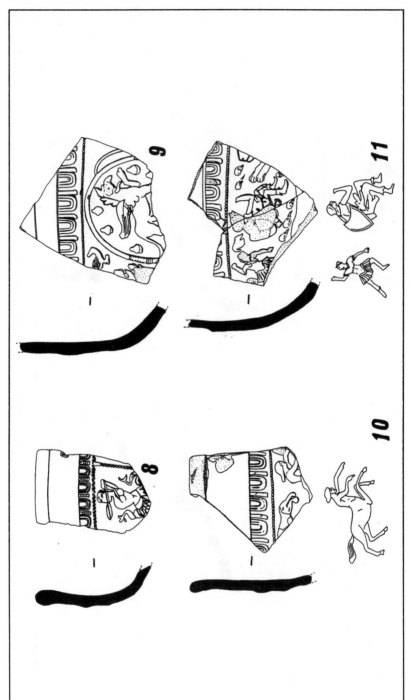

30.1,b

festoon containing two heart-shaped leaves with crossed stalks. Rosettes cover the border terminals. For the leaf, see *Knorr* (1919) Taf.75A and motif 23, by Senicio of La Graufesenque. See also *Hermet* pl. 58, 19 and 20. *c.* A.D. 43–60.

4. (A9) Dr.37, with the small ovolo of Doeccus, see *Rogers* (1974) B160, and with his large beaded borders. Lexoux, Central Gaul. *c.* A.D. 160–190.

5. (A1) Stamp]IM on base of platter Dr.18 (not illustrated). South Gaulish. *c.* A.D. 65–80.

6. (A3) Stamp on base of bowl of form Dr.29 (number 1 above).

7. (A7) Stamp OF VITA on Dr.33 base (not illustrated), by Vitalis of La Graufesenque; see *Oswald* (1931), pp. 340-2. There is a groove on the outside at the lower edge of the wall. *c.* A.D. 60–80.

8. (A10) Dr.37 in the style of Iullinus of Lezoux. The triton is close to 0.21=D.17. His ovolo is *Rogers* B164, with the coarse roped borders. *c.* A.D. 150–180.

9. (A12) Dr.37 from cemetery, Lady St Mary's Church, at 2.4 m deep. A large scroll with a griffin, 0.864=D.501. Leaf-tips surround the griffin. The ovolo is one used by the Cinnamus group, *Rogers*, B143 or 144. *c.* A.D. 150–180.

10. (A11) Dr.37 from cemetery, Lady St Mary's Church. Freestyle design, showing a centaur to right, 0.732=D.431. Illustrated also as the complete figure copied from Oswald. The animal to left may be the bear 0.1627 or 1628. Style of Cinnamus, see *Stanfield and Simpson* (1958), pl. 163, 73. *c.* A.D. 150–180.

11. (A13) Dr.37 with a free-style design. In the centre is an Amazon with a shield on her back. Her right hand is broken off. 0.207A. The small warrior is 0.177=D.103. Cinnamus style, with the sides and tips of leaves in the field. For dating see number 9 (A12).

ALSO NOT ILLUSTRATED:
A2 Dr.24/25, a thin-walled cup with a rouletted side. South Gaulish. *c.* A.D. 43–50.

A6 Dr.37 base, probably from La Graufesenque. *c.* A.D. 70–85. This sherd was previously identified as from a Dr.31.

A8 Dr.33, a wall-sherd, slightly incaved, with a groove in the middle of the outside. Central Gaulish. Second-century type.

Bibliography
Hermet (1934) Hermet, F., *La Graufesenque*, Paris. (Reissued 1979, Marseille).
Knorr (1919) Knorr, R., *Topfer und Fabriken verzierter Terra Sigillata des ersten Jahrhunderts*, Stuttgart.
Knorr (1932) Knorr, R., *Terra Sigillata-Gefasse des ersten Jahrhunderts mit Topfernamen*, Stuttgart.
Oswald (1931) Oswald, F., *Index of Potters' Stamps on Terra Sigillata*, Margidunum.
Rogers (1934) Rogers, G.B., *Poteries Sigillées de la Gaule Centrale: Les Motifs non Figurés*. XXVIIIe Supplément à Gallia.
Stanfield and Simpson (1958) Stanfield, J.A. and Simpson, Grace, *Central Gaulish Potters*, Oxford.

Appendix 31
The Enclosure at Hodway Lane, Shillingstone

The outline of this minor enclosure is relatively easy to spot on older maps, but only now can its origin be linked to the vanished stretch of Roman road from the Stour crossing to the existing T-junction at the north-eastern termination of Hodway Lane. The ridgeway route that the Roman army upgraded has largely remained traceable elsewhere in one fashion or another, which perhaps makes this gap surprising. The place-name *Hodeweye* is recorded for the thirteenth century, implying access over the Stour before the enclosure came into being. However, a chain is no stronger than its weakest link and that applies very much to the supporting evidence for a 'new' Roman road. It is helpful, therefore, if the landscape itself explains part of the problem.

The enclosure is identifiable from the tithe map and the Ordnance Survey six-inch (first edition, surveyed in 1885). It takes the form of a rectangle four furlongs long and two wide (ABCD), aligned with that central part of Hodway Lane (EF). Like some other early land-allotments that have been noted in Dorset (*cf.* Appendix 18), the boundaries as first laid out were followed by a perimeter lane, which could still be traced in part a century ago. The area within measured 8 hectares (20 acres), the typical holding of an independent yeoman, a simple arrangement intended to separate arable land from permanent pasture. At the east corner (C) of the enclosure, a rectangular plot of rough copse and nettles apparently marks the site of a long abandoned cottage. Judging by the internal field boundaries (now mainly destroyed), it is likely that the enclosure resulted from several enlargements, the first being the 3 hectares (8 acres) of regular layout AFGH. Around the enclosed land, between it and the Stour meander, extended a belt of river-meadow, which was divided into smaller manageable fields for grazing or hay by hedges originally running from the perimeter lane to the Stour.

The question arises: What light does this small enclosure throw on the stretch of Roman road from the river to the surviving Hodway Lane? Why did the enclosure layout not fully respect the Roman course, if Hodway Lane observed it as far as the south-west side AB? We have seen that until a generation back there was visible evidence for the continuation and re-alignment of the Roman road itself just inside the area of the old enclosure (fig. 5J.4). Yet the latter seems to have been first laid out deliberately in line with the continuation of Hodway Lane (EFG) running from the south-west.

The explanation may be that the original small arable enclosure AFGH observed the old way to the Stour, part of which continued to be traceable until not long ago in the arable and meadows within the great meander. However, the through track gradually fell out of use. In 1548 there was a reference to *Hodwaysende*, indicating, as might be expected, that the enclosed arable holding was in existence before then.

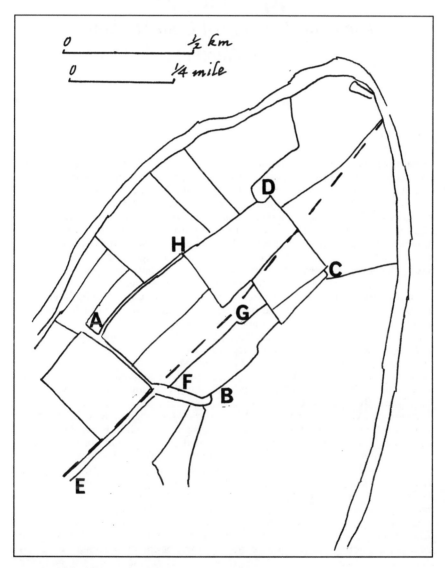

31.1 Land-holding at Hodway Lane, Shillingstone

Appendix 32
The Land-Holding at Cold Harbour, near Wareham

Certain details of the Roman branch-road (Chapter 5I) to Woolsbarrow are better appreciated if we consider local landscape history as it seems to have evolved over the centuries. It has been shown (Chapter 5F) that at Cold Harbour the early field-system supported the antiquity of the Roman road from Wareham to Woodbury. The argument for the Roman origin of that road rests partly on the claim that the general layout is pre-turnpike with significant deviations off-line to clinch the argument. In respect of the land-holding at Cold Harbour, a more subtle relationship will be proposed in which Iron Age, Roman military and Saxon elements may all play a part. No doubt more than one scenario could be offered, but what follows seems alone to fit all the emerging facts.

On tithe plans and the first edition of the large-scale Ordnance Survey maps, the land-holding that appears to have originated at Cold Harbour is seen as a slightly bent, but nevertheless symmetrical, sub-rectangle of land (fig.I.2: ABEG). It lies north–south and measures nearly 1.6 km long and a little under 0.8 km wide. The Roman road to Woodbury runs transversely (CH) across the area dividing the holding into two distinct unequal parts.

The southern part (CBAIH) was at one time demarcated by a circuit lane, which can still be traced on the ground. The slightly sinuous course of AH on the west is exactly reflected by the line of BC, especially as it curves north of Cold Harbour (C). Of these two parallel boundaries the original was the western, which continues the Roman road from Woolsbarrow (KGH). From the original nucleus at C, a pattern of small fields developed on that side of the Roman road with a smaller secondary settlement eventually appearing at J, which appears to have developed an independent access westward (at I). In the course of time, arable land nearest Cold Harbour came to incorporate a short stretch of the road, so that wayfarers had to deviate slightly. About half the land in this southern part seems ot have remained as rough grazing within the ring-fence.

The northern part (GECH) shows as a block of land that was, until recent times, mainly uncultivated. On this open heathland, which was traditionally left for furze-gathering, peat digging or grazing, early bounds were often marked by stones, unless some linear feature could serve. Thus, in this case, it was bounded on the west by a short length of Roman agger (GH). On the north the parish

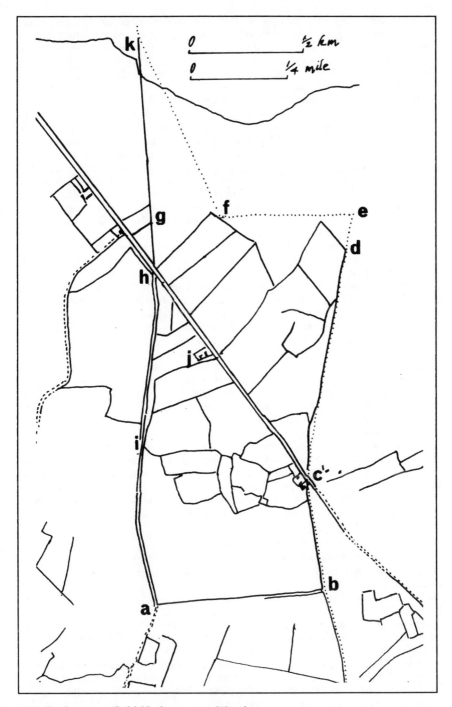

32.1 Enclosure at Cold Harbour, near Wareham

253

boundary between Wareham Lady St Mary and Morden once ran straight across (EF) but seems to have been diverted to K, a long recognized meeting point of three major estates in post-medieval times. On the east, the parish boundary (CD) was provided in part by the edge of a batch of early fields dependent on Cold Harbour; otherwise in the nineteenth century a short length (DE) of the boundary was still marked by stones on open ground.

The Cold Harbour estate apparently took in some 101 hectares (250 acres) and its regularity is a notable feature. At this stage one thinks of a land-holding probably of Saxon origin, such as the 64.75 hectares (160 acres) surrounding Mountain Clump and The Knoll in Corfe Mullen. There it can be demonstrated on the ground and from documentary sources that there was a pre-Domesday holding of precise proportions whose complete circuit was formed by a double-embanked lane. However, at Cold Harbour, the lane is seen only on the south of the Roman road, yet the whole circuit-boundary gives every appearance of having been laid out at one and the same time. The differences in land tenure and farming practice within the enclosure itself stemmed in the first place from observing the line of the transverse Roman road (CH).

Enclosures certainly developed in some numbers on the heathland in the medieval period, with frequent reference in Tudor documents. The association of the embanked lane and the parish boundary in the present example, however, points to an origin that is very much earlier. Fortunately, further clues to its general date can be gleaned from the linear features that have left their mark on the landscape. We have seen that the field-system related to the Cold Harbour settlement had grown up against (and even over) the line of the road that eventually became the turnpike, one important pointer to the origin of the whole road being of very early origin. In addition, the west side of the land-holding is aligned against what appears to be a cross-country route of very long standing (KGHIA), part of which is attributed to Roman military work. It is traceable from the Piddle to the south and runs northward past Woolsbarrow hillfort. As part of its west boundary, this heath-track must, *prima facie*, have been in existence when the Cold Harbour estate came into existence. Its behaviour is very revealing. South of the Roman road to Woodbury (where the track is an embanked lane) its course (HIA) is definitely sinuous, while, to the north, however, the enclosure-circuit is absolutely straight. Did the sinuous southern stretch arise as a later continuation of the Roman branch to Woolsbarrow, or was the whole heath-track from the Piddle northwards already in use at the time of the Roman conquest? In the second eventuality, we must suppose that the Roman engineers straightened a prehistoric route, an action which certainly took place elsewhere in Dorset during the military period.

To sum up:

(1) There was a rectilinear land-holding laid out at Cold Harbour;
(2) It was later than the Woodbury Roman road, but earlier than medieval parish boundaries;
(3) It was aligned on the west partly against a Roman road, partly against a heath-track;
(4) The old track was earlier than the establishment of parish boundaries, but it is uncertain whether the track came into use before or after the Roman roads were constructed;
(5) If the heath-track was pre-Roman in origin, then straightening took place earlier than the land-holding. The straightening was later than the original course of the old track and later than the Woodbury Roman road (arguably as an addition immediately secondary to the latter).

The fifth point raises interesting thoughts, but the subject of prehistoric routeways has always been fraught with difficulty. Only excavation, in the right place, where positive evidence awaits, can tell whether the track was indeed prehistoric and in use until the Roman army constructed its road from Wareham to Woodbury.

Appendix 33
Medieval and Turnpike Roads
at Trickett's Cross

If we examine the development of the medieval and turnpike roads that centred on Trickett's Cross the ultimate antiquity of the 5 km stretch from Stapehill is further emphasized. The latter, based on a Roman antecedent (AB), must be differentiated from the similar length of turnpike road (EB) reaching the Cross from the Angel Inn at Longham, which was, on the evidence, a new construction of mid-eighteenth century date. The original act of parliament (1758–9) planned that the new turnpike roads from Wimborne and Longham should join at Palmer's Ford (G) and go on from there to Ringwood. The fork (F) where the medieval tracks came together is indeed still marked by hollow-ways in rough heathland 350 m west of the Ford, close to a notable tumulus. However, the projected routes were soon changed to link at Trickett's Cross. Thence, to St Leonard's Bridge (BD), the combined turnpike took a slightly sinuous course as it was now clearly following an earlier highway, confirmed by the mention of a bridge at St Leonard's in 1620 (Mills 1980, p.231). The latter date is important, because Charles Drew (Drew 1942), in identifying the site of the Chapel, was mistaken (in company with the later editors of Hutchins, whom he quotes in support) when he thought that, before the creation of the turnpikes, people had reached Ringwood from Wimborne by the much longer journey via Palmer's Ford. Historically, from Trickett's Cross, three routes diverted in a generally easterly direction:

(1) the Roman road due east (ABC);
(2) a medieval road north-eastward to reach Ringwood via St Leonard's Bridge (ABD);
(3) a medieval track passing south of the St Leonard's estate to join the cross-heath route from Longham towards Ringwood via Palmer's Ford (ABFG).

Why had the Roman road eastward from Trickett's Cross (BC) been interrupted for some distance? As Ringwood grew in importance in medieval times, movement from Wimborne came to be diverted north-eastward. Furthermore, the 'ring-fence' (to use a modern term) around the lands farmed from St Leonard's Chapel apparently came to dictate the ways used by travellers passing to Ringwood from both Wimborne and Longham. The area thus bounded (BFGCD) corresponds fittingly to that of the manor, farm and common which Drew ascribed to the sixteenth-century settlement. When the turnpikes (AB and EB) were finally completed, the two forks at the Bridge (D) and the Ford (G) were replaced by the single fork at the Cross (B).

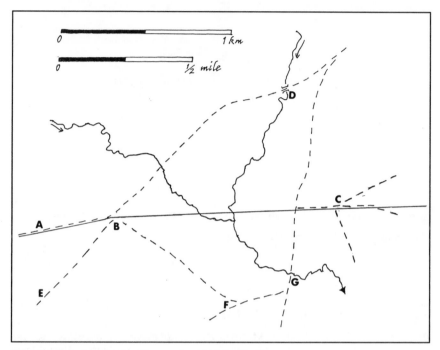

33.1 Medieval and turnpike roads at Trickett's Cross

Appendix 34
Profiles Across Six Early Roman Roads

Surviving evidence for the early Roman roads in Dorset takes three forms:

(1) Lengths of ridge (*agger*) with the right proportions and alignment;
(2) Hedge-lines and old boundaries possibly including stretches of medieval/ modern roads that may have remained in use (sometimes alongside telltale strips of the original ridge);
(3) Buried metalling or side-ditches, where, over time and for various reasons, an accumulation of soil has concealed the original road; probing with a metal rod may help, but final assurance comes from a dug section.

In Appendix 35 the lesson drawn from eight profiles belonging purely to the first category makes an overwhelming case for one single road. Here, half a dozen examples in the first and, sometimes, second, group, illustrate the visible ridge of a similar number of the early roads. The width of the causeway in each case is consistently around 4 m with the visible height up to 0.5 m, but usually much less. Later local remetalling may have played a part in the build-up that we see today. Thus Wareham to Bere Regis (and Woodbury Fair) must always have been a frequented route, which may account for the prominent causeway in Triangle Plantation. Even there, however, there is a sign of what often happened elsewhere, namely the development of the medieval road alongside the Roman original, with the latter then serving as a land boundary.

(1) North edge of The Down Wood, Tarrant Monkton (ST 91200695 and fig. 5B.3b). The bank on the south is the parish boundary with Langton Long Blandford, which soon cuts across the road to run north-west.
(2) West edge of Triangle Plantation, Trigon, Wareham Lady St Mary (SY 89609060 and fig. 5I.1a).
(3) Duddle Plantation, Ilsington (SY 73489120 and fig. 5C.10c). The modern road is that from Dorchester to Ilsington.
(4) Mount Pleasant, Corfe Mullen (SY 99069757 and fig. 5D.2a). In this small grassy paddock the road-ridge is observed to make a slight re-alignment as it reaches the crest of higher ground from Lake Farm. The massive field-bank looks to be of considerable age.
(5) South-west side of Triangle Plantation (SY 89609033 and fig. 5F.2ab). The

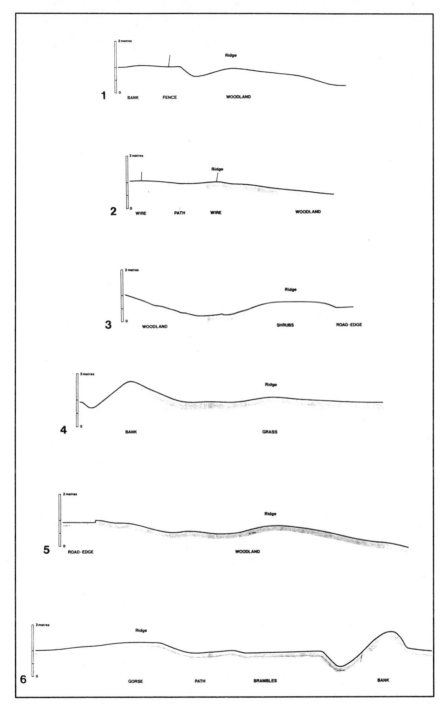

34.1 Some profiles across early Roman roads in Dorset

hollow-way development can be seen west of the agger, although it is uncertain how far there has been embanking for the turnpike/modern road on the far side. (6) Stoborough heath (Wareham bypass), Arne (fig. 5C.2 and SY 92628535). A section of this precise profile was later excavated by the Trust for Wessex Archaeology (*cf.* Appendix 27).

Appendix 35
Profiles in Avon Forest Park (South Block)

Since taking over the Avon Forest Park as a public amenity, Dorset County Council, through its Planning Department, has been making a detailed record of the landscape for which it is responsible. The possibility of a Roman road being detectable within the South Block provided a problem that could be tackled in the scheme of work. With the co-operation of the Warden and the County Archaeologist, eight surface profiles were surveyed by R. Matthews of the Planning staff. Each profile was effected by taking spot-heights at one metre intervals for lengths varying from 36 m to 60 m. At each end of the traverse (Profiles A and H, 500 m apart), the writer had noted indications of a significant ridge, crossed in each case by modern tracks running from north to south. Elsewhere, for the most part, the ground surface was masked by gorse and young conifers, which made normal visual observation impossible.

The line of what is established as the Roman military road from Lake Farm to the New Forest and beyond was detectable from the profiles once the results were set down on paper by Mr Matthews. Throughout the zone crossed there is a slope from north to south, with a slight gradient (3%) for the western part of the traverse (HGFE). The fall is more marked midway towards A (12%), where a spur of higher ground projects from the north, and then the north-south gradient settles at a steady 8% (BCD). Details from west to east with height and width of ridge:

Profile H 0.15 m x 6 m. Visible athwart modern cleared path.

Profile G 0.2 m x 5 m. Heather, gorse and firs.

Profile F 0.2 m x 6 m. Similar cover; slight ditch or terracing on north side of ridge.

Profile E 0.15 m x 6 m. Similar cover.

Profile A 0.1 m x 6 m. Modern gravel track, 2 m wide, on north of ridge, flanked by modern field-ditch.

Profile B Dense cover. Course of road betrayed only by break in ground; land here reportedly ploughed in past.

Profile C 0.2 m x 5 m. Scoop on north side (ditch?) producing prominent crest to ridge ('top of bank' on Mr Matthews' survey).

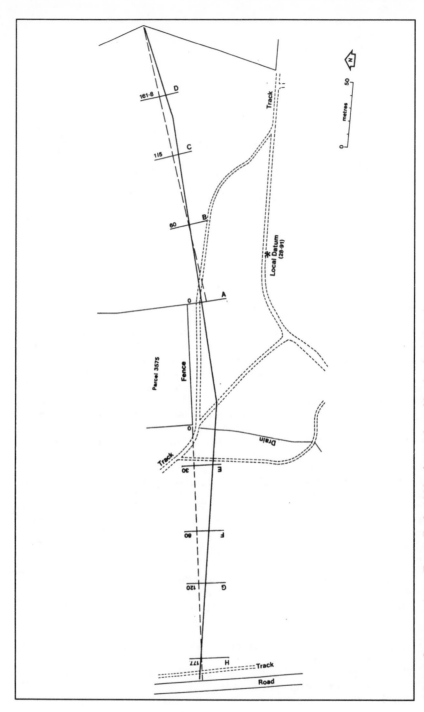

3.5,1–2 Survey at Avon Forest Park, 1989: plan and profiles (and opposite)

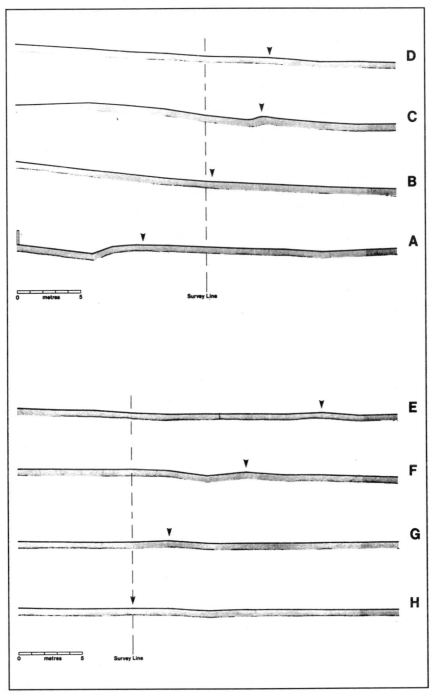

35.2

Profile D 0.15 m x 6.5 m. More open grassy terrain with larger conifers. Ridge ('remains of old track', Mr Matthews) unmistakable for some distance, crossed by north-south path.

In picking up the course of the road, the survey has demonstrated how and why the Roman engineers created this minor deviation, visibly starting just west of Profile H. The gradient of the Roman road itself from H to E was almost nil, with its height above Ordnance datum keeping between 28.5 m and 28.9 m. Thereafter, by skirting the southern end of the spur, a gentle climb of 2 m in 161 m (AD) to reach 30.9 m replaced the stiffer slope offered by the higher ground. An ascent to some 34 m would have been needed north of A, had the original line from Trickett's Close continued. However, that line, directed at Watton's Ford, was soon regained. Re-alignment angles are shown on the profiles to lie between E and A and between C and D. Certainly, Roman roads in very hilly country might well not have deviated thus for what would have proved a minor obstacle. However, the present example illustrates the careful survey carried out in the first century by the Roman military engineers in relatively unchallenging terrain.

Notes

Introduction
1 Frere 1987, 50.

1: DORSET BEFORE THE INVASION

Essential detailed reading for the Dorset Iron Age includes Wheeler 1943; Richmond and Brailsford 1968; Cunliffe 1975; and Wainwright 1979.

1   The county of Dorset, as such, did not exist, of course, in Iron Age times. As noted later, the term 'Dorset' will be used either to apply to the present county or to the tribe that largely lived in that area, but also extended its influence into what became the counties of Devon, Somerset and Wiltshire.

2   For details, Rieu 1951, Chap. 2.

3   Brailsford 1957, 118–21.

4   For tribal pottery distribution, Cunliffe 1975, 91. The boundary between these two tribes in the Wylye-Nadder area may well have played a part in the Roman campaign (see note to Chapter 9).

5   RCHM *Dorset*, Vol. II, Part 3, 619 and Aitken, 1990.

6   Cunliffe 1975, 151.

7   Woodward, 1987, 68 ff.

2: THE ROMAN ARMY

1   For the army itself, the best general survey comes in Webster 1969 and later editions.

2   Dudley and Webster 1965 is still useful for the background to the invasion and the landings in the south-east of Britain, but was written before the recognition of the Lake base in the south-west. Other accounts occur in Frere 1967 (third edition 1988), Salway 1981 and Hind 1989.

3   In the course of time, Roman legions had come to be further identified by the addition of an epithet to their original number. The word might signify an honour ('Augusta' was equivalent to 'Emperor's Own') or the first source or recruits (the Ninth Legion Hispana had been formed in Spain) or simply a duplicate force (the Second Legion Adiutrix, meaning 'Reserve', was assembled later in the first century A.D).

4   Johnson 1983 provides a wide survey of early Roman military works.
5   Webster 1964, 135.
6   Frere and St Joseph 1974.
7   Hawkes and Hull 1947, 177.
8   Woodward 1987.
9   Webster 1988, 9.
10 Webster 1960, 91, referred simply to 'cleared routes'. For its part, the RCHM *Dorset* Vol. V, p. xxix, stated that 'The Romans introduced ... planned and engineered roads ... designed to meet the needs – at first *military*, but increasingly administrative and economic – for fast and efficient communications ...'. In 1972 there was uncertainty about which of the known roads (1972) was military or not, while, as for the Roman fort at Hod Hill, occupied for some five to seven years, it was 'unlikely that a metalled road had been built'.
11 Collingwood 1930, 4.
12 Frere 1987, 5.
13 Quoted in Chevallier 1976, 83.

3: THE INVASION AND AFTER: SOME EARLIER VIEWS
1   Quoted in Webster 1965, 90.
2   Wheeler 1943, 61.
3   Richmond and Brailsford 1968, 2.
4   RCHM *Dorset* Vol. 1, 226.
5   Webster 1959, 54.
6   Webster 1960, 91.
7   Putnam 1970.
8   Beavis 1974 and 1975.
9   Field 1976a.
10 Field 1976b.
11 Field and Butler 1966.
12 The Fosse Way 'frontier' as the limit set by the Romans to their initial conquest has had doubts cast upon it, but the suggestion remains the best in the circumstances.
13 Eicholz 1972.
14 Manning 1976, 19. A similar view had been expressed in 1972: RCHM *Dorset* Vol. V 1975, p.xxxi: ' ... a large garrison was already established in Exeter before the end of Claudius's reign ... '.
15 Manning 1988, 10.
16 Salway 1982, 93–4.
17 Webster 1988. This scenario of the Roman campaign in the West of England is discussed in Chapter 9, note 1.
18 Todd 1984b, 1985a.
19 Putnam 1984.
20 Alcock 1972.
21 Roman Forts in Devon have now been recognized at Tiverton, Okehampton, and several other locations.

4: THE MILITARY BASE AT LAKE FARM
1   The date for the first Roman presence at Exeter is given as *c*.60 or a little earlier (*Britannia* xiv [1983], 321).
2   Webster 1988, 91.
3   David 1976–83 provides the results of the geophysical survey. A full summary of the various 1959–71 excavations at Lake Farm between 1959 and 1971 has been prepared by NHF and a copy deposited with Poole Museums in advance of the report on the 1979 work.

4   Road 3 was seen and recorded in 1962 (Davison), 1963 (Drayson and Hoy) and 1965 (NHF).

5   The name 'Lake Gates' may provide problems in the future. It was used to refer first, in the singular, to a gate on the turnpike from Wimborne through old Corfe Mullen and then soon after, in the plural, to the level crossing over the track of the Somerset and Dorset Joint Railway.

6   Volunteers came mainly from Poole Grammar School, Henry Harbin School, Poole, and the then Queen Elizabeth's Grammar School, Wimborne. J. Drayson, K. Hoy, R.J. Briggs and R.T. Tanner were particularly helpful. Professional archaeologists who undertook work on the site before 1971 incude B. Davison (for the then Ministry of Works) in 1962, and Dr. R. Butler (RCHM Eng.) in 1965. Both passed on their reports to NHF. Since then, work has been directed by Dr Graham Webster (1972-3) and I. Horsey and K. Jarvis (1979 and later).

7   The size of the base could be established once a south-west corner was identified. The west gateway must arguably have lain opposite the bend in the Hamworthy–Badbury road. Since that gateway would normally be sited half-way along the western defences, the full length of that side could be established. From that dimension, given the normal proportions of Roman military sites of this kind, a further provisional dimension could be reached for the length of the southern defences. The lines of the eastern and western sides of the buried fortress, which followed from these calculations, received some confirmation from the look of the ground in the fields involved.

8   B.R. Hartley said in 1962 of the samian from the pit cut by the side-ditch of Road 2: 'There would seem to be a strong case for suggesting an initial date soon after A.D. 43.' As the dating range of the pottery extended into Neronian times, the construction of the road may be put in the mid 50s, no earlier.

9   Frere and St Joseph 1974.

10   Horsey and Jarvis 1981. That brief report did not reconcile a continued belief in a one-phase 12 hectare fortress with this clue to a major re-planning of the internal features.

11   The latest calculation of the fortress area at Exeter is given as 16.37 hectares (40.45 acres): *Britannia* xviii (1987), 343.

12   Maxfield 1986.

13   As noted earlier, the evidence from beside Road 4 indicated that in the mid 50s the first tank served by the leat was remodelled with a reduced capacity. This was probably for a smaller fortress.

14   Webster 1979 gives the occupation of the Roman fort at Waddon Hill at between A.D. 50 and 60.

15   Manning 1988, 12.

16   An analysis of the internal dimensions and a comparison with other sites leads to one view (Henderson 1990) that the 12 hectare (30 acre) site at Lake (i.e. Lake II) could well have been organized to house a complete legion. This economy of space seems unnecessary on the terrain at Lake Farm, where there was plenty of room for Lake I. Nor was such economy apparently practised at Hod Hill.

5: THE EARLY MILITARY ROADS

1   Collingwood 1930, 2.

2   As quoted in Chevallier, 1976. Writers on Roman roads (like Margary 1966 and Johnston 1979) have not emphasized certain features of construction, like the foundation trench described by Statius. It is well shown below, for example, in the sections named in the text.

5A: Lake Farm to Poole Harbour

1   Jarvis 1982: the section described at Vineyard Copse possessed features shared with other exposures of the early military roads in Dorset: clearance of turf and topsoil down to bedrock whereon to bed the road; use of that spoil to create a camber; widening of road soon after initial build; and the possibility of a central rib and a kerb. Erosion had removed any later remetalling, while the widely spaced side-ditches (in this writer's view) were almost certainly not original features.

5B: Lake Farm to Hod Hill

1   Details with NHF (who also has slides) and Kingston Lacy Estate (per David Smith).

2   Widely spaced ditches were noted east of Badbury Rings in ploughed ground (*Proceedings*, **85** [1963], 106).

3   Excavation (directed by David Johnston) in Batt's Field, north of the trifurcation, has shown that the side-ditches of the Bath road were laid out to fit in with those of the Dorchester–Badbury–Sarum road. Since widely spaced side-ditches are not a necessary feature of military roads in Dorset, it appears that the Bath road was upgraded to fit into the 'new' civilian road from Dorchester. In that area ploughing had destroyed all traces of metalling over the chalk.

4   Crawford and Keiller 1928: feature x in illustrations of Badbury, pp.58–60.

5   Excavations by East Dorset Antiquarian Society (led by John Day) 1985–6.

6   Observations by NHF in 1976 at time of diversion of footpath.

7   Field 1976b.

8   RCHM *Dorset*, Vol. III, Part 2, 263.

5C: Lake Farm to Dorchester

1   Regarding the place-name BROG STREET, David Mills suggests that in the present case the element *street* has the meaning of 'a long, straggling hamlet' (Mills 1980, 16). The subsequent discoveries make more likely the conventional explanation that this was a Saxon term for a neighbouring Roman road.

2   In 1988 the BP pipe-lines were trenched across the line just north of the A31. Removal of topsoil revealed the harder ridge of the abandoned Roman agger, but there were practical difficulties to further investigation at this spot.

3   The Wessex Water pipe-line (June, 1989) exposure occurred 56 m north of the A31-Dullar Lane crossroads at ST 04249875. It was surprising to note that for a long distance north of the A31 trunk road there was no sign of the expected chalk bedrock. The overlying stony, sandy deposit is at least 2 m thick (*cf.* RCHM Vol. II, Part 3, 611 and *Proceedings* **85** (1963), 105 and 86 (1964), 115.

4   RAF vertical air photograph: 1934–5134.

5   Air oblique views by J.R. Boyden in present custody of NHF.

6   Copies of Drax Estate Maps by Taylor in Dorset Record Office.

7   On the 1845 Bere Regis Tithe Map the north-west side of what was then field 698 lies along the expected course. The new bypass cuts across the line.

8   The argument that these bridge remains are possibly of Roman date is given in Chapter 8C.

9   Crawford 1921, 176–8.

10   It is significant that John Hutchins believed in the existence of a Roman road from Dorchester, which he traced as far as Pallington, where he lost it in the expectation that it was leading towards Wareham (Hutchins 1774, Vol. I, p.xv).

11   There is some support for the antiquity of this straight stretch past Hastings Farm in an eighteenth-century plan of Tincleton estates (Alington papers 1936, 23, 27), in Dorset Record Office. It shows half a dozen numbered

plots aligned to the road on the south, which is hedged on both sides, whereas the diverted line from the east is not hedged and crosses what is called 'Symes Free Land'.

12   Dorset Ordnance Survey six-inch XLI SW (1902) clearly depicts the 400 m of parallel linear features, but, after ploughing, recent maps are less certain as to what is being shown.

13   There has been much confusion over the early roads leading into Dorchester from the east. Thus it has been stated (Good 1966, 111): 'In mediaeval times Bhompston, Bockhampton, Kingston Maurward and Stinsford were all small settlements, and there can be no doubt that an old road, which almost certainly left the present one at Heedless William's Pond ... ran through them into the town.' But on p.28, looking from the other direction, the view is expressed that 'there was no real exit from the town directly eastward along the line of the High Street until Grey's Bridge was built.'

A recent discussion on Heedless William's Stone would have benefited by the knowledge that it lay beside the Roman road from Lake Farm (C.L. Sinclair Williams, 'Heedless or Headless William's Pond and Stone ... ', (*Proceedings* 110 [1989], 161–3). A straightforward explanation for the siting of this stone and the so-called Roman milestone at the top of Stinsford Hill is that they were placed to mark the edge of the public road that was finally diverted round Kingston Maurward Manor and House (Chapter 14).

14   An extinguishment order dated 13 August 1778 (Dorset Record Office) is informative: 'An order for diverting and turning the Bridle Road from Stinsford Cross to the village of Bockhampton and likewise the Footpath from Grey's Bridge on the Turnpike Road from Dorchester leading to the village of Bockhampton aforesaid ... the diverting and turning the two Roads ... may be effected without any detriment or anyway inconveniencing the Publick.' The movement of the 'Bridle Road' was the final act in the diversion of a right of way through Kingston Maurward Park away from the original Roman line to the south. The latter had declined to become the 'Footpath', which cannot have been a new creation since 1748, when Grey's Bridge was built. A 'Footpath' as recent as that would have had no validity in law and no extinguishment order would have been needed. There is therefore the implication that the carriage-bridge of Mrs Pitt replaced an existing footbridge.

15   Hutchins, 1774, Vol. I, p.xiv.

16   The reports are specific on the alignment and early dating of these exposures: 'Excavations for the Dorchester Excavation Committee, 1970 ... Greening's Court, High East Street' (P. Greene), Proceedings 92 (1970), 137; and 'Discoveries during Building Work at St. Peter's Church, Dorchester' (C. Sparey Green), Proceedings 103 (1981), 124 and 126.

5D: Lake Farm to Wareham

1   Details of excavation west of Wimborne Road with NHF.

2   The apparent connection between the line of this road and the early field-system of Lytchett Minster is given in Chapter 14.

3   Details about the communication system within the grounds of the former Royal Naval Cordite Factory were provided by M.R. Bowditch, author of *Cordite-Poole* (1983).

4   *Proceedings* 110 (1988), 152–4.

5   Early ditches (28/22 and 32) were seen in 1974–5 running parallel to the presumed Roman line of North Street, suggesting that the westward bend is a medieval phenomenon (Hinton, D.A., 'Excavations in Wareham, 1974–5', *Proceedings*, 99 (1977), 42–83).

5E: Wareham to Flower's Barrow and Purbeck

1   There has always seemed a distinct possibility that the pre-turnpike road between Corfe Castle and Wareham had a Roman origin. The old route (still basically followed today save for the detour on Stoborough Heath) reached the Frome from Norden in two straight stretches. The re-alignment on Hyde Hill can be traced as a hollow-way in thick gorse. If Roman, it belongs to a later military period or the civil period. It is unlikely that the original military way, via Hill View, was totally abandoned, since it probably served the villa at Furzebrook. Certainly, the Flower's Barrow garrison moved on when the base at Lake was still operative (Chapter 9), so that a more direct road from Purbeck to Wareham from the Corfe Castle gap would have made sense. There is another possibility. Given the likelihood that the South Causeway, like the North (see note 4 to Chapter 5D), was substantially improved in Saxon times, it might have happened that the development of Corfe Castle as a pre-Norman strong-point necessitated a slightly more direct route to the mouth of the Frome.

2   From the general evidence where that parish boundary turns away a further well laid-out road once branched off to run due east over Norden Heath. South of Gallows Plantation, it was crossed by the later (?) line of the Corfe Castle–Wareham road (A351). It survives to the east of that intersection as a length of old drove (known strangely as New Line Lane) after which the alignment continues as an embanked boundary as far as Corfe river. The overall straight measures more than 1.6 km. The inference is that long ago the angle was indeed a road junction.

3   The *Stanwei* (Stone Way) occurs in one of the Saxon Charters for Corfe B910.K.435 (Grundy, G.B. 'Saxon Charters of Dorset', *Proceedings* 57 (1935), 123–8).

5F: Wareham to Woodbury

1   There may be a very slight adjustment in this otherwise straight Roman stretch opposite the Silent Woman inn. However, this is where the turnpike/modern road moves across the Roman line. The spot is marked by the start of a public path and a magnificent bifurcate oak. Just past is one of the old milestones for which this road is notable: 'Bere Regis 5 miles – Wareham 3 miles'.

5G: Wareham to Dorchester

1   Dorset Record Office: Strode manorial map, 1732 (D279/P3). The quotation ascribing this Worgret–East Stoke stretch to the turnpike engineers is from Good 1966, 58 and 139. It is extraordinary how this evidence has been misunderstood over the years.

2   RCHM *Dorset*, Vol. II, Part 2, Monument 42, 409.

3   Where this revealing side-step occurred in the parish boundary, the local right-of-way was so long established in the mid-nineteenth century that foot-passengers were left the chance to cross the new railway by means of stiles, which still exist. This curious concession took place only a few paces from the Wool level crossing.

4   Good 1966, 58.

5   A buried ditch observed at this point probably belongs to the Roman road. Information from Roland Smith, further to his note: 'Empool Pipeline, East Stoke to West Knighton', *Proceedings* 111 (1989), 111.

6   The new Dorchester bypass for the A31 sliced through Alington Avenue, but sadly did not evoke a close archaeological check on traces of the Roman road.

7   RCHM *Dorset* Vol. II, Part 2, 539.

8   Davies and Woodward 1985. With reference to the milestone fragment that

was found, one Roman mile (1480 m) from the south gate takes us a little way south-east of the excavations to a point where the bypass has now been cut through.
9   RCHM *Dorset* Vol. II, Part 2, 551.
10   C. Sparey Green makes pertinent comment on the probable road and its alignment in describing hitherto unrecognized Saxon burials: 'Early Anglo-Saxon burials at the 'Trumpet-Major' public house, Alington Avenue, Dorchester', *Proceedings* **106** (1984), 148–52.

5H: Sandford to Bulbury
1   This set of enclosures and others still surviving on the heathlands (*cf.* Chapter 8B and Appendix 32) deserve close examination.
2   Mills 1980, 35.3
3   There were apparently four opposing entrances still visible at Bulbury in Victorian times, a fact suggestive of Roman military activity (*cf.* Chapter 8E).

5I: Cold Harbour to Woolsbarrow
1   The first Ordnance surveyors were aware of the width of this agger. On the relevant Ordnance Survey 25-inch map north of Triangle Plantation the field-boundary runs for some distance on the east, then is shown diverting sharply for perhaps 5 m to continue on the west side. Today the property boundary has shifted entirely to the east, although the agger has been mainly spared from destruction and incorporation in the farmland to the west.
2   RCHM *Dorset* Vol II, Part 3, 487.

5J: Hod Hill to Rawlsbury
1   Crawford 1953, 61.
2   A line of spot-heights recorded by the surveyors for the 1st edition of the six-inch series in 1885 (Dorset XIV SW) strongly suggests that an agger could still be seen as a hedge bank at 84851060, about 280 m north-east of the present T-junction at the start of Hodway Lane.
3   Bowen 1961, Plate 1(b). The old road shows in the bottom right-hand corner. The original photograph cannot now be traced.
4   Good, 1966, 14 and 21, makes some useful comments on Hodway Lane which do not conflict with its Roman use.
5   The Celtic fields on Shillingstone Hill are illustrated in Bowen 1961, Frontispiece and Plate 1(a); and in RCHM *Dorset* Vol. III, Part 2, 340.
6   Hart 1964. The Ibberton charter named a *Walle dich* which is firmly identified as this length of parish boundary. The term *dich* can here be taken to mean an agger (*cf.* Ackling Dyke) rather than a defensive bank and ditch (*cf.* Bokerley Dyke or Wansdyke). Hart claimed a simple 'bank and ditch', but the reality is more complex.
7   RCHM *Dorset* Vol. III, Part 2, 259.

5K: Lake Farm towards Winchester
1   Col. Drew first reported the Park Farm stretch of Roman road to H.P. Smith in 1928 (Smith 1948), saying he had looked in vain for its continuation on the commonland at Hampreston, Parley and St Leonard's.
2   For discussion on the place-name KINGSTON, across the ford, on the opposite bank of the Avon, see Chapter 14.

5L: Dorchester to Eggardon, Waddon and the West
1   RCHM *Dorset*, Vol.V, xxxv.

5M: Other Roads?

1   Bere Regis must surely owe its ultimate origin to this long-lost crossroad.
2   Apart from following hedge-lines, this course runs over intensively worked chalkland arable where even the line of the Badbury–Dorchester Roman road, crossing it, has left no visible surface trace.
3   Hillamsland is situated on its own prominent knoll and owes nothing to the higher ground to the north, as suggested (Mills 1980, 126). This would have proved a vital sighting point for a Roman military road and a fine location for a later settlement (hill + ham).
4   The Western entrance to Dudsbury, at the end of the alignment from Ham Lane, is almost certainly Iron Age in origin, but has had a chequered history. A limited trial trench in 1921 revealed a buried causeway, deemed 'modern', *across* the outer ditch (Summer 1931).

6: WHERE WAS THE FORT AT DORCHESTER?

1   Further significant finds are recorded in note 6 below.
2   *cf.* Chapter 4.
3   For the size and date of the fortress at Exeter, see Chapter 4.
4   Johnson 1983, 36.
5   Aitken 1982.
6   Re-examination of Colliton Park finds from the 1930s has brought to light several ballista heads and pilum shafts, together with pre-Flavian decorated samian (personal inform.: Mark Corney, RCHM). This material of early date and military origin came from the sloping ground immediately north of the Library site to be discussed.
7   Draper 1983.
8   The section at the Library site recorded in 1965 by C. J. Sparey Green appears to confirm the eastward turn of Road 1: *Proceedings*, **104** (1982), 126.
9   A Roman marching camp of this early period at Tiverton had a residual rampart of 'turfy material' which was only 20 cm thick (*Britannia, op. cit.*, 323). The Okehampton fort, too, displayed the same type of rampart build-up, plus an *intervallum* road cleared of topsoil (*Britannia*, x (1974), 255–6).
10   Johnson 1983, 59.
11   Richmond and Brailsford 1968, 39.
12   Wheeler 1943, 254–65.
13   Todd, M. 1984a.
14   Johnson 1983, 31 and 33; also *cf.* Chapter 2 above.
15   Farrar 1959.
16   Draper and Chaplin 1982.
17   Keen 1983.
18   *cf.* Chapter 5G, note 7.
19   The 'road' has been traced on three, possibly four, occasions: (1) RCHM *Dorset*, Vol. II, Part 3, 552, no. 176. The road was laid (1955) in a trench cut into chalk, almost certainly a military technique thus early in the Roman period (*cf.* Road 1 above, Colliton Park, 1961–3); (2) 'Excavations for the Dorchester Excavation Committee ... Bowling Alley Walk', Putnam, W.G., *Proceedings* **92** (1970), 135. This interim report provides precise description of the early features, primary bank and road, without interpretation; (3) ' ... Dorchester Hospital Site E', D. Viner, *ibid.* 136. A 'chalk-lined' cut, the extreme edge of which was noted under the later western rampart, seems likely to have belonged to the early internal road rather than to a marking-out trench for the primary bank, a feature not noted elsewhere. (4) 'Excavations (1970) at South Grove Cottage, Dorchester', Viner, D., *Proceedings* **103** (1981), 24–5. The 'road' is here treated as an

unexplained 'feature'. In addition, there are possible signs of a trench for such an early road in Sections of N and W Ramparts (RCHM *ibid*, 546), where metalling may have been removed in building the later rampart.
20   Rodwell, 1975.
21   The interior of Hod Hill outside the Roman fort has long been suspected of being an exercise area for Roman cavalry. Such a function would serve a mounted auxiliary unit. See also Note 1 to Chapter 8a.

7: A MILITARY POST AT WAREHAM?
1 *Proceedings*, **65** (1943), 60.
2 *Proceedings*, **76** (1954), 82–5
3 Woodward 1987.
4 *The Making of Dorset* (series) No. 1.
5 Hawkes and Hull 1947, 147.
6 The handle from 'near Wareham' resembles A135 in *Hod Hill* i and bronze object 27 ('skillet-handle') in *Hod Hill* ii (where no. 26, however, has a slightly different pattern). That from Dorchester (RCHM *Dorset* Vol. II, Part 3, 552, monument 179a) was said to be like A134 from the same site.

8: OTHER SIGNS OF THE ROMAN ARMY IN DORSET?

8A Earthworks at Candy's Farm: a signal-station?
1   These medieval remains are sited on a belt of hillside, 150 m by up to 70 m, apparently terraced at an earlier date and lying between the earthworks at issue in this chapter and the Roman roads to Hamworthy and Dorchester.
2   Fox and Ravenhill 1966.
3   Farrar 1980. R.A.H. Farrar has looked at the earthworks on the spur, without feeling able, at this stage, to agree with this writer's interpretation.
4   There has been recent discussion on the nature and extent of military zones around legionary bases (Rodwell 1975; Mason 1988). The early situation in Dorset, however, cannot have been typical of what happened later around such British garrison towns, when the local populace had finally accepted Roman ways.
5   Donaldson 1988.

8B Two Earthworks at East Holton: Roman forts?
1   D.R.O. (D29).
2   Professor Frere points out that, on size, Enclosure B should have three gates, at least.
3   Collingwood 1930, 32–35.

8C Roman Bridge Abutments at Turners Puddle
1   Cunliffe 1971, 54–5.

8E Dorset Hillforts: causeways and cuttings
1   Todd 1984b.
2   To 'demilitarize' a hillfort in this way is merely saying that access was provided more in keeping with Roman thinking.
3   Richmond 1968, 90, in emphasizing the 'angle of rest' at the Ashfield Gate, Hod Hill, also referred to similar gaps in the Vallum south of Hadrian's Wall.
4   Crab Farm: 2.4 hectares (6 acres) Hod Hill (available area only) 3 hectares (6.86 acres)
5   The Roman road from Dorchester to north of Badbury is not early and almost certainly post-military, as various air-views appear to confirm (Chapter 5B and Field 1976a).
6   RCHM *Dorset* Vol. I, 13–15.

7   Reports on excavations at Pilsdon Pen directed by P. Gelling: *Proceedings* **86** (1964), 102; **87** (1965), 90; **88** (1966), 106–7; **89** (1967), 123–5; **91** (1969), 177–8; **92** (1970), 126–7; **93** (1971), 133–4; and by D.W.R. Thackray: **104** (1982), 178–9.

8   T. Williamson and R. Loveday: 'Rabbits or Ritual ... ' *Arch. Jour.* 145 (1988), 191–313.

9   For the neglected results of this examination by J. Forde-Johnston of the great ditch: *Proceedings* 80 (1958), 108.

10   For the railway burials and new information, see Chapter 13.

11   At the Water-gate on Hod Hill: 'The cutting ... did not go down to the base of the native earthwork' (Richmond 1968, 72).

12   RCHM *Dorset* 1970: Vol. II, Part 2, 246.

13   Richmond 1968, 79.

14   Todd 1984a.

15   The eastern entrance was given road-metalling both early and late in the Roman period. For one or other of these reasons, some link would be expected with the Dorchester–Radipole Roman road, only 700 m away down the spur that provided obvious access to Maiden Castle from that direction. This spur was indeed the traditional north limit of Winterborne Monkton, but the existing straight field boundary looks relatively recent and, on alignment, does not run to either of the Iron Age entry gaps.

16   Beavis 1985.

9: THE ROMAN CAMPAIGN IN DORSET

1   Webster (1988, fig. 12) puts forward his latest suggestion how the legions were disposed in Britain during the first century. His starting date for Lake probably has several sources, including the need to fit in both the role of Chichester and the symmetry of Roman movements. Another reason may be the unpublished appraisal of the continental pottery found in past excavations at Lake. That site has not yet produced examples of pre-Claudian material in the quantity that has turned up at Hod Hill. It is therefore assumed that, though much smaller and more westerly than Lake, Hod had an earlier foundation. This assumption makes no sense, given evidence for the road from Lake to Hod Hill via Badbury Rings (5B). Furthermore, from the writer's own knowledge of the site at Lake, the sample of the total fortress area so far investigated there is far too small for such conclusions. Coins from the two sites illustrate this point. Richmond's work at Hod Hill recovered one Republican issue, one of Caligula, and six of Claudius. Yet, if we went by Richmond's results from excavation alone, we would be unaware of the many pre-Claudian Roman coins that lay in the ground until discovered in the last century after ploughing. At Lake Farm, the coins found and recorded between 1962 and 1972 comprised one of Augustus and 21 of Claudius. If the Roman deposits at Lake were at the same shallow depth as at Hod Hill, can we doubt that the story would be similar? The same argument applies to the finds of pottery datable to around the invason year. Other unfathomable factors may have operated: for example, did the detachment at Hod receive slightly older stocks of coin and pottery from the quartermaster than those issued at the legionary base? Dr Webster's uncertainty is further emphasized by his offer of two dates for the departure of the Second Legion Augusta from Lake: *c.* 55 on the map and 60–61 in the text.

2   A.D. 45 for the arrival in Dorset is suggested by Peddie 1987. While this work does not offer new archaeological facts, there are some interesting ideas on the logistics of the Roman invasion.

3   Chapter 4, note 1.

4   Salway 1981 thought the transfer of bases might be gradual, without a clean break.

5   Richmond 1955, 26.

6   'During that day Caesar followed the enemy at the usual interval and pitched his camp three miles from theirs.' (Rieu, 1952, 52)

7   Some of the weaponry from the nineteenth-century finds from Spetisbury appears to include spear-heads and swords of Saxon type (Swanton 1974 and unpublished material at Dorset County Museum).

8   Further details of the problem of the roads at Badbury Rings come in Frere and St Joseph 1983, also important for its discussion of the earthworks at Hod Hill.

In 1982 the intersection of the Roman roads north of Badbury Rings was examined by a group under the direction of David Johnson of Southampton University. A brief report in *Britannia* xv (1984), 320–2, stated that 'the Old Sarum–Dorchester road ... was laid out before the Hamworthy–Bath road.' This excavation found that ploughing had destroyed all traces of both causeways and the conclusion was based on evidence from the widely set twin *ditches* only, both pairs of which had been cut at the same time. In this writer's experience, such ditches are *not* characteristic of the roads of the military phase in East Dorset, but belong to the later phase(s). The *original* priority of the road to Bath over that from Dorchester to the junction with the Badbury Rings–Old sarum road remains certain from discoveries elsewhere.

9   Branigan 1973.

10   Field 1976a.

11   Hanson 1978 emphasized the amount of timber, but considered for most forts local supplies could be found. However, imports of prepared timber by sea must have been needed for the rapid construction of a base like that at Lake Farm.

12   Based on Peddie, 1988, 187–90.

13   It is recognized that some of the 'gaps' in the Poundbury defences are probably of the Roman period (RCHM Vol. II Part 3, 487).

14   Salway 1981, 93–4.14.

15   Manning 1988, 10.

16   Tacitus: *The Histories* (trans. K. Wellesley), 1986, 277.

Chapter 10: PTOLEMY'S ISCA

1   Field 1968.

2   As noted earlier, Ptolemy used details of latitude based on a slightly smaller globe than is actually the case, while his figures for longitude took the Canary Islands as a zero meridian.

3   The finds of Claudian samian at Maiden Castle probably indicate military activity on the site (Todd 1984a) rather than native occupation which is the subject here.

4   Rivet and Smith 1979, 145.

5   Stamped ingots of lead, recorded as found at Cheddar and Blagdon, have been dated to A.D. 49 (Branigan and Fowler 1976, 183). Another view (Whittick 1982) that the Cheddar find may be a lead commemorative tablet does not seem tenable (*Roman Inscriptions of Britain*, 2404.1). The ingot from Blagdon, admittedly early and genuine, can be dated only with a little uncertainty (*ibid.*, 2404.2). The important ingot from Mendip discovered at St. Valéry-sur-Somme in 1883 (*ibid.*, 2404.24) is dated by Whittick to the years 55–60, when Lake Farm was still an operative base of some kind. But must be noted that Bitterne, Southampton (*Clausentum*) certainly shipped ingots to the continent (L. J. Keen in *Archaeologia Atlantica*, 1.2 [1975], 166–7).

6   Woodward 1987, 68.

11: SOME ROMAN PERSONALITIES

In respect of P. Anicius Maximus, the writer is grateful to Brian Dobson and Sheppard Frere for helpful suggestions.
1   Todd 1984b,c and Bidwell 1980.
2   Eicholz 1972, 157.
3   *op.cit.*
4   What follows is the revised version of a Presidential Address given in 1979 by the writer to the Dorset Natural History and Archaeological Society at Dorchester. He has since learned that around that time, at the University of Exeter, Professor T P. Wiseman gave an Inaugural Address centred on the same Roman personality. A coincidence, it may be said, that underlines the need to recognize P Anicius Maximus and his work.
5   Maxfield 1981 gives the full background to these and other Roman military honours.

12: AN UNEASY PEACE

1   For this important kiln, see J B Calkin, 'An Early Romano-British kiln at Corfe-Mullen', *Antiq. J.* **xv** (1935), 42–55.
2   Rieu 1951, 188.
3   *cf.* Chapter 10, note 5.
4   The possibly slow transfer of the legionary HQ (Salway 1981, 98–9) could have created a division of forces and responsibilities between Lake and Exeter. That might well explain the dilemma faced by Poenius Publius at the of the time Boudiccan revolt (Chapter 13)
5   Bidwell 1980, 41.
6   *ibid.*, 41.

13: DORSET AND THE BOUDICCAN REVOLT

1   The story is told in Webster 1978.
2   Chapter 12, note 4.
3   Chapter 9, note 7.
4   Alcock 1972, 105–6 and Manning, W. H. in Branigan and Fowler 1976, 37–9.
5   Wainwright 1968 and 1978.
6   Other Durotrigian sites where excavation shows that a shift of dwelling-location may have occurred early in the Roman period include: Holcombe, Devon; Bradford Down, Pamphill, Dorset; and Bucknowle, Corfe Castle, Dorset.

14: THE LEGACY OF SECOND LEGION TO DORSET

1   RCHM *Dorset*: Vol.II, Part 2, 310-12.
2   The place name *Beaminster* of A. S. origin has been taken to mean the minster church either within a boundary ('beag', a ring) or named after its founder 'Bega' (?).
3   Cam 1930, 172.
4   In addition to Chancellor 1942, with its discussion of the possible connection between KING-names and Roman roads, Bourne 1988 suggests there is further information to come on a topic very much involving Dorset local history.
5   The oval field-system still traceable in 1840 was related to a central road that had basically vanished. The ancient fields were once bounded by a circuit-lane, demarcating the original layout (*cf.* Appendices 31 and 32).
6   The enclosed area, around 64.75 hectares (160 acres) comparable to Buckland Newton (Keil 1965) and Corfe Hubert (the manor at Corfe Mullen centred on Mountain Clump and The Knoll), each of which observed a two-field system. The early settlement at Lambs Green, Corfe Mullen, seems also to have been arranged with the Roman road to Poole Harbour as its axis and had the same area (Field, 1988).

Bibliography

Proceedings refers to *Proceedings of the Dorset Natural History and Archaeological Society*.

Aitken, G. and N. 1982: 'Excavations on the Library Site, Colliton Park, Dorchester 1961–3', *Proceedings* **104**, 93–126.
Aitken, G.M. and G.N. 1990: 'Excavations at Whitcombe 1965–1967,' *Proceedings* 112, 57–93.
Alcock, L. 1972: *By South Cadbury is that Camelot* ... (Thames and Hudson).

Beavis, J. 1974: 'Excavations at Abbotsbury Castle', *Proceedings* **96**, 56.
Beavis, J. 1975: 'Excavations at Abbotsbury Castle', *ibid.*, 97, 51.
Bidwell, P. T. 1980: *Roman Exeter: Fortress and Town*.
Bourne, J. 1988: 'Kingston Place-Names: an interim report', *Journal of the English Place-Name Society*, **20** (1987–8).
Bowen, H.C. 1961: *Ancient Fields* (British Association for the Advancement of Science).
Bowen, H.C. and Farrar, R.A.H. 1970: 'A Trial Excavation on a Crop-Mark Site on Maiden Castle Farm, Dorset', *Proceedings* **92**, 127–34.
Brailsford, J. W. 1962: *Hod Hill*, Vol. I (Trustees of the British museum).
Branigan, K. 1973: 'Vespasian and the South-West', *Proceedings* **95**, 50–7.
Branigan, K. and Fowler, P. J. 1976: *The Roman West Country* (David and Charles).

Cam, H.M. 1930: *The Hundred and the Hundred Rolls* (Methuen)
Chancellor, E. C. 1942: '"King" in Place-Names and Roman Roads', *Proceedings* **64**, 25–33.
Chevallier, R. 1976: *Roman Roads* [trans. N.H. Field] (Batsford).
Collingwood, R. G. 1930: *The Archaeology of Roman Britain* (Methuen).
Crawford, O.G.S. 1921: *Man and His Past* (O.U.P.).
Crawford, O.G.S. 1953: *Archaeology in the Field*.
Cunliffe, B. 1971: *Fishbourne* (Thames and Hudson).
Cunliffe, B. 1975: *Iron Age Communities in Britain* (Routledge and Kegan Paul).
David, A. 1976, 1980, 1982, 1983: *Ancient Monuments Laboratory Reports*: Geophysics **G11**/76. **G21**/80, **G18**/82, **G21**/83.

Davies, S.M. and Woodward, P.J. 1985: 'Excavations at Alington Avenue, Fordington, Dorchester', *Proceedings* **107**, 101–10.

Donaldson, G.H. 1988: 'Signalling Communications and the Roman Imperial Army', *Britannia* ix (1988), 149–56.

Draper, J. and Chaplin, C. 1982: *Dorchester Excavations, Vol. I* (Dorset Nat. Hist. and Arch. Soc. Monograph 1).

Draper, J. 1983: 'Some Further Discussion of the Library Site, Colliton Park, Dorchester', *Proceedings* **105**, 157–9.

Eicholz, D.E. 1972: 'How long did Vespasian serve in Britain?', *Britannia*, iii, 149–63.

Farrar, R.A.H. 1955: 'Recent Discoveries in Dorchester', *Proceedings* **77**, 129.

Farrar, R.A.H. 1959: 'A Fragment of Mosaic in Glyde Path Road, Dorchester', *Proceedings* **81**, 97–9.

Farrar, R.A.H. 1980: 'Roman Signal-Stations over Stainmore and beyond', in *Roman Frontier Studies 1979*.

Field, N.H. 1968: 'Ptolemy's Isca', *Antiquity* xlii, 309–11.

Field, N.H. 1973: 'An Ancient Causeway at Lazerton Farm, Stourpaine', *ibid*, 95, 87–8.

Field, N.H. 1976a: 'The Discovery of a Roman fort at Shapwick, near Badbury Rings, Dorset', *Britannia* vii, 280–3.

Field, N.H. 1976b: 'A probable Roman fortlet on Keynston Down, Dorset', *Proceedings* **98**, 65–7.

Field, N.H. 1988: *Corfe Mullen: the Origins of a Dorset Village* (Richards, Corfe Mullen).

Fowler, P.J. 1976: *The Roman West Country* (David and Charles).

Fox, Lady A. and Ravenhill, W.L.D. 1966: 'Early Roman Outposts on the North Devon Coast', *Proc. Devon Archaeol. Explor. Soc.* **24**, 3–39.

Frere, S.S. and St. Joseph, J.K. 1974: 'The Roman Fortress at Longthorpe', *Britannia*, v, 1–129.

Frere, S.S. and St. Joseph, J.K. 1983: *Roman Britain from the air* (O.U.P.).

Frere, S.S. 1986: *Britannia – A History of Roman Britain*, 3rd ed. (Routledge and Kegan Paul).

Good, R. 1966: *The Old Roads of Dorset* (Horace G. Commin).

Hart, C. 1964: 'Some Dorset Charter Boundaries', *Proceedings* **86**, 158–9.

Hawkes, C.F.C. and Hull, M.R. 1947: *Camulodunum* (Society of Antiquaries).

Henderson, C.G. 1990: 'Aspects of the Planning of the Neronian Fortress of Legio II Augusta at Exeter' (*Report 90.03, Exeter Museums Archaeological Field Unit*).

Hind, J.G.F. 1989: 'The Invasion of Britain in A.D. 43 – An Alternative Strategy for Aulus Plautius', *Britannia*, xx, 1–22.

Jarvis, K.S. 1982: *Proceedings*, **104**, 194–6.

Johnson, Anne, 1983: *Roman Forts* (A & C Black).

Johnston, D. 1979: *Roman Roads in Britain* (Shire Books).

Keen, L.J. 1983: 'Dorchester: Finds and Observations', *Proceedings* **105**, 150.

Keil, I. 1965: 'Farming on Dorset Estates of Glastonbury Abbey in the Early Fourteenth Century', *Proceedings* **87**, 234–50.

The Making of Dorset (series) n.d.: No. 2 Hod Hill [N.H. Field]; No. 5. Hillforts [J. Beavis] (Dorset Archaeological Committee).

Margary, I.D. 1966: *Roman Roads* (John Baker).

Manning, W.H. 1976: 'The Conquest of the West Country' in Branigan and Fowler 1976.

Manning, W.H. 1988: *Early Roman Campaigns in the South-West of Britain* (National Museum of Wales)

Mason, D.J.P. 1988: '*Prata Legionis* in Britain', *Britannia* xix, 163–90.

Maxfield, V.A. 1981: *The Military Decorations of the Roman Army* (Batsford)

Maxfield, V.A. 1986: 'Pre-Flavian Forts and their Garrisons', *Britannia* xvii, 59–72.

Mills, A.D. 1977 and 1980: *The Place-Names of Dorset*, I and II (English Place-Name Society).

Peddie, J. 1987: *Invasion* (Alan Sutton).

Putnam, W.G. 1970a: 'Interim Report on Excavations on Black Down, Winterborne Steepleton', *Proceedings* **92**, 140–1.

Putnam, W.G. 1970b: 'Section across the Roman Road from Badbury Rings to Dorchester', *Proceedings* **92**, 147–8.

Putnam, W.G. 1984: *Roman Dorset* (Dovecot Press).

Richmond, I. 1955: *Roman Britain* (Penguin Books).

Richmond I. and Brailsford, J.W. 1968: *Hod Hill* Vol. II (Trustees of the British Museum).

Rieu, E.V. (ed.) 1951: *Caesar: The Conquest of Gaul* [trans. S.A. Handford] (Penguin Books).

Rieu, E.V. (ed.) 1957: *Suetonius: The Twelve Caesars* [trans. R. Graves] (Penguin Books).

Rivet, A.F.L. 1958: *Town and Country in Roman Britain* (Hutchinson).

Rivet, A.F.L. and Smith, C. 1979: *The Place-Names of Roman Britain* (Batsford).

Rodwell, W. 1975: 'Milestones, Civic territories and the Antonine Itinerary', *Britannia* vi, 76–101.

Royal Commission on Historical Monuments (England): *Dorset*, Vols, I–V, 1951–1975.

Salway, P. 1981: *Roman Britain* (O.U.P.).

Smith, H.P. 1948: *The History of the Borough and County of the Town of Poole* (Looker, Poole).

Sumner, H. 1931: '*Local Papers*', 22–3.

Swanton, M.J. 1974: *A Corpus of Anglo-Saxon Spear-Types* (B.A.R. series 7).

Todd, M. 1984a: 'The Roman Phase at Maiden Castle', *Britannia* xv, 254–5.

Todd, M. 1984b: 'Hembury (Devon): Roman Troops in a Hillfort', *Antiquity* lxviii, 171–4.

Todd, M. 1985a: 'Excavations at Hembury, Devon', *Antiquaries Journal* lxiv, 251–268.

Todd, M. 1985b: 'The Roman Fort at Bury Barton, Devonshire', *Britannia* xvi, 49–56.

Wainwright, G.J. 1968: 'The Excavation of a Durotrigian Farmstead near Tollard Royal', *Proc. Prehist. Soc.* **34**, 102–47.

Wainwright, G.J. 1979: *Gussage All Saints* (H.M.S.O.).

Webster, G. 1960: 'The Discovery of a Roman Fort at Waddon Hill ... ', *Proceedings* **82**, 88–108.

Webster, G. 1964: 'Further Investigations on the ... Roman Fort at Waddon Hill', *Proceedings* **86**, 135–49.

Webster, G. 1972: 'Interim Report on Excavations at Lake Farm, near Wimborne, 1972', *Proceedings* **94**, (1972), 76.

Webster, G. 1973: 'Interim Report on Excavations at Lake Farm, near Wimborne, 1973', *Proceedings*, **95** (1973), 86–7.

Webster, G. 1979: 'Final Report of the Excavations of the Roman Fort at Waddon Hill', *Proceedings* **101**, 51–90.

Webster, G. 1969: *The Roman Imperial Army* (A & C Black).

Webster, G. 1978: *Boudica* (Batsford).

Webster, G. (ed.) 1988: *Fortress into City* (Batsford).

Webster, G. and Dudley, D.R. 1965: *The Conquest of Britain* (Batsford).

Wheeler, R.E.M. 1943: *Maiden Castle* (Society of Antiquaries).

Whittick, G.C. 1982: 'The Earliest Lead-mining on Mendip and in North Wales' *Britannia* xiii, 113–23.

Woodward, P.J. 1987 in Sunter, N. and Woodward P.J.: *Romano-British Industries in Purbeck.*

Index
Main text and appendices